Dear Dr. Bloodstein,
With great respe ♡ appreciation.

Aaron L. Reichel
January 9, 2007

THE MAVERICK RABBI

THE MAVERICK RABBI

Rabbi Herbert S. Goldstein
and the Institutional Synagogue—
"A New Organizational Form"

Aaron I. Reichel, J.D.

Donning
Norfolk/Virginia Beach

The Donning Company/Publishers
5659 Virginia Beach Boulevard
Norfolk, Virginia 23502

Library of Congress Cataloging in Publication Data

Reichel, Aaron.
  The Maverick Rabbi.

  1. Goldstein, Herbert Samuel, 1890-1970. 2. Rabbis—
New York (N.Y.)—Biography. 3. Jews—New York
(N.Y.) Biography. 4. New York (N.Y.)—Biography.
I. Title
BM755.G624R44   1984   296.8'32'0924 [B]   82-9664
ISBN 0-89865-174-3
ISBN 0-89865-299-5 (pbk.)
Second Edition

TABLE OF CONTENTS

This second edition is dedicated to my dear and revered father, Rabbi O. Asher Reichel, DHL, on the occasion of his receiving the Rabbinic Leadership Award from the Manhattan Day School (Yeshivat Ohr Torah), whose Board of Education he has chaired for over a decade, and in recognition of my father's encouragement and assistance in most of my achievements, not the least of which is the publication (and republication) of this book.

New York City
March 2, 1986

Rabbi Herbert S. Goldstein, The Maverick Rabbi

FOREWORD

Fond personal memories combine with profound respect for enduring achievements in introducing this literary tribute to the late sainted Herbert S. Goldstein. He was truly a lifelong pioneer whose indefatigable labors throughout his career left an indelible mark on the Jewish spiritual and cultural landscape in America as well as in Israel.

At its beginning, the West Side Institutional Synagogue reflected the bold vision of its founder; at its peak, it became a singular landmark of Orthodox regeneration and respectability, helping to reverse what had been the ebbing tide of traditional Judaism in the United States.

His tireless work for the Harry Fischel Institute in Jerusalem likewise helped to transform this unique citadel of Jewish learning and scholarship into a monument to his enterprise and devotion.

Transcending Rabbi Goldstein's institutional accomplishments is the impact of his inspiring personality. Years of friendship and close collaboration during the evening of his rich life filled me with boundless admiration for his notable contribution to the stature and influence of the American Orthodox Rabbinate which he graced with such distinction.

This volume is more than a reverent tribute. It relates a remarkable story in the evolution and transformation of American Jewry, showing how the gifts and energies of a single individual can be brought to bear on the art of spiritual engineering and communal re-invigoration with lasting effect on the Jewish loyalties and the religious heritage of thousands. This work of love will be acclaimed not only by the many who cherish Rabbi Goldstein's memory and who are still touched by the spell of his inspiration but by everyone interested to explore the mystique of Jewish survival and revival.

SIR IMMANUEL JAKOBOVITS
Chief Rabbi of the British Commonwealth

1

PREFACE

The first American-born, Ivy League-educated, orthodox rabbi in history stepped into the twentieth century directly from his rabbinic education. Before his thirty-fifth birthday, Rabbi Herbert S. Goldstein was dynamically influencing the rest of the American Jewish community to join him. He had become the duly elected national president of American Jewry's leading confederation of orthodox synagogues, following the phenomenal success of his Jewish revival movement. This sweeping revival was powered by his new and creative mode for running a synagogue. His synagogue embraced many activities in one institution. He molded this form in New York City, and it spread throughout the country.

I was not surprised. He applied himself to the building of an institutional synagogue with the same indefatigable vigor and charismatic charm that he used in teaching *torah* and in his brilliantly moving sermons. I also had the good fortune and rare privilege of hearing him discuss his aspirations for a united Jewry. He had a huge vision, and he was determined to fulfill it. He believed every synagogue could become an irresistible magnet in drawing Jews to it. He was convinced the synagogue needed to be more appealing, warm, and inviting. He envisioned the synagogue as a home where prayers, community participation, and leisure-time pleasures could be enjoyed in a congenial atmosphere. He wanted the synagogue to provide a total religious experience. He succeeded.

The Institutional Synagogue may elude the easy recognition of a great many, but nearly all Jews who belong to a temple these days will find they participate in a synagogue possessed of the institutional characteristics that Rabbi Goldstein created. Every-

2

one, Jew and non-Jew alike, who enjoys the benefits of some community center should enjoy Rabbi Reichel's documentation of how the well-known Jewish and Christian religious/community centers were first implemented on a large scale, in modern Jewish settings, under the leadership of a man whose name will remain among the immortals of religious life in America.

You might argue: Y's existed before Rabbi Goldstein thundered forth from his pulpit. Indeed, Jewish synagogues have always been centers of community activity. Rabbi Goldstein, however, first formulated the multifaceted, superorganization that not only housed a synagogue, a Sunday school, social clubs, and a gym under one roof, but also made each facet inviting enough to draw those who had originally joined only to participate in others. His institution's programs at their peak drew through the building's doors each day up to 3,000 people from all walks of life—politicians and successful businessmen, laborers, and immigrants.

Rabbi Goldstein's relentless emphasis on the positive, which attracted even skeptics and cynics to the benefits of religion and patriotism, is sorely needed today.

In his allegiance, 100 percent kosher and traditional, Rabbi Goldstein held at the same time a remarkably progressive outlook. He had to defend each side of his beliefs before adherents of the other. Rabbi Reichel presents how this little known, and perhaps even less understood, combination of modernity and tradition worked miracles.

Only as Rabbi Goldstein approached his later years did I come to know him personally and hear his down-to-earth orations (which is not an oxymoron because of the rabbi's ability to mix the humdrum with the spiritual). Hence much of what Rabbi Reichel writes was new to me and sheds new light on a man with whom I was already deeply impressed. This book, I am confident, will open the eyes of many people to the constructive conceptions of a human being who had the energy and brilliance to implement and perpetuate his dreams for untold numbers of people in our generation.

Honorable David N. Edelstein
United States District Judge

Honorable David N. Edelstein is a former chief judge of the federal court that has jurisdiction over the Southern District of New York (including the Borough of Manhattan). He presided over the IBM case, widely considered to be one of the most complex litigations in history.

3

Acknowledgments

When I was fourteen years old, I received a letter from the protagonist of this book. In this correspondence, Rabbi Goldstein wrote: "I always enjoy your letters, because of the way [you] describe things." Little did he imagine, then, that shortly after he was destined to pass away, a little more than half a decade later, I would decide to undertake the project of researching—and then describing—his life in a full-scale biography. I was a college student in Israel when the rabbi passed away, and I wrote a letter to his newly-widowed second wife, in America, asking for her blessing and cooperation in this venture. She told me that she had just received a letter from Rabbi Israel Miller (former chairman of the Conference of Presidents of Major American Jewish Organizations), asking for just that authorization on behalf of Yeshiva University (the oldest and largest university under Jewish auspices). Rabbi Miller envisioned a graduate student writing a thesis on Rabbi Goldstein's significant life of accomplishment. Rabbi Goldstein's widow was struck at the coincidence of the timing of the requests, and granted mine. Little did she or he realize, at the time, that the wishes of *both* of them were destined to be fulfilled within a handful of years, for when I enrolled in Yeshiva University's Bernard Revel Graduate School (simultaneously with my enrollment in the university's affiliated theological seminary and Fordham University's Law School), I decided to major in modern American Jewish history and availed myself of the opportunity to savor virtually every single course on the subject offered by the venerable Professor Hyman B. Grinstein. Dr. Grinstein also served, at the time, as the official archivist of Yeshiva

5

University. It was my privilege to get to know the professor personally, and in the course of one of our conversations, he showed me some material in the university's archives that he knew would be of particular interest to me—minutes of the synagogue of Rabbi Herbert S. Goldstein, who at one time had been Dr. Grinstein's teacher, and who was none other than my own grandfather. When I broached the idea of merging my own literary project with a required research project under his sponsorship, Dr. Grinstein simultaneously demonstrated his instincts for propriety and for cooperation. He told me it would be inappropriate for a grandson to do a serious scholarly work on the life of his grandfather, but Dr. Grinstein *was* willing to sponsor a post-graduate thesis on Rabbi Goldstein's synagogue—the Institutional Synagogue. And so it came to pass. I then found that I had compiled so much information about the synagogue alone, that I decided to delay the presentation of most of the rabbi's simul-taneous and subsequent activities, and focus first just on the rabbi's early and most dynamic years. (If any reader knows of any anecdote or substantive development not covered in this book, please let me know, at 230 West 79th St., New York City, NY 10024, as I am now preparing the sequel.) I then took my scholarly thesis and totally transformed it into its current dramatic format.

When I began to compile the thousands of index cards that document my findings, I was based at my parents' home and spending most of my time fulfilling the requirements for profes-sional academic degrees at various graduate schools while doing my research on the side, but even as one who was rated one of the "most prolific" writers in his class, I will never be able to find the words that would be adequate to thank my dear parents for their encouragement every step of the way, not only in virtually every other venture I have undertaken, but in this venture as well.

God blessed me with grandparents and parents each of whom was or is worthy of not just admiration, but awe. Each in his or her own way or ways embodied piety, compassion, cleverness, efficiency, or any combination of these characteristics. God has also placed me in the midst of other relatives many of whom approach their elders in terms of various of the abovementioned traits. I am still amazed at the patience and concentration exhibited by each of Rabbi Goldstein's four children and two of his grandchildren in reviewing virtually every page of the manu-script and presenting me with written constructive suggestions, many of which were incorporated into the final manuscript. My uncles Messrs. Simeon H. F. and Gabriel F. Goldstein (the execu-tive director and president, respectively, of the Harry and Jane Fischel Foundation), in New York City, and my aunt, Dr. Naomi Cohen, in Israel, carefully examined the entire manuscript, as did my sister, Mrs. Miriam R. Bronner, and my brother, Rabbi Hillel

M. Reichel. My mother, Mrs. Josephine G. Reichel, examined the manuscript at various stages, each time coming forth with additional astute observations, and my father, Rabbi Dr. O. Asher Reichel, was invaluable with his long-range and short-range advice and assistance in conceptualizing, planning, and making important contacts. All of these individuals are unusually idealistic and brought a high level of intellectual honesty to their comments, notwithstanding their proximity to the subject and the author.

At the head of the list of the distinguished and detached professionals who gave my manuscript a thorough reading was Professor Grinstein, again, a few years after approving my project in its academic form. By this reading, the manuscript had undergone a thorough popularization, dramatization, and expansion. At this point, Grinstein—himself the author of monumental works—actually offered *more* substantive changes than he had when he had been my academic mentor. Professor William Helmreich (an author of Harper and Row and Book of the Month Club fame), and Professor (and Rabbi) Tzvee Zahavy (another author of a number of books) read the manuscript and gave me sound advice, not the least of which was to seek out a publisher of the caliber of the one with which, as you can see, I ultimately contracted. English Professor (and Rabbi) Maurice Wohlgelernter, another widely published author, notably under the Columbia University Ivy League imprint, read selections and made some helpful comments. Mrs. Rochelle Faverman Singer, a professional book reviewer, read the entire manuscript and made extensive stylistic suggestions. Israel Silverman, Esq., reviewed proofs.

I also benefited from an exchange of research information with Professor Jeffrey Gurock (whose book, *When Harlem was Jewish,* I reviewed in the Winter 1980 issue of *Tradition*) and with Rabbi Joseph Epstein, in connection with his work on the Central Jewish Institute.

Many newspaper clippings were painstakingly transcribed onto index cards by my late grandmother, Mrs. Lena Reichel, and Mrs. Ethel Halpern. Also of assistance in the transcribing, at various times, when they were teen-agers, were Messrs. David Grunhut, Yechiel Nachum Kahn-Frankel, and Moishe Spira (a grandson of Rabbi Israel Spira, the world renowned Bluzhover Rebbe).

I am also grateful to the following people who assisted in the typing: Mrs. Judy Convoy, Mrs. Marge Harvey, Mrs. Hannah Matathias, and the following people, when they were students: Rachel Yehudah, Susan Berzansky, Dale Eichenbaum, Ivy Kaufman, Bev Green, and Syma Niderberg, the latter of whom was helpful in her role as switchboard operator.

Rabbi Goldstein invariably was able to maximize the results he was able to achieve in virtually every one of his many undertakings. He thus succeeded in getting many of his thoughts published first in his synagogue bulletin, and then, again, in book form, for still wider circulation. The books, in turn, often commemorated specific events and honored people close to him.

His first book, a translation of Luzatto's classical ethical work, *Praise for Righteousness,* was co-written with his wife, Rebecca Fischel Goldstein, and distributed as a wedding souvenir upon their marriage.

His next book, *Comments on the Ethics of the Fathers,* was published in conjunction with the marriage of his wife's sister, Rose Fischel, to Albert Wald, who later became a New York State senator.

The first in Rabbi Goldstein's series of *Bible Comments for Home Reading,* on the Book of Genesis, was dedicated in loving memory of his father, Morris Goldstein, and in honor of the bar mitzvah of his son, Simeon Hai Fischel Goldstein.

The volume of Exodus was dedicated in honor of the bar mitzvah of his son Gabriel Fischel Goldstein.

The volume of Leviticus was dedicated to his mother, Sarah Miriam Goldstein.

The volume of the Book of Numbers was dedicated to his mother-in-law, Mrs. Harry (Jane) Fischel.

The volume of the Book of Deuteronomy was dedicated to his father-in-law, Mr. Harry Fischel, on the occasion of Mr. Fischel's seventieth birthday.

The final book in the series—the comments on the Book of Joshua—was dedicated to "my beloved wife—my self-sacrificing helpmeet, Rebecca Fischel Goldstein."

The first five books of the *Bible Comments for Home Reading* were republished in a two-volume second edition. Each volume was dedicated to "my beloved wife—my self-sacrificing helpmeet, Rebecca Fischel Goldstein."

The last book Rabbi Goldstein published in his lifetime, *Between the Lines of the Bible,* was dedicated "to my beloved, selfless, and self-effacing wife, Rebecca Fischel Goldstein, of whom King Solomon would have said, 'One in a generation.'"

Shortly before the rabbi passed away, he dictated some reminiscences in preparation for an autobiography. This book incorporates many of these recollections—in print for the first time and adheres to one of his final written requests, that the memories he recorded toward the close of his life be dedicated to his second wife as follows: "to my beloved wife—my guardian angel, Regina Krengel Goldstein."

Grateful acknowledgment is hereby made to Mrs. Herbert S. (Regina K.) Goldstein, for granting permission to reprint whatever passages of the autobiographical material of Rabbi Herbert S. Goldstein that the author feels will be helpful.

Grateful acknowledgment is also made to *The New York Times:*
© excerpts from selected news articles and features, by the New
York Times Company. Reprinted by permission.

I hereby express my feelings of appreciation to Dr. Stefan
Grunwald, the Renaissance man who recommended my manuscript to his colleagues at Donning, and to Mr. Robert Friedman,
who edited the manuscript with care, consistency, skill, and
restraint. I also thank all the other fine and cooperative people at
the publishing house, most notably Mr. Richard Horwege, for his
positive role regarding policy decisions, and Ms. Jamie Raynor,
one of the Donning production department's paradigms of
efficiency and alacrity. I have rapidly come to respect and
appreciate all of them for their high standards of professionalism
and courtesy.

I would like to take this means of thanking the directors of the
Harry and Jane Fischel Foundation, of New York City, for their
assistance and advice in connection with this project, above and
beyond the call of duty.

Norman Jaspan and Harry Grossman, Esq., gave me appreciated sound advice that I was able to put to good use in arriving at
mutually beneficial arrangements with my gracious and accom-
modating publisher.

Finally, grateful acknowledgment is made to all the entities
and all the individuals, living as well as deceased, who are quoted
in any way in this book, as well as to those who supplied the
author with background information or information that can still
be used in a sequel.

Aaron I. Reichel

Part One
INTRODUCTION

Chapter 1

A Vacuum Filled By A Charmer's Touch

When many community leaders examined Jewish law, toward the close of the most massive pre-World War I immigration of Jews to the United States (1880-1914), they drew an arbitrary line and said, "Enough; Jewish law as handed down from generation to generation can no longer apply in the 'New World.'" On the other hand, some leaders sought to erase the divisive line that this attitude created, one that relegated Jews into disjointed "wings." What they drew, instead, in some successful cases, were not lines of divisiveness, but overflow crowds of supporters.

When, at the other end of the spectrum, many rabbis filled their cozy synagogues with their familiar countrymen and women of European origin and said, "It is enough that we transfer our provincial customs to the 'New World'" without any attempts at adaptation, some of their colleagues foresightedly rose and said that unless Jews would, in the future, not merely *transfer*, but would rather *transplant* their culture, it would not take root.

When other rabbis were content to preach rousing sermons to bring their audiences to a dramatic emotional pitch, and then "quit while they were ahead," some were not content to leave their audiences in suspended spiritual animation. Instead, they were able to make an effective pitch of their own that could induce a positive and religiously constructive release of their listeners' pent-up potential energies. They were able, by these means, to transform the fixed *status quo* knotted together by ties of geographic kinship, into kinetic energy. Their inspiring words and positive deeds led directly to concrete action and material sacrifice—for otherwise neglected causes—by the thousands of people they were able to influence on the strength of their formal and informal positions of leadership.

13

When Rabbi Herbert S. Goldstein was still in his youthful thirties, a Jewish daily published an informal "Who's Who," whose entry under his name focused precisely on this knack of successfully filling gaps in the American Jewish community:

> I could list many worthwhile enterprises to which Rabbi Goldstein has successfully put hand and heart. The formation of Jewish clubs among the college and high school students [for the first time under the auspices of a national Orthodox organization]. The manufacture of actually kosher crackers and other edibles [launching the historic first generally accepted national kosher food endorsement program in the United States].* These are all vital things that should have been attended to by the previous generation but were neglected, whether for good and sufficient reasons or not makes no difference here. It took this man, with his fire and patience, to break the soil and to plant the seeds.

Rabbi Goldstein ascended to the rabbinate at a time when, on one extreme, sticklers for provincial customs quixotically attempted to transfer every aspect of their European mores to this country, and when, on the other end of the spectrum, pseudo-Reformers arrogantly claimed that many basic Biblical commandments were non-essential, and they thereby diluted Judaism beyond the point where it could sustain itself.

To begin to understand Rabbi Goldstein's role in transplanting a viable and powerful brand of Judaism—of an Orthodoxy that could attract the modern and young segments of the native American population—one must, first, briefly scan the spiritual wilderness which provided the setting for his daring pioneering initiatives.

Although the United States has always championed freedom of religion, it is no secret that the overwhelming majority of Jewish immigrants were *not* primarily motivated to come to this country, paraphrasing Genesis 12, in order to "Get themselves out of their respective countries and to go from their respective kindred and fathers' houses" out of an expectation of finding God's presence in the United States! From a point of departure anywhere in Europe, the Holy Land is the *opposite* direction. It was no accident that, to Jews of this period, two of the most well-known nicknames of the United States were "the golden land" and "the nonkosher land." At a time when shiploads of immigrants were regularly reaching United States shores, a social commentator once wryly remarked that a vast *geniza* (underground, or in this case, *underwater*,

---

* See our special Chapter 37 for a far more comprehensive panorama of his areas of activity beyond these representative examples mentioned in this early "Who's Who."

repository of precious articles) could be filled with the phylacteries*
thrown overboard into the Atlantic Ocean by immigrants to this
country!

The post-1880 immigrants—mainly of East European origin—
that dominated the streets of New York's Lower East Side in the
early part of this century were clearly the most impressionable
of the Jewish immigrants of this period. The Spanish and German
Jews by this time had either dug their roots solidly into American
soil or had become hopelessly assimilated. Yet, from an economic
point of view, the new immigrants faced more than the two strikes
against them that face all religious Jews—Sabbath observance on
Saturdays in a six-day work week that provided a day off only on
Sundays, and a traditional commitment to pay for a Jewish
education for children who were otherwise expected to supplement
family income. In addition, they faced a potent third strike at every
turn, threatening to break their will to remain religious. The
"villains," ironically, were none other than their very avowed
benefactors! Correctly sensing that bigots would lump all Jews
together, already-Americanized Jewish philanthropists were
interested in Americanizing their recently arrived Jewish countrymen as quickly and efficiently as possible. The most efficient way
to attain this end was by the Americanized "haves" inducing
immigrant "have nots" to discontinue virtually all of their
religious and "old country" practices. The young, with the weakest
such links, were the quickest to comply, thereby antagonizing
their parents and further quickening their alienation from their
heritage. American piety became, to many struggling immigrants,
"as tasteless as American cucumbers and American fish." By
contrast, Goldstein, in founding the Institutional Synagogue,
wrote:

> Our purpose can be summed up in one sentence: We want
> to Judaize Americans *and* Americanize the Jews.

An aggravating factor contributing to Jewish immigrant loss
of identity centered around their motives for deciding to relocate
in the United States. Immigration by members of most other
nationalities was prompted essentially by simple poverty. For this
reason, many other nationals intended originally to come to the
United States only long enough to accumulate some money to take
back with them to their native countries; Jews, however, left their
native lands under additional compelling pressures, such as
religious and political persecutions, as well as outright pogroms,
and were thus far more inclined to break all past bonds and not
even to consider returning. They could hardly have harbored

---

* Religious articles donned by observant males for their daily prayers.

strong nationalistic feelings towards lands dominated by their former tormentors. On the other hand, in their zeal to start life anew in America, and in their gratefulness for this country's abundant positive and democratic values, many of them subconsciously associated *all* of their European customs, both the secular and the Jewish, with their previous physical "homelands"— where they had often been treated as stepchildren. With this in mind, it should come as no surprise that between 1899 and 1943, only 4.6 percent of Jewish immigrants to America returned to their European birthplaces, whereas in a comparable period from 1908 to 1943, fully 35 percent of the general basically non-Jewish immigrant population returned.

Even if an immigrant overcame the obstacles to maintain his identity, the synagogue was the *least* attractive unit for him to join, when compared to the far more sociable atmospheres of *landsmenschaften* (clubs based on commonality of town of origin), socialist Workmen's Circles, Zionist groups, or, eventually B'nai B'rith lodges. Y.M.H.A.'s (with the "H" for Hebrew) sprang up as an answer to the Y.M.C.A.'s, but they were weak copies rather than strong answers. In accepting the national presidency of the Synagogue Council of America, Rabbi Goldstein observed that

> The Center Movement is highly secularized, with religion as a tail trailing behind it. Its workers in many instances are unsympathetic to a religious program. There is no need for additional Y.M.H.A.'s or Y.W.H.A.'s or so-called Jewish Centers. These institutions, well-financed usually through our influence, have unconsciously diverted our youth away from the synagogue. They are in many instances competing institutions.

In a constructive response to these "Y's"—which differ from Y.M.C.A.'s by their nontheological approach—Goldstein, early in his career, created the Institutional Synagogue—the main focus of this book. The novelty of the I. S. was that it combined the features of the traditional synagogue, the Hebrew School, and the "Y" into one integrated institution, thereby strengthening the religious lives of thousands who otherwise would have only attended a "Y" at best.

In creating the Institutional Synagogue, Rabbi Goldstein did more than simply restructure a bureaucracy. The rabbi was among the first to set the tone and a workable prototype for the widespread restructuring of the major social, cultural, and athletic facilities in Jewish life for countless American Jewish communities.

Anomalously, although America has been a home and a haven to Jews for centuries,* there was virtually no truly self-

---

* There is evidence that Columbus, if not himself a Jew, certainly had at least one with him in 1492, the year the Jews were expelled from Spain.

sustaining, complete Jewish community in America until well into the twentieth century. To be "sustaining," a community must be able to perpetuate itself, yet in the early twentieth century, the "Conservative" movement had to draw on rabbis from Orthodox backgrounds for its leadership, and the "Reform" movement had yet to prove itself in light of its assimilation rate and its dependence on former traditional Jews to replenish its ranks. A complete Jewish community must be one with a rabbi who can unreservedly relate to the youth—the future members of his community. In this respect, the Orthodox, too, could not have claimed to have been free of the tension between the two cultures— the American and the Jewish—not substantially free, that is, until Rabbi Goldstein and a select few other young rabbis began to make their marks.

Rabbi Herbert S. Goldstein was the first Orthodox rabbi* of American birth to receive a traditional ordination in America, and thus, in a sense, the first Orthodox rabbi to relate as a fully "Americanized" Jew to the young generation. For centuries, Jews in America had been led by either European rabbis or American *chazzanim*—cantors who served as spiritual leaders but lacked formal rabbinical ordination. Such legendary personalities as Gershom Seixas and Isaac Leeser were *not* rabbis but were *chazzanim*, cantors. Other notable English-speaking rabbis who will be noted later were either of European birth or education—or both—thus giving the distinction of being number one to Rabbi Goldstein so surprisingly late in American history.

The reader should not assume for a moment that Goldstein's pre-eminent role in building a modern but undiluted Orthodoxy in America rests on accidents of fate or on technicalities. He was to become not just a national president but a major initiative force in the historically most significant periods of the Union of Orthodox Jewish Congregations of America (U.O.J.C.A.), the Rabbinical Council of America (R.C.A.), and the Synagogue Council of America (S.C.A.).**

He was relatively unique in his de-politicized brand of "religious Zionism" which he supported from his positions in the upper echelons of the leading "ultra-Orthodox" world organization of his time (the Agudath Israel), and in the upper echelons of the most prominent "moderate" Orthodox world "religious Zionist" organization (the Mizrachi), as well as in the United Jewish Appeal.

The rabbi's close contacts in Washington and Albany (the capital of New York State) played a vital role in rescuing leading

---

* Certainly the first one of national prominence.

** He eventually repudiated the latter organization for reasons to be discussed later.

rabbinic authorities—as well as ordinary laymen—from Europe during World War II, and in landmark legislation of Jewish significance.

As the ranking professor at Yeshiva University's Department of Homiletics and Practical Rabbinics, Rabbi Goldstein had a strong and steady hand in the molding process of the first two generations of American Orthodox rabbis to be produced in this country's oldest Orthodox Jewish seminary. He was also a significant force in supporting the majority of the most prominent Talmudical academies of the United States and of Israel.

In his youth, Rabbi Goldstein's revivalism earned him the then-enviable nickname, even in the non-Jewish press, of "the Jewish Billy Sunday." In his prime, Goldstein was recognized by organizations as far away as California as not merely a leading Orthodox rabbi, but no less than as "the foremost rabbi in America."

Such recognition was by no means unanimous, even in the Orthodox community and even in his most influential years, but as Rabbi Goldstein's exploits leading up to and into his dramatic Institutional Synagogue experiment spring back to life in the pages ahead, he stands a good chance of picking up posthumous votes.

Part Two
BORN TO LEAD

Chapter 2

A Generation Apart

The very first childhood memory that Herbert S. Goldstein ever saw fit to record focuses on the spoken word, a tool he was destined to use most effectively all his life:

> At a very early age, I began to speak in public on political matters. I favored United States presidential candidate William McKinley as against [William Jennings] Bryan, and stumped for him on the corner of Clinton Street and Rutgers Place on the Lower East Side of New York. A crowd came to hear the young boy deliver a political speech. My mother happened to come along and, as soon as she saw and heard me, cried out, "Sammy! (that was [later to become no longer my first but] my middle name) you come right home." Whereupon an Irishman said, "Lady, leave that kid alone." Well, that was the first and last outdoor *political* speech [*emphasis not in original*] I made.

A writer for *The American Hebrew* supplemented this version by stating, in 1939, that "they still tell this story on the Lower East Side," referring to the future rabbi as a six-year-old standing on an egg box. His version has "the Irishman in the group around the young Demosthenes" interpose: "Let him alone. Begorra, he's the best we've heard tonight!"

Not only did this occasion represent his last purely political outdoor speech, but it also may have influenced his deeply religious mother to consider the possibility that his oratorical

21

talents could potentially be channeled toward the perpetuation of that which she saw to be more significant than party politics.

An aside arising from this incident gives us an idea, also, of his relationship with his father. Commenting about the incident in his autobiographical sketch that he was destined to leave for completion in this work, he wrote:

> I spoke for McKinley, although I heard later that my father made a small wager on Bryan, which hurt me very much that I crossed my father when I was apprised of this fact.

This incident is an isolated one, but it reflects the attitudes of this independent little thinker toward his parents that he was later to express so graphically in maturity as well—respect for both of them, but at somewhat of a distance from his father, while under the greater influence of his mother, to whom he often referred as "one of the two greatest influences on my life." (The other was his wife.)

Goldstein's sense of respect extended to his earlier ancestors as well. On his return from his first trip to what was then known as Palestine—an exotic trip in the year 1923—he made it his business to stop at his paternal grandfather's hometown, deep in the interior of Poland. Although presumably virtually *every* town has its pious people, the town of Ciechanow was particularly proud of its own acclaimed "Ciechanower *tzaddik*" (or saintly person) whose memory, apparently, was well preserved even after he had died. Indeed, people from this town claimed that the town was famous *because* of the still recognized reputation of this man. Aside from the lingering aura of the Ciechanower *tzaddik*, the town, according to Mrs. Goldstein's diary, "was the typical small town with all one story houses and no improvements." The Goldstein party's arrival in this insulated town was all the more dramatic since it came only moments after the arrival of the telegram announcing their planned visit! Mrs. Goldstein wrote: "Outside of the trip to Herbert's grandparents' graves and to the Ciechanower *tzaddik's* grave, the whole day was consumed in listening to the terrors endured by our people during the war, and the life of fear and dread they led." Although the visit was described as understandably "nerve-racking," "it meant much more to Herbert, for he even sat down in the spot where his grandfather used to learn in the *bet hamedrash* [house of study]." The impact of this visit was so strong that, in an interview nearly half a century later, his surviving sister described this thrill that had been experienced deep in the hinterlands *of Poland* as the highlight of her late brother's first trip *to Palestine*.

Herbert Goldstein was intensely proud of the stamina of his immediate ancestors, and, in fact, opened his until-now-unpublished autobiographical sketch with the unusually assertive statement:

> I give my forebears for what it may mean to my younger co-workers. My mother died at 79, my father at 76, my grandfather, whom I knew [he had visited the United States when the future rabbi was still a child] died at the age of 97, and my great-grandfather at the age of 106, having fallen off a horse.

When Morris Goldstein, at the age of twenty-four, came to America in 1874, his name was not Goldstein; rather, it was Schultz. Two different versions of the story of his name change have filtered down through the family. According to the simpler version, somebody informed the young immigrant, as he got off the boat, that Schultz was not an acceptable name in the New World. He had been told that the stones of this legendary country were indeed paved with gold, hence, the decision to change his name to Goldstein. The youthful newly-named Goldstein rapidly learned the actual meaning of this figurative legend. By industry and hard work, he became a successful—though not particularly wealthy—clothing manufacturer.

In fact, according to the second version of the story of his name change, Goldstein's very first experience with the clothing business influenced his decision:

> Jacob Joseph Schultz had a *landsman* [an acquaintance from his home town in "the old country"] by the name of Morris Goldstein, who was here when Schultz came, and who was very successful in the clothing manufacturing business. He couldn't turn over his goods fast enough, and Schultz became sort of a sub-contractor. He had a book in which to take orders, with the name "Morris Goldstein" on it, and somehow adopted the name, either out of gratitude or superstition, I suppose.

—or, very possibly, out of expedience.

Gradually, as Goldstein proceeded to emulate the person whose namesake he had become, he came to be affiliated with "a large number of charitable, philanthropic, and educational organizations of this city" in his own right, notably with the Beth Israel Hospital, and as vice president of the Beth Hamedrash Hagadol, the oldest Orthodox synagogue in New York among those tracing their roots to Eastern Europe or Russia.

When Morris Goldstein passed away in his sleep on a

Thursday evening at the age of seventy-six,* his son, the rabbi, insisted that Jewish law be adhered to and that he be eulogized and laid to rest before the sun would set Friday evening, marking the beginning of the Sabbath. Jewish law considers delays in burying the dead to be disrespectful to the memory of the departed. As it turned out, however, "due to the impossibility of getting the plot ready in time," the funeral was rescheduled for the first post-Sabbath opportunity, at which time Morris Goldstein was eulogized by no fewer than six rabbis,** including his own son, who "moved everyone to tears" and, significantly, "controlled himself wonderfully except when he spoke of his 'angel mother.'"

At the celebration commemorating Rabbi Goldstein's 45th year in the rabbinate, Rabbi Goldstein held center stage at a completely different kind of an emotional moment. Once again, his powerful voice*** seemed on the verge of faltering at only one point, and again this point was at the mention of his mother, who by this time had long-since departed. If his mother, both in life and in death, held such a special grip on his telltale heartstrings, it was for good reasons, some of which we will now record.

Sarah Miriam Mikler came to America from Sierpc, Poland, at five years of age in 1872, and after receiving a regular public school education, "you would never think she was born in Europe. She spoke the most perfect English." Orphaned at the age of eleven, she lived with friends and joined the work force before being joined in wedlock to Morris Goldstein. His first wife had passed away, leaving him with no fewer than six children by the time he met Sarah Mikler. His second wife was only eighteen years old at the time of their wedding. He was thirty-six.**** It was said that "she had married an orphan asylum." "My mother," wrote her only son,

> at the age of 18, was a very pretty girl, and married...for religious reasons, because my father was a religious adherent, and the younger suitors in her day did not live up to her standards of religious observance.

One might have expected some tension in a family with a stepmother of eighteen and a stepson as old as fifteen, yet in this

---

* According to virtually all printed and family sources except the *New York Times* which put his age at seventy-four.

** Rabbis Margolies, Hyamson, Schuchatowitz, Goodman, Jung, and Goldstein.

*** As recorded on audio-tape.

**** Twice *chai*—and, of course, twice her age. (*Chai* is Hebrew for "life," as in "*l'chayim*, to life." The letters of this highly symbolic word—each Hebrew letter in the alphabet is assigned a numerical value—add up to precisely eighteen.)

seemingly difficult situation, Sarah Goldstein became a model stepmother. As a mother, she was later described as:

> ...the type that if she would hear a fire engine, she would rush to the telephone to make sure that all her children were unharmed. If she would see rain outside, she would call up all her children to make sure they would put on their galoshes.

Her role as a stepmother was built on this foundation, and may have reached its highest step by the fact that a son of one of the children who had been born to Morris Goldstein's first wife was able to declare: "You didn't *know* they were 'step.'" In fact, they casually referred to each other as "brothers" and "sisters," never referring to the otherwise conspicuous and often uncomfortable prefix of "step," so that they were able to relate to each other as equals on a common plane.

Possibly the most telling justification of the statement that "Not a finger could be put on her as a stepmother" is borne out by a letter written in 1945 by Rabbi Goldstein to a congregant who questioned him about the role she should maintain as a second wife:

> I must tell you of my own family. My mother, God bless her, was the second wife of my late father, of blessed memory. It was she who used to remind my brothers and sister of the *yahrzeit* [date of the death] of their mother. It was she who would wake them up early to go to *shul* [synagogue] to say the *kaddish* [annual memorial prayer for the deceased]. It was she who encouraged them to go to the cemetery. She even encouraged my late father to buy a cemetery plot around the grave of his first wife. You can readily understand how my brothers and sister then felt toward my mother. You cannot go wrong by going out of your way and allowing the memory of your husband's first wife to be revered. If you do that, you will become bigger and kinder in the eyes of your husband's family.*

The rabbi's mother seemed to have had a natural inclination for treating in-laws better than many people treat their own blood relatives. Mrs. Harry Fromberg, the wife of one of Rabbi Goldstein's cousins, recalled how a week or so after she had married into the family, she (the new Mrs. Fromberg) had been in an automobile accident, and had been hospitalized for ten weeks as a direct result:

---

* Sure enough, it was not surprising when, in the next generation, after a stepbrother's son's wife's brother passed away, Rabbi Goldstein "said *he* would say *kaddish* (the memorial prayer) every day" for the initial eleven-month mandatory period prescribed for all bereaved Jewish children—but not for other relatives.

Mrs. Goldstein sent over a main meal every day [this was long before the dawn of the era of the kosher "T.V. dinner," and, in fact, of the T.V. itself!] for the ten weeks I was there—and she did things like that all the time!

Similarly, in the next generation, one stepson's daughter-in-law recalled visiting one of Sarah Goldstein's *natural* daughters "once a week when she was sick in later years," virtually until the end of her life.

As the youngest boy in the family, the future rabbi was the apple of his mother's eye—as *well* as of his step-siblings' eyes, as we will see later. The "apple" did not fall far from the "tree," and the tree provided more than shelter. As could well be imagined, the rabbi's mother did all in her power to assist him in the work of the synagogue he was destined to establish. On the very first holiday of Succot to be celebrated in the nascent Institutional Synagogue, it was none other than she who "baked cake and made all the necessary preparations for the [mid-holiday mini-celebration known as a] *Simchat Bet Ha-sho-eh-vah* given by the Institutional Synagogue boys [sic] at the Y.W.H.A. succah [special holiday hut]. Herbert furnished the refreshments." Later on, she faithfully and actively participated in synagogue bazaars, cake sales, and other such functions.

This loyalty on the part of the rabbi's mother did not go unrequited. On his cross-country train trip in 1927, Rabbi Goldstein:

> . . . made it a practice at almost every train stop to send a post card to my dear mother. Every Thursday night, no matter where I was, I left word with the telephone operator of the hotel to call me at 5 A.M. so that I could say Good Shabbat [Sabbath greetings] to my dear mother. . . . This was 8 o'clock Friday morning due to the difference in time.
>
> For the last twenty-five years of her life, not a day passed that I did not think of calling to see my dear mother to give her my usual kiss, or to telephone her. This practice has also been followed by my daughter, Josephine.

Chapter 3

An Auspicious Childhood

Nothing particularly unusual was noted about the festive religious circumcision ceremony that officially inducted Herbert Samuel Goldstein into the Jewish faith on the traditional eighth day after he was born, on February 8, 1890—other than the fact that his future father-in-law recalled, many years later, that he had been present! Both young Goldstein's famous philanthropic father-in-law to be, Mr. Harry Fischel, and young Herbert's father, Mr. Morris Goldstein, were active, by mere chance, in the same synagogue—the oldest Westernized one in New York City, no less—on the then overwhelmingly Jewish Lower East Side. Both, too, later moved their households to the fashionable Upper East Side of Manhattan, and both became regular worshippers at the same congregation—Kehilath Jeshurun—long before their off-spring were destined to spring into each other's lives.

Nothing particularly noteworthy can be said at this point about the name Herbert Samuel Goldstein other than the fact that this was *not* young Goldstein's given name, at birth. Like his father, he, too, underwent a drastic name change, but for a very different reason. The decision to change young Goldstein's name was based on a clear-cut religious practice, followed by the clear cut of a surgical knife. When he was a teenager, he was stricken by an acute attack of appendicitis. Before the operation, from which he recovered, his family adhered to a traditional Jewish practice of symbolically seeking to change an ill person's destiny by grafting the Hebrew word for life, "*Chayyim*," onto the endangered person's given name. In young Goldstein's case, his first name, Samuel, was superseded by "Herbert," corresponding to the Hebrew name, "*Chayyim*." Young Goldstein's given name, "Samuel," was thus destined to near oblivion when its primary usage became limited to that of a scaled down middle initial.

The young rabbi was closest to his brother Emanuel, whom he always referred to as "Manny." The two were roommates and shared a common appreciation of the game of baseball.* The other Goldstein brothers included Maury, the oldest, Nat, and Miller (a first name). One brother went off to fight in the Spanish-American War, and never returned. Of the two daughters born to Morris Goldstein's first wife, "Aunt Essy" is remembered fondly by the Goldstein family, but Pauline (Polly) was merely a name to them, since she died as a teenager as the result of a reaction to dental treatment.

Morris Goldstein's union to Sarah produced two daughters in addition to the future rabbi. Both Hannah and Lillian, and their respective spouses, Henry Blankfort and Jack Levine, were very close to both Herbert and to the institutions with which he involved himself.

As the youngest boy in the household, Herbert was naturally accorded quite a bit of attention. His younger sister recalled: "At home he was treated like a china doll. Essie [his stepsister] and Hannah would butter his bread, his corn...and if we could *chew* for him, we *would* have!"

His formal education is discussed from various angles in his autobiographical sketch:

> When I was six years of age, it was the custom then to send a child, especially a son, to public school. My mother was not opposed to my attending public school, but she certainly was for the Bible, Jewish tradition and law. So she wanted her son to learn the word of God as interpreted in the *Talmud* and found in Jewish Law.
>
> My mother wanted me to receive God consciousness, and that can only be found, as far as a Jew is concerned, in the Bible, the Talmud and the Schulchan Arukh, the Jewish Law.

Sarah Goldstein opposed the prevalent trend that existed—

* Manny often took his younger brother to professional games at the Polo Grounds, where they developed a strong sense of allegiance to the New York Giants. This bond was maintained even after the Giant franchise moved to San Francisco. Baseball was unquestionably *the* national pastime in the period of their youth. (As of this writing, the predominant status of baseball is being vigorously challenged.) Later in life, as a rabbi, Goldstein was able to endear himself to many of his youthful followers by peppering his language and assortment of anecdotes with occasional references to this sport. When he would notice some young people about to leave the synagogue before the service was completely over, he might quietly say to them, "Would you leave a *baseball game* before the last 'out?'" When he would overhear some boys talking about baseball during the service he would gently remind them what they were in the synagogue for, and then, with a friendly wink, add, "Besides, you're rooting for the *wrong team!*"

Little wonder that the inter-club baseball tournaments of the Institutional Synagogue received his particular personal encouragement. The synagogue newspaper on March 20, 1925 reminded its readers that "Rabbi Goldstein offers a baseball cup annually to the winning team."

even among observant Jews—that relegated religious education to a secondary status, and thereby often to the status of an easily expendable appendage. She "proposed," instead:

> ...that her son receive first [or, in this context, foremost] a religious education and then a secular education. She won out and, accordingly, my father engaged a teacher for my religious education at the age of 6.

One of Herbert Goldstein's early instructors on the Lower East Side was the father of the famous Zionist leader and orator, Rabbi Abba Hillel Silver. For a short time when about twelve years old, Goldstein attended the religious school at 85 Henry Street*, then known as Etz Chayyim, the tree of life, one of the two schools that later merged and grew together into the Rabbi Isaac Elchanan Theological Seminary, which, in turn, later became one of the major schools affiliated with Yeshiva University. At any rate, as he tells it, "Somehow or other I didn't make it that well; the Yiddish was not the Yiddish that I could translate into English." In fact, Yiddish was never one of his strong points. Although he could communicate in this language, the "Yiddish" he used leaned heavily on the German from which the more colloquially used language of Yiddish draws most of its roots. (Many of his teachers—not his ancestors—were of German origin.)

Whether in a private or a group setting, Goldstein's parents made sure he had some form of religious instruction in addition to his secular studies at all times until the day of his ordination. Even after his ordination and subsequent marriage, and throughout most of his prime in the rabbinate, he continued to make arrangements for private study with rabbinical scholars.

The only one of his elementary school memories recorded in his autobiographical sketch follows:

> At the age of about eleven, I went to Public School #2 on Henry Street, between Rutgers and Pike Streets. The principal was Mr. Oscar Birnbaum, a very strict disciplinarian. I was appointed one of the monitors to report to him any pupil who was disorderly in going to or coming out of the classrooms. I brought one of the boys to the principal for disorderly conduct. The boy denied it. When Mr. Birnbaum shouted, 'Do you mean to say that the monitor is lying?' The boy kept quiet. The principal then slapped the boy's face, the sound of which could be heard throughout the large assembly room. I

---

* Actually, he referred to the school, about seventy years after attending it, as "the Yeshiva on 38 Henry Street." From the context of his statement and the fact that the statement was made at the twilight of his life when his memory was no longer highly reliable with respect to details of his childhood, there is no doubt that he was actually referring to the school just mentioned.

shall never forget the remorse I experienced because of the boy's severe punishment.

Apparently, the time spent on Goldstein's religious studies did not have a very harmful effect on his secular studies, since he was elected salutatorian of his class upon graduating from P.S. 2.

Concerning his bar mitzvah, we read in his memoirs:

> As a rule a teacher is engaged to prepare [a] boy for his ceremony of Bar Mitzvah. My father engaged a teacher who was an elderly person, and whom I respected greatly. In addition to the portion from the Pentateuch that the Bar Mitzvah is to read, he is also to read a portion from the Prophets called the *"HAFTORAH."* Behold! About one week prior to my Bar Mitzvah my teacher came worriedly, breaking the news to me that he had prepared me for the wrong portion of the *HAFTORAH*. Of course, I had great respect for the old gentleman, so I quieted him and said, 'Do not worry, I will work harder.' The average Bar Mitzvah lad takes at least a month to master his portion, and [as soon] as I realized that my *HAFTORAH* was much longer than the average prophetic section, I did not complain, but I rehearsed the *HAFTORAH* so often that I knew it almost from memory. Thank God! For the glory of my parents, I was able to finish the task creditably.
>
> [T]he services...took place in one of the largest Synagogues on the Lower East Side, which was and still is called the Bet Hamedrash Hagadol, at 60 Norfolk Street, between Grand and Broome Streets. It still is one of the largest and most spacious edifices in the Lower East Side. That synagogue played an important part in my life.
>
> Many times the Bar Mitzvah celebrant delivers a short address referring to the wearing of the *Tefillin* (Phylacteries), or some other appropriate topic. As was expected of me, I did deliver a short address as it had been prepared for me by my teacher.
>
> At the conclusion of the service, many worshippers came to a spread which my mother, God bless her, prepared, namely a luncheon at our home which was then at 180 Henry Street, in New York City. At the home we were treated with listening to two speakers. One was the rabbi of the congregation; the other was Mr. Harry Fischel [who had attended Goldstein's circumcision ceremony]. Little did he then know that he would become my father-in-law. Both had as their theme the hope that, as I grew into manhood, I would remain faithful to our religion. As I recall, I nodded smilingly and willingly in the affirmative.

After the Bar Mitzvah, when I made application for admission to Townsend Harris Hall High School [which was a New York City-sponsored school for "the cream of the cream, for geniuses" with the highest academic averages in the city, and which was eventually closed by Mayor La Guardia who called it a "frill the city could no longer afford"], I was asked by the principal "Why are you Jewish boys so anxious to be admitted to Townsend Harris Hall High School?" I answered, "Because, thereby we save a year. Other high schools have a four-year program, but Townsend Harris has only a three-year program of studies." He remarked, "You Jewish boys are very ambitious, and always try to improve yourselves." He was right.

Herbert S. Goldstein was accepted into and attended the prestigious Townsend Harris Hall School.* During the better part of his high school years, young Goldstein's private instructor in Hebrew subjects was Rabbi Henry Guterman, himself at that time a student at the Rabbi Isaac Elchanan Theological Seminary. As was the case with most of young Goldstein's instructors, "He was like a member of the family," according to an actual member of the family. According to Rabbi Guterman's son, Dean Simeon L. Guterman (formerly of Yeshiva College), the elder Guterman at this point was so close to the family that he "preferred eating at the Goldstein residence, whenever it was appropriate."

Goldstein's years at the Townsend Harris Hall High School and then at Columbia University provided him not only with the polish that was to help him shine as an orator and public figure in later years, but also with an excellent opportunity to make a realistic appraisal of non-Jewish values and occasional discriminatory incidents.**

---

* According to a writer from *The American Hebrew*, "We read in the school paper of that day that he turned out for the football squad. His athletic prowess received no further mention."

** His recollections of this period sketch some of his more pleasant as well as some of his nerve-racking moments.

At Columbia no one was permitted, among the students, to smoke a pipe until he became a sophomore. However, I was permitted as were other members of my class . . . to smoke a pipe. Prior to this I did not smoke even a cigarette, except on my mother's birthday, which was on Purim [a holiday characterized by unusual merriment]. I had played checkers with a very dear friend who presented me with a good Havana cigar. I am very grateful to him because the cigar was too strong for me, and about twenty years elapsed thereafter before I tried to smoke any cigar again.

In my freshman year at Columbia I joined the class in a tug-of-war. It was usual for everyone to participate in different activities. However you can imagine my great excitement when I came home with a torn shirt.

Then, later, as part of our activities, I was chosen [after having led a debating team for the Henry Street Settlement against the Y.M.H.A.] as a member of the Freshman

31

Even back in 1911, Columbia University offered some of its more gifted students the option of substituting their fourth undergraduate year with their first year at its prestigious law school. Goldstein, apparently following his attitude regarding Townsend Harris Hall, was quick to seize this opportunity of graduating college, also, in no more than three years. At this point, he was considering both legal and rabbinical careers. Note his retrospective account of this juncture of his education:

> When the time arrived for my entering the seminary, I saved a year by taking the option of exchanging my senior year for a year in the law school. I applied to Columbia Law School, and my application was accepted.

His sister recalled that he went to law school at Columbia for a short time and he came home and said, "I'm not studying law.

Debating Team. [He later represented the Sophomore Debating Team as well.] . . .

[As to incidents with religious overtones:]

. . . When we had an examination scheduled to take place on [the holiday of] Shavuot, Professor Carpenter of the English Department, who wrote books on rhetoric, was in charge of the examination. I went in to see him, so that I could arrange to take a special examination some other day, permission of which was granted to me. He at that time said to me, "Mr. Goldstein, you asked to be relieved on Saturday or on your holiday, but what would we do if a Mohammedan asked for similar relief on the day of his observance, Friday?" I was about to say, "But what about the Christian religious boys? No examinations are scheduled for them on Sundays." But I felt that discretion was the better part of valor. I remained quiet and was granted a special examination on another day.

There was another incident I overcame [this time by successfully concluding that an affirmative act was appropriate]. An upper classman, George Christian Miller, would always put out his foot when he saw me coming down the library steps. This time when he repeated this act, to have me trip, I threw the books that I held in my hands, down the steps, and said, "are you looking for a fight?" Luckily for me, he did not accept my challenge. He was a tall, strong, six-footer and could no doubt [have gotten the] better of me with very little effort on his part. Luckily, also, my neighbor in class, Jay Gould, an expert in squash tennis, a very decent fellow, coming from one of the richest families in the country, as well as a student named Stuart, who also came along, separated us without [our] getting into a fight.

The result of this incident was in my favor, for the next morning, when I was undressing in the locker room, lo and behold, I took off my *tzitzit* [fringed undergarment worn by Jewish males for religious reasons] and was asked by Stuart, whose locker was next to mine, "Goldstein, what is that little garment for?" I said jokingly, "That is my chest-protector," but then I explained the purpose, that it was a reminder to daily observe our religious commandments. Stuart became impressed, and from that time on, I was taken off the hazing list, and we became closer friends.

Upon graduating from College, all of the seniors marched into the gymnasium, but I was greatly saddened when I noticed a Negro, George Washington Scott, walking alone without a white man beside him, for we were to walk in two abreast. As soon as I saw this occur, I went over to Scott, and said, "Scott, I will join you. Let us walk in, together." I shall never forget this incident. Shame! Shame! on my fellow classmates. I overheard another classmate say: "I like the Jewish boys, but may not invite them to our home." I said to myself, "Shame! upon my beloved United States." However, this was balanced by my faculty advisor, the professor of Astronomy, who called me and said, "Herbert, I would like you to come over to my home Sunday afternoon at a reception." I accepted, but could not, of course, participate in the food, because of my adherence to Kashruth.

I can't see myself getting up and taking the part of an accused person." Although there is a public policy encouraging lawyers to represent the interests of all people, surely no lawyer is obligated by the legal code of professional responsibility to represent causes against which he finds himself personally biased, and, in fact, criminal law is only one of many areas an attorney can choose in which to specialize. His decision to reject a career at the bar was influenced to a greater degree, obviously, by the positive considerations that prompted him to become a rabbi, than by his disenchantment with the thought of practicing before the secular bar.

After leaving law school, young Goldstein lost little time in finding a discipline of post-graduate study at Columbia that was more suitable as a supplement to the rabbinic studies that he was pursuing simultaneously. He proceeded to earn a Master of Arts degree in Judaica, and his thesis was a translation of excerpts of *Praise for Righteousness*, an ethical work by the mystic moralist, Moses Hayyim Luzatto, together with a biography of the author.

His rabbinic training, as well as his later-acquired honorary doctorate, merit separate discussions in light of the particularly unique circumstances involved.

Chapter 4

Idyllic Romance Of Two Idealists

Some people meet their future spouse at a social gathering, at a party, or simply by chance. This was not to be the case with Herbert and Rebecca Goldstein. The most significant day in the social life of Herbert S. Goldstein was December 5, 1909, for on that day he first

met Miss Rebecca (Betty) Fischel at the memorial service for Rabbi Joseph Mayer Asher, at the United Hebrew Charities Building, now called the Jewish Social Service Building, at 22nd Street and Second Avenue. After the services were over, my very close friend, Samuel M. Roeder introduced us to each other, and we walked home from 22nd Street to 93rd Street, where [she lived with] her parents. Sometime later, she told me, that she wrote in her diary, that she met a young man, a seminary student, by the name of Herbert Goldstein, whom, were he a girl, she would like to have as a friend.

Tall and handsome, he was obviously not a girl, and destined to become significantly more than just a friend! Apparently, *"two kindred spirits met."*

As close as their spirits may have been to one another, it was clear, even from this early diary entry, that some force—although not insurmountable—stood between them. It was the force of social standing. Betty's father, Mr. Harry Fischel, had risen literally from rags to riches, and was one of the most highly regarded Orthodox Jewish philanthropists in the country. His entire life's story was one of phenomenal and unrelenting upward mobility. He had no surviving sons, and was a very powerful personality—both in public and in personal matters. He strove for excellence, and wanted nothing but the best for each of his four daughters. Although at the time of the Asher funeral young Goldstein was more of a Columbia man than a seminary man, the events of this day, and their aftermath, had a tremendous impact on his own personal and professional attitudes. Partly out of a sense of loss of the unusual English-speaking Rabbi Asher,* and partly out of a sense of *finding* the ethically uplifting Betty Fischel, Goldstein was strongly moved to give serious considera-tion to a career in the rabbinate.** Since the Fischels, the Goldsteins, and Asher were Orthodox, he could have had in mind only the Orthodox rabbinate. But as of this point in time, virtually no fully Americanized person had become a fully accredited Orthodox rabbi. Most European rabbis were associated with unpretentious small-town synagogues that were facsimiles of those they had led in Europe, and thus were seen as remnants of the past and without a future. Under these conditions, the notion of marrying a person considering launching the type of a career that had practically no precedent and thus barely a minimum likelihood of stability, must have seemed unthinkable. Therefore, Betty Fischel, at first, tended to think only in the restrained terms of a "platonic relationship, at most."

It was inevitable that their paths would meet again, since they both lived in the same neighborhood, attended the same syna-gogues, studied worldly disciplines at the same university (he at Columbia and she at Barnard), and delved into religious studies at the same institution (he at the Jewish Theological Seminary and she at its Teachers' Institute).

If all this were not auspicious enough, both of their families vacationed at the same town in the heart of the Catskill Mountains,

---

* In addition to the void Rabbi Asher's untimely passing created in a pulpit, Asher's passing represented a dramatic setback, from an Orthodox point of view, to the Jewish Theological Seminary, which was rapidly losing its Orthodox identity. Only a few months earlier, in this same year, the Orthodox Rabbi Drachman, formerly the dean of the faculty, was involuntarily dismissed from the Seminary's faculty.

This also marked the period of the death of Mordecai M. Kaplan's father, after which Mordecai began to more openly shed his moderate approach to Orthodoxy in favor of the ideas he began to develop that, in relation to historic or traditional Judaism, are often considered heretical. Kaplan later termed his approach "reconstructionism," although most traditional Jews—including Rabbi Goldstein himself—regarded and continue to regard many facets of it as "*destructionism*."

** One of the closest first-hand observers of Mrs. Goldstein's role in influencing her future husband's decision to abandon the secular bar in favor of the rabbinate was an orphaned relative, who was very close to them particularly in the early years of their marriage. She stated without reservation that Herbert Goldstein "was inspired to change his profession because of Betty. She said the idea of someone going into that profession was one of the highest ideals. Falling in love with her, he therefore decided to enter the rabbinate." This appears to be an oversimplification, but at the very least, it certainly shows the type of support the rabbi could expect from his wife once the decision was to be reached.

in Hunter, New York. It was in the serene brisk air of this summer resort town of Hunter that Goldstein began his hunt, in earnest, for a permanent place in Betty's heart. In 1911, in order to become better acquainted, but so as not to attract undue attention to his long-range designs, he arranged to teach her shorthand, although it is still not clear precisely how he had come to master the skill of shorthand in the first place or why, for that matter, he *wanted* to master it, if not to shorten his quest for her hand in marriage. Gradually, the "tutor" and his "pupil" became tennis partners, walking partners, and partners in many other areas of endeavor before deciding, of course, on the ultimate partnership. During the school year, they regularly walked home together after classes.

By the end of the summer of 1912, young Goldstein concluded his vacation only after leaving the following letter and memento for her who had long since become his sweetheart:

> I leave not out of choice, but because I must. I shall never forget both the parting words of yesterday, and the day before. Take the enclosed flower as nature's parting gift. May our relationship be as beautiful, simple, and innocent, as this offspring of mother earth. Your own, Herbert.

By March of 1913, Betty Fischel wrote in her diary that, "He said this evening that my word would be law for him, in all matters, especially in those which regarded me. He told me to write this fact down, so that I can hold him by it in the future."

By this time, two factors were keeping the two from formally revealing their plans: the fact that the oldest Fischel daughter had yet to wed, and the reluctance of Betty and Herbert to marry before Goldstein would actually become ordained and in possession of a full-time position. Even when attained, the salary of a rabbi would not begin to maintain the young couple in the standard to which the Fischels were accustomed. Betty Fischel was rather philosophical about the prospect of marriage to a person with a minister's modest salary. She wrote in her diary, one day:

> In the evening, Herbert and I went to the second of the "Nations of War" travelogues, which was on the Allied Powers, England, Belgium, and France....
>
> There are so many inexpensive yet very enjoyable forms of amusement that I'm not worried about how much enjoyment Herbert and I will be able to afford on a limited income. We are so happy and contented with our love alone that we need little else.

A far more unusual form of "entertainment," but one no less suited to their unusual tastes was described in this diary entry:

In the evening, Herbert and I went down to the Public Library and did some work, he on his sermon, and I writing up texts from books on sermons. I love to work for and with Herbert. That unity of interest is one of the strongest bonds between us.

The following "adventure" tells more about their relationship than any other:

Herbert and I planned an adventure which we enjoyed most thoroughly. We wanted to stay down at the library all day without coming home for supper. Therefore, when supper-time came, we went out on 42nd Street to buy our supper and eat it wherever we could, preferably in the park near the library. We had not counted on it raining, which it did when we started out marketing, and since we had no umbrella with us, the park was out of the question, so we therefore walked along Sixth Avenue till we came to 45th Street, where fortune favored us by leading us into a store were we obtained figs, bananas, tomatoes, chestnuts, and milk. The storekeeper gave us glasses for the milk, salt for the tomato, and made us feel perfectly at home. What we bought formed a pretty nourishing supper, but even if it hadn't, the enjoyment we derived from the experience could not be compensated for by a twelve course dinner. Herbert and I realized for probably the millionth time, that no matter what we do, provided it is *together*, we are completely happy. We returned to the library after our repast, and stayed there till ten o'clock. It was pouring when we went home, but that didn't worry us, except insofar as the folks would scold us for the absurdity (from their point of view) of our conduct.

This unity of interest was deep and all enveloping. On another occasion:

Herbert and I took our usual Friday night walk and stopped at the synagogue to review the sermon, as we usually do. [On occasion, she would read to him a paper of her own as well.] We enjoy the spiritual element in this procedure more than other people enjoy the finest theatre.

Although there was a tacit agreement for at least three years prior to their marriage that they would eventually marry, this understanding was verbally expressed in increasing degrees of formality.

Although they were not to be married until March of 1915, Betty recalled that:

The summer that Herbert was courting me, in 1911 [one can deduce, from this choice of words, that thereafter, in her eyes, he had *already* won her heart] we were both in a highly spiritual and ethical frame of mind. Thus it happened that we decided at some time to write a book together—an ethical work of some kind.

When he proposed to me, he did so in the words, "Don't you think it would be a good idea to write our book as a wedding favour, at our wedding."*

The first record we have of an informal but actual verbal proposal from him to her was on August 13, 1912. He noted at the time that the Hebrew date was the first day of *Rosh Chodesh Elul*, the period in the Jewish calendar characterized by introspection and general penitence. Furthermore, the Hebrew letters of the month *Elul* have been said to constitute an acronym for the famous Biblical double-entendre, *anee l'dodee v'dodee lee,* "I am for my beloved and my beloved is for me."

Not until August 10, 1914, did Goldstein formally approach Mr. Fischel, in Long Branch, to ask for his daughter's hand in marriage. According to Mrs. Goldstein's diary:

He...said, we have "sown in tears" [having met at a memorial service for Dr. Asher]; therefore we would "reap in joy"** and that he loved me the first time he saw me....[by this time, any Fischel family opposition to the proposed union had disappeared, and] Papa said, "Here under the open heavens, I grant you my full approval and blessing."

Like the coach of a team of relay racers, Mr. Fischel was so anxious to release his patiently waiting second daughter after the marriage of his eldest, that he engineered the announcement in this typically (for him) flamboyant manner at the reception immediately following Sadie's Thanksgiving Day marriage at the Hotel Astor:

Herbert called me [his future bride] down to the room of Mr. and Mrs. Kahn of Rochester, who were staying at the Astor, and in whose room he changed from his minister's frock coat to full-dress suit, and then he gave me my engagement ring....

My ring is a dream! It is every bit as pretty as Sadie's, and even if it weren't, I would be just as happy, for the love between Herbert and myself is infinite and doesn't require

*This was precisely what eventually took place.

**These are quotes from the Book of Psalms 126:5.

material things to add to it.

After I got the ring, I went up to his folks...Then we went into the dinner, which was beautiful. There were a number of after-dinner speeches including [one by] Judge Rosalsky who was toastmaster. Judge Sanders said that besides being the occasion of a wedding, the evening marked the wedding anniverary of the folks, and tomorrow morning, the papers would contain the announcement of the engagement of Mr. Fischel's second daughter. Of course, all eyes turned on me, which made me quite embarrassed, and Rosalsky said that a judge ought to know better than to make public announcement of a thing told in confidence, without Dr. Goldstein's permission. This let the cat out of the bag completely.

The cat, of course, did not have to blink in unaccustomed daylight once it bounded out. Nor, in fact, did anybody else blink in surprise. An article in a newspaper the very next day was uncharacteristically informal when it expressed the wry observation that, "This announcement [of the Fischel-Goldstein engagement] will scarcely come as a surprise to any of their friends, as they have been seen together almost constantly during the last few years."

The engagement reception, which took place about three weeks later, was likewise a glittering milestone on their carefully charted road to marital bliss. The bride described the impressive social highlights of the occasion* in addition to some very pressing mundane matters of consequence.**

*"From a quarter to three in the afternoon, when Dr. and Mrs. Mordecai Kaplan [the controversial figure destined to break away from Orthodoxy and found the Reconstructionist "branch" of Judaism] came in till half past six when Dr. [Samuel] Schulman [president of the "Reform" Central Conference of American Rabbis and rabbi of Temple Beth-El, which later was "consolidated" with Temple Emanu-El, the leading "Reform" congregation in the country, where his spiritual leadership continued] came, [It is conceivable that these two notables intentionally and thoughtfully arrived before and after the 3-6 p.m. designated hours in order to avoid creating a stir among the predominantly Orthodox guests] there was one constant stream of people (fully 400) in spite of the fact that we didn't send out any cards. It was so interesting to see people come, for we didn't know who would be present, and there certainly were a number of people I didn't expect to see. Mr. Jacob H. Schiff [later of Our Crowd fame, and one of the leading Jewish philanthropists of the period], I must say, was the most unexpected of all."

** When Pop spoke, he announced that Herbert and I are to be married on March 7—i.e., the Jewish date of my birthday, and everybody applauded. Before Pop announced this, he had spoken to Herbert and me about it, and, anxious as we were to be settled in a little home of our own, we were very reluctant to say "yes," for we would have liked to be more independent financially than Herbert's present salary permitted us to be. Herbert said to Pop that he didn't feel he was in a position to talk about marriage, and that he would rather wait till the [about-to-be-instituted Central Jewish Institute] would be up and his salary would be raised. Pop said that would take a very long time, and furthermore, at the beginning of the year, God provides for everybody's prospects during the year, and He has probably provided for us also. This settled it, and Papa shook hands with and kissed Herbert and me and set our wedding date

Although Rabbi Goldstein was destined to develop close bipartisan ties with illustrious occupants of City Hall later on in life, his unheralded trip to the seat of the city's government with his fiancée to pick up the document signifying the knotting of his own *marital* tie revealed some unusual features in their relationship:

> Herbert and I went down to City Hall today and got out our marriage license. . . . Herbert felt badly [sic] that he was unable to give me any jewelry, as Dave gave Sadie when they went down for their license, but I don't need any jewelry to make me happy. Herbert's unselfish wholehearted love is enough of a priceless jewel for me.
>
> From City Hall, we went to the printer's where we got the proof of *"Lahyishariem"* [the wedding favor that the two of them translated] which I have gone over and corrected.

No detail appears to have gone unnoticed by the bride on her wedding day.*

for March 7, the date he had decided upon in his own mind, and the date I had decided upon some time ago. [Mr. Fischel waited until more than two weeks elapsed after the wedding to reveal what God had provided to give Goldstein the means to attain some of the "accoutrements" of the Fischels' more majestical standard of living. Practical "Papa was waiting till we got a safe to keep the deed in, and now we have the deed and the safe."] Finally, [Mr. Fischel, back at the engagement, now] called upon Herbert to speak. Herbert made such a beautiful and feeling speech that nearly everybody cried. He told of the beauty of our love, and how there always was a spiritual element in it, even at the height of its physical expression. He also said that I was the jewelled mirror of his ideas and ideals; and that I was a true helpmeet to him, and that he would always try to make me happy, concluding by quoting what I always say, "If it depends upon us, we will be happy."

*It is noon of my wedding day, and the snow has been falling for the last twenty-four hours. . . .

My wedding is over and I think it was lovely. The ceremony at the synagogue was conducted beautifully with the assistance of a [corps] of about twenty-six ushers—boys of the synagogue and the lodge. . . . The synagogue was decorated with white lilies, daisy plants, and smilax. The ceremony began at six and lasted half an hour. We received congratulations on the platform in the center of the synagogue and about 700 or 800 people came up to shake hands. Being faint from our fast [observed by all observant Jewish couples on their wedding day], this was some ordeal for Herbert and me, but we went through it all right.

At the dinner at the house, which began at about 8 o'clock, there were 108 people present.

Judge Rosalsky was toastmaster and the speakers included Dr. Mendes, Prof. Schechter. . . and Sam Roeder [the "soul-mate" and closest confidant of young Goldstein before Roeder himself introduced Goldstein to the person who was to become a far deeper soul-mate and confidante—Goldstein's bride]. All of them spoke in the most laudatory and admirable terms of Herbert and some of them laid stress on the sacrifice I was making by marrying a minister. The beautiful things they said of Herbert, however, made me feel that perhaps I was being compensated for my sacrifice of material things by the whole-souled and unselfish love of a fellow like Herbert.

Luzatto's *"Praise for Righteousness"* [a classic allegorical play] which Herbert and I translated [from the original Hebrew] as our wedding souvenir, was distributed towards the end of the dinner and was favorably commented on by all the speakers and guests. . . .

The ceremony was performed by Professor [Solomon] Schechter [president of the Jewish Theological Seminary, which was rapidly turning away from its traditional moorings to become the monopolistic seminary of the Conservative movement], Rabbi [M.Z.] Margolies [who was recognized by many as the leading Orthodox pulpit rabbi in the country] and [Rabbi] Dr. [H.P.] Mendes [the co-founder and first president of the Union of Orthodox Jewish Congregations of America], who delivered the wedding sermon, and told me to make my home a home for the whole congregation, just as I always intended to do.

The Goldsteins' romance completed a full cycle with their return to Hunter as husband and wife the following summer:

It is heavenly for Herbert and me to be up here [in the Fischels' summer home] alone together. Every step we take is full of the most beautiful and lovely associations. There is no place under the sun where we could have spent the first summer of our married life more delightfully than up here—the seat of our romance—the place where our love was knitted together by indissoluble ties, and the place where Herbert first asked me to marry him. We have such fun recalling the days when we were afraid to be seen together in the village for fear of the gossips and we revel in our freedom from restraint. There too it is wonderful for Herbert and me to be master and mistress of the house, to do all the bossing and not to be bossed by anybody, to have the authority to invite whomever we wish. It is just too good to be true. It is more like a story than real life—(just like the rest of our beautiful romance)—and Herbert and I are too happy for anything. We are up in the clouds[;] not down on *terra firma*. Thank God!...One of our ideals and dreams after another becomes realities. U.B. [*Um B'shrien* is an expression of thankfulness and humility], and there is nothing in the world that we wish for.

Goldstein would occasionally describe his love in Biblical terms:

...My entire love [is] just like the *o-lah*, [the technical classification of a certain kind of Biblical sacrifice], which was given wholly to the Lord, so I am yours devoted wholly....

It is no wonder that the couple was described by an orphaned relative they often invited to their house as "my Romeo and Juliet."

The first summer after he founded the Institutional Synagogue, while his wife was in the country with one infant and another was on its way and he was in the city to be at the synagogue for a few days, he was in a contemplative frame of mind, writing to her:

The trip to the city gave me a chance to do a lot of thinking. I need to work myself up to the best possible spiritual, exemplary stature as possible. Just watch and you will see. Of course, you will help me, and grow with me, won't you darling."

Many pages of this book will testify that her life most emphatically was dedicated to not only helping and growing with her ambitious husband, but to reinforcing his resolve in periods of crisis as well.

Chapter 5

Ordinations To Satisfy Both Extremes

As if destined by a conspicuous cosmic plan of spiritual reincarnation to succeed the brilliant charismatic young British Rabbi Joseph Mayer Asher, who was destined to be cut off by the hand of God in the prime of his life, Herbert Samuel Goldstein and his life as a rabbi seemed to be linked up to the former's heart, and set by a cosmic time clock to spring off the starting line just as his mentor was to cross the threshold into the world to come. Both Goldstein and his then bride-to-be had looked up to the prematurely deceased rabbi as the embodiment of all that could be noble in a spiritual leader. At the funeral service, Goldstein began to arrive at what he himself considered the most important decision of his life.

While a student at Columbia, he had originally intended to become a lawyer, but, as he recalled more than half a century later:

> At the same time, one of my closest friends, Samuel M. Roeder, Esq., was constantly urging me to study for the rabbinate, and offered me a clerkship in the law office of his father, of which he, his brothers, Judge Jehiel and Joseph, were partners. He suggested that, if I studied for the ministry and changed my mind, for law, I could do so, saving [by using this training as an approved substitute for law school]...the time required...for...law school....
>
> At about that time I prayed often at the Congregation Orach Chaim at Lexington Avenue and 95th Street, I received a great inspiration from Professor Joseph Mayer Asher who was the rabbi of the congregation and professor of homiletics at the Jewish Theological Seminary. Rabbi Joseph Mayer Asher died [on Nov. 9, 1909]. I was present at the funeral held

at the Orach Chaim Synagogue. It was then that I made up my mind as to the future. I said to myself, "Why should I become a lawyer? And, even if I do become an able lawyer, do the Jewish people need another lawyer?"

I also thought to myself, "If I become a Rabbi and become a mediocre English-speaking rabbi, will the Jewish people need another English-speaking Orthodox rabbi— especially for the young people?" My answer to myself was "yes." There and then I finally decided not to pursue the study of the law,* and made my application to enter the Jewish Theological Seminary of America.

For decades, the only institution in America offering even a semblance of an Orthodox rabbinical degree was the Jewish Theological Seminary (J.T.S.). That, however, was the problem, since in the eyes of many Orthodox rabbis of stature, this was *all* that the Seminary offered—a *semblance* of a universally acceptable degree. Although the Seminary was formally incorporated with "the purpose" of "the preservation in America of the knowledge and practice of historical Judaism, as ordained in the law of Moses and expounded by the prophets and sages of Israel in Biblical and Talmudical writings," a virtual definition of Orthodox ideals, the school's direction changed radically after its founders passed away. Moreover, even in its pristine original state, the J.T.S. never offered the intensive course of study in the *Talmud* and *Codes* traditionally considered prerequisites for a universally acceptable rabbinical degree, nor did it set up the type of personal standards of religious commitment which likewise are expected in a generally recognized Orthodox rabbi.

The dilemma was solved when Goldstein consulted the rabbi of one of the two synagogues he attended, Rabbi M. Z. Margolies, the "dean of the American orthodox rabbinate." He recommended that young Goldstein should study privately and intensively with a scholar by the name of Dr. Zadok Kapner, and thereby gain the knowledge and expertise in Jewish law needed to sit for a traditional private oral examination with a leading nationally recognized rabbi, which would lead to ordination. Goldstein decided to strive for both a Seminary and a traditional ordination, thereby obtaining rabbinic credentials that could satisfy the broadest range of views feasible within the Jewish community.

This decision set the stage for an unprecedented challenge. It meant that he was destined to become probably "the first American-born to receive his ordination from a prominent Orthodox rabbi of this city." This distinction was attributed to

*As indicated earlier, this was only a provisional decision, since in 1911 he clearly *did* at least present his schedule to study law.

him almost as soon as he received his traditional ordination and, as of his death more than half a century later, it was recognized to an even greater extent, since it passed the test of time, and the word "probably" was dropped. Thus he actually became known as the first Orthodox rabbi* of American birth and education to receive a traditional ordination anywhere in America.**

Although Goldstein always differed theologically with the views of Dr. Solomon Schechter, the fiercely independent president of the Jewish Theological Seminary, a mutual sense of admiration developed between the two. Goldstein as a student used to accompany Schechter to numerous functions and picked up insights and valuable intangible tidbits of information, as well as Schechter's personal friendship. This friendship seems all the more remarkable in light of Schechter's apparent hostility to another militant and outspoken defender of unadulterated Orthodox values in the Seminary, Rabbi Bernard Drachman.

Schechter also was a close friend of Goldstein's then father-in-law-to-be, Harry Fischel. One of the Fischel daughters recalled that during their summer vacations, "Schechter used to come down from the Grand View [Hotel in Hunter] to have *gefilte* fish (a Jewish delicacy) at Papa's." This personal relationship existed even though Fischel was known for his philanthropy which benefited virtually every major American Jewish institution that was not hostile to Orthodoxy, yet Fischel's thorough, authoritative biography makes absolutely no mention of any contribution to the Jewish Theological Seminary. When Fischel asked Schechter for an analysis of his then-prospective son-in-law, Schechter's reputed reply was positive, with one caveat: "He is a little *too* religious." Coming from Schechter, this was the best recommendation Fischel would have liked to hear!

Goldstein introduced his stay at the Seminary in his auto-biography as follows:

I entered the Jewish Theological Seminary in the Fall of

---

*Certainly the first one of national prominence.

**People continue to be astonished that a man who died as recently as 1970 could hold this distinction. The explanation is rooted in American Jewish history. For centuries, Jews in America had been led by either European rabbis or American *chazzanim*—cantors—who served as spiritual leaders but lacked formal rabbinical ordination. Such legendary personalities as Gershom Seixas and Isaac Leeser were *not* rabbis but were *chazzanim*, cantors. Other prominent English-speaking Orthodox preachers were either of European birth or education —or both—thus giving the distinction of being number one to Rabbi Goldstein so surprisingly late in American history. Other rabbis who, in the minds of many people, inaccurately seem to merit this distinction are rabbis Joseph Hertz, Moses Hyamson, and Mordecai Kaplan (before he reconstructed his views and founded "reconstructionist Judaism"), but they were all born in Europe. Rabbi Bernard Drachman was ordained in Germany, and Rabbi Sol B. Friedman was ordained in 1919, five years after Rabbi Goldstein had been, even though Friedman may indeed have been the first native Yankee to graduate the Rabbinical Seminary later associated with Yeshiva University. By this time, Rabbi Goldstein was *teaching* there.

1910. Our sessions started at 9 A.M. and ended at 1 P.M. Thereafter, the students would have their lunch and then go to synagogue schools to teach religious subejcts. I realized there would be little opportunity then to pray *Mincha* [the daily afternoon service], and I suggested that we have a regular *Mincha* service or afternoon service at the close of our sessions.

Needless to say, I met with some opposition which only encouraged me as to the intensity of my efforts toward that end (for the service). Finally I succeeded, although when I entered the classroom I was teased and called "Mincha Goldstein," which I recognized as a title of honor. This service was continued throughout the four years of my stay at the Seminary, and I believe it was continued for some time thereafter, perhaps to this very day.

Another mark of religious distinction that he brought upon himself, both literally and figuratively, was the skullcap, or *yarmulkeh*. Other students wore such religious articles too, on occasion, but many did so only when they felt obliged to out of a sense of conformity with their peers or parents—a respect for others. Goldstein wore *his* with an unconcealed aura of *self*-respect. No trace of a skullcap appears on the heads of any of his classmates in their yearbook photographs; Goldstein, the class valedictorian, was the only student photographed with one on, and he wore it as a crown—which covered the entire crown of his head, actually reaching down across the top of his forehead.

Notwithstanding—or perhaps in part *because* of—Goldstein's unreserved stance in favor of unadulterated Judaism, despite the corrosive influences to it that often prevailed at the Seminary, his popularity grew. At a well-attended meeting, likewise in his senior year, he was elected president of the student body, then known as "the Morais-Blumenthal literary society of the Jewish Theological Seminary."

Goldstein, as president of the society, did not try to *equal* the achievements of his predecessors—he sought to *surpass* them. Not content with ordinary social gatherings, the society, in Goldstein's administration, did not stop at winning the participation of students, but it also succeeded in engendering the presence of professors—and the professors' families. The society's Loan Fund Committee aided students in "financial straits" most concretely not by merely making recommendations to a school-sponsored or other outside financial agency, but rather, by dipping into a fund which was "made up chiefly of a monthly assessment on the members."

Likewise on the practical side, the society's own Employment Committee "secured employment"—mostly afternoon teaching positions—"to the amount of sixteen hundred dollars." The society's Social Service Committee, were it to be given a more accurately descriptive name might have been legitimately called the Subtly Religious Inspirational Service Committee as well, in recognition of its members' successful efforts "establishing Friday evening services in the different sections of the city," and launching or aiding the "Anti-Mission League," "Young Israel," "the young Judeans," and "similar movements."

Most objectively unprecedented was the society's ability to justify its reputation as a literary society with a substantial publication of its own—beyond the scope of the bi-monthly literary meetings arranged by the Literary Committee.

> For the first time in the history of the Seminary [wrote Goldstein in his Presidential Report on the achievements of the society], though similar attempts were made by the student bodies of the past, the Morais-Blumenthal Society, through its General Publication Committee, has fulfilled a long-felt want—the publication of a *Seminary Annual.*

Going beyond the realm of an ordinary yearbook, it was replete with major substantive articles by both students and distinguished faculty members, and, reflecting Goldstein's boundless optimism in establishing precedents organizationally as he was destined to do throughout his life, the very *name* of the publication—*The Seminary Annual*—consciously laid both the actual and the psychological groundwork for the future.

No matter how many mountains Herbert Goldstein may have moved as a student leader, he reserved his most forceful assault for an ideological attempt to cut down to size the people at the top. Goldstein dared to challenge two of the most charismatic and powerful personalities in the institution, and yet he was able to walk away from the commotion he had caused with a reputation that was only enhanced from the point of view of Orthodox Jewry.

> In the beginning of my sophomore year at the Seminary, I was given as my assignment in homiletics for preaching before the Sabbath congregation the *sedra Veyechi*, the closing [portion] of the Book of Genesis. It was the custom to give the students an opportunity to preach before an adult congregation.
>
> Before addressing the congregation, [each student] was to preach his sermon in the presence of the president of the Seminary, the late Dr. Schechter, the professor of homiletics,

Dr. Mordecai M. Kaplan; and the instructor of public speaking, Mr. Grenville Kleiser, who wrote a number of books on public speaking for the Funk and Wagnalls Publication Company. They were the first to be called upon for the criticism of the sermon, followed by a number of students who were called upon to offer their remarks. This was held every Wednesday before the Sabbath day of preaching, to give the student time and opportunity to improve his sermon for the coming Saturday.

[After Goldstein delivered the first draft of his sermon,] Dr. Schechter, who was always the first speaker, made some remarks and then left the room. Professor Kaplan attacked my sermon, and was very displeased with it. He was then followed by Meyer Waxman, a student who later wrote a very important work entitled, *The History of Jewish Literature* in four volumes. He came to my rescue and defended my stand and point of view.

Dr. Abraham Neuman, an able student who is now president of Dropsie College in Philadelphia, a pet of Dr. Kaplan, sided with him. The class was then adjourned. As he walked from the classroom there was turmoil...Professor Kaplan spoke to me in the hall alone and told me, his face flushed with anger, 'Goldstein, you cannot preach your sermon on Saturday." I did not want to lose my equilibrium, so I simply answered, "I'm sorry," and walked away.

The next morning, Dr. Schechter sent the superintendent of the building, Mr. Breuer, who said to me: "Dr. Schechter would like to see you in his office." I immediately went up to his office.

As I entered, Dr. Schechter said to me, "Goldshtein (that's the way he used to pronounce my name), sit down. I should have criticized your sermon yesterday afternoon, but I rather like your "Frumkeit" [religious commitment]. I would like you to go home and rewrite your sermon, and bring it back to me tomorrow," to which I replied respectfully, "Of course, Dr. Schechter, I will rewrite the sermon, but there are certain parts which I may not or should not omit." He then replied, "Goldshtein, you are excited now. Go home, and do as I ask."

Thereupon I went home, worked on the sermon and brought it back to Dr. Schechter the next morning. When I returned I said to Dr. Schechter, "I will read the parts in which you are interested." He answered, "Oh, no, read to me from the beginning to the last word of the sermon."

Of course, I did as I was commanded. When I came to the subject of Revelation of the Torah [Five Books of Moses] on Mount Sinai, [a cornerstone of traditional Jewish belief,

48

which Kaplan had repudiated], Dr. Schechter [asked me to tone down my intended remarks] by merely putting these words into my sermon: "He who does not teach that the law was revealed on Mount Sinai is not fit to be a teacher of Israel." He then said vehemently, "That is Jewish theology, and that is my subject. No one here has a right to teach that here." To which I replied, "and that is not what I learned here."

On the Wednesday that I was to deliver my sermon before the student body, I [had] said to my mother, "I may not remain a student at the Seminary after today." I delivered my sermon as revised and approved by Dr. Schechter, on Saturday morning, to the Seminary congregation. I took as my text, "For thy salvation I hope, oh Lord." I said, "Why should I speak of hope in regard to the laity when rabbis and aspirant rabbis and some of their teachers violated the Biblical commandment that "Thou shalt eat, be sated, and bless the Lord, thy God." I complained that, at a recent Chanukah gathering, delicatessen sandwiches were served, and I did not hear anyone saying grace either before or after the meal. I further made reference to our Zionist organization called the "Collegiates Zionist League," which was composed mainly of our rabbinical students. There would appear regularly on the blackboard in our restroom the following statement: "There will be a meeting of the Zionist Collegiate League this Saturday night, followed by dancing," No Torah inspiration was indicated on the agenda....In my sermon I complained that we were not being taught that the Torah was revealed on Mount Sinai....*

It was Dr. Schechter's custom to invite the preacher for the Sabbath to his home for lunch. After the sermon, I walked over to Dr. Schechter's home on Riverside drive. [H]e had told me on Friday that he had a cold and might not be able to come up to the synagogue for services. As providence would have it, Dr. Schechter was unable to be present....There was a very long hall in his apartment from the door to his study. [Upon returning from synagogue after Goldstein did] Schechter's daughter Amy cried out, not knowing that I was in his study with Professor Schechter, "Dad, you ought to be glad that you were not at the services. It was awful." We were invited into the dining room, and I enjoyed a real delicious lunch. We spoke about many subjects, but no reference was made to the sermon....

I must say that this sermon was the steppingstone

*Many years later, in a deposition under oath in an unrelated matter, Goldstein was called upon to testify as an expert witness on Orthodox Judaism. When questioned about the Seminary, he volunteered the comment that "One of our professors did not teach us Orthodox Judaism, but taught us, theologically speaking, Heresy, and, as a matter of fact, I have preached a sermon in the Seminary charging him with that...."

[leading to my being] called to share the pulpit occupied by the senior revered rabbi, called "the dean of the Orthodox Jewish rabbinate," Rabbi M. Z. Margolies, of Congregation Kehilath Jeshurun.

When told of this incident many years later, Dr. Louis Finkelstein, a successor of Schechter, listened in horror and replied, "*I* believe in *Torah Misinai* [that the Bible was revealed by God at Mount Sinai]. Certainly while *I* was chancellor, there was no policy of forcing people to take positions."

Although the impact of Goldstein's spunky sermon was felt, its sting was somewhat mitigated by the fortuitous circumstances that Schechter "was unable to be present" to hear the final version of the Sabbath sermon because he had a cold, and Kaplan lived "too far away from the Seminary" to attend its Sabbath services.

Ironically, later in life, Rabbi Goldstein frequently commented, "I shall never forget the late Dr. Schechter's admonition about professors, as I was about to enter my post-graduate studies at Columbia University. He said: 'I want you to promise me to be an *apikoros*, a doubter, to their *apikursus*, their doubts.'"

Many of Kaplan's preachings were far more subtle than his simple outright denial of revelation. He was a brilliant and persuasive person, so much so that even Goldstein later confided, "When I was a student at the Seminary, I remember clearly walking home one day and praying to God to give me strength to withstand these teachings, and to make clear my vision." God granted Goldstein the strength, but many people under Kaplan's sway did not have this strength or Goldstein's patience in studying Jewish sources for answers anticipating and responding to Kaplan's attacks on some of the most basic of Jewish teachings. Even Betty Goldstein recalled, before an audience of girls at the Hebrew Teachers Training Institute*, that:

Way back in 1909, there opened in this city a Hebrew Teacher's Training School, and being possessed, as most of you girls doubtless are, of a deep yearning for religious knowledge and inspiration, I immediately registered in that school.

Can you imagine my horror when I realized that the deep religious feeling and intense spirit of faith with which I entered the school was gradually being undermined by the lectures of the head of the school? At times I was simply miserable for I felt the bottom of my spiritual world was slipping from under my feet. But God was good to me. Just at

*In 1928, she had been among the co-founders of this school. It was to develop into the Teachers Institute of Yeshiva University's Stern College for Women.

50

this psychological time, I met that sincerely religious man who is now my husband. When I confided my trouble to him, he suggested that I bring my notes to him after each lecture, and that he would attempt to straighten out my spiritual difficulties. Fortunately he succeeded in doing this, for if he did not, I would today be an atheist or agnostic as so many of my classmates in that school have turned out to be.

Goldstein was not content merely to try to straighten out his future wife's "spiritual difficulties" that had been created by Kaplan, but, while still a student himself, he went directly to the source of her troubles. Kaplan recalled, not surprisingly, over sixty years later:

> My recollection of him dates back to the time when he and I were walking in the campus of Columbia University and arguing about some theological problem and he was trying to convince me of [the authenticity, superiority, and continued relevance of] his Orthodoxy [note who was taking the initiative in this first-recorded teacher-student confrontation] which I had by that time openly repudiated, although I was still the rabbi of Kehilath Jeshurun [although he was not destined to be for much longer, due, at least in part, precisely to this repudiation].*

---

*When Kaplan later flaunted his true colors by publishing his *Judaism As a Civilization*, Goldstein responded as follows to a letter co-signed by Milton Steinberg, Robert Gordis, Henry Rosenthal, Ben Zion Bokser, and Ira Eisenstein:

> I have your recommendation wherein you ask me to sign a letter of protest to the editor of *The Jewish Forum* for attacking Professor Kaplan's recent book.
> I cannot associate myself in your protest.
> I had hoped that this book would go the way of all diatribes against Judaism, and would be "damned with faint praise."
> I have advised a number of my colleagues of the Orthodox rabbinate to resist giving it any publicity. I have, therefore, up-to-date, refrained from saying anything in public about the book.
> However, since the issue has been made by *The Jewish Forum* and you seem to be willing to perpetuate it, I want to take this means of saying to you, and particularly to the members of the faculty of the Seminary, that they must let the Jewish world know whether their silence means consent, or whether they are biding their time to make a reply collectively or individually. . . .
> Academic freedom [in a Jewish seminary] means the right of any professor to state his views and interpretation of Judaism within the law. I have in mind Dr. Kaplan's denial of the Revelation of the Law. I have in mind, also, his permission to break the Dietary Laws outside of one's home. This is not creative but destructive Judaism.
> The *midrash* [Jewish homiletical writings] points out that a pedagogue is as a "nurse." Surely we would not permit a nurse to tell our children, "Hearken to father at home, but you do not have to listen to him outside of home." This is Dr. Kaplan's attitude in regard to the Jewish Dietary Laws.
> I can understand [the justification of] academic freedom when one rabbi wants to take his stand by [siding with] one *"posayk"* [decisor], as over against another. But certainly, there is not academic freedom involved in Dr. Kaplan's efforts to break the authority of the Jewish law [in a Jewish Seminary].

Goldstein never let up on his criticism of the teachings of leading members of the faculty, even while accepting honors they felt compelled to confer upon him. In his own words:

> In June [7], 1914, the Sunday after [the Jewish holiday of] *Shavuot*, I was graduated from the Jewish Theological Seminary. I received the Lamport prize for Homiletics, consisting of two volumes of the Jastrow English Dictionary of the Talmud. [Dr. Jastrow was a leading professor at the seminary.] I was also selected as valedictorian of my class. It was the custom of the valedictorian to close his address with the statement of "loyalty" to the faculty.
>
> I knew that I had to be very cautious in regard to this matter because I did not see eye to eye with some members of the faculty [—putting it mildly!]. The [Biblical passage read at the service, known as the] *haftorah* of that *Shabbat* [Saturday] was taken from the Book of Zechariah, Chapter 3, verse 7. "Thus saith the Lord of Hosts. If thou wilt walk in My ways and thou wilt keep My charge, then thou shalt also judge My house."
>
> I then turned to our teachers and declared, "Gentlemen of the faculty, we shall be loyal to you when we walk as the prophet Zechariah said, 'In the ways of God.'" That, I said, "will be the measure of our loyalty."

Although the eminent Jewish jurist Louis Marshall presided over these graduation ceremonies; although the charismatic Dr. Mordecai Kaplan was among the speakers; and although the words of the ailing, aging J.T.S. President Solomon Schechter were read aloud to the assemblage, the *New York Journal* saw fit to headline its coverage of the event with Goldstein's dire warnings of "disruptive perils" in Judaism.

Although Goldstein maintained a number of personal lines of communication with acquaintances he had met at the Seminary,

---

We cannot accept as academic freedom [within the framework of a traditional Jewish seminary], teachings of the absence of God as a direct revelation of the Torah, which amounts to atheism within Judaism. . . .

Perhaps the Seminary, by virtue of this issue, will return to the law and spirit of its founder, Sabato Morais. . . if those who guide the spiritual destinies of the Seminary. . . will once and for all. . . blink an eye at Dr. Kaplan. . . .

I trust, I may have been able to convince you that academic freedom has been converted into academic license.

A copy of this letter was sent to Cyrus Adler, the president of the faculty during Schechter's years as its functional head, and the acting president of the seminary after Schechter passed away, who assured Goldstein, in a letter dated six days after Goldstein's original, that various organs of the seminary, as well as the rabbis who had prompted Goldstein's letter, had decided to drop their counter-offensive.

he had very little to do with the institution *per se,* after getting in "the last word" at his graduation. This void in his academic life was quickly filled the year after he graduated by his joining the faculty of the Rabbi Isaac Elchanan Theological Seminary, the unwaveringly Orthodox school that later became part of Yeshiva University.

Despite Goldstein's election to the executive committee of the Jewish Theological Seminary Alumni in 1915, far more typical of his subsequent relationship to his Jewish alma mater was his participation in its semi-centennial in 1937. His wife reported:

> ...Herbert spoke on "The Synagogue as a Means of Preserving Tradition." He was well-received, even though he took the strictly traditional stand. Herbert and I have been somewhat estranged from the Seminary, for many years, due to their untraditional stand. However, we felt perfectly at home, and Herbert met a number of his classmates.

No less unusual than Goldstein's seminary experience was his course of private religious studies. It is impossible to conceive of his forceful stand against the Jewish Theological Seminary and so much of what it eventually came to stand for—or *stoop to* (depending on one's point of view)—without his family-arranged private course of study. Virtually each one of his private teachers or study partners was either well-known in his own right or the father of a nationally-known figure.* During his critical teenage years, as well as during the crucial years of rabbinical training, his personal relationships with these instructors were so close that his teachers were described as "practically members of the family"—*by* members of the family.

The man hand-picked by Rabbi Margolies to train his future protégé was a seemingly unassuming person** by the name of Dr. Zadok Kapner. Born about 1880, Kapner had studied at the Slutsk Yeshiva in Russia before coming to the United States shortly after the turn of the century. The young immigrant wasted little time earning a medical degree at Flower Medical School. Although Kapner served briefly in a rabbinical capacity at the Nachlat Tzvi Synagogue at 109th Street, and occasionally lectured at the Institutional Synagogue years later, he was best known as a radiologist and a roentgenologist. He had a particular knack for diagnosing illnesses, particularly when he was "one of the few who

---

*As we have already seen, and will continue to see.

**Not only was Kapner recommended as an instructor by Margolies, who, as a rabbi, was widely regarded as "number one" in his day, but Kapner also became a close personal friend of Rabbi Joseph E. Henkin, who followed Margolies, in the eyes of many, as the most erudite rabbi in America. At one time, Rabbi Henkin had been a boarder at Dr. Kapner's parents' house.

had X-rays and could *use* them. There wasn't a rabbi in America,"
it was said with some exaggeration, "who didn't come to him for a
diagnosis."*

The dapper doctor and his ambitious student managed,
somehow, to find the time to study Jewish law and lore together for
a few hours nearly every single day for a number of years. Kapner's
relationship with Goldstein rapidly evolved into one of not just
teacher-student but friend and confidant as well. Not only did they
continue to study together long after the student was ordained,**
but Kapner even joined the Goldstein family on extended vacations
in Hunter, New York, in the Catskill Mountains. Although neither
one of them, as a rule, ever exhibited anything remotely resembling Spartan tendencies, Goldstein's sister vividly recalled
frequently seeing the two of them studying while seated on a rock
that was visible from the main road running through the town.
One can only speculate that they chose this setting to get away from
the chatter of the house or to keep themselves from getting too
comfortable and thus less alert.

The two were always most welcome at each other's houses.
When Goldstein and his wife visited the Kapner residence, Mrs.
Goldstein remarked in her diary that Kapner's mother "always
makes such a fuss over us when we come." Kapner's presence in the
Goldstein home was equally, if less conspicuously, appreciated. As
late as 1931, Mrs. Goldstein wrote in her diary that "The whole
family, including Dr. Kapner, walked down to the Folks' home...
for a Chanukah party."

Kapner's close nephew, Harry Block, now a New York
attorney, rather liberally estimated that Goldstein and Kapner
spoke to each other on the phone "a million times a day." In
partial corroboration of this less than impartial claim, an active
member of Goldstein's synagogue recalled being in Dr. Kapner's
office one day, and hearing the phone ring. Suddenly, "Dr.
Kapner...began to discuss the *sidrah* [Biblical portion] of the
week, and Dr. Kapner gave the caller a *payroosh* [an opinion of a
prominent Biblical commentator]. In other words," the patient
concluded, "Rabbi Goldstein was preparing a sermon."

Apparently, Dr. Kapner prepared Goldstein well. Their
grueling study of the *Talmud and Code of Jewish Law* amply
supplemented the more narrative and less analytical subjects
emphasized at the Seminary. Goldstein was thereby elevated to the
novel status—for one born and educated in America—of being in a

---

*Kapner's prowess as a doctor was not lost on Goldstein either. When the latter anticipated
a potential health crisis in the family, Goldstein would occasionally ask Kapner to sleep over as
a house-guest.

**In fact, many of the thoughts that the quick-witted Kapner came up with, privately,
made national headlines when presented later in Goldstein's fluent and often dramatic style.

position to receive an Orthodox ordination independent of and beyond the scope of the Seminary's. He chose to have the traditional comprehensive oral examination administered to him by no less a personality than Rabbi Sholom Elchanan Jaffe, for twenty-four years rated by the Jewish Telegraphic Agency as "the leading rabbi of the Orthodox synagogues of greater New York." The *Jewish Daily News* referred to him as "one of the greatest rabbis in the land." Jaffe served at least one term as the national president of the Union of Orthodox Rabbis. Born in Kovno, Russia, in 1857, he was the rabbi of New York City's oldest Orthodox synagogue among those that catered to descendants of middle and eastern European Jews (Ashkenazim, now in the overwhelming majority among American Jews), the Bet Hamedrash Hagodol, of the Jewish immigrant capital of the Western hemisphere, the "lower East Side" of New York City. Rabbi Goldstein recalled:

> Rabbi Jaffe, who granted me the *Smicha,* the right to decide religious questions, added a postscript to the *Smicha* which increased, very much, my opinion of his spiritual stature. He wrote that if I accepted a call to a congregation which is not bound by our religious laws, then my *Smicha,* which he now grants me, will be null and void.*

In line with this unusual precautionary "postscript," Rabbi Jaffe pointedly required the precedent-breaking Goldstein to be prepared to be tested on laws relating to the construction of—and the separation of the sexes in the seating in—houses of worship, in addition to the standard subjects.

Goldstein was officially elected to his first pulpit the very night after passing this comprehensive test, which was seven months and a day before he officially was graduated from the Seminary.

Practicing what he preached—that a person's Jewish education should be continuous and should never end—four years after his ordination, and three years after he himself had ascended to a position on the staff of the Rabbi Isaac Elchanan Theological Seminary, Goldstein hired a fellow instructor at this institution to

---

*In this context, Goldstein added:

He [Rabbi Jaffe] was a man of great erudition, and after long preparation, in the knowledge of our [religious] laws, he granted me *smicha,* the diploma certifying ordination; after examining me in these laws, of Kosher and non-Kosher; of meat and milk foods; and their mixtures; the laws of mourning; the laws of slaughtering; and the laws concerning the knife used for slaughtering, which is to be so finely prepared that the animal feels the least pain, when slaughtered; the laws of family purity; of ritual immersion; the laws concerning intermarriage; circumcision; business ethics; concerning the construction of the house of worship; the segregation of the sexes involved in the seating arrangements in the synagogue as they relate to male and female.

"succeed" Dr. Kapner. Rabbi Samuel Gerstenfeld not only studied Talmud with Goldstein, but also assisted Goldstein in the research for a number of his books.* As Kapner had been before him, Gerstenfeld was also invited to the Goldsteins' summer residence, although the relationship was not quite so close. The depth their relationship may have lacked, in comparison to the intensity of the camaraderie of the Kapner years, was certainly compensated for in duration. "The tea rabbi," as the Goldstein children dubbed Gerstenfeld for the drink he would sip whenever he was over, consumed, over the years, a thirty-year supply!

Although Goldstein never formally pursued an academic doctorate after receiving an M.A. from Columbia, Yeshiva University recognized the contributions that he had made toward the institution in his capacities of communal leader, educator, and political power on its behalf, particularly with respect to his indispensable role in obtaining governmental approval of the expansions of its charter. The university expressed its appreciation by conferring upon him, in 1941, the first honorary Doctor of Divinity degree that it ever granted.

---

*This assistance was duly recognized at the beginning of each of them.

Chapter 6

A Pulpit Occupied Before Graduation

Although the congregation Kehilath Jeshurun was led by the acknowledged "dean of the American Orthodox rabbinate," Rabbi M. Z. ("Ramaz") Margolies spoke in Yiddish. For this reason, at least, the American-born young people of the congregation could not fully relate to him. This helps to explain the keen sense of loss felt in the community at the premature death of the English-speaking Rabbi Joseph Mayer Asher of the neighboring Congregation Orach Chaim. It also explains why Rabbi Margolies was compelled to share his pulpit with an English-speaking rabbi. This American presence in the congregation's pulpit was conspicuously vacant as Goldstein entered his senior year as a rabbinical student. Thus, while still a mere "mister," he was invited to preach on *Rosh Hashanah*, the Jewish New Year, and on *Yom Kippur*, the holiest day of the year. His topic on this holiest day was "The Casting of the Lots." Although Goldstein could not have known it then, God was to cast a lot in his general direction countless times, and Goldstein invariably took the initiative to make the most of his lot. The same Rabbi Margolies who headed the prestigious Kehilath Jeshurun synagogue came from none other than the very European home town of Goldstein's famous future father-in-law, Mr. Harry Fischel. Margolies, in fact, had been Fischel's godfather. They were so close that when the Fischels stayed in Hunter during the summer beyond the opening date of the school term, two of their daughters were cared for by the Margolies family in New York City. Rabbi Goldstein's illustrious eventual successor, who married into the Margolies family—and congregation—once remarked that "few people...were closer to each other than the sainted Rabbi M. Z. Margolies and the sainted Harry Fischel." The decision, however, of who would share the pulpit was not that of one man alone, but of the board of directors.

Two objections were voiced, at first, to Goldstein's candidacy —his youthfulness and his comparatively undeveloped rabbinic credentials. Regarding the first, he later wrote, the directors:

> . . . inquired at the Seminary, as they thought I was too young to assume the rabbinate of one of the most influential and outstanding Orthodox congregations in the city of New York. They spoke to Dr. Samson Benderly [the director of the Bureau of Jewish Education of the *Kehilla*—the only Jewish community organization that ever attempted to harmonize internal Jewish life in the city of New York in a carefully structured manner], who heard me preach at the Seminary. He told them, "This young man has enthusiasm, and I advise you to elect him," which they did.

The fact that Goldstein had not as yet been formally graduated from the Jewish Theological Seminary was not counted against him by those directors who at first opposed his candidacy. If anything, the fact that he had chosen to attend the semi-Orthodox Seminary at all disturbed some of them, for reasons Goldstein himself eloquently championed. His predecessor in the English-language pulpit had been Mordecai Kaplan. During the first five years Kaplan occupied the pulpit, the minutes of the synagogue subtly revealed dissatisfaction with a mere J.T.S. ordination in referring to him only as "mister," "reverend," or "doctor," rather than "rabbi." Kaplan, therefore, travelled to the town of Lida, Russia, in the summer of 1908 to receive a traditional ordination from Rabbi Jacob Reines, the founder of what is now Israel's National Religious Party. Reines was a close friend of Kaplan's father, who was an uncompromisingly Orthodox scholar. Apparently, the old style ordination came too late to have the desired effect. Although Kaplan *did* win the synagogue's full recognition as an Orthodox rabbi, he resigned by October, 1909, and then continued to drift toward the concept of "Reconstructionism," which he was to create, and which has come to be known as the fourth "wing" of Judaism.

The Kaplan experience gave the synagogue's leaders all the more reason to be wary. What disturbed some of them was their presumption that Goldstein did not have, nor could he ever acquire, on American soil, what they considered to be a recognized traditional ordination like that of the European rabbis that they knew they could respect. On November 6, 1913, "the foremost rabbi in New York" conferred this precedent-shattering traditional ordination on Goldstein, making him "the first American-born to have this authority conferred on him" in America. The last vestiges of opposition were therefore shattered as well, giving way to a "unanimous appointment" in his favor at a meeting of the directors the following evening.

Although Fischel himself had originally been among those who doubted that the ordination Goldstein had sought could be obtained, one can only smile in amusement at Goldstein's formality reflected in his "consulting" his future father-in-law about accepting the choice offer. An official invitation was issued by the congregation to the general public to hear, on November 29, 1913, the inaugural sermon of its newly elected "minister and superintendent of its religious school."*

While pastoral calls might be a chore to some ministers and beyond the call of duty to their wives, no sooner was Goldstein's engagement to be married formally announced than he began taking his willing and eager fiancée with him on his rounds. The first "pastoral call" he made with his fiancée was actually mislabelled. His fiancée candidly commented in her diary, "Herbert had a [Hebrew School] Committee meeting" at the residence of one Marcusson family, "so he took me along, thus killing two birds with one stone. We enjoyed the visit immensely."

While other fiancées might have been spending more time on wedding arrangements, the Goldsteins chose, instead, to begin a systematic series of pastoral visits, and they took to them as if they had been doing it for years. They paid their "first real pastoral call" on the president of the congregation, Mr. Davis. Then they began "the rounds of the trustees first." Mrs. Goldstein's diary entry for each pastoral call includes the words, "We are enjoying it immensely." One of the keys to Goldstein's success was his ability not merely to *enjoy* virtually every phase of his activity, but actually to relish them. He exuded exuberance. Where other rabbis may have seen their calling as a labor of love, *he* loved so to labor. Where others may have had a zest for life, he had a zest not only for life, but for everything about *Jewish* life as well—and his enthusiasm was contagious.

The Goldsteins literally opened their house to their congregants. Mrs. Goldstein regularly recorded the names of her visitors in her diary, and was prompted to remark, on one occasion:

> Our Saturday afternoon "at homes" are working very well. There is only one inconvenient part of it and that is that Herbert isn't able to be at home all afternoon, but that isn't so terrible, for, except on the days of the Study Circle, he's here for two hours at least.

*Less than half a year later, while he was still a Seminary student, he was given a three-year term and an eight and one-third percent increase in salary. The year after that, "very lovely things were said about him" at a meeting which saw his salary rise by fifty percent above that agreed upon in his original contract.

I'm so glad that my dreams of having "open house" are being realized.

Within a week of assuming his post, Goldstein began to change the complexion of the relatively staid congregation whose employ he had just entered. "My first effort," he wrote:

> ...was to disprove the statement that no young people's group could be organized in [the] Kehilath Jeshurun Congregation. Thank God I was successful in forming the Young People's Welfare League [Social Welfare Circle].

The aim of this group was no less ambitious and idealistic than:

> ...to reach all our coreligionists both in and out of our section of the city, so that we can better serve our mutual interests. Our hope is to aid and assist those who are in need, and to lend the little help, or say the little word, that shall make us a little happier than we were before. Our purpose is to spread abroad some of that old-fashioned, kindly, Jewish spirit...for the good and glory of our people.

"At our first meeting," Rabbi Goldstein recalled with remarkable specificity more than fifty years later, those in attendance:

> ...were addressed by Judge Jonah J. Goldstein [no kin] who urged them to enlist in Jewish social service. He stressed, particularly, the value of becoming Big Brothers and Big Sisters as part of that movement indicating that, in performing this act of social serice, the boy or girl who is visited [is] directed along the line of ethics and morals; and secondly, the visitor would improve his own stature and growth by taking on such responsibilities. Furthermore, when the Big Brother or Big Sister appeared, they were examples to the little brother or little sister of cleanliness and deportment.

After the Social Welfare Circle was in existence for a single month, *The American Hebrew* was able to report that, "Within the Circle a number of groups interested in Big Brother and Big Sister work...have been organized." Physical welfare was not beneath the dignity of the members of the Social Welfare Circle, either. "They also participated in visiting the sick in the wards of our Jewish hospitals." The young women met on a bi-weekly basis "to sew [clothing] for the poor" and "at the same time spend a social afternoon." In its first half-year of existence, "250 garments for the poor" were produced and distributed.

Goldstein molded affiliate clubs within the Circle such as "the

Achva—the Jewish fraternity—club which was formed," according to an article in the *Hebrew Standard*, "first to foster a wholesome sentiment of good fellowship; second, to advance, study and practice the tenets of Judaism; third, to encourage athletics." To celebrate festivals, the Circle also planned and directed dramatic presentations for children. Participants included "sons and daughters of the prominent members of the congregation." Scions of the families of the first two men to contribute $100,000 to Yeshiva College became vice president and treasurer of the Circle. In addition, on her own merit, a one-time member of the Circle's executive, Judith Epstein, was later to become national president of Hadassah. Philanthropy under such leadership became a significant focus of the Circle's efforts.

Fund raising for charitable causes not only came naturally to the members of the Circle, but activities in this unusual domain for young people produced unusually concrete results. In its first half-year of existence, the Circle netted enough to donate $500 to the Central Jewish Institute, and this figure grew at a steady pace—an equally unusual achievement. About a year and a half later, the Circle reported:

> We have paid $2,000 thus far toward the $3,000 donation we have pledged to the Central Jewish Institute, for which sum we are to have the privilege of dedicating one room in that institution.

On a global level, they contributed to the Central Committee for the [World] War Sufferers, while on a local level they helped to furnish candy for local Hebrew School children on festivals. The fund raising was on a highly sophisticated level. Small-time amateurs do not usually run successful affairs the way the Circle did, at hotels like Delmonicos and the Biltmore in its prime. At the same time, professional fund raisers rarely follow the Circle's attitude of pride in, rather than suppression of, their Jewishness. To the Circle's members, an "evening was very appropriately and Jewishly concluded with the singing of the *Hatikva* [thirty years before it was to become the Israeli national anthem] by all members."

The all-embracing Social Welfare Circle prominently featured cultural events. A "Study Circle" met "in the vestry rooms...the first and third Sabbath afternoons of the month" for an extended period of time "under the leadership of Rabbi Herbert S. Goldstein" to "study Jewish history" and "discuss problems of Jewish interest." The Circle also regularly arranged public lectures by prominent speakers including Professor Israel Friedlander, whose series-opening lecture drew 150 people.* Courses were offered ranging from "Reading and Exegesis of the 'Five Scrolls'" to "Some Great Women in Israel." On three different days of each week, Goldstein himself conducted classes on the Talmud, the prayer book, and Jewish ceremonials of the home.

Business meetings were convened in no less pleasant atmospheres than those provided by places like the Hotel Bon Ray on Madison Avenue. The meetings, which drew, on occasion, "more than 100 young folks," featured dancing and refreshments as well as discussions on "current Jewish events."

The Circle also took the initiative in opening an Employment Bureau to:

> ...place those of the [Hebrew School] children who must work, in positions where they will be able to keep the Sabbath. This will allow the child to carry into practice and live in accordance with the teachings which he has received while at the school.

Goldstein's role in the Social Welfare Circle was all-pervasive. The entire first page of the Circle's own journal in 1914 acknowledged its "deep gratitude and indebtedness" to Goldstein, "through whose personal efforts and inspiration, each and every one of the numerous and varied activities of the Social Welfare Circle had been organized and fostered." The centerfold of the journal consisted of cartoons of personal interest, no fewer than three of which focused on Rabbi Goldstein. One of them compared him to the leading evangelist of the day, who went by the name of "Billy Sunday." The cartoon's inscription was in the form of a notice to hear "Rabbi 'Billy' *Shabbat*." (*Shabbat* is Hebrew for the Jewish Sabbath day.) The adapted nickname stuck.**

Although the Circle had an accomplished set of officers, and "hundreds of enthusiastic supporters" by 1916, Rabbi Goldstein himself presided over the discussion at which a proposal was made for the amalgamation of the neighboring congregation's *Orach Chaim* League with the Social Welfare Circle. Rabbi Goldstein's presiding role assured the maintenance of the Circle's identity, as "the young people of *Orach Chaim*...joined the Social Welfare Circle."

---

*Subsequent lectures featured, among other notables, Rabbi Dr. H. Pereira Mendes, founder of the Union of Orthodox Jewish Congregations of America, and Rabbi Dr. Judah Magnes, founder of the Kehilla.

**In fact, this was to be only the first of a number of variations.

The Synagogue's Hebrew School

Within a month and a half after his inaugural sermon at the synagogue, Rabbi Goldstein had already begun to have a significant impact on the synagogue's Hebrew School. Children, in particular, are more impressed with actions than words. Goldstein did not simply welcome the students with an address; he welcomed them with a challenge. By offering to donate two prizes in the middle of the academic year for the best essay by a boy and the best essay by a girl, he not only came across as a person interested in giving them something concrete, but he also generated the excitement and the positive achievements that naturally come with competition. Another idea he was to develop, at the outset, for this synagogue and elsewhere as well, was that of a Sabbath afternoon service set up by the Hebrew School for its pupils. The synagogue thereby became a familiar part of their lives. The major changes the rabbi introduced, however, will be discussed in the context of the historic Central Jewish Institute into which the school was to grow during Goldstein's brief tenure at the synagogue.

Chapter 7

Two Phases
Of A Dream

When Goldstein joined the rabbinical staff of Congregation Kehilath Jeshurun in 1913, its Hebrew school was in the synagogue building's basement. Its location in the subterranean depths of the otherwise impressive edifice was symbolic of the esteem in which it was held by many of its sponsors—but certainly not by Goldstein. By contrast, the rabbi, qua educator, repeatedly emphasized that if children are expected to be motivated to supplement their secular education with a Jewish one, a minimum requirement is a light, airy, and esthetically attractive school building. The burden of constructing such a building and a suitable institution to promote its most effective use became the personal challenge of one Mr. Samuel I. Hyman, a prominent businessman in the feather business. When Goldstein joined forces with him and converted Hyman's dream into a reality, the Jewish community, which had been burrowing its collective head in the sand in relation to Jewish education, suddenly had a right to lift its head and place a special feather in Hyman's deserving cap.

The rabbi, meanwhile, found himself with *two* educational hats atop his towering brow. The task was his to simultaneously phase out the old synagogue-affiliated school and forge the nuts and bolts of a new entity, both of which, for a time, actually existed side by side.

An authoritative study on the Central Jewish Institute, as the new school came to be known, concluded that "Hyman, the lay leader, worked well with Goldstein...Hyman saw in Goldstein the ideal religious type that he would like to see head his modern [Hebrew School.] Both men combined a modern style with a deep zeal for Orthodoxy which made them ideal and compatible working partners....Both were involved with raising funds for the school...They were developing the first educational community center which was ideally suited for the modern American society."

Goldstein's well-publicized reasons for calling on the community's support were destined to meet with success, in his own fund-soliciting words of 1915:

Because: There is no [community Hebrew School] from Seventh Street up to 103rd Street.

Because: From the census taken, 5,600 Jewish children within a radius of ten blocks, north and south of the Institute, are without any Jewish education.

Because: This institution is planned so that 2,000 children can be taught every day.

Because: This institution will not merely be [an ordinary Hebrew School], but also a Jewish Social Centre, wherein there are provided a gymnasium, room for club work, kindergarten classes, and a kosher kitchen; in short, a centre where the ideas of traditional Judaism will be fostered and encouraged in the minds of American youth.

The institute (known as the Yorkville Talmud Torah until the New York Board of Regents approved a revision of its charter on April 27, 1916) was obviously to be far more than a Hebrew School or synagogue appendage. It was to be completely independent of the synagogue. Because of this projected independent status, many people objected to the new construction since it was only seven short city blocks south of the famous Young Men's Hebrew Association (YMHA) of 92nd Street. "Sam Hyman," however, "wanted this to be Orthodox and the 'Y' was dominated by the 'Reformers.'" For reasons discussed earlier, Goldstein welcomed this first opportunity to demonstrate to the administrators of the "Y," right in their own shadow practically, what a positive force a community center could be in the promotion of religion.

Although there had been a tacit understanding going back at least to April of 1914 that Goldstein was to be the top active official directing the Institute, as of January of 1915 he was listed as a mere member of the Committee on Finance, and as of the day of the cornerstone-laying ceremony of May 16, 1915, Goldstein was still listed along with M. S. Margolies and M. M. Kaplan as a mere honorary director. Not until January 20, 1916 was Goldstein officially appointed director,* the very first one to lead the institution.

*Or until March, according to another authoritative source, was he chosen general director.

The ambiguities in the perceptions of his formal title reflected the numerous functions he was called upon to carry out. He was variously described, in addition to the descriptions just noted, as the person in charge of "guiding the Educational Department" of the Institute and concurrently as a member of the board of trustees, a position often considered incompatible with that of a salaried executive. Thus, even at the very beginning of his career, Goldstein displayed his uncanny ability to jockey successfully for maximum latitude and authority. His extra leverage enabled him to make the most of the power vested in him—power he converted into creative energy relatively uninhibited by bureaucratic restraints. In fact, his dedication was so absolute that his wife wrote in her diary:

> Papa [her father] says [with his typical hyperbole] that Herbert's position is undignified and takes so much of his time that he cannot do any studying.*

The extent of the Goldsteins' personal involvement was apparent even before the cornerstone was laid. It was at the Goldstein residence that Mr. and Mrs. Sam Hyman discussed invitations to the cornerstone-laying ceremony; the Goldsteins prepared the program for the printer; and Mrs. Goldstein even bought the baskets for the anticipated contributions.

The cornerstone-laying ceremony was presided over by the famous philanthropist, Felix M. Warburg, who was destined, years later, to be memorialized in the best-selling *Our Crowd***. The venerable Rabbi Margolies opened the program with a prayer, and the controversial Mordecai Kaplan, not yet ostracized by the Orthodox community, joined Goldstein on the speaker's podium. Kaplan had originally suggested the idea of the Central Jewish Institute to the leaders of the Kehilath Jeshurun, and he is often given the credit for having founded it; however, he himself

---

*Rabbi Goldstein's starting salary at the Institute was almost equal to that which he had originally received from the congregation on whose payroll he remained simultaneously at an increased monetary level. When he had signed his three-year contract as "Minister" of the Kehilath Jeshurun, he had been clearly led to believe that he would receive an additional salary for superintending the new school, yet when the synagogue Hebrew School was phased out, some Kehilath Jeshurun directors sought to tamper with his contract—and with the earlier assurances on which he had relied. Pressure was exerted on him to unilaterally accept a reduction in his rabbinical salary. He did not succumb to this initiative that may have bordered on moral blackmail, and although in standing his ground he may have raised some eyebrows, he had occasion within the year to raise them even higher by voluntarily resigning, thus precluding the possibility of ever accepting another Yorkville raise. Ironically, his comfortable salaries—when combined—at his prestigious "silk stocking district" positions made his eventual decision to resign from both positions and start from scratch all the more self-sacrificing from a materialistic view.

**Warburg's position as the first and longtime chairman of the national Joint Distribution Committee, then the leading Jewish charitable organization in the country, made him, in a sense, the symbol of philanthropy for Jewish causes in the United States.

conceded that, "The only member that I succeeded interesting in the project was Sam Hyman."

The challenge was left to Rabbi Goldstein to co-establish and to mold the institution that has been referred to as "the first major attempt at amalgamating Jewish social, cultural, and recreational programs with religious educational activities under the auspices of an established Orthodox congregation."

The dedication of the $140,000 building took place a year after its cornerstone had been laid. This time, the organizers asked for more than small change. Goldstein delivered the direct appeal for funds, using imagery he was to conjure up a number of times, to motivate numerous future audiences:

> We have given slips to every man and woman in this audience. Some of us can do great things for the support of the institution, some can do smaller things to the best of their means...life has been compared to a grand symphony, with every man and woman in this world as a player in that symphony. Some of us have many notes to play...but every one of us has at least some note to sound. And so in the great orchestra of Jewish life, in the great symphony of religion I ask every man and woman to sound some note so that there will be no discord, no disharmony. If in the large orchestra one note is not sounded correctly, there is discord. The men of wealth and the men of average means must give if they want our faith to survive.

At the C.J.I.'s inception, the New York press heralded the new organizational entity as one destined to become "one of the largest and best-equipped Jewish schools and settlements in this country." Although statistical figures are sketchy for this pioneering period, the record does indeed show that even at an early stage of the C.J.I.'s development, 448 children were already enrolled.

An advertisement with the "Motto: Judaism and Patriotism," listing just some of the activities of the institute, outlined the three major areas of involvement under Goldstein's overall direction: religious and civic,* social,** and physical.***

---

*This category included:
—Outdoor nursery and kindergarten
—Day school classes for children
—Afternoon and evening classes for children
—Evening classes for adults for the study of Hebrew literature
—Evening lectures in civics, American history, etc.
—Educational moving pictures, stereopticon talks
—Public speaking course
—Plus Bible study, ethics, school of philanthropy, modern languages, and neighborhood forum.

At a reception for the National Education Association held in the C.J.I., Goldstein proudly invited principals, teachers, and persons intending to open up schools and other institutions:

> ...to investigate the building, that they might profit from the many interesting devices installed...

> ...The institute's auditorium can be converted into a synagogue [this was done only on special holidays] by opening doors at the back of the platform, thus revealing the tablets of the Ten Commandments and the scrolls. It can be turned into a dancing floor by folding up the chairs and packing them into drawers which slide under the platform, making it possible to have a stage for theatricals, and a complete moving picture outfit lurks behind the wall opposite the platform, ready for use. [Recall that this was back in 1916!]

All of the gadgets and sophisticated equipment were less significant in Goldstein's personal opinion, it appears, than the single improvement he saw fit to mention in his autobiographical sketch:

> The Hebrew School of the Congregation...was...moved from the basement of the synagogue into the light and airy rooms of the Central Jewish Institute.

At a speaking engagement in Massachusetts in 1917, Goldstein informally remarked, after his prepared address was concluded, that the main shortcoming of most synagogues is that:

> ...most of them have the main auditorium on the first floor

**This category included:
—Public entertainments and lectures
—Library and reading room
—Literary, social, and athletic societies
—Social rooms, club rooms, chess rooms, play rooms, study rooms, roof garden, and playground
—Employment bureau
—Penny provident fund
—Plus choral music, orchestra, camera club, and dramatics.

***This category included.
—Gymnasium
—Indoor and outdoor handball courts
—Indoor and outdoor basketball courts
—Businessmen's and students' gymnasium classes
—Calisthenics drills, athletics
—Gymnasium classes for women and girls, showers and lockers
—Classes in first aid to the injured
—Health talks by medical experts
—Children's classes in physical culture
—Shower baths, needle spray
—Plus volleyball, boy scouts, folk dancing, and physical examinations by medical director

68

and the Sunday school room in the basement...[C]hildren should be kept in the sunlight and clean air, if their minds are to be bright and pure.

Women Not in Closet Either

Whether or not the Ladies Auxiliary of the Institute chose to meet in well-lit and ventilated rooms, its goals were certainly as bright and pure—and its activities were as open and apparent—as any director could desire. Its own social service committee changed its name to "the co-workers league," but this organization retained "the same objects as heretofore, i.e., helping the work of the Institute in whatever way possible."

Pied Piper Blows Horn of Future Fiddler

Rabbi Goldstein's personal interest in the Institute's children was such that he went out of his way on their behalf when he saw untapped talent, even in nonreligious areas.

A case in point was preserved in the files of Felix M. Warburg. In late January of 1917, when Rabbi Goldstein was already thinking of leaving the Institute, he nevertheless was moved to use up a "favor" he might have otherwise later attempted to solicit for some other purpose by writing the following to the Warburg family:

> Enclosed you will please find a letter from one of the boys who attends the...Central Jewish Institute. [Characteristically, the rabbi insisted that the boy participate, himself.]
>
> I have watched the boy and have observed that this is a most worthy case for encouragement. From what I have heard from people that know, this boy is a prodigy in music. I feel confident that with the training he receives in our Religious School together with a professional course in music, we could expect to see in him the flowering of a Jewish genius in music.
>
> May I ask you please, if it would be possible to have a scholarship granted for Philip Geller, at the Loeb Conservatory of Music?

Goldstein's personal follow-up led to a successful audition for the boy with the head of the violin department of the Music School Settlement in New York, and finally to the following conclusion to Rabbi Goldstein's part in the *beginning* of what might have otherwise become a stunted career. His letter to Mr. Warburg thanked the latter:

> ...for the interest you have displayed in endeavoring to place

our young prodigy...in the hands of Mr. Damrosch.

In your last letter there was an enclosure from Mr. Damrosch in which he states it would be necessary to contribute $40.00 for the boy's tuition through June 2nd and that next year he would receive a scholarship.

I am enclosing a check of $40.00 for this purpose....

No matter how Goldstein acquired the pre-inflationary fee, his willingness to put money on the table is an indication of more than a fleeting whim of the moment, but of a deep and abiding personal interest in his students worth far more than money in the bank.

Resignations from C.J.I. and K.J. Send Shock Waves Through Community As Goldstein Waves Good-Bye And Appears To Waive His Rights To Two Golden Opportunities

After more than three years in his comfortable and coveted position at the prestigious Kehilath Jeshurun, a significant part of which time had also been devoted to the model Central Jewish Institute, Goldstein decided to resign in order to launch a new synagogue movement. His personal resolve to pull up his roots and leave all but the immediate members of his family, to give up his community ties and to renounce his secure office with his strong, deeply entrenched supporters, to create a new synagogue without a guaranteed salary, building, or plot of land, was not an easy one.

His experience on East 85th Street, however, whetted his appetite irrevocably to take on one of the most daring challenges the American rabbinate, at this point, had ever seen. Goldstein's activities on the Upper East Side were reaching a limited audience in a static population whose Orthodox Jewish composition was actually declining. If Goldstein wished to create a vibrant American-ized Orthodox synagogue on a large scale, the time was ripe and the place had to be in a different neighborhood. Even regardless of the Yorkville Jewish community's decline, in terms of numbers, the Kehilath Jeshurun at its pre-1917 height had drawn only from a basically elitist layer of Orthodox Jewish society, "from among the most affluent element in the East European Jewish community." "The members of the Social Welfare League came from respect-able, comfortable homes, and did not have the weighty serious problems which Rabbi Goldstein had discovered [in other areas of the city]," and with which the rabbi yearned to grapple.

Another factor in his decision to leave revolved around the simple political reality that strong personalities often cannot comfortably share a top leadership position. At the Kehilath Jeshurun, Senior Rabbi Margolies was a dominating personality

70

on one hand, and Goldstein was a maverick in his own right on the other hand. Although there is no evidence of any open friction between the two, either personal or professional, and possibly in part *because* of the deference Goldstein unquestionably felt obliged to pay, Goldstein's flower could not fully bloom in its original garden, no matter how green the garden may have been.

Goldstein began to investigate alternative areas of potentially fertile ground more than half a year before his contract at the Kehilath Jeshurun was due for a renewal. His sights settled on Harlem, then a solid middle-class community that housed a substantial number of Jews who had risen above the crowded immigrant atmosphere of the Lower East Side.

The actual proximate force that propelled him into his decision, in the spring of 1917, came as a result of a cycle he had set in motion as he lay the groundwork for developing a potential nucleus of adherents. The nucleus almost exploded prematurely, according to his wife's diary account:

> The Y.M.H.A. of Harlem, a group of 75 young men who have been waiting impatiently for the realization of Herbert's idea for the past three months, with the intention of affiliating themselves with it, sent word to Herbert that if nothing is done by March 10th, they will take quarters by themselves. Since it would be a pity to lose such a large following of young men and since Herbert himself is getting tired of the inaction, delay, and uncertainty, he has decided to announce his resignation from the synagogue this coming Saturday.

The decision to resign was not an easy one to adhere to. Fully a month after the original decision had been reached, Mrs. Goldstein found it necessary to write that her husband "definitely decided to resign from the synagogue this week." Nobody will ever know how many times he changed his mind in between.

On the second day of Passover, the holiday commemorating the ancient Israelites' crossing of the Red Sea, Goldstein crossed his own point of no return.* Although he had carefully planned his every move, he had not, apparently, done so at the expense of the drama of his official announcement:

> Contrary to his custom, he read his [resignation] sermon from notes....After explaining the idea of the Institutional Synagogue, declaring his intention of dedicating his life to a Jewish revival movement, and reading the call from the young

---

*Curiously, although he delivered sermons regularly on ordinary Saturdays, his resignation sermon was delivered on the second day of Passover and his farewell sermon was delivered on the second day of the Shavuot holiday (also known as the Feast of Weeks).

men of Harlem, he announced his **RESIGNATION** as associate rabbi of the congregation. The sermon...created a great stir and furor in the congregation....As many people expressed it, 'It came as a bombshell' out of the clear sky for it was a surprise to practically the whole congregation.

Goldstein's resignations from the Institute and the synagogue, and his decision to establish an institutional synagogue combining the attributes of both—and creatively responding to the criticism that the influence of the Kehilath Jeshurun synagogue over the social and educational Central Jewish Institute was "small"—were all the results of a single complex decision. We have seen the political factors motivating him to leave his first synagogue, and we will see the idealistic factors motivating him to begin his own synagogue in a later chapter. No less significant were the practical factors that bore down on him from his position at the hub of the Central Jewish Institute: "We came to the conclusion," his wife commented, echoing in this case her father's—if not her husband's—views, "that staying at the Institute was swamping Herbert's individuality, taking all his time and energy, and preventing him from studying."

In weighing the components of even *this* analysis, however, it seems that the intrusions on Rabbi Goldstein's *independence*, more than on his *time*, were at the heart of his decision to move on. In the first place, the launching of a new and larger combined venture from its very foundations would be far *more* time-consuming than the continued stewardship of already-established institutions. Secondly, regarding the then-existing allocations of his energies, we have seen—and will return to see further—evidences of his simultaneous non-C.J.I. creative, organizational, and intellectual pursuits in this period. In the final analysis, there is no way to get around the realities that the rabbi had to confine himself and conform his ideas, to a degree, to satisfy both a senior rabbi on one hand and two boards of directors of his elders—many of them European and fixed in their ways—on the other. The opportunity to occupy an undivided pulpit and work with a board carved along his own innovative American grain must have been irresistible.

His formal resignation from the C.J.I. was submitted to the Board of Directors on May 2, 1917. "Speeches of praise were made by nearly every director." Then the Social Welfare Circle, on May 23rd, tendered the Goldsteins a lively farewell dinner.*

---

*Parodies were sung, at the dinner, to the tunes of the songs of the day. Typical among them were the following stanzas:
Social Welfare leader, finest of them all,
What could we have done without that figure spare and tall?
Always optimistic, always smiling bright,

The most memorable farewell of all, however, was not witnessed by a board of directors or a ballroom full of diners, but took place in the privacy of the Goldsteins' own home. Mrs. Goldstein's diary captured the atmosphere:

A very touching incident happened this afternoon. A little girl and boy of about 10 and 7 years respectively came up and asked for Dr. Goldstein. When Herbert asked them what he could do for them, the little girl who was the spokesman said, "Do you remember, Dr. Goldstein, that I asked you when would be your last day at the Institute and you told me on Thursday. Well, I couldn't come to Hebrew School yesterday and the reason I asked you that question was because I wanted to say goodbye to you and that's why my brother and I came up here." With that she walked up to Herbert, shook hands with him, and said, "Goodbye, Dr. Goldstein. I wish you much luck in your new work." And the little boy who had been shaking his head in approval all the time the girl was speaking, came up and did the same. I considered that a greater tribute to Herbert than the speeches of the whole Board of Directors of the Institute combined for I felt that it came directly from the heart and was full of feeling.

That's the rabbi whom we're bidding our farewell tonight.
The most poignant, perhaps, and not idly prophetic, stated:
    That you're going from the Institute is giving us regret,
        Rabbi Goldstein, Rabbi Goldstein,
    For the splendid things that you have done we never can forget,
        Rabbi Goldstein, Rabbi Goldstein,
    Though we all applaud your courage, and we're sure you'll win fame,
        we'll miss you just the same.
    So we take this opportunity to cheer the man we love,
        Rabbi Goldstein, that's you.

Chapter 8

Fighting Words For Fighting Men

Throughout history, in times of crisis, Jews have been scapegoats for evils with which they have had no ties. Although World War II is generally considered to have been the major contemporary war that victimized Jewish minorities disproportionately, Jews and their institutions were pillaged by invading armies and berserk citizens more severely than non-Jews and their possessions, as a rule, even in the *first* World War. Despite the all too predictable prevalence of such persecutions in Europe following the outbreak of World War I, American Jews, along with their Christian neighbors, were strongly tempted to turn the other cheek, to look the other way, to thank God that they were not personally involved, and to hope or pray that the status quo would continue in this regard, come what may in the European theatre. Others, Goldstein among them, could not stand idly by while their European relatives and coreligionists suffered. Although the Jews in the United States may not have lost too much love on their often anti-Semitic countries of origin in Europe, the cherished Talmudic concept that all Jews are responsible for each other created a very real sense of anguish and urgency among caring American Jews on behalf of their relatives who had been left behind.

Many European centers of higher Jewish study, in particular, were severely damaged by the ravages of World War I. This was all the more demoralizing in light of the fact that such centers played—and their successors continue to play—a greater role in the mainstream of Jewish life than their often monastic and isolated counterparts do in non-Jewish life. Every traditional Jew strives to attain at least enough of a Jewish education to endow himself and his children with the knowledge necessary to enable both himself and his progeny to avoid infractions of the intricate all-embracing Jewish law. (Christians, by comparison, have fewer technicalities for the rank and file to follow on a daily basis.)

It should come as no surprise, therefore, that the Central Committee for the Relief of Jewish War Sufferers was founded, in October of 1914, not by wealthier "Reform" Jews, who do not even claim to follow many Biblical and Rabbinic laws other than in the breach, but, rather, by Orthodox immigrant East European Jews. At this early stage in the war effort, the Central Relief Committee immediately assumed the responsibility of raising funds on behalf of European Jews and institutions. It exerted, thereby, a very real gravitational force on American Jewish bank accounts long before the United States officially declared war in 1917.

Only a few weeks before the Goldsteins were married, the rabbi saw fit to come to his fiancée's house to join her in pasting stamps for the European War Relief Fund onto their wedding invitations. At a *Kol Nidre* night appeal for this cause on *Yom Kippur*, 1916, at Congregation Kehilath Jeshurun, Rabbi Goldstein said, "We must give even if it hurts us to, even if it is at a sacrifice." His wife observed, with her eye on his checkbook, that:

> He practiced what he preached for he pledged $100. Later on, when I asked him about it [note that the buying power of this sum was so high in those days that even his wife, the philanthropist's daugher, was surprised] he said he is making ...more this year than last [although he also had the additional responsibility of supporting his first child born in the interim] and if he gave $60 last year, he can give $40 more this year...$6,600 was raised.

Goldstein also went on trips out of town for the exclusive purpose of speaking "for the War Relief" as, for example, to Paterson, New Jersey, in November of 1916.* Once the United States entered the war, Goldstein took a two-edged rhetorical sword wherever he went, rousing his audience to heights of both patriotism and Jewish service, stressing that the concepts of a good Jew and a good American not only were harmonious, but promoted each other. A Southern newspaper summed up his attitudes as reflected in one of his public addresses as follows:

> Judaism to his mind was the practical application of loyalty to one's country and its interests, and to attain the goal of better Americanship, the Jew had but to be true to his

---

*On a Fourth of July during the war, Goldstein made a special trip to New York City from his summer retreat in Long Branch for the sole purpose of speaking at "some patriotic demonstrations."

Judaism.*

In a similar vein, during Economy Week, the *New York Herald* excerpted the convention sermon on food conservation he delivered to the Young Judeans assembled at Asbury Park, New Jersey. He said, in part:

> Today America faces the same situation as Joseph of old did in Egypt. He held the key to the granaries of the world. . . . The grain was sold only by measure. . . . Americans, be ye modern Josephs! [His appeal was not only to his listeners as *Jews,* but as *Americans,* with an added reason to be *proud* of their Jewish heritage.]

The world war also provided Goldstein with an opportunity to present his perception of how the changing political status of Palestine should have been treated.**
To Goldstein, however, the war effort was above politics. Individual and nationalistic concerns—both Zionist and American—were clearly secondary. A wartime diary entry of his wife could simply state: "I served lunch to Herbert. . .and a soldier who had dinner with us." There was no mention of the name, nationality, or religion of the soldier. To them, apparently, it was irrelevant.

---

*He harped on this theme long after the war ended, since in this period this idea was not at all taken for granted. Most New York Jews were first or second generation Americans bombarded by the assimilationist influences that asserted that one could not be truly loyal to Judaism and to America at the same time.

**His conception of Zion—as later outlined in his widely circulated and reprinted article on "Torah-cratic Zionism"—was in religious and not nationalistic terms. His views thus had potentially universalistic appeal among all but some non-Orthodox Jews. Most of the leaders of "Reform" Jewry, in particular, insisted, for decades, that the Biblical idea of Jewish settlement of Israel was "out of date." In 1885, the Reform leadership's Pittsburgh Platform stood for the enlightened principle, among others, that the long longed-for Biblical city of Jerusalem should no longer be an ultimate residential goal but should be substituted, in modern times, by the American land of opportunity—and other such utopias—as viable alternatives to the then-barren slopes of Judea in the promised, but then unpromising, land of Israel. It took more than a generation for these sophisticates and their successors to recognize the realities of modern Zionism and classic Orthodoxy.
The *New York Times,* in a sub-headline, cited Rabbi Goldstein's unifying exhortation that the "Uppermost Thought of All Must Be Toward Winning the War," before quoting his specific remarks to the effect that:

> Jew and Christian alike must welcome the opportunity this war has brought about of evolving in Palestine a centre for the intensification and the spreading of a pure spiritual message to the whole world. Let all mankind help to make Palestine again the holy land.

Just as Goldstein saw a Jewish obligation to help the cause of freedom in America, so he saw an obligation binding all individuals to endorse freedom of religion and the dignity of all people in a civilized Zion, and thus, of course, incidentally, to encourage Jewish settlers in their struggle to tame both the land and its often tyrannical overseers.

A ringing headline in the *New York American* stated: "Subscribe to [Victory] Loan As Religious Duty, Says Rabbi Goldstein." The article proceeded to quote him as follows:

> We must approach this loan with a double-barreled motive: first, to back the government, and second, to show our gratitude to God for the cessation of the war. [In his characteristic all-out hard sell, Goldstein added:] We must subscribe as liberally as we have done in the past, but in addition, all of us ought to secure at least one more bond. Let the added bond represent our thanksgiving offering. [Presumably, he was not playing on words when he mentioned in the next paragraph that:] Passover marks deliverance from bondage..."

J. W. B. Speaking Tour

Goldstein's most dramatic contribution to the war effort was made by direct contact with the soldiers. He was not content with merely serving on a local New York City committee to meet them—even 14,000 of them—and he was not content with merely serving as chairman of the American Soldiers and Sailors Welfare League of District Number 1 of the B'nai B'rith. Rather, he found fulfillment in bringing his oratorical skills to bear directly on the temporary home turf of those who were to bear arms for America, by going on a one-man speaking tour of many of the major military bases in the southern part of the country:

> I was asked by the Jewish Welfare Board if I would volunteer [in the sense of receiving no financial remuneration] to deliver a message to the boys in the service, which I gladly consented to do. I felt that it was my duty to render some service to the men who were sacrificing their lives for the United States. When I left to go on such missions, I would take with me two valises, one for my clothing, and the other filled with prayer books, *taleitim* [prayer shawls], **and** *tefillin* [phylacteries].
> My opening statement to these men was usually that I had not come to speak to them about patriotism because being in their uniforms was sufficient evidence that they were performing the highest form of patriotism and were prepared to make the supreme sacrifice.

As much as Goldstein may have had a golden tongue, his success was measured not so much by what he *said* as by what he *did*. He, in turn, judged his own impact on people not by what they *said* to him after his sermons, but by what they did to express their enhanced Jewish identity. It was no wonder that his businessman father-in-law wrote to Mrs. Goldstein in reaction to a letter from her husband: "I received a seven-page letter from Herbert telling me how he was successful in disposing of several hundred pair of *tefillin* and *tzitzit* [religious articles that are donned daily by religious men]....He is certainly...wonderful...in that line." After one of Goldstein's first stops (in Augusta, Georgia), he wrote to his wife: "I...feel delighted at the success God is sending.... [The] Welfare Board had a supply of their own and ran out of them after the address." Simply having them on hand without stimulating interest, as had been the sorry status quo, was clearly not enough. Goldstein had the power to generate the necessary interest. "Wasn't it wonderful, dear," he wrote to his wife, "to get so many boys [to] ask for *tefillin* and *tzitzit*.... The whole town is talking about it."

Not all of his talks were in army camps. From Augusta, Georgia, he wrote that he was "motored to the federal prison and spoke there. I feel at home when it comes to interned people, thanks to my experiences at the Magdalene Home [for "wayward" girls which he addressed periodically for many years]."

Goldstein toured the South with a repertoire of five titles: "Before the Battle," "Battle of Valley Forge and Religion," "How to Be Happy," "Who Is Happy," and "Reveille and Taps."* His address at Camp Jackson was typical both in terms of the major theme and the enthusiastic reaction. According to a local South Carolina newspaper, a General French introduced the rabbi, who:

> ...[w]ith an eloquence that was characterized by its earnestness and devotion, showed that the world in the last century was following the materialism of Mammon and licentiousness of Belial. They have gone astray from God. The war is God's chastening rod urging them to return. Such a return in the form of a religious revival is necessary for the winning of the war for "Not by force of physical or military might alone is a war won, but more so by the spirit."**

He also urged the soldiers to be clean and not pollute themselves while they are engaged in this mighty struggle. Heroism demands as a prerequisite the complete control of an individual's evil inclination and passion.

---

*He spoke at Camp Lee, Petersburg, Virginia; Camp Morrison, Newport News Virginia; the Armory, Norfolk, Virginia; Camp Jackson, South Carolina; Camp Gordon, Georgia; and Camp Jessup and Fort McPherson, Georgia, before swinging back up to speak at Camp Devens, Ayer, Massachusetts.

**Another version of the talk at a different camp quotes him as follows:

...The people chose Mammon, or the search for wealth; then Belial, or the passion for immorality. Next they raised the god Thor, with the cannibalistic desire for brute force. The nations of the world have called on God for the past four years. The present need is for the revival, the recalling to power of the spiritual God. We must not wait for the Big Stick of the Lord. [Theodore Roosevelt, the father of Big Stick Diplomacy, was a figure with whom soldiers obviously could identify.]

The five hundred soldiers, Jews and non-Jews, who composed the audience, were highly pleased and affected by the sermon. In this sermon was weaved [sic] the charming personality, and the sterling sincerity of the rabbi.

Still another meaningful barometer of Goldstein's success was the material sign of appreciation shown by the following extract of a letter written to the rabbi by the president of a Mizrachi Zionist society in Atlanta:

> ...Was at Camp Gordon last Sunday. You have no idea how your lecture inspired the boys. Some of them ask me if there is any chance for you to honor them with another visit—they are willing to pay the expense, whatever it may be....

Regarding Goldstein's sponsors at the national headquarters of the Jewish Welfare Board, Louis Kraft wrote:

> ...All the men in the office think most highly of the value of the meetings you have addressed, and the men in the camps are loud in their praises of the enthusiastic gatherings and the splendid spirit that you have aroused.

His successes were not without cost—to Goldstein's *own* spirits. In a tender letter to his wife back home, the relatively newly-wed rabbi had written, at one of his first stops in the South:

> ...Thus far [on arrival at the hotel] I have really no news of special interest—except that I am only a fraction of a *mensch* [a person] without you.... Every man should get married, yes, but have his wife with him, too.

If he considered himself a fraction of a person emotionally, he undoubtedly felt that way physically too, experiencing sensations of drying out or melting down beneath the sweltering midsummer Southern sun. Clearly, this climate must have been a self-imposed living Hell to a northerner like Rabbi Goldstein coupled with the challenging, exciting, and tension-creating packed schedule he had undertaken, which built to a climax at every stop. Although this was long before air conditioners were used—even at the best hotels—and he certainly was aware of the heat, he calmly and uncomplainingly coped with the situation. Midway through his trip, he wrote to his wife:

> Just got into this town [Spartanburg, South Carolina]. Of late, I take *three* baths a day—one when I get into town, one before I go to the meeting, and one when I come back before

going to bed. Believe me, I need all three of them—the first, because the roads are so dirty; the second, to make me fresh; and the third, to take off the perspiration after my lecture.

Without having seen this letter, Mrs. Goldstein's father wrote her:

You can see how well it is to listen to Pa [Mr. Fischel had obviously urged her not to accompany her husband on this Southern trip]. Picture to yourself how you would feel in the South in this weather. Herbert can stand much more heat because the Al-mighty has given him additional strength in order to be [better able] to deliver the message of God to the people. You certainly remember the story [in a famous Biblical homiletical writing] that our Father Abraham was thrown into an oven and he came out, like from a Turkish bath, feeling fine. Herbert is the same. He preaches and spreads the name of God so the biggest heat will not affect him.

The impact of Goldstein's orations was so strong that in the mid-1920's he was cited on one of the published ballots in a *Jewish Tribune* poll as one of the ten Jews who had done the most for America, and in 1939, a writer commented in the *American Hebrew* that:

It is quite likely that this selection was based in great measure upon his forgotten activity during the war when Rabbi Goldstein appeared before every large camp in the country [slight exaggeration, presumably] exhorting the soldiers. . . . His sermon, "Before the Battle," became famous for the confidence with which it inspired the soldiers who listened.

The Institutional Synagogue And the War
Whether or not the fact that the Institutional Synagogue was founded the day the United States entered World War I was a coincidence, it is clear that the wholehearted devotion and self-sacrifice for an ideal that the war inspired, was cleverly and effectively simulated—and emulated—by Goldstein and his synagogue, leading to increased service *within* the synagogue for both "God and Country." Shortly after the conclusion of the war, Goldstein wrote an article for the *Jewish Immigration Bulletin*, stating, in part:

Before the war, we were more or less engrossed in material things, in material pursuits. . . . During the war, however, the body politic of our American people underwent a sweeping...change for the better....We refined the material sense of our people into a sense of service—especially for our young...Before the war, to concentrate [consecrate] one's life to service was indicative of the extraordinary young man or woman or the peculiar young man or woman. The war enlisted activity...for spiritual pleasures, and for serious thoughts and devotion to a cause. All this may be summed up by the word service...for a great cause—for our dearly beloved U.S.A.—and for the maintenance of its fundamental ideal—Democracy. An infinite amount of good has resulted from all this. Clubs and groups organized for war work have in many instances been reorganized into Social, Literary, and Social Service societies....A number of churches have banded themselves together to raise $10,000,000 for the post-war work. We of the Jewish faith must strive to do this same work through the medium of a most serviceable and beautiful Institutional Synagogue or community centre in every section of our cities....The Jewish community...has its best opportunity now....This is the psychological moment....

Regardless of the timing of the Institutional Synagogue's founding, the I.S. certainly gave to the war effort more than it took. In September of 1917, before the first I.S. building was even completed, a newspaper reported that "[a] large number of Institutional Synagogue members have joined the colors, and an honor roll is being prepared which will be placed in the foyer of the new building." At first, a white slab was put up memorializing the men who lost their lives in this war. There were at least ten. Later, the memorial was formalized.

Never one to let an opportunity go by, Goldstein utilized the occasion of a eulogy—for one of these fallen soldiers—to influence public opinion against the restrictive immigration laws that threatened to put an end to the waves of Jewish immigrants who had been steadily reaching America's shores until the World War erupted. "Who was Herman Kantrowitz?" he asked, in his occasionally used Socratic style.

He was the only son of foreign-born immigrant parents. May our Congress remember this fact in Washington this week, and act according to the knowledge that the sons of the foreign-born laid down their lives that this country might continue a leader of the human race.

The Jewish element in America is but 3 percent, yet of those who died in France for Old Glory, 5 percent were Jews.

For those not eligible or available for actual military service, there was a middle ground, between those in action and those in total *in*action, and the Institutional Synagogue members plunged into it at every opportunity. About four months before the synagogue moved into its first building, for example, a newspaper informed the Jewish community that "Rabbi Herbert S. Goldstein...with the assitance of members of his congregation, has begun to collect books, magazines, and newspapers of interest for distribution among the boys at the front and in camp." Later we will see, too, how extremely systematically the synagogue sisterhood knitted clothing for the troops to supplement the bare essentials. The I.S. welcome mat—even for temporary visits—was always ready to be rolled out, going as far back as Day One, in the sense that the first Jewish New Year services at the Institutional Synagogue were graced by the attendance of more than 300 soldiers in uniform. "They came from cantonments and from military stations in the city."

By the beginning of 1918, the Institutional Synagogue's involvement with the emotional, spiritual and physical conditions of its soldiers in the war effort had attracted the attention of New York's incumbent Governor Charles Whitman, who:

> officiated...at the unfurling of a...sixty-six star...service flag at the Mount Morris Theatre....The ceremony was arranged by the congregation of the Institutional Synagogue in honor of sixty-six young men who are serving the nation in the army and navy.

The Institutional Synagogue did not limit its patriotic activity to events where it received all the credit—or even most of it. When President Wilson proclaimed May 30, 1918 as a day of prayer and fasting, the Institutional Synagogue suggested that all synagogues in Harlem combine to hold one service *not* at the Institutional Synagogue—to avoid appearing unfairly self-serving—but rather at "the synagogue at 26 West 114th Street." Mrs. Goldstein's diary entry said nothing about her husband's talk, but it *did* mention that he "was fasting." He was as observant of his patriotism as he was of his Judaism.

The armistice agreement certainly did *not* put an end to I.S. involvement in the effects of the war * For example, a third of a

---

*Mrs. Goldstein's diary entries at the time of the actual armistice announcement capture both the excitement of the occasion, her reactions and the synagogue's:

Nov. 7   Spent the afternoon preparing a peace ad, for *peace was declared at 2 P.M. this afternoon.* [Note that the first mention of the occasion was with regard to *her activity* in reaction to it.] The sirens blew, the church bells tolled, and all the people went mad with excitement...parading, horn blowing...and all kinds of noise all day and night. In the evening I went over to the Institutional Synagogue where wild excitement reigned like everywhere else.

Nov. 8   The peace report was a false one. (cont'd)

year after peace had been declared, the I.S. sponsored a public meeting at the neighborhood Mount Morris Theatre to discuss "War Saving," with the participation of officials of the French High Commission, the *New York Times* and the War Savings Society. In a single shipment in 1922, the Institutional Synagogue sent $1034.33, collected in charity boxes, to the "War Relief Headquarters."

The honoring of the memories of those who had made "the supreme sacrifice" became an annual event, and, in a sense, a daily event. A four-foot high bronze tablet memorializing these heroes was placed on prominent display in the synagogue foyer, and unveiled on November 19, 1922, the 59th anniversary of the Gettysburg Address. A medallion reproduction of the head of Abraham Lincoln was engraved onto the tablet, accompanied by the text of the Gettysburg Address. The occasion was highlighted by an "Address of Dedication" by Dr. Nicholas Murray Butler, the president of Columbia University. Elias Lieberman, the poet, associate editor of the *American Hebrew*, and author of the poem "I Am an American," agreed to read a poem he had written especially for this occasion.

Armistice Day was a regularly commemorated event at the I.S., drawing, one year, 900 people* to a Friday night talk on disarmament.

In June of 1924, a "Central Relief Committee" was "temporarily [re-]organized" for the express purpose of "subsidizing the *Yeshivot* [schools of higher Jewish study] of Europe, whose existence [was] threatened by the aftermath of the war." In December, a city-wide conference was called "to decide upon plans as to how a permanent organization may be effected."** The original Central Relief Committee had become, a decade earlier, the first of three recognized agencies working in cooperation with the Joint Distribution Committee (JDC), of which Goldstein was a director and member of the National Council. Goldstein was to be active on behalf of both of these committees for the better part of

---

Nov. 11   I was awakened at 5:30 A.M. by the blowing of the sirens [and the other noisemakers described above]...and I realized at once that peace *was really here at last*...I went down to see about the beginning of the United War Work for which the I.S. is also working. We have a booth in Riker's drug store, and after I settled Bertha [one of her younger sisters] there to take care of the collection in the booth, I went down to the Red Cross auxiliary on Fifth Avenue to get instructions for the pajamas we are making at the sewing circle of our Sisterhood. .I went over to the I.S. where I...discussed matters concerning the United War Work Campaign.

*By Mrs. Goldstein's usually conservative diary estimate.

**The headline speakers were Rabbis Goldstein and Meyer Berlin, the world Mizrachi leader in whose memory the then-yet-to-be-built Bar Ilan University in Israel was to be named.

his life.* Once the committee was re-established, its meetings, during at least one period, "used to be held at the Institutional Synagogue." In the course of this time frame—and possibly beyond it, as well—"[a]ll their propaganda came out from there."

Goldstein's nonmilitary wartime activities were revived following the outbreak of World War II, and then, once again, during the Israeli War of Independence. In both of these campaigns, Jewish involvement was far more pervasive than it had been in World War I. The rabbi's efforts during World War I and its aftermath may be all the more striking precisely because Jews were *not* singled out, in the public eye generally, as the group with the most at stake.

---

*In 1936, he was to speak over the radio for the JDC in his capacity as the Honorary Secretary of the Central Relief Committee, a title conferred, obviously, on the basis of services rendered as well as anticipated.

Part Three

THE INSTITUTIONAL SYNAGOGUE— A DARING EXPERIMENT

Chapter 9

Surveying A Fertile But Fallow Field

One of the major factors in the failure of Orthodox Judaism to capture the fancy and the enthusiasm of many American-born Jewish young people in the early 1900s was these youths' tendency to reject, without careful analysis, what they perceived to be the alien and "irrelevant" ways of their European parents. Their parents' religion, as an inherent part of their foreign "way of life," was thus an inevitable casualty of the overriding attitude that mandated a complete break with the past.

Rabbi Goldstein refused to write off this vanishing Jewish generation. Imbued with a sound appreciation of both the Jewish and the American cultures, he was able to see a future for the two cultures where they would not only co-exist but actually support and reinforce each other. He felt that there was nothing inherent in the American way of life that could not be reconciled with the Jewish. To the contrary, he felt that the primary reason for the failure of the Orthodox Jewish culture's transplantation was the unwillingness, even if at times unintentional, of the transplanters to give the flower of Jewish life in America an opportunity to draw nourishment from, and adapt to, its new surroundings. Instead, well-meaning Jewish immigrants attempted to turn all roots back inward, a self-destructive act to the young fledgling American Jewish spirit. Rabbi Goldstein chronicled the situation, while still in the budding stage of his career as a rabbi, as follows:

When the Jewish immigrants from Russia, Poland, Austria, and Hungary first began to come to this country, they were interested in erecting houses of worship, not only wherein they might pray, but wherein they might also meet their countrymen, their *"Landsleute."* Thus congregations sprang up styling themselves after the name of the province of or the town from which the members of the congregation came, as for instance: The Ciechanower, the Suvalker, and the Byalostocker *Chevrot* [societies].

The members of these congregations would come together not merely for Sabbath prayers, but would attend the three daily services during the week as well. After *Shacharit* (the morning prayers), they would listen to the exposition of a chapter of the *Mishna* [the writings on which the *Talmud* is based]. They would spend the interval between *Mincha* [the afternoon prayers] and *Maariv* [the evening prayers] hearing someone give a course in *Schulchan Arukh* [the Code of Jewish Law]. After *Maariv* they would stay an hour longer poring over the Talmud, until it was time for them to return to their respective homes. The religious services on all occasions represented the chaos, the lack of decorum, and the peculiarities of the European communities from which these people came. These provincial synagogues as a rule merely represented the transplanting of the Russian, Polish or Galician synagogue to American soil.

Rabbi Goldstein's view as a seasoned rabbi well over a decade later accentuated this point:

> ...Why has the synagogue [—in general, not his—] failed to hold the young? Because we [again, present company excluded!] transplanted to this country the environment [of European countries] and expected the American youth, cradled, nursed, and brought up in American surroundings to be at home in these quarters. For our parents this type of synagogue was a haven of protection...the stranger to this land was made to feel at home, and often given his first real start in life by his friends who knew him, his family, his character, and his whole history.... But we, the children, born in this country, did not feel at home in these synagogues.

Goldstein emphasized the shallowness of the clannish approach. The immigrant Jew was devotedly attending synagogue services, but often, at least partly, for the wrong reasons. Inevitably, attendance on such terms proved to be almost as worthless, in influencing or impressing the "new generation," in the long run, as no attendance at all! Goldstein spelled out the last phase of the all-too-frequent progression, as follows:

> As soon as these men were able to save money and open businesses for themselves, they became so absorbed in their enterprises, that they went beyond the pale of the Ghetto, took up their habitations among non-Jews, adopted the customs of their neighbors and ceased to attend the Synagogue three times a day, nay, many of them came not more than once a week, namely on the Sabbath. Moreover, as these men began to have families of their own, their interest in their country-people *(Landsleute)* waned....

The problem is a particularly American one. When Goldstein was in his prime, a study was conducted regarding the position of Orthodoxy in the two most prominent English-speaking countries in the world. While Orthodoxy was firm in England, it was eroding in the United States. The author dismissed the suggestion that this was due to more of a "relish for change" in the American personality than in the British. Although the English, he conceded, might be slower to change consumer buying habits, when it came to ideas and entire modes of living, the British voted a Labor Party to power long before Franklin Roosevelt dealt his New Deal to the American public!

In a 1924 interview, Rabbi Goldstein likewise rejected the explanation that held that differing American and British personalities, alone, were responsible for the status of Orthodoxy in America and England. "Orthodoxy in America," Goldstein pointed out, "was Yiddish, whereas Orthodoxy in England was English." "We judge," Goldstein pragmatically continued, "by appearance. Orthodoxy here expressed itself in a foreign language—Yiddish; ergo, Orthodoxy was foreign. In addition, the Yiddish-speaking generation of the Orthodox, unacquainted with conditions here, knew not how to interpret it to their offspring. Orthodoxy's hold was consequently impaired.

"Immigration into England, on the other hand, was on a much smaller scale, and there was always the nucleus of English-speaking Orthodox rabbis and laymen who could assimilate the immigrants into their own fold."

Now about to unfold is the story never before fully told of the experimental process by which Rabbi Goldstein engineered the creation of an unabashedly Americanized Jewish community atmosphere around a single building, on an unprecedented scale, without taking any liberties with purely religious matters beyond the religious parameters of the Yiddish mother-tongued Orthodox community out of which he had flowered.

Chapter 10

Three Institutions Combined

We have already alluded to the potentially fatal shortcomings inherent in many of the "traditional" or Orthodox synagogues in America at the turn of the century. The educators produced by Yiddish-speaking, European-thinking leadership similarly could not realize their potential effectiveness in reaching and relating to American-born, English-speaking young people.

Goldstein summed up much of his dissatisfaction with the dominating and intransigent "old school" of Jewish leadership in one uncharacteristically sharp—although characteristically straightforward—sentence: "The feeling that Orthodoxy has been opposed to all social, educational, and athletic activities is responsible for the fact that our young men have drifted away from the religious path of their fathers."

At the other extreme, Y.M.H.A.'s, in their zeal to play *down* their traditional roots, likewise left much to be desired. Although the Hon. Irving Lehman, as president of the Jewish Welfare Board, proclaimed that his organization's policy was "to further the religious observances and loyalty of those who came under its sway," he conceded in the same address "that the Y.M.H.A.'s and the centers affiliated with the Welfare Board were not intended to replace the synagogue, but to lead the Jewish youth of America toward the synagogue." Rabbi Goldstein questioned even that limited claim:

> ...[S]peaking at [the] Mount Morris Theatre...under the auspices of the Institutional Synagogue, [he] attacked the Y.M.H.A. and expressed the belief that its work ought not to be extended. He said that it represented a failure to solve the religious problem.

"The synagogue failed to hold the young, and instead of attempting to cure and remedy the existing evils within the synagogue, a new institution which did not cure the one spiritual ache, but brought on another pain, was created.

These institutions are mainly negative in character. They do not represent any positive religious conviction. They are neither Orthodox nor Reform, neither fish nor fowl, and as a result produce men that have neither the historic faith nor the soul saving message of the synagogue."

The furor raised by this public stand—taken despite the risk of offending many of his own supporters—led to this follow-up report a week later in another secular New York City newspaper:

...Dr. Goldstein said yesterday that he had not attacked the work of the Y.M.H.A. as an organization, but as a religious institution....

"What I insist on and say, is that organizations like the Y.M.H.A. do not fill the spiritual vacancy or give the spiritual awakening which the young men and women of the day need."

In short, an institution that did not give its members a sense of religious direction, Goldstein felt, could not legitimately claim "to lead the Jewish youth of America toward the synagogue," especially since the "Y" was widely perceived as a self-contained entity.

On another occasion, he discussed the root of the problem—and the roots of the organization:

Let us briefly review the history of our well-meaning efforts to remedy the then existing malady. We began imitating the Y.M.C.A., the Young Mens Christian Association of our neighbors, substituting an "H" for Hebrew, in place of the "C." We felt that if the synagogue was derelict or unable to grapple with the problem, we would create an institution that could, and perhaps would, tackle the problem successfully.

Recently we celebrated the fiftieth anniversary of this movement, which has accomplished a great amount of good. It has given our young men a social and recreational atmosphere. No institution in this country has done better. As far as giving our young men a religious message, however, I believe we will agree that this phase of its work has been only an appendix. Furthermore, it caters largely to young men and does little for the other growing members of the family. As a result, we find ourselves almost in the same, or perhaps worse, condition from the point of view of Judaism than we were when the Y.M.H.A. movement was first started.

Rabbi Goldstein had been ordained for fewer than three years when he began to agitate, publicly, for the establishment of an all encompassing organization which would provide the functions of the synagogue, the Y.M.H.A. (and Y.W.H.A.), and the Hebrew School in one financially efficient and esthetically pleasant framework. He felt that this arrangement would generate an irresistible appeal to every member of the Jewish family. His proposal, in September of 1916, immediately made front page headlines in Jewish newspapers throughout the country. The candor, cogency, and eloquence of his presentation render any attempt to paraphrase pointless and presumptuous.

I speak from the point of view of one who is fully imbued with the tenets of our faith as handed down in the Bible in its completeness, [i.e., as explained in] the *Talmud*, and codified in the *Shulchan Aruch* [the code of Jewish law], and therefore what I have to say I want viewed [as being presented] from an uncompromisingly Orthodox point of view...
...My plea for the future is the Institutional Synagogue, which would embrace the [functions of the] Synagogue, the *Talmud Torah* [the Hebrew School], and the Y.M.H.A. movements....
The institution that is to live and that is to contribute a most potent force in the future will be an Institutional Synagogue. The Institutional Synagogue must, first of all, be as Orthodox a house of worship as is prescribed in Jewish codes. It should then be a place of study for the elders in the evenings, and for the children in the afternoons (in large, light and well-ventilated classrooms). It should be a place where men and women may come after plying their daily cares and spend a social hour in an Orthodox environment and in a truly Jewish atmosphere. In short, if we desire to perpetuate the real Judaism of the past we must so shape Jewish spiritual activity that it will all find expression in one institution.

This institution would be a revival of the historic synagogue. The synagogue of old was the center for prayer, study, and the social life of the community, all in one. The restoration of this type of synagogue would spell the salvation of Judaism. Aside from all this, it would serve the practical purpose of helping to solve the problem of support of religious institutions. Let me show you concretely how this can be accomplished. Suppose a synagogue has a mortgage of $50,000, a Y.M.H.A. a mortgage of $50,000, and a [Hebrew School] a mortgage of $50,000, together making a total mortgage of $150,000, and perhaps an equity in each institution of $25,000, making a total cost of three such institutions $225,000, and a total cost for maintenance about $60,000. A building similar in structure to that of the Central Jewish Institute for a high-class synagogue, a well-equipped [Hebrew School], and a model Y.M.H.A. could be built for $150,000 and maintained for $30,000 per annum.

Now instead of a man belonging to three separate institutions, he could pay a little higher membership fee in the Institutional Synagogue which would include all the activities and advantages of the three separate institutions. This organization would, by reason of the greater income, be able to do superior work to any of the three institutions, individually; and an added advantage to Judaism would be that the father and mother, the son and the daughter, the young boy and young girl, would all come to the same institution for Jewish pursuits. The father and mother would go to the synagogue with their children; the young man and woman would go to the building for social work; the children would go to the [Hebrew School] and thus there would be brought back to the family life that religious unity and enthusiasm which is so sorely lacking today. It is my firm belief that the Institutional Synagogue would mean a rejuvenation of the American Jewish life. It would mean the preservation of traditional Orthodox Judaism; because as has been my experience already, when you give the young man or young woman opportunity to express their social instincts in good American style, under the auspices of the synagogue, their respect for the synagogue and its authority increases; but when the synagogue stands up as a barrier between the young folks and social life, they rebel and lose interest in the synagogue altogether.

As I see it, there are two problems that American Jewry must solve at the present time. First and foremost is the economic problem, a solution of which is beginning to appear faintly on the distant horizon, and with God's aid, I think that we may be able to tackle that phase. Already efforts are being made to interest manufacturers and the laborers in a five-day week, so that the Sabbath may not be transgressed by working thereon. The second problem is one of environment. If the home is typically Jewish, the child will unconsciously absorb Judaism; but it has been the unfortunate experience of American Israel that young men and young women have come from good Orthodox traditional homes and yet are not Orthodox Jews.

What is the reason? The chief reason is that when the young men and the young women left their homes, entered into companionship with their friends, and spent social hours in institutions they were divorced from the influence of the home, and the force of social life overpowered and overmastered the force of the home. If, however, the social life of the young man and young woman would have the opportunity to express itself in an Institutional Synagogue where the young folks might run a dance, attend the gymnasium, do social work, or study, in a thoroughly Jewish atmosphere, then the outer social environment would aid and assist the home environment and keep the boy and girl thoroughly Jewish. We would then have men and women who would be loyal to their faith and a pride to their people.

At present some rabbis are attempting to introduce a little social and educational work in their synagogues, but they are merely wasting their time and duplicating work that is already being done. It is impossible to accomplish good results with poor material, and no synagogue, as the average synagogue is constructed today, can possibly compete with any Talmud Torah [full scale Hebrew School] or any Y.M.H.A.

Difference Between the Free Synagogue And the Proposed Institutional Synagogue

The difference between the Free Synagogue, headed by the Rev. Stephen Wise and the Institutional Synagogue which I am advocating in this article is that the former socializes religion and the latter will religionize the whole of social life. Nay, it will go farther than that, it will tend to keep intact the Jewish ceremonials of our people. It will bear a generation of knowing Jews and Jewesses, who will be imbued with the ideals and practices of their people, and who will ever strive to make the future of Israel as glorious as its past.

Dissatisfaction with the existing Y.M.H.A.'s and Jewish community centers of this era was publicly acknowledged by the Jewish Welfare Board itself in a far reaching historical survey it sponsored in 1948, under the direction of Professor Oscar I. Janowsky. "The synagogue center or 'Institutional Synagogue'" did not achieve a "clarification of purpose" until the period beginning with the year 1920, according to his study. This coming of age of the Jewish community center, which in its improved and refined form was "fathered," according to Janowsky, "by Mordecai Kaplan, Herbert S. Goldstein, and others," produced an entity that was "frankly 'religious'" in its emphasis, "with the synagogue functioning as the central and motivating factor in the activities of the institution."

Although the credit for the idea has been divided between Kaplan and Goldstein, the latter appears to have been the first to *implement* it. We have seen that Goldstein had been the first actual director of the Central Jewish Institute, after Kaplan had failed to get the idea off the drawing boards. In addition, even one of the leading experts of the Harlem Jewish community conceded that the founders of the youth groups (in which Goldstein was deeply involved) that eventually amalgamated into the Institutional Synagogue, "foreshadowed" the self-named Jewish centers per se, of which Kaplan's was *later* to become the first.

Since the Institutional Synagogue and the Jewish Center were founded almost simultaneously, the priorities the two leaders set in implementing their ideas takes on added significance. Although the founding dinner of Kaplan's Jewish Center took place in November of 1916* and the Institutional Synagogue was founded four months later, the Jewish Center did not start to *function* as a synagogue center until 1918, whereas the Institutional Synagogue's actual activities and impact on its community in 1917 was almost instantaneous. It did not wait for the construction of its ultimate fully-equipped building.**

Even before the Institutional Synagogue moved into its first and temporary building in 1917, the *New York American* stated that the then-nascent Institutional Synagogue was in fact "the first movement of its kind in America," and "something new in religious endeavor." Another reason why the Institutional Synagogue could not have been considered even "the second movement of its kind" was that Kaplan and Goldstein were simply not two of the *same kind*. By this time, as we have seen, the very ideals and religious identities of Goldstein and Kaplan were as similar as day and night—or night and day, depending on one's perspective—but either way, they were clearly near opposite extremes within the broad "modern Orthodox" spectrum at that time. Although Kaplan was still considered at least nominally Orthodox by many people in the Jewish community, he had eased himself out of his Orthodox rabbinical position at the Kehilath Jeshurun due, at least in part, to his noticeable lurch to the left after his respected father had passed away. Goldstein, by contrast, was considered acceptable enough to win unanimous support in his bid to succeed Kaplan.

Chronological and religious factors aside, the very organizational aims of the two institutions were significantly different. Kaplan himself openly conceded this point in print in 1918 and

*Goldstein's monumental article describing his proposed "Institutional Synagogue" first appeared in the *Hebrew Standard*, which at that time claimed the title of "America's leading Jewish family paper," in September of 1916, whereas Kaplan's comparable article on his "Jewish Center" did not appear in this publication until March of 1918.

**It *certainly* did not wait for the reconstruction of its religion either! (Kaplan, of course, later tried to tear down some fundamentals of traditional Judaism and founded "reconstructionism.")

orally more than half a century later. "We state frankly," he wrote, at the outset:

> that we are establishing the Jewish Center for the purpose of deriving from it for ourselves pleasures of a social, intellectual, and spiritual character. We are not building a settlement, nor a communal center, nor a Young Men's or Young Women's Hebrew Association; nor do we expect the Jewish Center to be an institution for the doing of so-called uplift work.

Even before these words were published, Mrs. Goldstein had written in her diary, contrasting the Center with the "Institutional Synagogue idea," that they had noticeable similarities:

> ...except that the former caters to the classes and the latter to the masses. The former is to be enjoyed and participated in by the members only; the latter is to be conducted for the benefit of everybody who wishes to take advantage of it.

When Goldstein received his Doctor of Divinity degree from Yeshiva College years later, Rabbi Joseph Lookstein, a successor at the Kehilath Jeshurun of both Kaplan and Goldstein, referred to Goldstein, in his formal "remarks upon conferring the degree," as "the initiator of the Jewish Community Center." Although Kaplan had founded a center—for his affluent members—Goldstein had created a model center for an entire *community* to share.

Kaplan unhesitatingly described the Institutional Synagogue as Goldstein's "own idea," differentiating between the two ventures, from his unique point of view, as follows: "The Institutional Synagogue was a religious 'Y,' whereas the aim of the Jewish Center was to have the synagogue *itself* for worship and study, and then in *addition*, to have the young people socialize." It was thus clear that even his own concept of his own creation was of one entity with another as an appendage for only one segment of the population of the first. The Institutional Synagogue geared each facet, in varying degrees, to *every* member of the family.

Kaplan's immediate successor at the Jewish Center, the unquestionably Orthodox Rabbi Dr. Leo Jung, who came four years after its founding and molded it to his dictates for over half a century, likewise made a clear distinction between his Jewish Center and the I.S. The biographical sketch of Rabbi Goldstein which Jung prepared for the *Universal Jewish Encyclopedia* states that Goldstein's Institutional Synagogue..."combines the features of the Jewish Center with those of the Young Men's Hebrew Association."

Goldstein never tired of contrasting his synagogue with "Y"'s and "Jewish Centers" to emphasize their differences. One of the differences that gave him particular pride was the fact that he could say, in 1927, without fear of contradiction, that "the Institutional Synagogue is the only center bearing the name Synagogue." This distinction cost the synagogue dearly, but the principle was worth more to Rabbi Goldstein than the added revenue. One of Goldstein's close confidants recalled that many people "said if we would change our name, they might give a large donation, and Rabbi Goldstein answered straight from the shoulder." There is evidence that Jacob Schiff offered Rabbi Goldstein a considerable sum on the condition that he would change the name of the Institutional Synagogue, "but he refused." Goldstein's emphasis on the word "synagogue" went far deeper than mere semantics. When his creation was still only in the proposal stage, he wrote:

> I am unalterably opposed to the getting away from the synagogue. I feel that if we get away from the synagogue idea, we are getting away from the root, the sentiment and the practice of the Jewish religion. Interest in the synagogue implies a love for religion; interest in the Talmud Torah [Hebrew School] does not always imply a love for religion, [but] perhaps a love for education or culture only. These two must walk hand in hand. They are separate only as the branch is separate from the root.

Not only was Goldstein able to restore and maintain the identity of the synagogue per se, but he was also able to build his own on such a massive scale that it came to be known as "one of the largest community centres not only of New York City but of the country."* Before we begin to look behind the scenes at the actual first steps by which Rabbi Goldstein brought his idea to life, we will briefly explore in the next two chapters two additional motives that figured in Goldstein's plans: his desire to lead a red-blooded revival movement, and his desire to lead a bloodless war against crime in a community that had ample need for both of these challenges.

---

*Notice that it was not referred to as merely one of the largest *Jewish* ones; rather, as one of the largest community centers in the country, period.

Chapter 11

Out "Billy-Sundaying" Billy Sunday

William "Billy" Ashley Sunday (1863-1935) was one of the most well-known evangelists in the country in the early part of the twentieth century, just as Billy Graham has been during the middle of this century. By the very definition of the term evangelist, there could not have possibly been a true Jewish counterpart to Billy Sunday. Jewish law, in fact, prohibits prosely- tizing, and requires that if a non-Jew wishes to be converted, the approached Jewish potential converter is obligated to attempt, in good faith, to convince the non-Jew to change his mind and remain a non-Jew. Rabbi Goldstein, however, foresaw the need to utilize *methods* similar to those used by some successful evangelists in an attempt to win back ebbing Jewish souls, even though it meant incurring the wrath of some Jews and non-Jews who misunderstood both his deeds and his goals and incorrectly thought that Rabbi Goldstein was out either to convert non-Jews to Judaism or Jews to Christianity. Particularly in his early years at the Institutional Synagogue, Goldstein molded Jews on an individual level as steadily as he molded the synagogue on an institutional level, and rapidly established a reputation as "the first rabbi of modern times to have started a religious revival movement." Rabbi Goldstein was so successful in his approach that he was often referred to even in the *non*-Jewish press as "the Jewish Billy Sunday," after first being referred to as "Billy *Shabbat*" (Hebrew for Saturday) by his coreligionists. *The World Magazine* actually carried a feature on the rabbi that clearly portrayed Rabbi Goldstein out-"Billy Sundaying" Billy Sunday!

Although Billy Sunday and Rabbi Goldstein employ the same tactics in getting people to hit the sawdust trail, still

Rabbi Goldstein is going just a step further in his campaign than is Billy Sunday, the man who, it can be truthfully said, revolutionized religion. While the noted evangelist is content with having people hit the trail and then lets the local churches take care of the trail hitters, Rabbi Goldstein prefers to stay in one spot—for the present at least—and have his flock under continual care. And always the flock is growing, because the rabbi has the personality to keep them interested in his work.

In an interview with the *New York American* shortly after the Institutional Synagogue was formed, Rabbi Goldstein observed that, "The Institutional Synagogue was designed as a permanent revival to take care of the religious instruction of the young, and to cause adults to continue to keep in touch with the temple."

During its early years, the Institutional Synagogue sponsored "Revival Rallies" every Sunday morning at various theatres—the original synagogue building was not large enough to accommodate the throngs that attended. This fulfilled a "campaign promise" Goldstein had made in his resignation sermon at his previous synagogue. He was also scrupulous in pointing out in this very sermon and ever after that these rallies featured "lectures, not Services—do not misunderstand, not Services, but Jewish lectures on Judaism for Sunday morning." To those who insisted on misunderstanding, nevertheless, whether intentionally or not, and mistakenly linking him with those pseudo-Reform Jews who aped their Christian neighbors by switching their Jewish Sabbath from Saturday to Sunday, he calmly explained:

> ...Sunday morning revival meetings—not services, mind you, but meetings, merely with the object of bringing a word of Scripture home to those hundreds of young people who are prevented by reason of the unfortunate economic conditions [the six-day work week] from attending a house of worship on the Sabbath.

These events were entertaining as well as uplifting. Nobody attempted to pretend they were not. At the same time, they afforded Rabbi Goldstein positive exposure which he used to introduce spiritual and educational values to hundreds of people simultaneously, many of whom would never have considered entering an actual synagogue. At every rally, a massive recruitment effort was made for the various social, athletic, educational, and religious activities of the synagogue.*

---

*We will describe specific aspects of these unusual rallies in a separate chapter.

Goldstein's message was clear to those who heard it directly. Those who heard *about* him, indirectly, were prone, at times, to arrive at hasty, inaccurate conclusions since superficially they could mistakenly associate him in their minds with Christian missionaries. These doubters could be classified into two categories, those who did not know any better and those who *should* have. Goldstein himself recalled instances of the former:

> We commenced an advertising campaign with billboards on Fifth Avenue reading as follows: "God is calling. Institutional Synagogue, 112 West 116 Street."
>
> I also had advertisements in the subway trains, and there were some parents who became suspicious because of these tactics, believing that, perhaps, I was a missionary. They were quickly disillusioned after attending our services.

The few members of the press that concluded that his "propaganda" was saturated with Christian overtones, however, should have known better, because in so doing they violated their duty to the reading public to research properly and follow up their articles. A scathing editorial in the *American Jewish Chronicle* took him to task by stating that:

> [T]he task of a rabbi is not that of an agent of society to prevent vice, nor is it Billy Sundayism; his task is to study and to teach the law and to spread the knowledge of Judaism. . .no revival mass meetings will make our boys and girls religious.

The failure to realize that these rallies were basically set up to promote Orthodox Judaism in general and one Orthodox Synagogue in particular was truly startling. His approach was so novel to them that they refused to pay attention to what was actually happening at the rallies, or what was said at them. Goldstein was hardly an unknown quantity by this time, having occupied a prestigious Orthodox pulpit for over three years and serving at the time of this criticism on the staff of the oldest Orthodox rabbinical seminary in America.

In reaction to the insinuation that the "revivalist" idea had its roots in the Christian Billy Sunday, Rabbi Goldstein had this to say:

> The revival idea. . .is an intrinsically Jewish one and not an imitation of a Christian movement. We are told that such eminent rabbis as Rabbi Jacob Joseph [1848-1902, the first and only chief rabbi of the Orthodox Congregations of New York City, following his tenure as *Maggid* or preacher of the famous Lithuanian city of Vilna] and the Dubner Maggid

[1741-1804, Jacob Ben Wolf Kranz, whom Moses Mendelssohn called "the Jewish Aesop"] arranged for so-called revival talks in which they used plain, direct language and urged the people to return to the faith of their fathers. It is recorded that following these revival talks, hundreds of pairs of *tefillin* [religious articles] could be sold in one week, housewives would buy new dishes and would revive their scrupulous observance of the dietary laws and such like phenomena would take place.

In a sense, Goldstein's revival methods, if anything, taught some zealous *Christians* a lesson! Gently and indirectly chiding some Christian missionary methods from the Crusades to the present, he advocated at the outset of his revivalist campaign "a popular religious movement, not through vulgar means, not through threats and scares, but by the more proper method—through [giving individuals opportunities to learn about] the *Torah*, [and their] Rabbinic and Jewish background."

Chapter 12

A Religious
General Leads
A War On Vice

No matter what was to happen to the Harlem community afterwards, the fact remains that in the early years of the twentieth century, Harlem harbored a middle-class Jewish community. Shortly after moving into the neighborhood, Rabbi Goldstein was quoted in the *Harlem Home News* as having referred to his newly adopted neighborhood as "the hell of Harlem." Rabbi Goldstein selected this choice of words not because he considered Harlem a physically uncomfortable or unpleasant place in which to live but rather because of the numbers of loiterers, gamblers and prostitutes in the neighborhood.* What he found particularly distressing was that many of them were Jewish, and a significant part of the challenge he undertook by setting up his synagogue in this community found expression in his two-fold resolution both to dissolve these unwholesome elements and, simultaneously, to give the young people more meaningful pursuits with which to fill their time. In this atmosphere, the Institutional Synagogue's success was doubly remarkable. Each young participant in its numerous programs was regarded not only as Judaism's gain but as a loss to the forces of vice as well. Some of the synagogue's supporters, in fact, including a Supreme Court Justice, appeared to be more enthusiastic about the synagogue's role "as a curb to crime" than about its more obvious roles.

Congressman Siegel was able to proclaim in his presidential anniversary message of 1927:

*His criticism, at this point had nothing to do with the factors that were later to force the middle class to abandon the community, when the crimes turned from the spiritual to the physical, from the "victimless" to the violent, and when the *real* gamblers became not those in the poolrooms but, rather, those innocents who risked their lives by remaining in the nearly nonrecognizable neighborhood.

Thousands pass through our building each day. What better proof can we offer to this community that we are entitled to their support than the fact that no boy or girl who has come into our [Hebrew School] has ever come in contact with the police authorities. Thus we have been the insurance companies which have protected thousands of men and women, and you have been the premium payers.

In 1929, he came up with the more concrete, albeit remote, statistic that "92% of those committed to penal institutions never received a religious education." In 1931, the synagogue newspaper reproduced the highlights of a survey demonstrating a reduced number of Jews in prisons and reformatories to "practically a negligible quantity." Although 27.4 percent of New York's population at the time was Jewish, the House of Refuge, a state institution for delinquents, had a 58 percent population of Jews in 1914 and only a 3.56 percent Jewish population in 1931. Ernest K. Couter, who first published the survey, attributed "the amazing decrease to the efforts of the Jewish communal leaders, who set about to do the necessary preventive work." Long before these statistics were released, Goldstein himself had been quoted in the *New York Times* on the subject:

To say that more judges, heavier fines, longer terms of imprisonment, [and fewer] suspensions of sentence will prevent further crime is but suggesting at best palliative measures. When the fear of God is made the norm among our people, then as it always has been, it will deter our youth from the performance of any criminal act.

In precisely the same context, Goldstein once again made headlines in the *New York Times*, on this occasion for the following proposal:

We speak of the three R's of reading, writing, and arithmetic as the foundation of our education. Therein we have failed, because we have neglected to give equal consideration and time in the child's educational life to the Fourth R—Religion.

Even those members of the Institutional Synagogue family who were slow to maintain or develop this fear of God gradually found that they had no cause to develop a fear of the police authorities either! By virtue of the Institutional Synagogue's wide scope of activities, athletic and social in addition to the religious and educational, young people in the neighborhood simply had more of an incentive to take advantage of the alluring facilities and activities in the ever-expanding synagogue complex than to stand around, loiter, and eventually get themselves into trouble.

Independent of this indirect approach to the fight against juvenile delinquency, Rabbi Goldstein led a very active campaign to close the crime-sheltering pool halls in the area. Before he had even left the employ of his previous congregation and moved into Harlem, a headline in the *Evening Telegram* publicized his goal "to uplift Harlem conditions." The article referred to his intention to launch a campaign "to eliminate from Harlem all questionable resorts, and for the further enlightenment of youthful Jews of both sexes in questions of religion."

In October of 1917, only a few months after the Institutional Synagogue had been founded, the *New York American* carried a headline declaring "Rabbi in War on Gamblers." the gist of the accompanying article was that:

> Rabbi Goldstein's revival meetings will not only serve to reclaim Harlem's Jews who have strayed far away from the teachings and doctrines of the Talmud, but will make for a better Harlem in many ways. It is his intention to hurl a bomb in the camps of all loiterers and good-for-nothings that make 116th Street and Lenox Avenue their hang-out in a way that will do Harlem the most good. Rabbi Goldstein has in his possession the names and addresses of a score of gamblers that will soon be taken into custody by the police.*

Rabbi Goldstein was still in the forefront of the war for "moral purification" in the city four and a half years later. The *New York Times* saw fit to print the following extract from his Saturday morning sermon of March 18, 1922:

> Some time ago. . . a committee after great difficulty obtained an interview with Commissioner Enright informing him that there were forty pool rooms between Ninety-sixth Street and 116th Street and twenty more about to open. The Commissioner sent this committee to the 67th Street Precinct, and there the committee was informed that the police department was short-handed and could not send even one man to supervise the poolroom, though there are always enough policemen to special for parades
>
> I shall call together the heads of the social and recreational institutions of Harlem and see whether as a united body we cannot prevent the further encroachment of the moral evils and perhaps get the police and detectives, now a stationary fixture, to become active in wiping out the moral filth of this

*Publicizing the fact that he had such a list was an obvious invitation to trouble, but, apparently, this was the type of a risk that the rabbi was willing to take.

end of town.

Rabbi Goldstein worked in close concert with the Union Settlement and the Federation Settlement on this matter.

Goldstein was not afraid to cite specific down-to-earth examples as he unified the masses behind him. For example:

> Since I came to Harlem, a little more than five years ago, the City of New York has been spending a lot of money to keep a policeman at the corner of Lenox Avenue and 116th Street. What good is he doing at that place when all around him, behind closed doors, all kinds of gambling is going on?

By 1926, Rabbi Goldstein was referred to in an article in the *New York Evening Journal* as "[t]he prime figure in the struggle to make poolrooms inaccessible to uptown youths." This phase of the seemingly perpetual struggle was described as follows:

> Poolrooms are laying the foundation for our future criminals. With this declaration, hundreds of uptown mothers have set out to rid Harlem of these crime-breeding places, behind whose green curtains the police charge many of the uptown holdups are planned. These mothers have organized a strong body to demand city aid "to save their sons."
>
> The passage of a city ordinance which would close billiard rooms at 11 P.M. instead of 1 A.M. and raise the minimum age of patrons to 18 is their goal.
>
> The failure of their first attempt to pass such a law has actuated mothers to a more vigorous and determined fight. The ordinance introduced at the closing session of the old Board of Aldermen was disapproved by the general welfare committee. The opponents of the bill contended their business now is over-regulated.

The article went on to discuss Rabbi Goldstein's role, and then quoted some of his remarks:

> The poolroom presents fertile soil for our budding criminals. The poolroom paves the way to the wrong road for gullible youths, mere boys hardly out of their teens.
>
> It is a place where our boys get their first lessons in gambling. Hundreds of mothers have come to me, tears in their eyes, asking for help. Their sons have gotten beyond their control. They were hanging out in poolrooms, gambling and worse.

Normally, once young people get beyond the control of their

parents, it is a safe bet that they are certainly beyond the control of any synagogue. Nevertheless, occasionally I.S. officials were able to save the day even at the eleventh hour. According to the synagogue newspaper in March of 1925:

> The other day a parent came tearfully into the building exclaiming that his son was about to be put away at the Hebrew Protectory Home—that all his other previous efforts to get the boy out of the jurisdiction of the court have failed, that he did not want the stigma of the reformatory on this Jewish boy, that the parents would do all in their power and anything asked of them if we could only save the boy from being sentenced. Through the medium of our Social and Educational Department, this boy has been taken from the prison atmosphere, has been saved from an obviously miserable career, and has once more been given the chance to hold his head up in the world. This only happened three days ago.

Goldstein's fight against crime also had positive effects on people who were not the least bit involved but who simply were intrigued by or admired his efforts. A most prominent example of such a person was Mr. Max E. Sanders, who eventually became a vice president of the synagogue and chairman of the dinner marking the rabbi's twenty-five years in the rabbinate. On this occasion, Mr. Sanders reflected on his initiation into the synagogue:

> About twenty years ago, I had heard so much about the war that was being waged against gangsterism in Harlem that I inquired of some of my friends the name of the warrior. I was introduced to a young rabbi, Herbert S. Goldstein....Little did I realize that this brief introduction was the beginning of a lasting friendship between us and was responsible for a complete change in my somewhat undetermined religious views.

Chapter 13

An Idealistic Dream Becomes A Reality

An eloquent description of the societal climate that prevailed during the "incubation" and founding periods of the Institutional Synagogue appeared in its "Twentieth Anniversary Souvenir Program" that was published in 1937:

> All significant movements have grown out of, or have resulted from their times. No consideration of the development of the Institutional Synagogue would be complete without a word concerning the time that witnessed its organization...1917 and 1918.
>
> The world was dancing in a frenzy to the discordant music of a Dance Macabre. To the tempo of cannon, to the theme of death cries, to the counterpoint of tragedy, death, sorrow, Youth and Age danced. They gyrated crazily, purposelessly. They seemed to be disjointed mannikens of a marionette show responding to the careless handling of a drunken showman. Man killed man. Wealth and utility were dumped into nothingness....Gold stars appeared in windows and gray hairs drowned dark hairs of parents.
>
> The war ended. In the period of economic and social readjustment that followed, new ideals, new concepts, and a new outlook were evident among the youth of the world.
>
> In New York, the cosmopolitan city, the trend was clearly seen. The uncertainty of the period of readjustment reacting in the Youth turned a placid generation of boys and girls into a hard, caustic, ideal-less generation. The era of the "flapper" and the "wise guy" was in full blast. It seemed as though there was still a war going on, a war not of bullets and shrapnel, but a war conducted with broken youth.

In this atmosphere the foundation of the Institutional Synagogue was laid. . . .

The foundation actually was laid, in a sense, in Rabbi Goldstein's mind, while he lay in a reclining position, a most unusual one, to start with, for this generally hyperactive individual:

> In the summer of 1916 we stayed at Long Branch, in New Jersey. One afternoon, while relaxed on our lawn and day-dreaming, my thoughts began to wander regarding the young people and the synagogue. I came up with an idea for the future synagogue for all Jewish congregations. These thoughts led me to [what I eventually formulated into the concept of] *an Institutional Synagogue.*

Rabbi Goldstein's first article describing the Institutional Synagogue idea, which was excerpted in a previous chapter, "attracted the attention of the whole country and made a particular impression upon a group of young Jews in Harlem." Although, or perhaps because, in an addendum to this article, Goldstein carefully distinguished his proposed synagogue from the famous "Free Synagogue" of the tradition-shattering "Reform" preacher, Stephen S. Wise, Wise himself took the trouble to respond and express an intention to "come and see the Institute [Goldstein at that time headed the Central Jewish Institute] and discuss with you our common problems." Although theologically Wise and Gold-stein were worlds apart, their personalities and accomplishments had much in common; both men were creative, charismatic—and successful. The similarities between the two were so apparent even to the elder clergyman that, at a chance encounter with Goldstein, Wise once introduced his up-and-coming young colleague to his (Wise's) wife with the most glowing compliment Wise could possibly bestow—from his point of view: "This," he said, "is the *Orthodox* Stephen Wise."

Ironically, although Rabbi Goldstein's article attracted wide-spread attention throughout the country, his own congregants did not actually expect him to implement his proposal outside of his then-present synagogue, and certainly not on a full-time basis. This is additionally ironic in light of his remark in his resignation sermon that, "This thought of revival is not a mere ambitious enthusiastic ideal of the moment, but one to which I have given my most deliberate thought and due consideration. I have both in conversation and in my public utterances expressed this thought." (We will see a reference to one of these pre-resignation "public utterances" later.) Many of his congregants undoubtedly thought that the article was meant theoretically, and others believed he was merely describing the Central Jewish Institute which he had already founded. Although the Congregation Kehilath Jeshurun and the C.J.I. were separate institutions on paper, in practice they served the same constituents and together fulfilled many of Goldstein's projections for his Institutional Synagogue, which was portrayed in the article in sweeping, conceptual terms. The first phase of the concretization of the Institutional Synagogue thus took place without any noticeable effects on his duties at his original congregation.

The very first discussion on the subject of the Institutional Synagogue to be recorded in the daily diary of Rabbi Goldstein's wife took place on October 29, 1916. Although superficially this discussion seems to have been casual, having taken place with Mrs. Goldstein's parents in an automobile ride, the timing is noteworthy, for this was the day of the cornerstone laying of the expanded Home of the Daughters of Jacob, a pet charity of both Mr. and Mrs. Fischel. This home for the aged was founded in the Fischel residence. Mr. Fischel had served as chairman of the original building committee, had lain the first cornerstone (on October 6, 1907), and had expressed the hope at that time "that the time would come when the institution would grow to such size that it would occupy an entire block. That this prediction should have so soon come true filled him with unusual happiness." At precisely this auspicious point in time, with one dream just realized, he was "ripe" to be receptive to another person's dream. According to Mrs. Goldstein:

On our way down in the machine [automobile], [following the cornerstone laying ceremony in which Mr. Fischel had played such a prominent role], pa, ma, Herbert and I discussed Herbert's plans for an Institutional Synagogue in Harlem. Herbert has decided to launch his plans at once because the Institutional Synagogue idea is very much in the air now and Herbert thinks he ought to start it before somebody steals a march on him. He intends to send out copies of his article on "The Institutional Synagogue" which appeared in the *Hebrew Standard* some time ago, to a number of people in Harlem to call a big mass meeting for the purpose of stirring up enthusiasm, to lease a house and start services which will be Orthodox and at the same time very decorous and orderly.

The diary entry says nothing about a Fischel endorsement during or even following the discussion. At most, the absence of any explicit comment to the contrary implies, rather, a Fischel acquiescence.*

Mrs. Goldstein's diary entries for the next couple of weeks often went something like this one.:

> I...spent the entire morning addressing envelopes to people in Harlem whom Herbert hopes to interest in his Institutional Synagogue movement, and enclosing Herbert's pamphlet on the Institutional Synagogue in them.

She also spent time "fixing up" a card index mailing list for the projected Institutional Synagogue.

On November 3, 1916, only about a week after Rabbi Goldstein had privately announced his intention to launch his venture "at once," he took a walk up Seventh Avenue with his wife for the express purpose of looking for a "suitable house" in which to start his Institutional Synagogue. After midnight, according to his wife's account, they:

> found something very favorable on 122nd Street and Seventh Avenue, northeast corner, [which] greatly encouraged and enthused [them].

Although they were eventually to acquire a different building, since they found the interior of this one "unsuitable" for their purpose, this four-story brownstone house with a high stoop and an imposing entrance gave a good indication of what they were

---

*Mr. Harry Fischel, Mrs. Goldstein's father, was one of the most prominent Orthodox Jewish philanthropists in the country at this time. Contrary to the presumption of many, incidentally, Mr. Fischel did *not take it upon himself to erase any deficits the synagogue was destined to incur—as he had* done in the case of charities otherwise independent of his family—although he *did* become, like many people, a generous supporter in accordance with his means. In fact, to the contrary, some of the people most directly involved in the I.S. stated with certainty that the public knowledge of Fischel's relationship to Goldstein actually *hampered* fund-raising efforts on behalf of the synagogue since many would-be donors refused to believe that Mr. Fischel would not automatically foot the synagogue's accumulated debts. A member of the Goldsteins' inner circle wrote: "I remember Rabbi Goldstein commenting that the fact of having Harry Fischel as a father-in-law very often made people feel there was no need for outside support."

As if that were not enough, Mr. Fischel was already the president, at that time, of the huge and virtually unprecedented Uptown Talmud Torah (Hebrew School), located in Harlem. This facility boasted an enrollment that fluctuated over the years, from 1,800 to 2,800 students. Goldstein himself called this Harlem school "then the most important Jewish educational institution in America." The proposed I.S., as described to Fischel, had the potential to develop into a competing organization! For these reasons, it thus appears doubtful that Goldstein broached his idea so early to Fischel with the primary motive of gaining a financial commitment of support. At this stage, Goldstein probably spoke to Fischel to get the latter's advice as an experienced philanthropist regarding the feasibility of the project and its implementation. More importantly, he sought the strong-willed Mr. Fischel's blessing—or, at least, acquiescence—as a father-in-law in a close-knit family. For a father-in-law who was a sensationally successful businessman to react favorably to a son-in-law's avowed intention to renounce the security and prestige of a prominent position at two well-known institutions in favor of a speculative experiment, the idea would *have* to be cast in an unusually receptive light.

looking for. Two days later, Rabbi Goldstein dictated the speech he was "contemplating making at the inauguration meeting of his Institutional Synagogue Committee."

Appropriately, at a dinner of the then-forming Jewish Center on West 86th Street, which itself was a variation of the proposed Institutional Synagogue, Rabbi Goldstein had an appointment with Judge Rosalsky. Quietly removed from the milling throng of elegant New York Jewry assembled at the Hotel Astor for the affair, the rabbi sounded out the judge about the idea, and asked Judge Rosalsky to head the movement. The judge endorsed the movement but indicated that he was not in a position to devote the time necessary to do justice to such a responsibility.* After conferring with Rosalsky, Goldstein resolved that evening to "proceed by getting an interview with Congressman Isaac Siegel who lives up in Harlem and who probably knows the correct condition of things in Harlem."

Three days later, the congressman was in Rabbi Goldstein's home discussing the Institutional Synagogue idea. On the basis of this very first meeting, Mrs. Goldstein was able to correctly forecast, "He may be the president of the organization, for he approves of the idea very much." He was destined to co-found the institution, and, like Rabbi Goldstein, to remain at its helm until his death. At a lunch meeting on November 21st with the congressman, the rabbi and Mr. Fischel in attendance, "[i]t was decided that the congressman should ask for an interview with [Messrs.] Schiff, Warburg, and Lewisohn," three of the most prominent Jewish philanthropists of this era, and approach these people together with Rabbi Goldstein. No records have been discovered of any meetings on the subject in this period with Mr. Warburg—who later *did* contribute to the Institutional Synagogue—but references *are* available regarding early negotiations with the other two of the three. In fact, the first meeting with Mr. Lewisohn, on November 29, 1916, proved to be the very first recorded fund-raising call made by the two co-founders. Mr. Lewisohn said he would "refer it to the committee for philanthropic research, and with their approval, he would help the cause." Exactly one month later, Mrs. Goldstein recorded that, "The committee has approved on it and today they sent their report to Mr. Lewisohn." Keen was the disappointment of all concerned when Mr. Lewisohn's letter to Congressman Siegel stated "that he couldn't do anything for the Institutional Synagogue at the present time," but not keen enough to discourage the highly motivated fund raisers from trying again. They managed to induce Mr. Lewisohn not to leave them empty-

*Five years later, this same Judge Rosalsky formally delivered the official appeal on behalf of the I.S. at a theatre party held for its exclusive benefit.

111

handed, coming away with his pledge of "the last $250 of the $12,000 budget of the Institutional Synagogue as a MINIMUM—if he saw fit, he would give more later." The fund raisers were certainly not the type to put all their hopes in one basket. Long before they were disappointed by Mr. Lewisohn, the rabbi and the congressman had been down "to see Mr. Goldwasser, who is the expert on all educational institutions and who is actively connected with the Council of Y.M.H.A.'s and kindred organizations. He has promised... the cooperation of this body for the I.S. movement," wrote Mrs. Goldstein in her diary, "and he has told Herbert that he expects to get large sums of money for a building from certain men. This building will be erected as an Institutional Synagogue, and will be put under Herbert's charge. That surely sounds most encouraging." The next step, all agreed, was "to enthuse those rich men to give the money quick[ly] and towards this end Herbert is to write interviews for the leading newspapers, setting forth the value of this movement."

The enthusiasm, apparently, came quickest from the grass roots, from the intended beneficiaries, rather than from some of the sought-after donors, who, apparently, like Mr. Lewisohn, wished to see something concrete before sinking their vast economic resources into the project. First a committee of boys from the Harlem Y.M.H.A.*—whose membership was seventy-five—who wanted to become affiliated with the Institutional Synagogue, and who were accompanied by the congressman and one R. Korn, visited the Goldsteins to express their interest.

After the Y.M.H.A. delegation issued its "call" to the rabbi, another "group of boys" visited for this same purpose, this time from the Jewish Orthodox League. This latter organization was formally referred to later as the "Young Men's Hebrew Orthodox League"**—although it presumably had few occasions of formality despite its somewhat imposing name. It consisted of an unimposing thirty-five enrolled members, and, according to an estimate by one who was present at the time, "about a dozen people" were actually active in its core. This represented a net gain of twenty-five enrolled members and two solidly active members since the group's founding in April of 1915 by ten members of the Harry Fischel West Side Annex of the Uptown Talmud Torah.

---

*The organization had been founded *not* in a fully-equipped "Y" building of its own but rather, at Harlem's Temple Mount Zion, in 1915, as a separate Harlem branch of the National Y.M.H.A. movement, on "a limited non-denominational basis."

**Its avowed aim was to provide the young adults of the community with an "institution that would create an Orthodox environment..." and "spread a better knowledge of Jewish history, culture, and the Hebrew language, and...aim for a better observance of Judaism among the Jewish youth of New York City." They aimed to demonstrate, experientially as well as intellectually, "that by study, Orthodox Judaism will be found to be entirely compatible with modern ideas."

Despite the league's limited membership, its members were able to draw in people from outside of the league's small nucleus, after they had organized a rally "to better acquaint the people of Harlem with their aims." The league established what it self-assuredly referred to as "model" youth synagogues* at the Annex along the lines to be drawn by the I.S. The year-round activities of the league were both social and cultural, as well as religious. Although such Harlem-based luminaries as Rabbis Drachman and Dolgenas were among the rabbis that lectured at their activities in rotation with Goldstein, it was the *still-Yorkville-based Rabbi Goldstein* who "was elected Honorary President of the League in recognition of his constant encouragement of its activities."

Even before these Harlem groups had officially come to discuss their common interests with Rabbi Goldstein, the West 35th Street Synagogue, together with the West 28th Street Synagogue and the YMHA of that neighborhood, by Mrs. Goldstein's account, wished "to build an Institutional Synagogue if Herbert will assume the leadership of it." These organizations, even when combined, however, could not begin to muster up the type of a grass-roots groundswell that had been set in motion up in Harlem. Mrs. Goldstein reduced the decision to most pragmatic terms: "There are only 1,700 Jews in that section of the city [around West 30th Street] in comparison with 124,000 in Harlem; therefore, Herbert doesn't feel the field to be big enough." Not only did Goldstein have the numbers on his side in Harlem, but he also had the supply and demand on his side, if he could only make the community realize what it was missing. Two years after he had moved in, he alleged "there is not a similar institution from 92nd Street to the Bronx," a statement he later modified by narrowing the area to that between 112th and 157th streets.**

---

*The first fall of its existence, the league already attracted the attention—and sponsorship—of the prestigious city-wide "Kehilla" as the league organized a "provisional synagogue" to combat the abuses of the "mushroom synagogues" that sprouted up High Holiday time every year. These "mushroom synagogues" were commercial ventures established to accommodate Jews who wished to attend a synagogue only in this single brief annual period. Unsuspecting innocents were lured annually by often unscrupulous and irreligious businessmen to rented quarters whose ticket sales competed with legitimate synagogues desperately in need of funds to tide them over in their year-round activities.

**He could be forgiven such liberties since, technically speaking, one could just as well have said that not a single truly similar institution was to be found anywhere in the *world*. Certainly within Harlem its position was clear. No less heavy a thinker than Dr. Nicholas Murray Butler, the president of Harlem's own prestigious Ivy League school, Columbia University, referred to the I.S. at its peak as the "Light House of Harlem."

First All Homo Sapiens Were In Minority...
Then Some Sought To Keep Others From Getting Foothold

The soil of Harlem was not always receptive to penetration by Jewish roots....

What has been billed as "the first account of Manhattan Island by an eyewitness" described Manhattan as "full of trees, and, in the middle, rocky, but the north end has good land in two places," both of which were positioned in what is now known as Harlem! The town of New Harlem was first settled by the Dutch who "broke ground near the foot of 125th Street on August 14, 1658." From a Jewish perspective, nothing substantial took place in the community between then and the late nineteenth century when many Jews who felt they had outgrown the immigrant air of the Lower East Side sought greener pastures "uptown" in Harlem. By this time, of course, the pastures of Harlem which had once been the agricultural showpieces of Manhattan were no longer green, and the land once known for its agriculture was soon to flourish with Jewish culture, although, as already pointed out, at first the Jewish culture of Harlem was almost as dormant as the agriculture had become.

The Jews were not exactly welcomed to Harlem with open arms. If German *Jews* in America often resented the influx of alien East European Jews, it is not difficult to imagine the reception the Jews of Harlem received from the German *non*-Jewish element that dominated the neighborhood when they arrived. "The sometimes bitter response that they received...was symbolized by a to-let sign which hung on one building: *'Keine Juden, und Keine Hunde.'* No Jews, No Dogs." This attitude, however, was not to prevail.

...To live in Lower Harlem became a symbol of good times to many East European Jews. Some families who moved into the neighborhood, one contemporary recorded, "speak apologetically and at times are actually embarrassed when their former residence in the lower parts of the city is mentioned." The newspapers called this section of Harlem, "Little Russia."

By 1909, 46 percent—nearly half of all the families in Harlem south of 134th Street and west of Park Avenue were Jewish. These 12,893 Jewish *families*—which on the average were larger than the families of today—were served by only eleven synagogues, not to mention the dearth of community centers. There were "enough churchless Jews to fill forty synagogues with a seating capacity of 1,000 each." Furthermore, while only 11 percent of the Catholic families and fewer than 40 percent of the Protestant families were churchless, fully 79.5 percent of the Jewish families were "churchless." By the time the I.S. arrived on the scene eight years later, there were *shtieblach* (small provincial synagogues) and *landsmenschaften* ("old country" town societies) "all around," but, of course, the impact of these institutions on young American Jews was negligible. The stage was set for a religious revival.

Once Goldstein had firmly committed himself to the idea of organizing an Institutional Synagogue, he began to utilize even seemingly remote opportunities to get his idea before the public. On March 1, 1917, a few days before his first face-to-face meeting with all of those interested in actually founding the synagogue, and over a month before resigning from his Kehilath Jeshurun post, he was called upon to deliver a speech at a Hotel Savoy dinner to "spread the idea of" the then-recently revitalized Rabbinical College. In the course of his remarks, Rabbi Goldstein took the liberty of making "a strong appeal for the Institutional Synagogue," and actually announcing "that [he]...hoped to lead this revival movement." The "wonderful introduction" which Judge Rosalsky—the very judge who had refused to head the Institutional Synagogue himself—gave Rabbi Goldstein that evening sent the rabbi away from the dinner with "infinitely increased enthusiasm and hope for the Institutional Synagogue."

The Formative Meeting

Not one to burn his bridges behind him until sure of his followers' loyalty, Rabbi Goldstein was very much still the English-speaking rabbi of the Kehilath Jeshurun when he conducted the formative meeting of his proposed experimental Institutional Synagogue. On the evening of March 6, 1917:

> The meeting was held at Hollywood Hall, 41 West 124th Street, and the audience consisted of the membership of the Harlem Y.M.H.A. and the Young Men's Hebrew Orthodox League. The purpose of the meeting was to amalgamate these two bodies and get them to pledge their allegiance and support to the Institutional Synagogue. This purpose was accomplished and much enthusiasm was displayed.

In his autobiographical sketch, Rabbi Goldstein recalled stating on this occasion, *inter alia:*

> My dear friends: I suggest that we organize not merely a synagogue, but that it be an Institutional Synagogue. I want

115

that synagogue organized to attract not only men of wealth, who generally are the ones using their funds to build synagogues, to attract not merely the older men who generally manage and supervise the details in conducting the synagogue, but my ambition is to gather around me a large mass of American-Jewish young men and women.

I want to revive and intensify Judaism among the young people living in Harlem. I want to bring them no new-fangled ideas, no fads or fancies that change with the times....I shall endeavor, with God's help, to bring back to our young men and young women, some of whom have strayed away from the fold, the Jewish religion, as [it has been] handed down to us from the pages of history, as every loyal Jew is expected to practice. That Judaism is labeled Orthodox Judaism, or perhaps a better term, authentic Judaism. Many are the questions that may suggest themselves to your minds as I make these statements.

What is an Institutional Synagogue? What demand is there for an Institutional Synagogue? Why has the rabbi chosen Harlem for his field of endeavor?

I shall take these questions up in their proper order. First: What is an Institutional Synagogue?...An Institutional Synagogue is the means by which we shall Judaize our outside environment....The emphasis that must be put upon the [Hebrew School] is not so much education, but "chinuch," which [is the Hebrew term for education but which also] means [in the versatile Hebrew language] dedication or consecration, as, for instance, in Psalm 30, which we read and recite in our morning prayers, "mizmor sheer chanukat habayit"—which translated means "a psalm for the dedication of the house of God." To teach a language in the [Hebrew School] is insufficient. [The school's] atmosphere must at all times come from the synagogue, the root of the Jewish religion.

I say the same about the Y.M.H.A. or Y.W.H.A. These associations are partial and negative. It is partial in so far as it makes an effort to take the youngster off the street. It is negative—I could really say "colorless"—because it does not stand for religious Judaism.

My thought is that, where young men and women gather, for whatever purpose they see fit, for social, literary, or athletic purposes, there must be the atmosphere that springs from the synagogues, that lends a note of dedication even in their literary or athletic activities.

The Institutional Synagogue is that institution of the future that will provide for a high-class, clean, American structure for purposes of prayer where there will be decorum at all times, as well as a dignified and reverential, spiritual, Orthodox service. . . . We frequently find too much conversation heard throughout the services conducted in the synagogue, and . . . find, thereby, the synagogue has lost its dignity, and there is no reverence . . . evidenced by the "shnodder" system . . . on Saturday mornings, as well as holidays [whereby people are expected to announce donations upon being honored by being called to recite a pair of blessings at the Torah] intensified by calling upon wealthy men . . . so they may make large contributions to the synagogue.

In the realm of the social and physical activities which are taken up today by the Y.M.H.A. and Y.W.H.A., a rabbi should always be present to see that the influence of the synagogue is always uppermost, above all else, to see that it lies at the root of the entire institution, sending its sap to its many branches, religious and social, with the spiritual nourishment of the synagogue proper.

Religion, as represented in the synagogue, must permeate the whole of our lives. In short, the Institutional Synagogue is that center to Judaize, and must Judaize, or religionize all activities of the Jew outside of the synagogue.

The next question, I believe, that you will ask yourselves, is, "Is there a demand for an Institutional Synagogue?"

I think that I can give two answers to that question. First of all, there is a demand for such a synagogue in Harlem, and secondly, if there were not, such a demand must be created.

The young men and women who volunteered, immediately after they arrived home from work, to go and devote their time and energies in behalf of the Institutional Synagogue, who helped to create and organize it, they are our scouts, our religious scouts, in Harlem.

I ask you gentlemen whether we can leave the building of such an institution to the next generation. It is for the future, to plant the seed for those who will come, who will do their duty, and then water the seeds by throwing themselves wholeheartedly into the growth of the seeds, thereby consecrating and dedicating themselves, and, by their example, stimulate others to do likewise.

You, my friends, I hope, will plant the seed, and you will build the institution so that the young men and women can come and cause it to flourish. It is problematical whether they will build it of their own accord.

My friends, I am going to Harlem because that vicinity has practically not been broken. My idea is a popular one. I would have gone downtown on the East Side, but I am told we have over-uplifted the East Side, so to speak. . . . I believe there are more young men and women who traverse Lenox and Seventh Avenues than any other two thoroughfares in the city. I believe these young men are unattached to any religious institution.

It is my idea to attach these young people to a religious institution, have them belong to an institution where their social needs and play instincts will be encouraged and provided for, and at the same time protected in the environment of a Jewish atmosphere. I propose to commence this at once, to rent a building in Harlem for the purpose of carrying on daily and Sabbath services, as are prescribed by the Shulchan Aruch [Code of Jewish Law], for the purpose of carrying on self-supporting educational classes, for the purpose of carrying on social clubs.

Towards this end I propose to lease—and, listen to this, dear friends—the Mount Morris Theatre in Harlem for Sunday mornings between 11 and 12 [noon] so as to reach a large mass of the young men and young women in Harlem who, unfortunately, are required to go to business on the Sabbath and cannot then attend our services.

It is my purpose, also, to write letters to every member of my congregation [from which he was about to resign, asking them] to help me in assisting these young men and women, and [I] propose to form a Sabbath Observance Bureau whereby these young people can be aided along these lines. These youngsters come to me often and say, "Rabbi, I would love to observe the Sabbath, but there are no positions open to me where I can follow that practice."

I propose, on these Sunday mornings, to talk to them, and bring them back to the synagogue, and to have them affiliate themselves with the synagogue, which I am sure they will do.

I pray firstly that we will all join together in succeeding in our undertaking by aspiration, by perspiration, and for realization of this worthy purpose. This will mean, I am sure, that the Al-mighty will bless our institution and let us hope and pray that the Al-mighty will bless our intention, and let us all say AMEN! AMEN!

After the meeting,

The proprietor of the Hall was so enthused that he said he would not take a penny for the use of the hall that night nor any other night that they met for that purpose. From 40-50 boys were present. They all had one day's notice; otherwise, the attendance would have been very much larger, but from those few boys (all in very mediocre circumstances), pledges of membership amounting to $150 yearly were made on the slips handed out....[T]he upshot of it [the meeting] was that five boys from each of the organizations should meet together with Congressman Siegel at our home [the Goldstein residence was at 1186 Madison Avenue at that time] and discuss plans to proceed with the work.

This meeting took place six days later as scheduled.

[T]he conclusion reached was that the boys should get together as many names of people from 25-40 years of age in Harlem [as] they think will be sympathetic to the cause, and all these people should be invited to all mass meetings shortly and further [become] enthused about the cause.

The *American Jewish Chronicle*'s edition of April 3, 1917, reprinted a letter from Harry G. Fromberg as president, and Morris Horowitz as chairman of the executive committee, of the "Young Israel." The Lower East Side organization they represented was the first synagogue of the then still gestating "modern Orthodox" Young Israel movement. By means of their public letter, they wished Rabbi Goldstein, "as a pioneer for revival work throughout the city. . . . God-speed" in his Institutional Synagogue revival movement.

Far more significant was the letter reprinted in the same issue, signed by Congressman Isaac Siegel, as president of the Young Men's Hebrew Association of Harlem. Describing Rabbi Goldstein's proposed Institutional Synagogue movement as the "salavation for the future Jew in America," the letter, in the form of a resolution, stated that the Y.M.H.A. had asked the Young Men's Hebrew Orthodox League to amalgamate with the Y.M.H.A. as a preliminary step, and then continued:

We have. . .on Sunday, March 25, 1917, amalgamated both organizations into the Institutional Synagogue. . . . We hereby highly resolve to invite Rabbi Herbert S. Goldstein. . . to lead this revival movement.

On April 4th, the day after this resolution appeared in the press, and fully ten days after this resolution of amalgamation into an Institutional Synagogue was passed, Mrs. Goldstein still referred to the amalgamated organizations by their original identities, and for good reasons:

In the evening, I went with Herbert to a joint meeting of the Y.M.H.A. and Y.M.H. Orthodox League in Harlem at Hollywood Hall. [Apparently they had taken up the proprietor on his generous offer.] A certain discordant element among the Y.M.H.A. boys brought up the issue of giving up their identity and there was a very heated discussion. It showed Herbert and me that it would not be all smooth sailing and though things were

119

finally settled our way, we went home quite discouraged.

Rabbi Goldstein did not remain discouraged for long. Although by this time it was common knowledge in the community that he had founded the synagogue, it was generally assumed that his "extramural" experiment would continue to be conducted simultaneously with his official duties at the Kehilath Jeshurun. This assumption was unquestionably justified, particularly in light of the fact that it was not until April 3, 1917, that Rabbi Goldstein himself "definitely decided to resign." He held his resolve firm despite the disconcerting outburst of April 4th, and, to eliminate any doubt regarding possible impulsiveness, he departed from personal precedent by carefully preparing, in advance, a written statement for his resignation sermon, which he read. The pages of this text also served as an informal launching pad for the Institutional Synagogue. The rabbi's skillful integration of his personal revival theme into his Passover sermon was instantly recognized as a classic of historic dimensions, judging from the fact that it was published, *in full*, in the following week's *Hebrew Standard*. Since parts of it have already been quoted earlier in this book, the following passages will be limited to those that tie in the *timing* of the announcement to the auspicious announcement itself:

> . . . Passover stands for the redemption of Israel and the birth of a national life. Its renewed observances have always marked in our history great revivals. Its first observance in the wilderness meant the revival of Israel from bondage to freedom.
>
> In the days of Joshua, as we have read in the *Haftarrah* [portion of prophets read the previous morning in the synagogue], it meant the revival of the natural life. No longer did the Jewish people [eat] of the manna, but [they] ate of the natural products of the land. In the reign of King Hezekiah, as we read in the second book of *Chronicles*, the festival of Passover marked the great religious revival of his day. It was on the festival of Passover that Hezekiah tried to unite the people, banded them together to turn from idol worship to the true God, the God of Israel. Later, in the reign of King Josiah, as we are told in the *Haftarrah*, this morning, we find the Passover festival again the reason for revival. A copy of the Torah was found while the Temple was being repaired. The people had lapsed into idolatry. They forgot their God, and when the *Sefer Torah* [Pentateuch] was read to them, the king and the people rejoiced, and once more there was a religious revival on the Passover festival. "For there never had been held such a Passover from the days of the Judges that judged Israel, nor in all the days of the Kings of Israel and of the Kings of Judah." Finally we read in the Book of Ezra of the last great Biblical Passover. We read how the people returned from the exile with Ezra and rebuilt the temple. It was a Passover festival that

gave a concrete expression to the revival of the religious emotion of zeal among the people.

Thus you have seen that the Passover Festival always meant to the Jew and the world a reawakening, a break from bondage and, above all, a revival. The rabbis tell us that [the Hebrew month of] *Nissan*, marking the rejuvenation of Israel, also marks the rejuvenation of nature. "The month of bloom, the season of blossoms, is ushered in with *Nissan*." *Nissan* brings with it Passover, the festival of freedom from Egyptian bondage. Spring brings with it the freedom of nature from the ice and hoary frost. That is not merely a coincidence. It is an evidence of the spiritual law that man and nature are indissolubly related. Thus, my friends, when the spring of the year comes, nature puts us in the tune for a reawakening, in tune with the message of Passover. It brings to us a call for a new life, a call for a revival. I have endeavored to show you, through our Biblical history, that Passover was always the season for an awakening. The Passover in Egypt, the revival of freedom; the Passover in the plains of Jericho, the revival of the natural life, the Passover of Hezekiah, the revival of the worship of one God; the Passover of King Josiah, the revival of the Torah; the Passover in the time of Ezra, the revival of the Temple; and today, this Passover in America [by means of the proposed Institutional Synagogue], the revival of Judaism in America.

The immediate reaction of the stunned audience was described in the chapter dealing with Goldstein's first congregation. The highly charged atmosphere following this dramatic oration engulfed the Goldsteins' chance dinner guest that day, one unsuspecting Charlie Jacobs, "a young man of the world." Not surprisingly, Mrs. Goldstein reported:

> We minutely discussed the management of the Institutional Synagogue. [Young Jacobs, under the circumstances, had little choice but to offer, as he did,] his services throughout the winter as an usher at the proposed Sunday morning lectures at the theatre.

Although one can question the true level of the enthusiasm instilled in the Goldsteins' captive dinner-table audience of one, there is no question that the reaction that freely greeted Rabbi Goldstein's announcement where it mattered was enthusiastic, immediate and city-wide. Letters of encouragement as well as unsolicited offers of cooperation streamed into the Goldstein residence. An excerpt from Mrs. Goldstein's diary two days after the announcement, for example, disclosed that:

Two men who were very active in the social service work of the

Free Synagogue [headed by the "Reform" rabbi, Stephen Wise] voluntarily came to Herbert and offered their services and affiliations for the Institutional Synagogue. Mr. S. R. Travis pledged a donation of $500 for the cause and things look very promising...

In addition to the expressions of actual and financial participation (notice which form of participation Mrs. Goldstein had seen fit to mention first), reaction from the press was highly encouraging as well. An editorial on the first page of the English section of the *Jewish Daily News* stated, in part:

> The announcement, in another column, of Rabbi Herbert S. Goldstein's assumption of the leadership of a new movement among Young Jewry in this city will be hailed with gratification.
>
> For many years past, young men and women, deeply attached to traditional Judaism, have been very desirous of launching a citywide movement. The Young Israel Synagogue, the Young Men's Hebrew Orthodox League, the Adath B'nei Israel and similar organizations are the tangible expressions of these sentiments. They have done splendid work and have succeeded in a measure to stem the tide of de-Judaization which threatened to engulf our young folks. Lack of funds and the indifference of the community hampered them in their labors. The greatest drawback, though, was lack of cohesion and co-ordination among the various forces working for the strengthening of traditional Judaism. The step taken by the Young Men's Hebrew Orthodox League, the Harlem Y.M.H.A., and Young Israel in extending a call* to Rabbi Goldstein promises that in the future there is to be concerted action. The fact, too, that Congressman Siegel will take an active part is, too, encouraging.
>
> Rabbi Goldstein, Congressman Siegel and those associated with them will have no easy task. It is pioneer work; [i]t will be going up-hill and, to some extent, against the stream....
>
> The new movement is going to be watched and measured and weighed. Every word and deed of its leaders will be scrutinized, and endeavors will be made to pick up flaws. We utter this warning. It is just as well to know what is before them. All the more reason for them to be stout-hearted.
>
> We promise Rabbi Goldstein and Mr. Siegel every cooperation in their way-back-to-Judaism efforts.

*The Young Israel's voice in the "call" was not quite as loud as that of the other organizations—although it certainly came from further away (the Lower East Side). It was more of an echo of endorsement, if anything. The most concrete statement in the Fromberg-Horowitz Young Israel letter seemed to revolve around the statement, "[W]e sincerely hope that at some future date you will be able to co-operate with us."

We call young Jewry to rally to the standard which has been unfurled.

The non-Jewish national press also gave coverage to Rabbi Goldstein's plans. Under the headline, "To lead Jewish Revival in Harlem," the *New York Times* published excerpts of Rabbi Goldstein's letter of resignation from the Central Jewish Institute, in which he designated the geographic center of his projected life's work as "the heart of the most distressing Jewish conditions in the United States, namely, Lenox Avenue and 116th Street."

The first meeting of the members of the Institutional Synagogue following the official announcement of Goldstein's intention to resign from the K.J.—and the C.J.I.—took place two weeks after this announcement and a month and a half before it was to take effect. Mrs. Goldstein's account of the meeting, at the Uptown Talmud Torah, stated: "The constitution was adopted which included, among other things, a clause stating that Rabbi Herbert S. Goldstein should be minister of the Institutional Synagogue for his natural life." Further indirect assurance against potential efforts to ram through the board reforms contrary to Jewish law was subtly guaranteed by an additional clause stating that "no innovation in traditional Judaism may be inaugurated" into the synagogue's ritual "if there be one dissenting vote at a meeting of the corporation."

Four officers were elected to serve under Congressman Siegel and over the ten directors who were also elected at this meeting. The commitment of all the "approximately 12" active members of the Young Men's Hebrew Orthodox League was further solidified at this meeting when, "The old Y.M.H. Orthodox League announced a donation of 40 chairs, 12 Bibles, and 12 *Talaitim* [religious prayer shawls]." The early commitment of the newly elected members of the first board of directors was apparent. There was 100 percent attendance at their first meeting, which lasted three and one-half hours.

Eleven days later, the house that the Goldsteins had considered "by virtue of its location and interior...admirably suited to our purposes" was purchased at 112 West 116th Street. Five days later, the *New York Times* reported, "The Rev. Dr. Herbert S. Goldstein [many newspapers conferred doctorates on him before he received an academic one] announced yesterday that an anonymous donor had given a five-story house at 112 West 116th Street to be used as a head-quarters by the synagogue."* Until the building was sufficiently re-modeled to assume its new identity as a synagogue, the synagogue organization's activities revolved around the Y.W.H.A. on West 110th

---

*The identity of the mysterious anonymous donor does not seem to have been revealed or "leaked" to the press, and it was not even identified in Mrs. Goldstein's diary. The circumstances seem to have pointed to her father who was in the real estate business and who donated real estate and buildings to numerous other religious enterprises. The circumstances

Street. In this setting, a hundred young people attended the first meeting to be held after the new I.S. building was purchased. The encouragement their presence gave the Goldsteins was reciprocated by the encouragement Rabbi Goldstein gave *them* by announcing the actual acquisition of the building. About a month later, under the headline "Y.W.H.A. Notes," a newspaper article casually referred to regular Friday evening and Saturday morning services at the Y.W.H.A. conducted by the Institutional Synagogue. Although the I.S. had ready access to facilities at the "Y" as well as to facilities at other institutions, its first few board of directors meetings were all held in the Goldstein residence. This generated a strong sense of intimacy and fellowship that bound the group together around the rabbi into a cohesive unit.

The actual meeting at which the Institutional Synagogue completed the formalities necessary for the filing of a certificate of incorporation took place on a Tuesday morning, October 30, 1917. Rabbi Goldstein was the presiding officer although Congressman Siegel was present. The Congressman, as president, presided over all *subsequent* meetings at which he was present. Eight people personally executed the document that day before the Commissioner of Deeds of the City of New York. Mrs. Goldstein used to remark in later years that, "The founders were so young that they had trouble rounding up enough people who were *old* enough to sign the necessary documents!"*

were not nearly that conclusive, however, to the members of the Harlem community, most of whom did not know Goldstein personally at this point. Furthermore, he had not even moved to Harlem and his father-in-law never moved into the neighborhood, nor did his father-in-law ever become a member of the board of directors of the synagogue, even though Fischel and Goldstein were destined to sit on many other boards together. Besides, Goldstein's original discussion with Fischel *and* his public pronouncements all spoke only in terms of *leasing* a building for the first phase. In addition, Goldstein's plans and potential for further success were known nationally, and non-Orthodox prominent wealthy sources had been approached for their assistance. It was, therefore, conceivable that any one of them may have had a motive to make his contribution anonymous due, perhaps, to the experimental nature of the venture, or, possibly, due to Goldstein's outspoken and unflinchingly Orthodox views. Even the widow of Congressman Siegel, when asked about the anonymous donor in an extensive interview many years later, conceded she could do no more than speculate as to the donor's identity.

*Hyperbole aside, the fact that their time was sought on a workday morning should not be overlooked.

Chapter 14

Serving The First Services To A Receptive Community

The very year, 1915, that the two Y.M.H. organizations mentioned in the previous chapter were formed (a year before Goldstein recalled having even first *thought* about an I.S., and two years before he conclusively decided to start one in Harlem) Goldstein was involved, in what was then a purely altruistic voluntary capacity, in helping a group of boys in Harlem to organize at least a weekly schedule of prayer services at the Harlem Y.W.H.A. At that time, he himself was entrenched in a neighboring but distinctly different community of his own. What added to the idealism of his involvement with the "Y" under these circumstances was the fact that the two neighborhoods were within walking distance of each other. They were so close, in fact, that some Harlem boys regularly used to walk all the way down to his weekly *Oneg Shabbat* (Sabbath gatherings) on Friday nights at the Kehilath Jeshurun in Yorkville. From a purely personal point of view, therefore, it would appear that Goldstein was helping what in some respects was then his "competition," to get on its feet in its crucial formative years, causing all of its members to feel less moved than they may have otherwise felt to use their *own* feet to take the three-mile round trip—Jewish law prohibits the use of vehicular transportation on the Sabbath—all the way down to his Yorkville synagogue.

Thus when Rabbi Goldstein needed the Y.W.H.A. building two years later in which to conduct regular services until the first I.S. building would be ready for use, poetic justice in a positive sense was being served. He was not only *permitted* to run his own religious services temporarily in the very same building, but he actually had a built-in nucleus of worshipers who were eager to join him in the Institutional Synagogue as soon as he would be ready to lead them to it.

Precisely on the day his contract at the Kehilath Jeshurun expired, June 1st, which happened to have been a Friday (the day of the traditional weekly joyous Sabbath eve service), Goldstein "went up to the I.S. services for the first time." "Hardly any one" of the participants at the first I.S. service was over 21.*

In preparing for its first high holiday service, the synagogue administration undertook a massive advertising campaign, taking advantage of the fact that:

At that time, upper Fifth Avenue had no houses but was all empty lots closed in by wooden fences. These fences were used for advertisements. The Institutional Synagogue rented advertising space one block long between 107th and 108th Streets.

Not only did this provide a ready showcase to promote the aims of the synagogue, but it also helped to bring in the 960 people who attended these services at the Parkview Palace on 110th Street and Fifth Avenue before the I.S. even moved into its own building.

The *Hebrew Standard*'s coverage of the services stated:

One of the most impressive services held during the recent High Holy Days was conducted under the auspices of the Institutional Synagogue....1,000 worshipers were present

---

*Few idealists get the opportunity, as Goldstein did, of putting their good intentions to the test by launching their ventures in a full time capacity without accepting any remuneration from their beneficiaries for an extended period of time. Yet the *New York American* reported: "Goldstein is serving at the synagogue without compensation, and will continue to do so for the next year." Mrs. Goldstein made absolutely no reference to his personal source of income in this period beyond her previous reference to some property deeded to him by her father for the purpose of supplementing his salary, when he had been at the Kehilath Jeshurun congregation. The day after his K.J. employment contract had expired, she wrote in her diary:

Herbert's wonderful faith in being willing to take a chance to work for the Institutional Synagogue for one year without any salary and his willingness to gamble with the Lord is surely being rewarded and we cannot help seeing God's direct leading, for Herbert has made on weddings this week (the first week in which his salary ceases completely) more than he used to make a week when he drew a salary from both the Synagogue and the [Central Jewish] Institute.

The record shows that Goldstein held firm in his resolve and did not succumb to the temptation to accept any payment from the synagogue within his first year of employment, despite its instant success and dramatic and productive membership campaign. In fact, he even went beyond his original pledge of self-sacrifice for the cause. It was not until the Fourth of July of 1918—more than thirteen months after he had ceased to draw his K.J. salary—that Mrs. Goldstein was able to write in her diary (the capitalization is hers):

HERBERT RECEIVED HIS FIRST CHECK OF $250 FROM THE INSTITU-TIONAL SYNAGOGUE TODAY. Till the synagogue is on a firmer financial basis, Herbert is to return $100 a month as a donation to the Synagogue. Thank God we have lived to see the day when the I.S. can afford to pay a salary. It is not the matter of a salary which is so important, but the fact that the I.S. is supported by the people to such an extent that it is in a position to cover its expenses.

both at the Rosh Hashanah and Yom Kippur services; many of these included persons who have not entered a synagogue in years.

The entire service was conducted by young men, and all the [honors] were given to young men. On the whole, it was as completely American and thoroughly Jewish as any service ever held in this country heretofore.

On account of the impressive and dignified services, more than 200 persons signified their intentions of becoming members of the synagogue, and helping it in its great work.

The very first service to be conducted in the first building that the I.S. was able to call its own was as auspicious as the synagogue's founders could have possibly hoped for in their most optimistic projections. According to a firsthand spontaneous account of the event:

[At] the first service in the I.S. House, 112 West 116 Street...the synagogue was packed to the doors, and it is beginning to be feared that the building will soon be too small.

It was a "fear" that was happily to be proven well-founded! As daring and fearless a "pioneer" as Rabbi Goldstein may have been, generally, this was *one* "fear" that could have obsessed him without diminishing his stature. In fact, this highly desirable fear was most necessary to induce him to set his sights, in earnest, on his yet-to-be-created but well-described ultimate target.

Chapter 15

Rallying Around
The Rabbi

An earlier chapter in this book focused on Goldstein's concept of a Jewish revival movement and emphasized what it was *not*. Here an attempt will be made to try to revive at least the spirit of what the revival rallies *were* like.

In addition to having people plaster printed flyers throughout the streets of Harlem announcing Rabbi Goldstein's first "Monster Revival Meeting," scheduled for May 20, 1917 while the rabbi was still employed by the Kehilath Jeshurun, the Goldsteins sent about 200 cards to individuals, likewise, to spread the word. The most comprehensive announcement of this historic first rally appeared the day of the rally, in the *Harlem Home News*, under the headline, "Jewish Revival Strikes Harlem with a Bang."

> The great Jewish revival will strike Harlem this evening when the first big mass meeting will be held at the Y.W.H.A. Auditorium, 31 West 110th Street at 8 o'clock.
>
> An appeal is here made to the young men and women of Harlem to come to the meeting which will be the beginning of the Institutional Synagogue under the direction of Dr. Herbert S. Goldstein, who is to devote the remainder of his life to working with young Jewish people.
>
> Last night young men of Harlem paraded along Seventh and Lenox Avenues in order to interest the people of Harlem in tonight's mass meeting. Boy Scouts will patrol the block on 110th Street from Lenox to Seventh Avenue this evening to take care of the crowds.
>
> Rabbis back of [backing] the Jewish revival movement (which is the first Jewish revival in 1800 years*) are Moses

*Goldstein himself later refuted this claim.

128

Hyamson, of Temple Orach Chaim, former Acting Chief Rabbi of England, and Bernard Revel, Dean of the Rabbinical College of America.

The program for the evening includes the singing of the Star Spangled Banner, singing of Jewish Airs by the Judah Halevy Choral Society, an address by Congressman Isaac Siegel, President of the Synagogue, and an address on the need of a Jewish revival movement, by Dr. Herbert S. Goldstein.

The Board of Directors of the synagogue will act as ushers.

The rally was so successful in attracting people that the *New York American* reported that:

[H]undreds of people were turned away from the meeting last night because the hall was not adequate to accommodate the throngs. Two companies of Boy Scouts were stationed in the assembly room to aid in seating the people.

Mrs. Goldstein was naturally enthusiastic in her diary entry of May 20th, but whereas her entries on the Institutional Synagogue thus far had not, by and large, contained information overlapping that which was cited in the press, this one did. It presents a first opportunity to compare her reporting accuracy with that of the broad-based non-Jewish press. As will likewise be apparent later, not only did she pass the test of objectivity, but, in addition, her entries in relation to the reporting of the less biased press indicated a tendency to *understate* the achievements of her husband. Whereas she reported that merely "more than 100 new members were enlisted in the cause," the *Harlem Home News* reported, after describing the "hundreds" who had to be turned away for lack of room to accommodate them, that "Those few hundred who remained [the emphasis was obviously intended to be on the word *hundred*, and *not* the word few] became so enthusiastic over the prospect of the revival movement that *one hundred and twenty-five* of them [italics were not in the original] immediately signed up as members of the Institutional Synagogue, which is to be the synagogue behind the movement."

Although the Institutional Synagogue was to be based in Harlem and focused on the Jews of this particular community, "because of the power of the preacher," it was "expected that Jews from every part of the city" would attend the second mass rally three weeks later. Mrs. Goldstein's account follows:

Herbert and I awoke very early this morning for we were all excited and nervous about the revival meeting of the Institutional Synagogue which was to be held this morning. Although several hundred people had to be turned away from our first revival meeting at the YWHA, that place only seated about 300, but the Regent Theatre has a capacity of 2,000 and we were doubtful whether we could draw a sufficiently large crowd not to have the place look empty. Well, Herbert and I got to the Regent Theatre at 10:15, and by 11 o'clock the theatre was three quarters full. It was marvelous to see the crowds coming in. The Jewish Protectory Band of Hawthorne, New York, played first outside then inside...Congressman Siegel... presided. There was a vocal selection, some announcements, and then Herbert delivered a masterpiece of a sermon on the text, "How long will ye halt between two opinions." He explained the work of the Institutional Synagogue. He urged the people to become actively affiliated with it, and to sign blanks designating what activity they were interested in, and he pleaded with those who had strayed to come back to the right path. His sermon...met with tremendous applause...it was estimated that there were from 1,200 to 1,500 people present. Altogether our second revival meeting was a howling success.

A typical checklist distributed at this and subsequent early I.S. rallies asked for people to designate their fields of interest within five distinct areas: "Religious and Educational," "Social Service," purely "Social," "Athletics," and a "Sabbath Employment Bureau." The first two categories were each further subdivided into eight specific activities alongside of little boxes to be checked, and the next two each featured five subdivisions at this still formative stage. In answering one of his early critics, Goldstein referred directly to his second rally, at which "of the 1,200 people* who were handed slips of paper...of the activities of the I.S....about 400 designated their interest in Religious and educational pursuits." The lives of the 800 others were not to remain religiously untouched either.

Normally newspapers are notorious for inflating figures, particularly estimates of crowds, but if any group of people is *more* notorious for inflating such statistics, it is the sponsors of an event themselves. In complete contrast to this universal tendency, two of the largest circulating English-language Jewish weeklies, the *Hebrew Standard* and the *American Hebrew*, each estimated the crowd at at least 2,000; not only was Mrs. Goldstein's estimate far lower, but even when she quoted *other* people's estimates, she refrained from quoting the higher ones, and chose, instead, the lower ones. Similarly, the *American Hebrew* stated that, "More than 200 new members were recruited to the cause"—well above Mrs. Goldstein's approximation—"as a result of this meeting."

*Note that his estimate of his own achievement was even more conservative than his wife's!

130

Although compared to the newspaper reports her figures appear deflated, in *absolute* terms, of course, the numbers even as *she* gave them certainly appear to be impressive. Even the lowest estimate for this second revival meeting was no less than four times the estimate of the attendance at the first...and overflow...one!

Numbers alone, however, are of limited value. The question of far greater significance is whether this rally, with its merry music and three companies of smartly dressed Boy Scouts, did more than just entertain. The following excerpt that appeared in the *Hebrew Standard* answers this question rather eloquently:

> ...A most touching scene was witnessed after the meeting when fathers and mothers, with tears in their eyes, came up to thank Rabbi Goldstein. The most encouraging feature of the morning's revival was the fact that a throng of both young men and young women came up to the rabbi to tell him of their return to traditional Judaism, and of their joining this "Synagogue movement."

The *Harlem Home News* declared that, "Thousands of Jewish young men and women are going back to the faith of their fathers as the result of the revival movement."

Not only did Rabbi Goldstein inspire others, but he set in motion a beautiful cycle. Every individual success he achieved inspired *him* to renew his efforts. After a lecture on the *Ethics of the Fathers* by the rabbi at the Institutional Synagogue, his wife wrote:

> He brought home with him for *kiddush* [a religious ceremony over a cup of wine] a young man who was a wonderful example of the possibility of an irreligious fellow becoming religious. He said that it is not long ago since he knew about as much as a lay Catholic and now he is an ardent advocate and even preacher of Orthodox Judaism. He was an inspiration to Herbert and me to put all our energies into the Jewish revival movement.

The rabbi spent a good part of the following summer on trips into New York City on I.S. matters while the rest of his family remained in the Goldsteins' rented vacation bungalow in the Catskill Mountains. His negotiations with the neighborhood Mount Morris Theatre for a hall in which to conduct his rallies led, once again, to results people normally might only dare to dream about. The early phase of his negotiations left the matter wide open. He wrote to his wife on June 27th:

> I was at the Mt. Morris Theatre [which certainly had an

appropriate enough name for a platform from which to preach a return to the law of Moses—a Hebrew name which is often Anglicized to "Morris"]...and they asked for $1000 for 40 Sundays. I offered $500. The matter will be put to their board for further consideration, as well as to our board.

By the time the negotiations drew to a close, it was later revealed, the I.S. was "fortunate in securing the free use of...the Mt. Morris Theatre." Had the negotiations continued any longer, the theatre management might have ended up *paying* for the privilege!

After the summer and the high holidays, with the Institutional Synagogue beginning to function on virtually all of its intended levels, the revival meetings, lectures, or rallies, as they were interchangeably called, began to be convened, as promised, on a weekly basis. The kickoff rally of the season included a message from New York City's mayor, then John P. Mitchel, and, of course, addresses by Rabbi Goldstein and Congressman Siegel. By December, the New York press was able to refer to the revival meetings as a regular feature in the Harlem community: "More than one thousand people attend these meetings regularly, at which either Dr. Goldstein or some other prominent person speaks." Even when he did not deliver the main featured address, Rabbi Goldstein was on the program nevertheless. Those who attended could count on hearing the likes of Louis Marshall, one of Jewry's most influential jurists, Dr. Nicholas Murray Butler, president of Columbia University, and a wide assortment of congressmen, most of whose names are no longer meaningful today, as well as other federal, state, and local figures. Those who attended could *not*, apparently, count on such political "heavyweights" as "has beens" Theodore Roosevelt and William J. Bryan, who had circled United States presidential arenas so charismatically and who had promised to participate, but who apparently came short of fulfillment in the I.S. arena as well as in their final forays in the *political* arena.

When Congressman Julius Kahn of California joined Rabbi Goldstein on the speaker's platform in March of 1918, Mrs. Goldstein reported:

> ...for the first time since we began to hold our Sunday morning lectures, baskets were passed around and a collection was taken up for our Social Service activities. $77.00 was realized* to our great surprise and satisfaction.

Gradually, the point was reached where, "Hundreds of dollars

*It cannot be over-emphasized that these were in 1918-valued dollars.

were raised in this way every Sunday morning."

There was nothing static about these events except for their underlying purpose. The speakers changed from week to week, the entertainment was varied (featuring, on occasion, artists who claimed "to have their own musical recitals where admission [was] from 50¢ to $2.50"), the meetingplace was moved (to the Grant Theatre, in December of 1919), and even the very nature of the event defied a single set classification.* Yet any difficulties in defining the rallies did not, apparently, impede the recognition they received. By March of 1919, the New York *American* credited the Institutional Synagogue with the sponsorship of "one of the best forums in the city," without limiting the field to other *religious* or *Jewish* forums, but "one of the best open forums," period!

Rabbi Goldstein was not afraid to take strong stands on highly controversial issues. As early in the series as November 25, 1917, he dared to discuss, with advance notice to the whole community, "Judaism's Challenge to Socialism," in which he showed, according to his wife's capsulated summary,

> that Judaism contains all that socialism contains, as well as the good that it lacks, but having a highly socialistic audience I think he aroused some antagonism—nothing public, though.

The best way to see the effects of these rallies is through the eyes of people whom they affected. One such person wrote an account of his own experience (in the third person) for the synagogue newspaper. Note the *lack* of the fanatically zealous style of the typical missionary convert:

> ...Sam listened to other Jewish boys who drifted from their religion, and for a while, as a result of associating with Jews who violated the Sabbath, became a *Shabbos goy* [Sabbath violator] himself for about five years. His father pleaded in vain that he put on the *tephillin* [religious article worn by males during daily prayer]...
> One Sunday, Sam walked near 116th Street and 5th Avenue, and saw a sign at the Mt. Morris Theatre, stating, "Jewish Revival Meeting, Free Music, Admission Free." Sam walked in...listened to the rabbi's appeal for Judaism... joined as a member...attended one Saturday service. When Sam saw boys of his age read the Torah [Bible scroll, from the

---

*In addition to the labels that were mentioned earlier by which the events were known, they were also referred to as forums, and, for at least one period, "reconstruction lectures," featuring, consequently, "reconstruction and education," "social reconstruction," "political reconstruction," and "industrial reconstruction."

original parchment] he opened his eyes and couldn't believe his own eyes. [The thought that] a young man of twenty [could be] reading the Torah appealed to Sam, and he said, "That's what I call marvelous...No more shall I listen to Jews who have drifted from Judaism."

Later on Sam...remembered his father saying "Your *tephillin* are rusted [figuratively—since they consist only of small parchment scrolls in leather boxes and straps]. Put them on!"...Sam put on *tephillin* regularly, also attended services on Saturday for a year, and finds he is better off than he ever was.

The *Jewish Daily News*, from a perspective of ten years later, recalled that the Institutional Synagogue had "held during the War [World War I] the most successful forums in Greater New York at the Mount Morris Theatre."*

Goldstein's revivalist theme and approach met with equally enthusiastic responses practically wherever he brought them. The reactions he generated in Ottawa, Canada, were par for his course:

Those who were present at the initial Open Forum meeting of the season last Sunday night could not fail but be impressed with the crusading militant spirit of Judaism as exemplified by the brilliant and potent message delivered by Dr. Herbert S. Goldstein. What a maze of misconception has been lifted from many of those who smarted from the "legalism" of the faith of their fathers. Many who came doubtful of the value of some of those laws, which on the surface are irksome and appear [to be] unnecessary cumbersome restrictions, remained to pray, catching a first glimpse of their beauty.

That the remarks did not fall on deaf ears but took deep root in the hearts and minds of the audience may well be illustrated by the comment of one young married woman, who in her household observed the dietary laws simply because her forebears and a goodly portion of her Jewish friends did likewise, and often she was in a rebellious mood, failing to see the object, the utility, and the idea encompassing unnecessary restrictions which added to her labour without any apparent value. But when the "idea" of our Jewish dietary laws as expounded by Dr. Goldstein was revealed to her, the idea of "peace lovingness," the train of thought where by virtue of our laws our people are instinctively lovers of peace was explained to her, she saw the beauty of that religious law, and it may well be that hereafter the same practice, which hitherto was burdensome, will be carried out with a happy heart.

...Dr. Goldstein, pioneer and trail blazer in the campaign for the revival of the Jewish faith...not content with waiting for the Jew to return to Judaism...brings Judaism to the Jew. He makes it part and parcel of his being, of his everyday life.

Although Rabbi Goldstein never wavered in his advocacy of revival rallies, once all of the features and institutions of his Institutional Synagogue were installed, he found he could preach best by example, by letting people see for themselves what his institution was like, and by drawing them in to the religious and educational aspects of the institute. Direct exhortations at special public rallies became almost superfluous compared to the word-of-mouth publicity transmitted by the participants themselves. Goldstein concentrated on generating such a strong sense of pride in the synagogue that participants in all phases of the institute unconsciously became walking advertisers.

Never running out of novel ways to promote his revivalistic message, Rabbi Goldstein, in a 1926 sermon excerpted in the *New York Times*, claimed:

America is ripe for a new and different kind of drive. A drive not for funds, but a revivalistic campaign for religious practices.

There are many noble men and women who participate in every drive, whether it be for Palestine, for war relief, or even for Jewish education; but they are always driving for someone else. These people are altogether too unselfish....The time has now come when we must make a drive on behalf of the drivers. We must wage a campaign which will benefit the campaigners. A concentrated effort must be made to revive in the hearts of all these good men and women a spirit of complete loyalty to the glorious historic faith into which they were born.

We are about to see how the rabbi himself faced a different and unique kind of a loyalty test just as his own synagogue movement was beginning to change the face of Jewish institutional life in America.

Chapter 16

Temptation To Accept A Gilded Pulpit On A Silver Platter

Temptations often surface from the most unexpected points of origin. A spiritual leader tends to be removed from many of the usual and more obvious temptations. To an enterprising young rabbi, a temptation can somewhat paradoxically take the form of a call to a congregation where money is no object, fund raising is no challenge, and the rabbi would have *more* time for his own spiritual advancement, but at the expense of those left behind who may still need his inspiration to maintain even their minimum commitment. This was the siren call that beckoned to Rabbi Goldstein.

Just as old wine increases in value with age after years of mellowing in a dark barrel, so, it can be said, does the prestige of a congregation increase with added years in the national limelight. By this objective measure, added to the subjective social standings of the day, the Shearith Israel Congregation, otherwise known as the Spanish and Portuguese Synagogue, was the most prestigious, and certainly the most historic synagogue in the country when Rabbi Goldstein and the I.S. were approaching their prime. No matter how it will be judged regarding its past and future performance in the community, nobody will ever be able to take away its distinction as the first Jewish congregation to be organized in this country—and hemisphere—in 1654. As if that were not enough, in 1898, the Union of Orthodox Jewish Congregations of America (U.O.J.C.A.) was founded in this congregation's building, as had been the now-"Conservative" Jewish Theological Seminary of America (J.T.S.), in 1887, when, in accord with the wishes of its founders, the J.T.S. had been religiously traditional.

The first president and acting president, respectively, of these two organizations had been a man we have seen earlier, Rev. H.

Pereira Mendes. Rabbi Goldstein not only was destined to succeed him eventually as the president of the U.O.J.C.A., but was also destined to succeed him immediately as the head of the homiletics* department of the future Yeshiva University's affiliated Rabbinical Seminary. As one of the officiating rabbis at Goldstein's wedding, Mendes had observed, according to an eyewitness account, that "when God sees fit to take him [Mendes], he would like somebody like Rabbi Goldstein to succeed him." Little did the senior rabbi realize how close events were destined to come not only to fulfill his wish, but to go, in two senses, *further* than it. Not only "somebody *like* Rabbi Goldstein," but Rabbi Goldstein himself was destined to be offered his long-term position, and the offer did not have to be deferred until God would see fit to take him, since it was destined to be issued while Mendes was a very much alive, alert, and consulted Rabbi Emeritus!

The most striking aspect of the momentous offer was that "the invitation to other than a rabbi of Sephardic [Spanish or Portuguese] descent mark[ed] the breaking of a precedent of over two centuries." (The precedent would have been of a still greater duration had it not been for the fact that for the first few decades after the then-fledgling congregation had been organized in 1654, it had not had *any* formally ordained rabbi.)

The decision to break with such an old precedent in such a traditional congregation undoubtedly did not come easily, but it hardly came as a sudden thunderbolt from Heaven—or the "Hell of Harlem"—either. Not only had Dr. Mendes himself raised the prospect, in people's minds, on Goldstein's wedding day, but some years later, while Goldstein was still occupying the pulpit in the original small I.S. building, Goldstein accepted the express invitation of the elder rabbi to preach from *his* pulpit one Sabbath morning in 1919. After Rev. Mendes' retirement and Rev. David de Sola Pool's later-to-be-withdrawn resignation, Rabbi Goldstein was bombarded with invitations, for an entire year, to preach at the congregation again.

Finally, on or around the 6th of October, in 1921, an informal "call" was issued to Rabbi Goldstein. The first mention of it in Mrs. Goldstein's diary clearly indicated that the offer, as tempting as it may have been, was by no means "an offer he could not refuse"! At her parents' home that very day, "we discussed Herbert's call to the ministry of the. . .synagogue. We didn't come to any definite conclusion." That was putting it mildly. The better part of two months were to elapse, in agonizing soul-searching and analysis, before a final decision was to be reached.

Over a month after the informal "call" had been extended, Goldstein was still willing to risk not receiving a formal call at all

*Homiletics is the preparation and delivery of sermons.

by telling the president of the congregation "not to present his name for election at the present time unless the sentiment there is unanimous." Sure enough, two evenings later, according to Mrs. Goldstein's diary, her:

> phone rang and it was Mrs. Goldstein [the rabbi's mother] who called up to say that Dr. Rosenberg had called her up to tell her that *Herbert* had been *unanimously elected minister of the Spanish and Portuguese Synagogue.* Right after that, Esther Hirsch phoned to tell us the same news. This was followed by calls from Mama, Sadie, Dave, Henry, and Bertha and finally *Captain Phillips*, president of *Shearith Israel*—who had been trying to get us the whole time, called up to congratulate Herbert and tell him the news. At first, I cried, for I didn't want that *call* to come [had the congratulatory calls lasted any longer, the *official* call might very well *not* have come that evening] because I don't think Herbert has a right to leave the I.S., but then when I realized that Herbert was happy about it, I tried to be happy with him. There is no question that a call like that, from the oldest congregation in the city to a young fellow like Herbert...is a wonderful tribute, especially coming as it did, entirely unsolicited. After the folks left, Herbert and I sat down in the library and read some psalms to ourselves....

Three days later, the formal vote was backed up by the most formal of personal invitations imaginable, clearly befitting a congregation with such a dignified reputation:

> At 8:30, a committee of 7 members of the Board of Trustees of the Spanish and Portuguese Synagogue came up attired mostly in tuxedos ["frock coats, and silk hats"], and formally presented the call to their congregation to Herbert, in writing. Captain Phillips first got up [and] made a speech in which he stated that Shearith Israel had only had three ministers in 100 years; that they were all men of renown, that they had never taken anybody except a *Sephard* before; but Herbert's wonderful success in the work he was doing and his fame and ability forced them to set aside all questions of sect and to invite Herbert to become their minister. They said their minister was to be the minister of all Jewry and that they hoped nothing would stand in the way of his acceptance. They felt that though their congregation was old, Herbert could bring to it that pep and enthusiasm which would make it young again....
> Herbert responded by telling them the history of the Institutional Synagogue, that it would be very difficult for him

to separate himself from it, that for one year he had to be very close to it, and that he had called a meeting of the Institutional Synagogue Board of Directors for Saturday night, and until then he couldn't give them any definite answer....

The considerations in favor of acceptance of the offer were obvious. From a financial point of view, there were 7,500 very compelling reasons. At a time when he was living on a $4,000 annual salary in a still-experimental venture, he was offered a guaranteed $7,500 annually, for a five-year period, nearly double his then-existing salary—*plus* the use of the elaborate "parsonage" adjoining the glamorous historic synagogue building—and "telephone service." All this from the most time-tested synagogue in the country! What seemed, particularly, to impress a Reform publication as far away as the mid-western United States, was the apparent public knowledge that the salary offered to tempt Rabbi Goldstein was "half again [1½ times] as much as Dr. Mendes [himself] ever received"!*

One of the first members outside of the family with whom the Goldsteins had confided on the subject was the widow of the saintly rabbi who had so influenced their lives, Rabbi Joseph Mayer Asher. Surely she could have been counted on to give the question an objective and noble perspective. Mrs. Goldstein's diary reported:

> She strongly advised the acceptance of the *call* on the grounds that the prestige which that position lends would enable Herbert to do big things for Orthodoxy as a whole instead of for just one group. Also, only a man of Herbert's youth, vigor, and personality can bring that stronghold of Orthodoxy to life again....

The following evening, Mrs. Asher told Mrs. Goldstein that she had discussed the matter with Mrs. Hyamson, the wife of Asher's successor in the *Orach Chayim* pulpit, and that Mrs. Hyamson, likewise, encouraged acceptance of the call.

With the full knowledge that although the principles of the venerable synagogue "were 100 percent Orthodox," many of "its members were far from Orthodoxy," one confidant warned Rabbi Goldstein that "it is very essential that Shearith Israel should get the right kind of rabbi, for if the wrong man, with wrong principles comes in there and does harm to Judaism, Herbert will be morally responsible." Rabbi Goldstein was deeply troubled by

---

*This figure did not account for inflation nor for the outside positions of prominence and leadership that Mendes had assumed but that seemed unlikely, at that point, to be assumed, in full, by anyone, all at once—and least of all by a person just over thirty.

139

this prospect, and later spoke in public about the "irreparable harm" that "would come to Judaism" under this scenario. With most observers' failure to suspect Goldstein's early misgivings, however, the prevailing assumption appears to have been that the "right" kind of a rabbi was on his way. The *Hebrew Standard* editorialized not that the call was a feather in *Goldstein's* personal top hat or even merely that it was a wise decision for the well-being of the historic congregation that had issued the call, but that it actually was a strong indication of a strengthening "revival of Judaism."

> [A]s if to give point to the ever-new strength and vitality of traditional Judaism in this land today, one or two recent events of religious moment in the community may be adverted to briefly.
>
> The first of these is Rabbi Herbert S. Goldstein's election to the pulpit of Shearith Israel...that looks back on great traditions of its own....But...it needs a man of Rabbi Goldstein's spiritual forcefulness and vitalized touch with modern Jewish life in its very aspect as its leader and guide....He...knows what is necessary to vitalize our glorious faith in its undying traditions...[H]e is just the virile leader whom Shearith Israel needs in its present hour, for, from this venerable but militantly Jewish pulpit Rabbi Goldstein will dispel a new Jewish ambition over our community.

Not only was Goldstein destined to shock, and to go against the personal advice of, almost everybody he had consulted in the American Jewish community outside of Harlem, but in so doing he was even going against the generally well-heeded counsel of his powerful parents-in-law, who:

> said it seems to be the unanimous feeling of the general public that [he] ought to accept and it doesn't seem fair to [the Shearith Israel Congregation at] 70th Street to turn them down now, after it has been in all the papers.

In this particular instance, however, Rabbi Goldstein did not feel obligated to submit to transitory considerations of timing and protocol. Ironically, although his wife had grown up in luxury and had originally been reluctant to leave the Kehilath Jeshurun (the Goldsteins' established congregation in New York City's glamorous posh "silk-stocking district"), to start the I.S. from scratch in the "Hellhole of Harlem" (not her language, of course), it was Mrs. Goldstein who expressed more reluctance than the rabbi to leave Harlem just as the I.S. was on the verge of coming into full bloom. Even after the Goldsteins' early discussion with Mrs. Asher who had forcefully favored *acceptance* of the enticing offer, Mrs. Goldstein wrote:

> We left. . .after 12 and my mind was still clouded by the fact that I felt Herbert's first duty was to the I.S.; that his leaving the I.S. would be regarded by the public as a sign of failure; that the men now working would lose courage, and the whole thing would go to pieces.

It took more than a day after Goldstein's actual election for its import to be digested. Even at an I.S. wedding on the day after the election, Mrs. Goldstein observed that "everybody seemed to be agreed that it is a marvelous thing for Herbert and that he shouldn't turn it down, but I'm not sure yet." Sure enough, by the *next* day, after the initial congratulatory excitement had worn off, public opinion within the I.S. began to emerge. Mrs. Goldstein unburdened her thoughts into her diary:

> Felt very much unstrung and worried as to whether Herbert ought really to accept the call. . .I couldn't even eat all day. Herbert had lunch with Captain Phillips [who, though a military captain, was the *civilian* captain—in this case, president—of the congregation] and they talked the whole matter over from all points of view.
> In the afternoon I went to the [I.S.] Sisterhood meeting and all the ladies made me feel that it was terrible for Herbert to leave the I.S. I came home heart-sore and cried. . . . Went over to the I.S. for the congregational singing class and everybody there felt terrible at the thought of Herbert's leaving. . . .

The next night, Rabbi Goldstein received the formal personal call, and the night after that, the following scene, as recorded by Mrs. Goldstein, unfolded:

> The synagogue (in its Friday Night Circle) was as crowded as it has been the last few weeks, U.B. [*Um b'shree-in* is a religious expression of humility in a situation where others would express pride.] After the lecture was over, a mob of young folks got around Hebert and me, and with tears in their eyes started to plead with Herbert that he shouldn't leave them. They said they would get up a parade with 1,000 banners and march through the streets of Harlem, protesting against Herbert's leaving. Herbert pacified them by saying he wasn't leaving just yet. Herbert and I came home quite perturbed and didn't fall asleep till near 3.

The rabbi had promised to meet with the I.S. board of

directors the following evening before arriving at a final decision. If anything, however, the meeting only served to neutralize his tentative decision. Mrs. Goldstein reported:

> Herbert and I took the matter up by ourselves and reached the conclusion that he ought to accept. He rested a while and then the men began to come. Twenty of the I.S. directors were present, and not one was in favor of Herbert's going. They just couldn't see through it. A committee then came from the Young Folks League to tell Herbert that if he would leave, their whole inspiration would be gone, and they wouldn't work any more for the I.S.... Herbert and I sat up and talked till 2 and before we retired we were quite convinced that we ought to stay where we are. There seemed to be a load off our hearts, and we went to sleep feeling easier than we have in quite a while.

The "load" on their hearts returned the next day as they received delegations arguing the opposing point of view. After Rabbi Goldstein emerged from a long meeting at which acceptance of the offer was encouraged, however, the rabbi found that I.S. "grass-root" supporters had dug themselves in around his hearth, determined to continue to appeal to him to hold his ground in Harlem. Mrs. Goldstein wrote:

> ...We came home and found the house just mobbed with young people who had come to plead with Herbert that he shouldn't leave them. Such a wonderful tribute of love and sincerity rarely comes to mortals, and I wept bitterly, both because I was deeply touched and because Herbert, [then considering maintaining ties with *both* synagogues simultaneously] was undertaking such a Herculean task, and as he himself said, "It might take a few years off my life, but it is worthwhile, for the sake of Judaism."

The idea of serving more than one congregation at a time was by no means unprecedented, and the closest precedent was close in more ways than one. At a time when not a single rabbinical seminary had been available for traditional ordinations in this country, Rabbi Bernard Drachman, one of the first American-born Orthodox rabbis (though unlike Goldstein, he had not been ordained in America) had once been in such demand that for a period of time he served both the congregation he had founded, the Zichron Ephraim (now known as the Park East Synagogue) *and* the Ohab Zedek (the first Hungarian congregation), which was right across the street from the I.S.

Still earlier—and still in the United States—Max Lilienthal

had served no fewer than *three* synagogues simultaneously,* and in Europe, the chief rabbis of the British Empire traditionally served as "circuit rabbis,"** so the idea of serving more than one synagogue at a time was not only precedented but even, in a sense, traditional!

It was clear that the only real alternative available to Goldstein that might have been acceptable to all factions of both congregations was the one whereby he would serve both simultaneously and delegate lesser responsibilities to others. Realistically, some I.S. directors, while preferring that their rabbi stay with them one hundred percent of the time, suggested, outright, "that perhaps there would be some kind of amalgamation." One confidant specifically urged the rabbi to work out an agreement committing himself to:

> preach twice a month uptown and twice a month down at 70th Street. . . .[H]e should get capable assistants in all departments at the I.S. and at 70th Street, and then there is no quesion that he can do both. . .provided he doesn't do any outside work or anything that doesn't belong to a rabbi. . . .The man who does most is the man who has the most work.

Mrs. Goldstein recognized this fully, and commented, "hard work never frightened Herbert yet!" Three days after the informal call had first been issued, she recorded her husband's summary of his early exploration of this angle:

> Herbert called up William Solomon. He answered, "Take it by all means." In response to Herbert's question as to his duty to the I.S., he said Herbert can do more for the I.S. from there than up here, because the people down there always back up their minister in whatever he does [and Rabbi Mendes certainly *had* done quite a lot!]. Furthermore, there is a large group of Levantine Jews on 116th Street whom the 70th Street people feel it their duty to take care of. They could be provided for in the I.S. with fund[s] given by Shearith Israel. . .*A New light has come into my heart* and I am just beginning to feel that Herbert is fully justified in *accepting the call*. . .as far as the I.S. is concerned. Herbert is much happier now that I am beginning to see things his way. . . .

---

*Sha'ar Hashamayim, Rodeph Sholom, and Anshei Chessed.

**Three of them, Rabbis Hyamson, Hertz, and Jakobovits, happened to have served, at some point in their careers, in pulpits in Rabbi Goldstein's one-time community on New York's Upper East Side, and all of them were his personal acquaintances. The last of the three, in fact, wrote the Foreword to this book.

Another inspiration in this direction came from an unexpected source. After the solemn Yom Kippur Day of Judgment—during which Rabbi Goldstein undoubtedly grappled with a judgment of his own—the keyed-up Goldsteins went to unwind, by Mrs. Goldstein's account, at:

> the Longacre Theatre where we had passes to see *Thank You*. It was a play dealing with a minister's life, and gave Herbert and me much food for thought. Between the acts we came to a decision. . .that Herbert should become a "lay rabbi" instead of a "pay rabbi" of the I.S. That he should accept 70th Street, get as large a salary as he can, and finance part of the activity of the I.S. at his own expense, so that he will be doing practical Judaising work; so that he may be able to change from the role of appealer to answerer of appeals. Of course he intends to make it clear to 70th Street that he will not sever his connections with the I.S. totally, because his heart and soul are there after all, but insofar as his reputation will depend upon his success at 70th Street, if he goes away he will go into it wholeheartedly.

As dramatic as this idea may have been, it was, after all, conceived in a theatre, and was not destined to be implemented in real life—although it certainly *did* come close. The day after the last formality of the three-stage "call" was completed, Rabbi Goldstein wrote to Congressman Siegel, who was in the nation's capital at the time, about the call that he himself was issuing.

> . . .I am calling the members of the Board together for Saturday night when I expect. . .to tell them that I am prepared to accept this call with this understanding, that I can never disassociate myself with the Institutional Synagogue* and that for one year I pledge myself to be very closely affiliated with it. I told the committee of the Spanish and Portuguese Synagogue these things and they said to me that they do not object. They felt that, as minister of the mother congregation of North America, it was my function, not merely to lead them, but to help any Jewish cause that needed aid, which of course is a broad attitude. . .
>
> I am about to marry off the Institutional Synagogue, the child of my spirit, but I want to act to it as a parent does after marriage, not neglecting it but watching and aiding it in every way possible.**

---

*Many people independently felt that if Goldstein would maintain some ties to the I.S., "the prestige coming from the 70th Street position will elevate the I.S. in the eyes of the world."

** On other occasions, he had elaborated, "you take care of every little need of the child while it is young and helpless; then, when it grows up. . .[y]ou give it over to other hands, but don't lose interest in it and you always keep a watchful eye over it and you are always ready to make any sacrifice for its well-being."

Furthermore, I feel that as far as a new creation is concerned, that God has sent me to create whatever I could in Harlem and that now I am receiving another call, as Abraham was called "to leave his home, his birth and his nativity to another home that I shall show you." Genesis, Chapter 12.

A little over a year ago, as I think you know, I received a call from the president of the same congregation and I turned it down because at that time we were still at 112 West 116th Street, and the new building, the promised land, was not opened yet. And all of last year I have been called to preach there for Sabbaths and I steadfastly refused to go because of what I thought that might lead to.

I could sit back in the Institutional Synagogue for the rest of my life now and after God will call me to the great beyond, I would be leaving a monument to Herbert Goldstein. But now I am gambling with my future. I am going to the Spanish and Portuguese Synagogue for five years, and God alone knows the probabilities. I will go there with the hope that God may put in me the youthful energy of four years ago and breathe into those decaying limbs [of the venerable Spanish and Portuguese Synagogue] a new spirit. And from those ancient moorings, this watch tower of the Jewish people since their landing in America [will] send a note of warning and encouragement to all our people....

I have been offering special prayers this week that what I may do will be *lishmah,* for the sake of His [God's] name.

Almost to the very day of the rabbi's final decision, however, he never stopped seeking ways, with reference to the congregation whose birth he had brought about, to have his congregational birthday cake, so to speak, and eat it too. A mere five days before his final decision was made, he decided, according to his wife:

to tell the 70th Street people that we will only accept their call if they permit us to remain living in Harlem at least till the summer, and permit Herbert to take care of the I.S. as much as he thinks necessary, and to preach at the I.S. at least once a month.

Eventually, however, he was influenced by his old mentor whom he had consulted. Rabbi Mendes wrote him an eloquent letter from London, whose essence was:

...As minister of my [former] congregation, you will have to give your whole time, your life, to it. You must in prayer weigh the relative value of the two spheres of work, your I.S. and mine, in the eyes of God, your Master....

It appears that Congressman Siegel, possibly in large measure due to the fact that he had been out of town so long and thus was in a position to get in the *last* word, had the most *influential* words to offer as well. Mrs. Goldstein's diary entry for the late date of November 26th demonstrates the influence of the Congressman in the single decision relating to the I.S. and *not* relating to religious policy that Goldstein *could* have made completely independently of any of its other leaders—whether or not to resign. Goldstein, however, had ruled out the option of an absolute resignation; the only *real* question he had left open was the feasibility of actively occupying leadership roles in two tremendously challenging congregations simultaneously. Goldstein's final decision was all the more remarkable in light of his resolve to the contrary only moments before his pivotal discussion with the congressman began, as recorded in Mrs. Goldstein's diary:

Saturday, November 26. Chatted with Herbert and felt that we ought to try to hold both the I.S. and 70th Street. . . . Herbert. . . . came back (from the children's *Mincha* [afternoon] services) to the house, with Congressman Siegel, who stayed here about two hours trying to convince Herbert that it would be impossible for him to handle both the I.S. and 70th Street. He said that Herbert wasn't fair to himself, me, or our children to even try it. He felt the I.S. was an infinitely wider field of activity. We had supper at which we were joined by Hofstadter and later Henry Blankfort came up, and we all seemed to get to feel that the I.S. was after all a broader field of activity for real Jewish work, and although it was a big sacrifice in money and position for Herbert to give up 70th Street, he would be really happy if he took it. [The sacrifice, she presumably meant; not the position.] Herbert went to his mother's to tell her of his decision and to convince her that it was right. I told Papa over the phone, and he said he couldn't advise us for it was entirely up to us. [He also undoubtedly saw that the Goldsteins' minds were irrevocably made up at last!]

Once the final decision had been made in his mind, Rabbi Goldstein lost no time in conveying it to President Phillips the very next day. Instead of stunning him with a painfully point-blank negative answer, however, he decided to attach such an obviously unacceptable condition to his answer that he would thereby enable those who had issued the call to save face by refusing to accept his proposed condition. Rabbi Goldstein thus told Phillips over the telephone:

that the only way he could accept Shearith Israel was if he could have perfect freedom with regard to the I.S. indefinitely, as long as he felt it necessary, but on the whole he felt that perhaps it was best that he shouldn't take 70th Street altogether because he wouldn't be true to his ideals if he let anything happen to the I.S....

Goldstein then gave him the courtesy of hearing the formal letter of declination he planned to send *before* he sent it, and then the rabbi sent it the following day. The *Hebrew Standard* quoted it in full. We will omit, here, the conciliatory words of praise and regret with which the rabbi padded his devastating verbal blow, and cite only his official reasoning:

> ...I...find the the work which God has privileged me to undertake through the Institutional Synagogue which I have founded, still requires careful guardianship on my part.
>
> In the interest of Judaism, I have determined, therefore, rather to sacrifice myself than an institution, and deny myself the great historic privilege of accepting the call of your congregation, which I hereby regretfully decline....

Goldstein's decision may have been a difficult one to *make*, but to many people it was even more difficult to *believe*. Many prominent individuals close to *each* of the synagogues involved, as well as newspapers, assumed, even before the formal invitation process had been completed, that Goldstein had *already* accepted, for all practical purposes.

The day of the final decision, somebody told the Goldsteins:

> that betting had been going on in his club as to Herbert's decision, the majority feeling that he would take it and follow the laws of self-preservation.

The day after the letter of declination was sent, the rank and file members of the I.S. responded with the most that they had to offer—their *own* familiar active participation in synagogue programs. According to Mrs. Goldstein's account:

> Went over to the I.S. The building was a bee-hive of activity. The Young Folks League were meeting. The lobby was filled with Directors, and there seemed to be a new spirit pervading the building. Everybody was delighted and happy that "their rabbi had decided not to leave them," and there were congratulations all around. The spirit among the young folks was especially lovely. For it was such genuine love and worship [a term used with flexibility in this period] of Herbert. They were working very hard for their Bazaar and their enthusiasm was positively an inspiration to me.

Their direct expressions of appreciation to the rabbi for deciding to stay with them were equally wholehearted. Nearly a month later, Mrs. Goldstein wrote:

> We went to the Chanukah celebration at the I.S. The place was so jammed that several hundred people had to be turned away and the police had to be called. When Herbert got up on the platform to speak, he got a wonderful ovation. Everybody yelled and cheered for several minutes.

The most tangible expression of appreciation, of course, came from the board of directors the following month, when its members:

> decided to show their appreciation. . . by raising his salary from $4,000 to $6,000 a year.*

The Goldsteins had clearly not misjudged the effect their decision would have on every level of the I.S. membership. The actual day of their final decision, Mrs. Goldstein had written:

> The great determining factor in the decision we are about to make, is the infinite faith and trust that has been placed in Herbert and the wonderful love, admiration, and almost worship of the people up here for him. We feel, that even if the people never realize what a tremendous sacrifice of money and position we have made, it will be sufficient satisfaction for us to know that we have been true to our ideals, that we had the moral strength to withstand one of the greatest temptations that has ever faced anybody. We feel confident that God, knowing our motives to be only of the best, will always lead us in the right direction, for good. . . .

Nearly half a century later, Rabbi Goldstein recalled:

> My decision to refuse to accept this invitation was printed in The *New York Times*, and I received a letter from Mr. [Felix] Warburg [the world-famous philanthropist who had been one of the three men who headed Goldstein's original list of potential donors at the very first phase of the I.S. fund raising effort, as we have seen] telling me he was very much impressed with my decision.
> Mr. Warburg also said he would show me in a practical way his appreciation ["of the fact that you were willing to give

*This was *not* in addition to the parsonage and other "perks" the rabbi would have received at the Shearith Israel Congregation.

up an easy berth for a hard one"]. When I called to see him, he wished to know whether it was true that I would not admit any un-Orthodox Jew to my synagogue. I, of course, immediately said, "Oh, no, Mr. Warburg. It is my desire to influence as many non-Orthodox Jews to come to my synagogue as possible, not only for their own sake, but for the sake of their families." This seemed to satisfy Mr. Warburg, and I received a check for $5,000.00, which, of course, I turned over to the Congregation.

The cover letter accompanying the check, on the stationery of Kuhn, Loeb, and Co., stated:

> Following my conversation of the other day, I take pleasure in sending you the enclosed check for $5000 as Mr. and Mrs. Warburg's contribution towards your center.
> I gladly make this contribution as an expression of appreciation of the unselfish work which you are doing for the community in that quarter, where it is so badly needed, and with the understanding that your center will be conducted in the open, broadminded spirit of which you have given me assurance. I also trust that your organization will join hands with the other Jewish educational institutions, called the Jewish Welfare Board, Metropolitan District. I ask this simply because I know that Judge Lehman, the present head, has full confidence in your ability and intentions, and I feel that through such affiliation, your organization will help to strengthen this chain.

Nearly half a century later, seated on the comfortable cushions of time and success, Goldstein's decision, in retrospect, appears to have been much easier than it had actually been!

> ...[O]ur families were quite thrilled [with the offer]. Whilst I was also thrilled, I had some misgivings concerning the young people who were gathered around me. They were anxious that I remain with them. As a matter of fact, I was told they had said, "If Rabbi Goldstein [would have] accepted this call, we would not [have continued to] believe in idealism."
> Needless to say, this provided me with much soul-searching, and I determined, after hearing of this kind of report, I could not disappoint young idealists. . . . I, therefore, refused this call.
> I can now say I never regretted having come to this decision and remaining with my congregation. . . .

If he never regretted the decision, he certainly had come close, as late as the very day he had sent out his letter of declination. According to his wife's diary of that fateful day:

> Went with Mama to a Board meeting [of the philanthropic sponsors] of the Daughters of Jacob at which all the ladies congratulated me on Herbert's election to Shearith Israel, and when I told them that he had declined it, they were quite stunned, but admired Herbert's courage nevertheless.
>
> Went over to the I.S. where we spent the evening. Very few of the people were as yet acquainted with Herbert's decision, but those that were, were wildly delighted. [They] said that they were congratulating both the Rabbi for his stand and themselves for having him 100 percent again.
>
> Herbert and I, however, went home quite depressed, feeling that we had pushed aside an opportunity of a lifetime.

An editorial in the *Hebrew Standard*, entitled "Self-Abnegation," commented on the decision to decline the offer:

> What anguish of mind must have possessed Rabbi Herbert S. Goldstein in the moment when he reached his decision definitely to decline the election tendered to him to the pulpit of Shearith Israel to become the successor of Rabbi H. Pereira Mendes! What worldly delights and satisfactions he thereby forewent! But what heartening proof he thereby gave us and all Israel that with him the Torah is not a spade to dig with,* and that with him the rabbinate is a noble and holy calling, entailing sacrifices from those who embrace it. Rabbi Goldstein has raised the rabbinate by his act out of the slough of materialism into which, thanks to the labors of the Reformers, it threatened to descend.
>
> There is not the slightest doubt that Rabbi Goldstein will continue to shed lustre on the Institutional Synagogue, his own creation as it were, which is doing and where he is doing the best and noblest kind of work for Judaism. But what an opportunity to rank as a communal and religious leader would have been his in the world-famous pulpit of *Shearith Israel*, the great historic fane which has so Jewishly and adequately stood for the Jewry of our city well over two and a half centuries! For a rabbi deliberately to put aside such a prize in these days, for a rabbi whole-heartedly to continue to dedicate himself to a great and valuable Jewish task, but one that is cast along modest byways, betokens a nobility of soul and an intensity of devotion to a splendid ideal which are so

---

*The *Ethics of the Fathers* (7:4) uses this expression to discourage people from studying the Bible for concrete material gain rather than as an ideal.

infrequently displayed as to provoke this comment and, we doubt not, the laudatory remarks of all who speak of current matters Jewish.

Well off, indeed, is the Institutional Synagogue which possesses such a spiritual guide. Happy is the community in whose midst dwells a rabbi with an eye single to that community's highest well-being, who is utterly regardless of self-interest, and who nobly works in and for that great faith into which he was born. To be rightly envied is that religious profession whose glory throughout the ages it has been that its leaders were men of high idealism, of ungrudging devotion to the eternal verities, of complete self-abnegation in the pursuit of their noble goal. Rabbi Herbert S. Goldstein is well entitled to a high place among such men, the generation of which has not perished even in our days.

Ironically, poetic justice in a positive sense was destined to steer *more* opportunities for national communal leadership in his direction,* despite his decision of "self-abnegation," than could have possibly come his way had he been caught in a self-imposed, all-consuming, perpetual shuttle between two synagogues!

*These opportunities are outlined in the final chapter of this book.

Chapter 17

Membership And Membership Campaigns

All the charisma in the world is of limited value, of course, in the formation of a movement without a growing nucleus of people committed to following up on the ideals that brought the movement into existence.

From a nucleus of forty to fifty boys forming the Institutional Synagogue on March 6, 1917, the movement grew not by leaps and bounds, but by well-organized spurts. The first public rally drew from 101 to 125 new members, and the second drew from 150 to more than 200. After the summer and the high holidays, individual members of the synagogue's board of directors pledged to recruit an additional 250 members by the end of the following month. A formal membership campaign was launched November 29th with a goal no less ambitious than 1,000 new members twenty years of age and over. No fewer than "100 were procured" the first night! The membership drive was to continue from Thanksgiving to Chanukah. Not only did this timing reflect Rabbi Goldstein's blend of Americanism and Judaism going hand in hand, but it also set the tone in a holiday—almost carnival—atmosphere that characterized much of his success. To most Americans, Orthodox Judaism is considered ascetic, yet Rabbi Goldstein managed to envelop traditional Judaism in a lively and dynamic atmosphere enticing enough not only to attract already religiously affiliated Jews, but to draw in completely unaffiliated Jews as well, and immediately, to harness their energies and excitement to the cause.

It would be hard to conceive of a traditional Orthodox synagogue, prior to the Institutional Synagogue—or even of an un-Orthodox one—inspiring anything resembling the goals outlined in the following article excerpted from the *Harlem Home News*, December 5th, 1917:

1,000 members before December 16th is the quota assigned to the campaign workers, who have been divided up into teams of fifteen with a captain at the head. The workers are making a house-to-house canvass in this section and are visiting 3,200 people in Harlem whose names have already been listed as dispensers of charities.

The districts have been divided into blocks. The novel part of the campaign is that both young men and women and old men and old women are doing the work. At the conclusion of the campaign, ten prizes will be given to the team securing the largest number of members and to the individual securing the largest amount of money.

The article also included a list of captains *and* workers. *Everybody* who participated was made to feel important, and everybody who participated enjoyed the experience, and felt he or she was serving a vital mission in the process. All this was so despite one observer's assessment that "[t]here were no rich people among them."* One who was certainly in a position to know recalled:

> They were all working boys and girls and at the end of a day's work, instead of going home, for their evening meal, they would go first from door to door in the thickly Jewishly populated neighborhood of Harlem and campaign for members.

A progress report that appeared a few days later in the *New York American* was captioned "700 'Go over the Top' in Institutional Synagogue Drive for 1000 members."

> ...[A] divisional army of workers...have canvassed practically every home from 100th Street to 125th Street.
>
> A large clock...has been erected on the outside of the Institutional Synagogue, where the community can tell the progress of the drive by the hand of the clock. [More specifically. "A big oilcloth sign was put up...It had numbers from 1-1,000 by tens, in a circle, and a hand was pushed every night to indicate the progress."] Thus far fifty members in one day has been the lowest recorded.

The tenacity and success of the young amateur recruiters comes across strikingly in a most unrehearsed incident reported by the *Harlem Home News* on December 9th:

*This was not literally so.

It appears that there was an attempted robbery in one of the apartments where...two volunteers appeared to explain their mission. The only one at home was an elderly lady who thought she recognized one as one of the trio who attempted to rob her flat.* She grabbed one and screamed. The young man did not know what the trouble was.

The neighbors ran to the lady's rescue. She then began to explain why she held on to one of the young men, while he looked on with astonishment. When she got through, the young man explained his mission and his object in canvassing the various flats. The lady then released the fellow, and joined as a member; five other members were obtained from the various neighbors who came to her rescue.**

The campaign workers were so resourceful that they actually managed to neutralize objections raised by people who had formed fixed objections to the movement before they had even been approached. Under the provocative sub-headline, "A Matter of Silk Stockings," a secular newspaper printed up an unusual dialogue:

> ...One man told a story of going to an East Harlem House and asking a young woman to come back to the religion of her fathers and join the revival movement.
>
> "Oh," said the woman, "Is that the Dr. Goldstein who said that the young women shouldn't wear silk stockings? I wouldn't join anything like that."
>
> When the young woman was told that Dr. Goldstein didn't exactly disapprove of the wearing of silk stockings but did disapprove of Harlem girls' displaying much more silk stocking then was necessary, she decided to think the matter over.***

Before this first full-fledged membership campaign of the I.S. had begun, there had been 650 "old members." Ultimately, "The campaign which was for 1,000 members closed with 1,170." One did

---

*One of the aims of the I.S., it may be recalled, with a touch of irony, was to root out juvenile delinquency!

**Even "one man who was out of work wanted to give his contribution."

***Actually, in this era, language was more restrained than it is today, and the statement the young woman objected to was one which in context simply was a dramatization of his commitment to weed out "vice," which in reference to young women was a commonly used substitute word in polite society for what today would openly be referred to as prostitution, which the young woman, as a candidate for membership in a synagogue, presumably opposed as well. In other words, even the objection had been based on a misunderstanding.

not have to be as close to the situation as Mrs. Goldstein had been to consider it "a wonderful success."

About a month after the official conclusion of this drive, Congressman Siegel had been able to announce that "the membership had reached over nineteen hundred." A little more than a year later, the membership passed the three thousand mark.

Formal membership drives were hardly necessary to inspire infusions of fresh blood into the rapidly expanding synagogue. One individual in particular who stood out when it came to signing up new members was a Mr. Samuel Silver. Not only did he not need gimmicks to motivate him, but he himself was credited in a synagogue newspaper headline with singlehandedly inspiring the entire board of directors. Silver, who was destined to serve the I.S. (and then the West Side Institutional Synagogue) as an officer from 1919 until the day he died, over half a century later—a distinction not even *approached* by anybody else—personally secured no fewer than "85 new members" in a single two-week period in 1919!

We continually see the stress within the I.S. on people and personal involvement rather than the more frequent communal organizational emphasis on bank notes and financial contributions. Thus, time and again, satisfaction was expressed not in terms of *money* pledged but rather in terms of how many *members* were pledged. Dollars are cold, inanimate, and limited to their face value. People, however—particularly when not just their faces but when their hearts and minds are imbued with the contagious I.S. spirit—are warm, dynamic, and potentially irrepressible both when it comes to their own activities on behalf of an organization as well as the people whose enthusiasm they in turn can ignite in a perpetual chain of human attachment to a cause. The leaders of the I.S. perceived these truisms and capitalized on this philosophy promoting personal involvement.

The "Join Week" campaign of 1917 (the year the synagogue was founded) represented a formidable act to follow, and, indeed, no full-scale emulation of that momentous event was attempted for years. A dramatic event would have been needed to spark the type of enthusiasm required to recreate the unique atmosphere of 1917, when the entire future of the organization was still ahead of the newly mobilized young canvassers. An event of sufficient magnitude took place in 1924, when the long-heralded gymnasium and swimming pool were finally completed in the synagogue building, representing the final elements of the physical construction of the synagogue.

At this point, the I.S. was ready to appeal to those who lacked even the minimum amount of vision or patience which thousands of previously unaffiliated young Jews had already demonstrated, in working for the Synagogue "on faith" that its athletic facilities would eventually meet their original expectations. By this time, of course, the priorities of many of the I.S. pioneers had shifted slightly due to their maturity and exposure to the synagogue which considered athletics significant, but not quite the most important end in itself. Such priority shifts, however, were gradual, and, of course, yet to begin in the new "generation" then being wooed.

On the evening of November 13, 1924, a meeting was held "of 75 Institutional Synagogue folks at the house [of the Goldsteins] to launch a membership campaign for the Institutional Synagogue and start a JOIN WEEK drive. Teams were formed [of five people each] and the meeting was a success." It would be unrealistic to suggest that the eager teams were motivated by the synagogue newspaper headline launching the drive with the words "We Want You" or even by "their fighting slogan—'Rabbi Goldstein Wants to See You.'" One can imagine, however, the thrill that must have pulsated through their muscular young limbs when they read in the synagogue newspaper after seven athletically lean years,* that "The campaign will open on Saturday Evening, November 15, at the same time that the beautiful gymnasium and swimming pool, recently completed, will be thrown open for inspection." The campaign, originally scheduled to last until December 1st, called for a commitment to carry out the following mandate:

> ...Our campaigners—250 strong—are going out this week to canvass 10,000 Jewish families of this community [representing, by an estimate in a different article in the same issue, 30,000 Jews]. They are going to [try to] make every member, of every one of these families, above the age of 12, an active participant in at least *one* of our building's activities....

As usual, the synagogue supplied the necessary gimmicks and incentives to sustain the excitement for such a broad-based army of people facing no tangible enemy. In addition to the now familiar huge "clock" set up outside the building with hands denoting the progress made, the "contestants" were informed that:

> There will be a permanent trophy with the names of the winning members of the successful campaign team....put up in the building. There will be a little silver loving cup for each one of the members of this team...There will be an individual loving cup for the campaigner who brings in the greatest number of members.

---

*Lean only in terms of facilities and equipment; not lean in terms of success.

Although "at the request of members of the various teams, because of the number of demands...being made upon them by people who desire[d] to join, it [was] decided to extend Join Week until Sunday, December 14...the opening day of the Monster Bazaar [at which time] the winning teams [were to be] announced," the festivities and the long anticipated opening of the gymnasium could not have possibly been contained or postponed.

"Red, white, and blue electric lights strung across the front of the I.S.....announced the gala event." An outline of its electrifying program follows:

> At 2 P.M. [on November 30th] a march of directors and [Hebrew School] children started from the Institutional Synagogue, went down Fifth Avenue to 110th Street, over to 7th Avenue up to 120th Street, over to Lenox down to 116th Street, and back to the Institutional Synagogue. [The marchers were] led by Hon. Isaac Siegel, Rabbi Herbert S. Goldstein, and Rabbi Isadore Goodman [Goldstein's first assistant]. The Hebrew Orphan Asylum Band provided music for the occasion, and members of the clubs paraded with banners describing the work of the building.
>
> At 2:30 P.M., a dedication programme was featured in the Auditorium [which included a] salute to the flag by the Institutional Synagogue Troop 524, B.S.A. [Boy Scouts of America]....
>
> An inspection of the gymnasium and swimming pool followed.
>
> Mr. Elias Cohen played several violin selections.
>
> At 8 P.M. in the gymnasium...there was held a dance and gymnastic exhibit.

A personal touch was added to the reporting in the weekly "Around and About" informal feature of the synagogue newspaper:

> We could not help but notice our own Rabbi as he sat back in his chair on the evening of the opening dance and we all saw with him the fulfillment of that vision of seven years ago....

To illustrate the team effort expended in the five-year reconstruction of this building, the synagogue newspaper listed the names of the contributing "patrons," although in small print, and approximately a hundred names per column. The whole newspaper normally was four pages long, but on this occasion four pages would not have been enough, since the list was laid out over eighteen columns and contained over 1,800 names. At four columns to a page, this meant that the list itself covered more than the usual length of the entire publication!

Once members were enrolled in the I.S., the synagogue had little trouble holding onto them. Unlike many major congregations, which set high membership dues as a principal source of revenue and thereby tacitly encourage exclusivity and snobbery, the I.S. advocated virtually universal membership of the people in its community. One of the foundations of Americanism is democracy. And so the message went forth that:

> ...The Institutional Synagogue of New York has no class membership. It is open to all. Any individual who enrolls in the varied activities of our institution, be they social, recreational, educational, or religious, automatically becomes a member of the synagogue and receives all the literature and announcements which it issues.*
>
> Membership dues represent a free-will offering. We have a few members who pay one dollar a year, some two and three, and others five dollars up to $175.00 per year; the average paying from $5.00 to $15.00 per year.**

One of the many remarkable features about the I.S. membership was that despite the stress on youth and egalitarianism in its ranks, many high-ranking politicians and judges were actively involved as well.

Congressman Isaac Siegel, of course, stood head and shoulders above the others in his dedication to the synagogue. It is easy and even self-serving for a politician to permit his name to be attached to the stationery of a charitable organization that is known and respected by many potential voters, or that has a large mailing list. It is easy for a politician to join an uncontroversial bandwagon. It is infinitely harder and rarer for a politician to undertake not just to push the bandwagon from its starting point before it even has wheels, but actually to *build* the wagon—and an experimental type of wagon, at that—to oil the wheels and to fuel the motor. This is exactly what the congressman undertook in agreeing to co-found the Institutional Synagogue with Rabbi Goldstein, two years after he had already become an incumbent congressman on his own.

---

*It was thus almost impossible for a person who signed up only for athletic or social activity to ignore the educational and religious activities.

**This approach was so ingrained in the Institutional Synagogue rank and file that even when the synagogue moved to the comparatively affluent West Side, although a fixed minimum was indeed eventually established, as late as the 1950's the West Side Institutional Synagogue was charging a mere $10 for membership while neighboring synagogues were already charging $100 or more.

His outside credentials on behalf of Jewish causes were almost heroic even without considering the role he played at the I.S. After World War I, it was he, according to the *Universal Jewish Encyclopedia*, who "led the fight against immigration restrictions," on behalf of Jews who wished to relocate in the United States. In 1923, he locked horns in a U.S. District Court against the Attorney General of the United States and succeeded in saving 3,200 immigrants faced with being returned to their oppressive points of departure.*

Rabbi Goldstein did not want a figurehead for a president, and Congressman Siegel was certainly *not* a person to stand on the sidelines. Not only was he a forceful president at board meetings, but he did not seem to miss a single major synagogue event. His presence was felt at all levels. He was a regular congregant at the synagogue services, and even "often used to invite the young people over to his house for *kiddush* [a blessing over wine] after services. He lived on Park Avenue and 116th street." He lived with "the people" and shared his home with "the people," without regard to their political influence—or lack of it. At one point, the congressman himself even found the time to lead a regularly meeting boys club at the synagogue.

Not only did he talk *and take action* on behalf of the synagogue, but, in addition, his wife recalled that:

> Whenever my husband would get a gift, he would transfer it to the Institutional Synagogue. He would always tell people who insisted on paying him for his many favors rendered as a congressman, to give the money, rather, to "his pet organization."

The strongest financial support the I.S. received from the personal pocket of any individual, although posthumous, came from the estate of one Fanny Henning, a cousin of Congressman Siegel. Siegel was named the executor of her estate, which originally consisted primarily of $50,000 worth of Canadian Sugar Stock, but which eventually yielded an income of $12,000-$16,000 per year. The funds were particularly vital in that they became available for use in Harlem well after the main supporters of the I.S. had moved to the West Side and focused their attention on the West Side branch.

Siegel's I.S. co-founder, the rabbi, generally succeeded in maintaining close personal ties with politicians of both major political parties in order to promote specific Jewish interests

---

*Also of interest, while on a European trip as *chairman* of a Congressional Overseas Committee in the vital World War I year of 1918, he helped to establish several headquarters of the Jewish Welfare Board in France.

without becoming a partisan on behalf of either. On the rare occasion when Rabbi Goldstein *did* step into a political clubhouse, it was in the nature of a social call. The only record in Mrs. Goldstein's diary of such a visit occurred on Election Day of 1918, when, after casting her ballot, she:

> ...went with [her husband] over to the Republican Club where we stayed till 12:15 chatting with Congressman and Mrs. Isaac Siegel and listening to the returns. Siegel was re-elected by a large majority.

A few months later, Rabbi and Mrs. Goldstein "went as the guests of Congressman Siegel to the Entertainment and Ball of the Republican Club at Palm Garden." One cannot help noticing that this politician was not accepting payment for favors but was *granting* a favor to a person whose support was assured anyway as a co-leader of an institution in which Goldstein had far more at stake than did the congressman anyway.

Both the congressman and the rabbi had powerful personalities, and both were used to having their way. Inevitably, they differed on some issues, and just as inevitably, one of these issues emerged into the open. In January of 1921, they differed in public on the issue of opening a parochial all-day school offering both full religious and secular educations. Siegel considered the idea un-American, while Goldstein argued that a better Jew would be a better American, and that an after-hours Hebrew School following a full day at public school could not possibly reach its potential in building knowledgeable and good God-fearing Jews, and, as a related result, better citizens. Goldstein felt obliged to wait until his synagogue's branch on the West Side became independent of the congressman before launching what developed into the nationally acclaimed Manhattan Day School. As a result, in large measure, of this confrontation, the relationship between Siegel and Goldstein became cooler, but it is a tribute to both of them that they were able to attain their greatest achievements on behalf of the synagogue *together*, despite their personal differences.

Although there were fewer than twelve Jewish congressmen in the United States at one point in the 1920s, three *active* members of the board of directors of the Institutional Synagogue were elected to Congress in this decade, and the terms of these congressmen covered a span of three decades—from 1915 to 1949. Their terms ran consecutively, with no overlap, and none of them ever ran against each other. The first, Isaac Siegel, was a Republican, and the next two were Democrats.

The second I.S. director to be elected to the U.S. Congress was Samuel Marx. His credentials as an authentic I.S. *active* director were unquestionable. In 1920 he played no less than a central role in a synagogue theatre party, if Mrs. Goldstein's diary is at all indicative:

> ...all the girls ["who", she wrote elsewhere in this entry, "are to sell the programme and collect funds during the appeal tonight"] came up [to the Goldstein residence] and Sam Marx gave them detailed instructions as to what to do....Then... [Mrs. Goldstein] went with Herbert in Mr. Samuel Marx's machine to the I.S. Theatre Party at the Cohan and Harris Theatre....Mr. Marx made the appeal....We sold all our tickets and some standing room and the whole evening was a tremendous success....

In 1921, Marx actually "pleaded the cause of the I.S. from the pulpit," presumably in conjunction with a direct appeal for funds, on the holiest night on the Jewish calendar, *"Kol Nidre* Night" on *Yom Kippur,* the solemn day of Atonement.*

Only about two months before he was elected to Congress— and four months before his heartbreaking death as a congress-man-elect:

> [T]he I.S. gave an entertainment at Hotel Lorraine, Edgemere, Long Island....An appeal was made by Rabbi Herbert S. Goldstein and the Hon. Samuel Marx [campaigning not for himself—and not even in his own Harlem District— but for the I.S. in prime election campaign time] in response to which $2,000 was raised.

One hundred dollars was the maximum contribution recorded, and one of those to match this sum was Samuel Marx himself. Politicians active in the I.S., once again, apparently, were able to win with consistency even though they only bought good deeds rather than votes.**

Marx's impact on the I.S. was marked most vividly in an article written for a newspaper located as far away as Indiana. After his untimely passing, the *Indiana Jewish Chronicle* eulogized him as a national figure by stating, in part, "That the Institutional Synagogue has become the most successful synagogue in the United States is due to a great extent to Mr. Marx's untiring efforts."

---

*This appeal is generally considered the most important of the year also because it is made to the largest audience of the year.

**Strange to relate, in light of present political perceptions, Marx had been an executive member of Tammany Hall. Tammany Hall, however, long after Tweed had been replaced by men unscarred by his image, was coming under the reformist influence, in this period, of Governor Alfred E. Smith.

One morbid but telling way to dispel doubt as to a person's primary synagogue allegiance—especially in the case of politicians who, as a class, try to make whatever group they are with at a given moment feel it rates their principal loyalty—is to see in which house of prayer the person's funeral takes place. For Marx, as for most mortals, there was only one. Fifteen thousand people, according to the *New York American*, came to no other synagogue than the I.S. to pay him their last respects:

> ...Hours before the funeral, every seat...was filled....The overflow surged for blocks....

According to the *New York Times:*

> ...the twenty-five policemen outside soon found it impossible to handle the overflow crowd of thousands and reserves were called. Rabbi Herbert S. Goldstein of the Institutional Synagogue gave the eulogy.

Shortly after the funeral, another member of the I.S. board of directors, Sol Bloom, who had preceded his career in finance as a theatrical producer at the presumptuous age of seventeen, asked Rabbi Goldstein to introduce him to a certain influential politician who would have a strong say in designating Marx's successor. Bloom was interested in the position.

Bloom's association with Rabbi Goldstein went back to the day when Goldstein was a young boy attending Congregation Kehilath Jeshurun with his father. When Sol Bloom moved into the neighborhood and began to look for a synagogue in which to pray, he went to what was widely considered the most prestigious synagogue in the city, the "Reform" Temple Emmanuel, but he found himself uncomfortable with its style of worship. Then he went to what was widely considered the most prestigious *Orthodox* synagogue in the neighborhood, Congregation Kehilath Jeshurun, and asked the sexton to introduce him to somebody who knew Hebrew and English and could, at intervals, show him the place where the congregation was up to, in the Hebrew language prayer book, so he could follow the services. The sexton fortuitously seated Bloom next to young Herbert Goldstein. Young Goldstein already was known as "the *misher*"—the page turner—for both his father and for the man seated next to him, a Mr. Gouled. Mr. Bloom simply became another "customer." This innocent relationship was not to be forgotten. Years later, Congressman Bloom recalled, in a published congratulatory message:

> I remember as though it were yesterday, a little boy who used to sit next to me in Schule [synagogue] long before you

were a Rabbi, and who used to help me find my place in the Good Book.

In fact, "Congressman Bloom always called him his *misher.*"

When the still unanointed Mr. Bloom asked Goldstein for the introduction to the political leader, it was unhesitatingly granted. Just how much weight Goldstein's introduction carried in the political decision that was made this December day in 1922 undoubtedly will never be known, but the record does indeed show that Sol Bloom assumed the seat of Samuel Marx in Congress. The rabbi and the politician remained on a first name basis, and just how useful this relationship became when Bloom was the chairman of the Congressional Committee on Foreign Affairs during World War II and Goldstein sought his aid in saving leading religious scholars from the holocaust, will be discussed later.

Admittedly, Congressman Bloom was not as involved in day-to-day I.S. matters as the other two congressmen before him, but he *did* stand out enough to be mistakenly referred to in an official I.S. publication as a founding director, and, in fact, he *was* one of the first among those to come forth with tangible support to the I.S. way back in 1917. By May 24th (within a few weeks of its founding), only three individuals had made greater cash contributions than had he and others who had likewise donated $100.00. Furthermore, he eventually *did* become a director of the I.S., and, in fact, was the synagogue's official anniversary dinner guest of honor in 1930, the synagogue's "bar mitzvah year."

Although many other politicians stepped into the I.S. for one reason or another over the years, virtually the only one who, after becoming an elected political official, had even a comparable degree of participation in relatively mundane matters was Alderman Samuel "Dick" Morris, who, for example, "helped in getting reductions when payments were made against the mortgage," and who was the chairman of the Publicity Committee for the ceremony of the laying of the cornerstone of the I.S. building. Perhaps his most significant contribution to the synagogue, however, was the encouragement he gave to his wife and daughter to work on behalf of the synagogue. Annie, his wife, one of the early Sisterhood presidents, was followed by Mrs. Harry (Lena) Ward, their daughter, as a super-active Sisterhood president. Her husband, in turn, became the president of the Men's Club, and their only child, named after the Alderman, became one of the liveliest leaders the Junior Congregation of the West Side Institutional Synagogue ever had.*

---

*On a memorable occasion in the 1950's, J.C. leader Sammy Ward coaxed the writer of this work, to the amusement of all present but himself, to lead part of those services at the shy and tender age of six years old.

163

Numerous judges, at one time or another,* played active roles at the I.S. in one way or another, usually as fund raisers. Some of the more prominent ones whose achievements in public affairs—and whose links with the Goldsteins' personal lives—went beyond both the courtroom and the synagogue are of particular interest:

State Supreme Court Justice Samuel H. Hofstadter was a boyhood friend of Herbert Goldstein. During the period when the rabbi-to-be had been courting his bride-to-be and life's partner, the future judge and the future rabbi had partnered themselves many times, along with Betty Fischel and other mutual friends, on the tennis court of Goldstein's then-future wife's parents in the summer resort town of Hunter, New York.**

At the meeting of the I.S. held to draft its official certificate of incorporation, Hofstadter was designated a trustee in the intermediate group of five people who were to serve "until the second annual election." By 1919, he was an officer—recording secretary.

Hofstadter felt so close to the Goldsteins that when Goldstein's own brother-in-law, Albert Wald, had been running against Hofstadter for the state senate seat that was eventually won first by Hofstadter and then by Wald, "we heard a complaint," Goldstein's politically inclined son Simeon recalled years later, "that Rabbi Goldstein's children were campaigning for Wald [their own uncle] againt Hofstadter." It was an embarrassing situation, but, Simeon Goldstein rationalized in retrospect, "I don't think that as teen-agers [when the voting age had been twenty-one] we could have had very much influence on too many voters."

Hofstadter's most historical claim to Jewish prominence was marked in his successful defense, before the United States Supreme Court, of the constitutionality of New York State's kosher laws (regarding commercial labeling and sales). Hofstadter's courtroom appearances in front of America's highest ranking panel of judges were made in his unique capacity as a special Deputy Attorney General of the State of New York for the exclusive purpose of arguing this case. He was appointed to this distinctive and pivotal

---

*Legislative and judicial positions were probably more interchangeable then than they are today when more specialization is often expected. We have, therefore, generally not sought to trace the dual legislative and judicial careers that many of these distinguished individuals pursued. We have generally singled out the titles by which these individuals were known during their years with the I.S. For the record, however, we will make an exception and note that Congressman Siegel in his later years became a magistrate of the city of New York and then a justice of the Domestic Relations Courts.

**Some years later, Rabbi Goldstein had occasion to visit Hofstadter in Mamaroneck and later recalled the baseball game he had played over there which had "ended early because Rabbi Schuchatovits [another mutual friend] was a *mohel* [performed ritual circumcisions] and was afraid of overexposing his hands"!

164

position upon the recommendation of Rabbi Goldstein, who was then the president of the Union of Orthodox Jewish Congregations of America.

Judge Max S. Levine, first a city magistrate and then judge of the General Sessions Court, was the founder, organizer and first president of the Grand Street Boys' Association, and vice-president of the *National* Democratic Club in 1926. Notwithstanding these other time-consuming interests in the public welfare,* he found the time to serve as a director of the I.S. and as an I.S. delegate to the convention of the Union of Orthodox Jewish Congregations of America in 1929. His personal warm feelings toward Rabbi Goldstein were best illustrated by the letter he saw fit to write, on the stationery of his judicial chambers, to the rabbi who, at that point, was recuperating from a health crisis widely believed to have been brought about by the rabbi's consuming devotion to his synagogue. The essence of the 167-word letter was captured in its second sentence:

> While you never felt your real condition, during your many efforts to do good for others, yet, as one of your admirers, I have had it on my mind, so permit me to remind you of my desire to have you consider that very important subject of your own well-being.

State Supreme Court Judge** Aaron Jefferson Levy was the orator who had "pleaded for the actual pledges" after delivering the official appeal for funds on behalf of the I.S. at its tremendous Tenth Anniversary Dinner. Although many judges are accused of *taking* money for somewhat less than the public good, this judge apparently made it a habit to publicly *raise* money for unquestionably charitable purposes. In this approach, he was not alone.***

---

*Our apologies for this characterization to Republicans and Independents. No specific political judgment is intended.

**Before his elevation to this position, he had been a Municipal Court judge and had served for six terms in the State Assembly where he had been a leader in the drive to impeach the one-time Governor Sulzer. Levy also served as president of the Hebrew National Orphan Home and of the Israel Home for the Aged.

***Still another colleague on the judicial branch. Judge Max Solomon (also known as Salomon) was a director of the synagogue, one of its delegates to a U.O.J.C.A. convention, and the chairman of the synagogue's annual dinner committee in 1929.
   President Justice of the Municipal Court Samson Friedlander may be judged the least active of all the judges in relation to the I.S., yet even after he moved to 94th Street—in a completely different neighborhood—where he passed away in 1926, the Institutional Synagogue in Harlem apparently was deemed to have remained the closest synagogue to his heart, and it was there that Goldstein delivered his eulogy. Friedlander had been the president of the Hebrew Convalescent Home, also of Harlem.

Glow of I.S. Aura Transcends Time and Space

The personal charisma of the synagogue's respected political and judicial figures, and the pleasant memories of fulfilling days spent at the I.S., lingered with many members long after they were destined to leave the neighborhood. The I.S. anniversary dinners regularly drew many past members, and the synagogue, which never seemed to miss an opportunity, capitalized on the nostalgic emotions it could induce. In March of 1936, an "I.S. Old Timers Organization" was organized, later re-named the "Institutional League"; however, as a practical matter, synagogue anniversary dinners and personal milestones were more effective in bringing often still youthful "old timers" together.*

Even when no organizational framework was at hand, former members still found ways to make their feelings felt. In the 1950s, on one of the Goldsteins' then-annual trips to Israel, Mrs. Goldstein wrote to her family in America:

> This morning a man by the name of Gottlieb walked in and said he had lived in Harlem 25 years ago, and his children used to spend all their time in the I.S. building on 116th Street. They have been living in Israel for a number of years, now. . . . He said he would be eternally devoted and indebted to us because of the indelible, spiritual impression his children's contact with the I.S. had on their lives.

Typical of the intangible, close, personal feelings that continued to hold past members spellbound long after they ceased to have regular contact with Goldstein's immediate sphere of influence were those evident in the reminiscence of Mr. Louis Simon, a principal early club leader and later a synagogue director:

> When Rabbi Goldstein "sat *shiva*" [observed the traditional seven-day period of mourning] for his mother [in the 1940s] there was a large crowd. When it came time to *daven Mincha* [recite the daily afternoon prayer], his custom was to put on a hat [on top of his skullcap]. He turned to me, and asked me to get him his hat. . . . This shows his attachment to the old bunch. [Actually, this conclusion is debatable. More objectively, this incident appears to demonstrate that members of "the old bunch" considered it a privilege, even in full manhood, to be recognized by the rabbi even to be asked to perform a trivial act on his behalf.]

Possibly the most tangible measure of a former member's attachment was expressed by one Ira Streusand, who wrote Rabbi

*You will be able to feast your eyes on highlights of these monumental affairs when you reach Chapter 33.

Goldstein a letter that was later published in the synagogue newspaper:

I am enclosing a check for $225.00 to cover nine years' subscription [a self-imposed highly inflated figure] to the I.S. During all this period I have been a member in spirit and I therefore feel that I ought to pay my annual contributions for the past, as I hope to in the future.

As close as any member may have come to Rabbi Goldstein, only one was ever destined to become an alter ego, and a most improbable one at that. Clarence Liberman's father had passed away shortly before the boy's bar mitzvah, which, in turn, had been "celebrated" shortly before the I.S. had come into being. If the axiom, "It is hard to be a Jew" applies today, it is not difficult to imagine how hard it must have been to be a religiously observant Jew when the six-day work week in a Sunday-Sabbath-observing Christian society made Saturday Sabbath observance an act of economic heroism, and when positive social reinforcement from Orthodox but Americanized day schools and peer groups was virtually nonexistent. On top of that, it is not difficult to imagine how hard it must have been to be a believing Jew for a boy of thirteen from whom God had just taken his father. Yet this was the single nonrelative to ever become an almost constant companion of the rabbi.

Clarence, like many other Harlem youngsters, looked up to the rabbi as soon as he met him, but, to Clarence, Rabbi Goldstein rapidly assumed a father image. The rabbi, in turn, who had two sons who were still only infants in 1917, took to the young Liberman boy who no longer had a father of his own. As Clarence recalled:

I started to attend the I.S. at 112 West 116th Street at the beginning... in 1917. I joined a club and was at the building almost every night in the social room. Rabbi Goldstein was also there almost every night, and before long he and I were the last ones out of the building and I would walk home with him....

Within a year or two, our relationship developed into a father and son relationship....

While most of Clarence's peers who were drawn to the I.S. spent much of their free time in the I.S. building, Clarence began to spend an increasing amount of *his* free time assisting Rabbi Goldstein both while the rabbi was on the run from one pastoral engagement to another as well as in the rabbi's personal household. By "about 1918 or 1919," young Clarence was at the Goldstein residence "almost every day," and continued to come at least two or three times a week until 1929.

Around the house, he would do the helpful little things that a son might be expected to do—to help to take down the window curtains for the summer season, to help with packing and unpacking, and to assist in other such chores. Rabbi Goldstein's son, Simeon, recalled that "Clarence used to put the dishes [that were used on Passover only] away after Passover, and I remember saying 'I look forward to being big enough to do it.'" Clarence also "took care of" the rabbi's two sons in the synagogue when they were very young and their father was seated in the front of the prayer hall next to the ark.

The most prominent role that brought Clarence into the public limelight was his informal position of assistant to the rabbi at weddings. The rabbi, having been uniquely in demand to officiate at countless marriages, clearly needed a reliable and efficient person to help him meet his taxing schedule.* Clarence accompanied the rabbi so frequently that people came to take it for granted that the moment the lanky Clarence would poke his head into a wedding hall, Rabbi Goldstein could not be far away. "People used to call me 'his bodyguard.'"**

It was only natural that on the traditionally fun-filled holiday of *Simchat Torah* (literally, the joy of the Bible), when comic performances are encouraged, Clarence was annually called upon to deliver the sermon, in which capacity he regularly regaled the congregation with exaggerated imitations of the rabbi whose every move he knew as virtually no other nonrelative did.

Many years after he was married, Clarence still recalled that at his own wedding, Rabbi Goldstein had "said he was a stepfather."*** This private relationship represented the very least of the rabbi's parental roles. Rabbi Goldstein's public position as a *spiritual* father to many was apparent to all.

---

*In fact, together, they came to know the interiors of many a taxi as they shuttled between wedding engagements.

**The single time his guard was down, however, was when Clarence developed an abscess on the lower part of his mouth. "Rabbi Goldstein went with me to the doctor's office. The doctor lanced it, and I fainted. After I was revived, the rabbi laughed and said, 'a fine bodyguard I've got.'"

***Clarence remembered the Goldsteins' birthdays and other happy occasions with the devotion and feeling of a relative, even after he had moved down south to Atlanta, Georgia. He fondly recalled:

After I moved to Atlanta, I would stop by their home on 78th Street to see both him [the rabbi] and Mrs. Goldstein whenever I was in the city [of New York]. It was usually two or three times a year. They were always so happy to see me as I was to see them.

In June of 1965, nearly half a century after they had first met, Clarence specifically "flew up to New York to be present at the dinner honoring his 50 years in the rabbinate." Their most touching reunion, of course, was their last:

In January, 1970, I received a phone call from my brother telling me of [the] rabbi's death. I flew up to attend the final farewell to a dear and beloved friend. I helped carry the coffin from the synagogue to the hearse, and as I closed the door in the rear of the hearse, I said, "Rabbi, *Lekh b'shalom*" [Go in peace].

Chapter 18

First The Big Name; Then The Big Building

Even a spiritual father cannot live up to his role as the head of a spiritual community "household" if he cannot provide a roof over the head of each and every member of his flock, and even the highly motivated young enthusiasts of the Institutional Synagogue could not really get their ambitious venture off the ground, along with their rabbi, without a home of their own large enough and well enough equipped to meet their rapidly growing needs.

We have seen earlier that the synagogue organization certainly *had* a home of its own. But we have also seen that its home could not match in size what it had in ambience. While the synagogue organizers were still grappling with this not entirely undesirable problem, they happened to depart from their usual procedure, for one time only, to relegate their synagogue's participation to mere co-sponsorship (with the Independent Order of the B'nai B'rith) of the synagogue's usually independent Sunday morning rally. The occasion had a triple significance to the I.S.: it marked the second anniversary of the day the United States had entered World War I—which, with the hindsight of the then recent victory of 1918, became a *happy* occasion—it also marked the second anniversary of the founding of the synagogue, and it marked a third milestone which was unveiled in the following unrehearsed manner as reported in the secular press:

Rabbi Herbert S. Goldstein was chairman...[U.S.] Senator Calder [Republican, New York] was the principal speaker. Senator Calder was waiting to be introduced when Rabbi Goldstein arose and said, "It is with great pleasure and almost unbounded joy that I—(Senator Calder was now beaming with delight, believing that the rabbi had reference to

169

him)—am privileged to announce that we have purchased a site for a new synagogue." The Senator then lost his smile.

When bought, the building on which the rabbi had set his sights was known as the Columbia Typewriter Building of 37-43 West 116th Street.* Extensive alterations of the structure were obviously required since the only similarities a typewriter has with a prayer service are a common aim to get a message across and an expectancy that the prayers that are chanted be sung on *key!*

Mr. Henry Blankfort,** a man who was so successful in the clothing business that he "learned the secret of happiness, 'Make it early, quit, and sit,'" and accordingly retired at a young age and lived to be ninety, was appointed chairman of the Building Committee, which more accurately could have been called the "Renovation Committee." The committee selected a builder with credentials that were both objectively and subjectively irresistible. G. Richard Davis and Company had already more than proved itself by building the Home of the Daughters of Jacob, the Central Jewish Institute (which was the forerunner of the I.S. in ways already discussed) and the Jewish Center, which was the only synagogue center of this era to share, in some measure, the distinction of becoming a nationally considered prototype of a synagogue center.

The renovation process was not an easy one. It was stalled, at times, by predictable problems like a temporary lack of funds as well as more unpredictable problems like striking water during the excavation!

An impressive ten-by-nine inch advertisement in the *New York Times* showed a "before" and a projected "after" illustration of the I.S., the latter under picturesque heavenly clouds, and nearly nine times wider than the former. The huge sign that was posted in front of the I.S. as the building began to be transformed must have been equally inspiring in stating that the building would even- tually contain an auditorium, a *Talmud Torah* (Hebrew School— with twenty-one classrooms), clubrooms, game rooms, a library, reading room, kindergarten, gymnasium, open air nursery, social rooms (one of which was to be equipped with a radio and a "victrola"), a kitchen, a dining room, a roof garden, chess room,

---

**For some unaccountable reason, the building was sometimes inaccurately identified as the *Visograph* Typewriter Company building and the address was inaccurately given as 45-49 West 116th Street.

**The Blankforts' son was destined to become the award-winning novelist of *The Juggler, The Widow Makers,* and *The Strong Hand,* and the Hollywood screenwriter of *Halls of Montezuma* and *Caine Mutiny* fame. Henry Blankfort's most relevant relative, for our purposes, was none other than his brother-in-law, Rabbi Goldstein, who was generally no less effective in enlisting the active support of relatives, whether by blood or not, as he was in attracting total strangers.

swimming pool, steam room, showers, bowling alleys, basketball courts, handball courts, and tennis courts. Of these projections, eighteen were built—the roof garden, tennis courts, and bowling alleys were not. In order to achieve this phenomenal metamorphosis, two entire stories were added to the already cavernous three-story "typewriter building."

The most distinctive features of the synagogue structure were the gymnasium and the swimming pool. The gymnasium measured 55 by 67 feet (17 by 21 meters). It had a balcony, fifteen showers, a steam room, and "a large airy, sanitary locker room with more than 1,000 lockers of varying sizes, each with a different combination lock." The tiled swimming pool measured 62 by 32 feet (19 by 10 meters). It had:

> a graduated slope from 3 to 8 feet [1 to 2 meters]....an intercollegiate diving board [and] a continuous flow of filtered water, renewed each day. Brilliantly lighted and heated, spotlessly clean, the water and atmosphere [were] kept at a normally required temperature for comfort and warmth.... [The pool was] equipped with every modern device for... safety, protection and health.

The facilities were "considered by experts the largest and best equipped in the city"—for a synagogue sports complex, at any rate.

Not only was the construction of the gymnasium and pool put off to the point where these facilities were the last to be built into the renovated building, but construction was delayed even further than had been estimated, originally, beyond that of virtually all other facilities in the structure since, in the words of a synagogue representative:

> Our contract does not permit the builders to work on Saturday or on Jewish holidays. The immediate result of this is that in looking back over the past month [the "high holiday" season] we find practically every week the builder has been allowed to work for two and at the most three days a week.
>
> The demand for a gymnasium and swimming pool has been steadily increasing, with the result that from time to time various changes have had to be made in the building plans so that we could comfortably accommodate our members.... [A]dded space had to be built in to accommodate additional lockers....*

---

*It was also pointed out that

[t]he actual work of excavating, because of the nearness to the city sewerage and water supply system, is a very tedious process requiring skill and caution.

The synagogue could never have successfully tested the patience of the majority of its young and restless members had it not cleverly ordered its priorities so that the religious facilities were ready *first*, the natural motivation for the athletic facilities was converted into almost a competitive fund raising "sport" *next*, and the *actual* gymnastic facilities, for which interest among the young would never wane, were ready *last*. Had the fully-equipped gymnasium and swimming pool come *first*, the long-range benefits of a synagogue and a Hebrew School would surely not have inspired typical half-assimilated young people to exert every fiber of their lithe young bodies to run activities and raise funds on behalf of facilities for the spirit. By dangling an athletic carrot, so to speak, in front of the religiously at-first-unexcited faces of the majority, the synagogue subtly induced those in the otherwise minimally motivated majority to intensify their fund-raising efforts, rather than to reduce them. With every passing day, they sensed that they were coming ever closer to their original goal, while simultaneously developing a sense of pride and affinity to the first fruits of their labors most evident in the synagogue—the prayer rooms, the club rooms, and the Hebrew School classrooms. Even without considering the sequence of emotions, the facilities for prayer, study, and socializing or social work can be operational with far less renovation of a building than that needed to install an indoor swimming pool, so the decision to construct the gymnasium and pool last was sound for practical reasons as well.

The first wedding to be held in the new building left a lasting fixture in its wake—a wedding canopy—with an unusual history.*

Finally, a finishing touch to the whole building was added a few years after its construction was completed. It came about at the initiative of a group of club members who suggested the addition of two flags, one Jewish and one American. Within the first few days of their announced intent, "a dozen clubs pledged the $5.00 minimum contribution" requested for this purpose. A special "flag drive" was successfully organized, and "the crossing of the American and Jewish flags" became "an impressive emblem," symbolizing in a tangible way the longstanding I.S. motto of "Service to God and country."

---

*The ceremony was symbolic in a variety of ways. Not only was it the occasion of the marriage of a bride and groom, but it also was an occasion to celebrate the wedding of a congregation to its new building. In addition, the father of the bride that November day was, in a semantic sense, more than a founding father of the synagogue itself. Aaron Wartels' nickname, adopted for usage by the whole synagogue family—not just his own personal one—was "Pop," and to this day a plaque hanging on a prominent wall in the West Side Institutional Synagogue is dedicated to the memory of one of the synagogue's key and most amiable early officers, "Aaron 'Pop' Wartels." At the conclusion of this historic wedding, "Pop" Wartels donated the wedding canopy to the synagogue for its permanent use.

Chapter 19

Fund Raising
Can Be Fun!

Financing the original Institutional Synagogue building had not been very challenging, considering the facts that, for the first few months of the synagogue's existence, all services had been conducted in the local Y.W.H.A., and the first synagogue building to which the Institutional Synagogue took title—the 20-by-100.11 foot building at 112 West 116th Street—had been donated.

Within two years, however, the expanding synagogue membership and the very implementation of the I.S. idea as it had been outlined by the rabbi required expanded quarters, and *this* time the financing certainly *was* a challenge. On March 31, 1919, a 100-by-100 foot plot of land whose existing building's conversion into the I.S. structure we have already discussed was purchased, for $95,000, by Rabbi Goldstein, Congressman Siegel, "and two Yeshiva boys" (rabbinical students).

In his autobiographical sketch, the rabbi recalled:

> ...I went to see Mr. Jacob H. Schiff [the nationally known philanthropist], who [had come] to congratulate me when I [had been] engaged. He knew my late wife's parents. When I told him the purpose of my visit, he said, "The Jews of New York embark on building projects, and then they say, 'How much will Schiff give?'" I answered, "Mr. Schiff! Now we need $50,000 [as a partial payment] to purchase this building. I can raise $49,000. Will you help me by donating the fiftieth thousand?" And he said "Yes." When it had all been pledged, he sent his check.

The building was renovated at an estimated cost ranging from $300,000 to $500,000. Even on the basis of the mere $300,000 estimate, it was heralded as being destined to become, upon completion, "the biggest institution of its kind in the country."*

The campaign for the new building began with a theatre party and reception at the Plymouth Theatre on West 45th Street. Presumably, this venue was selected for reasons other than the consideration that it may have conjured up images of the Pilgrims landing at Plymouth Rock to launch their quest to practice their religion freely in the New World. To get an idea of the kind of dedication exhibited by the Goldsteins as well as other key individuals in this undertaking, one can but read one evening's diary entry of Mrs. Goldstein, who had put in quite a bit of time, herself, preparing the theatre party journal for publication:

> I . . . was about to go to bed when Herbert came home with Mr. and Mrs. Silver and Mr. Metchick.** We went over the proofs of the journals, had some refreshments, and they didn't leave the house till 1:45 A.M.!

Although one newspaper claimed that "almost $50,000" was netted by this affair, the figure according to more reliable sources was considerably lower, yet for the dollar value of those days, still worthy of the *Hebrew Standard*'s headline report of a "large sum."

About sixteen people participated in a meeting of the Senior Building Committee at the Goldstein residence on May 28, 1919. At this meeting, the architect, Mr. B. Levitan, explained many of the details of the actual plans for the first time. The real fund raisers, though—the rank and file—did not have to wait for the architect to spell out his plans. . . .

On April 30, 1919, sixty people converged on the Goldstein residence to consume punch and cake, and "to discuss plans for the Institutional Synagogue Building Fund Campaign. . . . The last ones left near one [o'clock]." The following week, virtually every participant of the first meeting returned to the Goldstein residence, at which time "Captains and workers were chosen. . .[and] several speeches of advice and suggestions were given. . . ." Again "some of the people stayed till near one," and again, Mrs. Goldstein matter-of-factly recorded in her diary that "It was a very successful meeting." Mrs. Goldstein recorded three more meetings for the general campaign workers at her home, and at least three *more* meetings at the synagogue as well, not to mention the two special

---

*It may be recalled that the Central Jewish Institute, credited with a similar precedent-setting achievement on its completion a couple of years earlier, had been built from scratch for a mere $140,000.

**The latter was the only Englishman in the synagogue, a printer, and one of only about five or six men to come to synagogue on a typical Sabbath in a top hat and striped pants!

meetings held for the *captains* themselves, before the official kick-off was finally considered ready to get off the ground. At last the campaigners were put on the scent of enough crisp green dollar bills and were motivated with the necessary ideological and psychological incentives to begin. So the official green go-ahead light was flashed. The *Harlem Home News*, surely an authoritative source on the subject of Harlem-based fund drives, reported:

> One of the largest and best money drives ever staged in Harlem will be launched by the Institutional Synagogue today.
> Because of the great rivalry that exists among the teams for premier honors, the captains are devising original ideas* of their own in order to realize the most money.
> Open-air talks have been arranged at prominent street corners in Harlem. Rabbi Goldstein and Congressman Siegel, president of the congregation, will be the chief speakers.

Gradually, some of the more dramatic fund raising ideas filtered out into the press:

> A novel feature was injected into the campaign when the Maccabee Club of the Synagogue held a bucket parade through the streets of upper Manhattan on Wednesday evening. Led by a large band, the boys easily filled their buckets, thus raising their quota of $3,000.00.
> Through the permission of Harry Mount, vice-president of the Bronx Exposition Amusement Park, 177th Street and West Farms, a group of workers collected more than $200.00 in funds there on Sunday.

On June 10th, Mrs. Goldstein wrote:

> The Building Fund Campaign is on full swing. The young folks are out collecting with a vengeance and teams of them come streaming into the I.S. office which is just jammed. Great enthusiasm is rife.

As of June 13th, a Friday, the date that had been set aside for the drive's termination originally, it was still in full gear. "The entire Harlem district [was] well posted with campaign literature. Many merchants volunteered to give 10 percent of their gross receipts during one day of the drive." The figure released midway through the originally scheduled time period of the six day drive was $80,000, but on June 20th, the *Hebrew Standard* assured its

---

*Not divulged in this particular article for strategic reasons, presumably!

readers that the campaign would be continued "until the entire $300,000.00 is raised."

Special appeals earmarked exclusively for the building fund netted an average of about $10,000 in pledges on each of the four Yom Kippur holidays from 1919 through 1922. Although no synagogue member had to lift a finger to inspire these donations, one or two people did have to lift their voices in eloquent appeals. Without a doubt the overwhelming balance was achieved by the organized legwork of an overwhelming army of young "campaign workers." On a literally down to earth level, they "sold" figurative "bricks" for the building via "brick books" by all available means—in person, from bazaar booths, and through the mails. A house-to-house canvassing committee sustained interest for even a longer period than the *team* method used for membership drives.

> ...Mr. Morris Jablow, one of our new recruits,* has volunteered to organize a house-to-house canvass committee in Harlem, which will begin work...Nov. 22nd.... Mr. Jablow...is in the building nearly every evening.

This campaign was launched at a dinner in the Republic, on Lenox Avenue, "dutch treat," yet "everybody who was invited came." Interest was sustained for so long that on January 10th, sixty-five "young folks" were still involved enough to come to the Goldstein residence for a light dinner and "a lovely musical programme and a number of speeches concerning the work of the Institutional Synagogue and the House-to-House Canvass."

In the context of the initiative of the I.S. corps of fund raisers, the cornerstone laying ceremony of the renovated building presented a most concrete opportunity for financial advantage on the part of the synagogue. Naturally—for the Institutional Synagogue, that is—the festivities were preceded by a parade along the same "patented" route outlined in a previous chapter, headed by the rabbi's colorful young alter ego, Clarence Liberman, on a white horse, followed by "the officers of the Institutional Synagogue, followed by the Hawthorne Protectory Band, then by about 300 of the [Hebrew School] children." At the door to the synagogue, buttons were sold with a picture of the synagogue on them.

The program began at 2:30 with an estimated 3,000 people in attendance. Mr. Sol Lamport—brother of the donor of the main auditorium of the main center of Yeshiva University—not only was presented with the golden trowel in recognition of the fact that his $1,000 donation was the largest announced at the affair, but in

---

*He was destined to serve the I.S. as executive director on the West Side of the City many years later.

addition, after the ceremony, he was given the opportunity to read a paper on the place of the Institutional Synagogue in Jewry. Subsequent trowels were literally auctioned off. Messrs. Blankfort (chairman of the Building Committee), Fischel, and Aaron Wartels each paid $500 for their trowels. Mrs. Isaac Siegel paid $333.33 for hers.

> ...[A] great many [went] at $100.00, $50.00 and $25.00. Altogether this brought about $10,000. Then people began to inscribe their names in the Book of Life and this also brought a lot of money.*

The Dollar Drive of 1921 presented another example of the unusually successful coordination between the businessmen and the youth of the synagogue. Although six men, including Rabbi Goldstein, constituted the formal committee, an article in the *Harlem Home News*, captioned "Institutional Synagogue 'Dollar Drive' Exceeds All Expectations," had Rabbi Goldstein attributing much of this success "to the various clubs and sub-organizations of the synagogue." Even single dollar bills, the young troopers demonstrated, could add up.

The theme of this colorful campaign was none too subtly illustrated by Mrs. Goldstein's diary account of the Purim holiday carnival, March 19, 1921:

> ...[I] began to work on my costume for the Institutional Synagogue Young Folks League Purim Masquerade at Chalif's tonight. It consisted of my college gown...on the front it bore a sign, "Dollar Drive." The whole back was covered with green crepe paper down to the bottom, and on it was a sign, "Be a Builder for a Greenback," to resemble that slogan of the Dollar Drive the Institutional Synagogue is conducting now, "Be a Builder for a Dollar." All over the gown I had dollar signs made from crepe paper. Then I had several real dollars pinned on the back and the front. My head was covered with green crepe paper and a real dollar across the front. I was awarded the first prize, and I certainly had a lot of fun out of the affair.

Perhaps Rabbi Goldstein's most successful money-making innovation was his adaptation and development of a dollar match plan idea that had sprung up on the other side of the continent. Rabbi Goldstein's successes, from the very idea of the Institutional Synagogue—and even its name, which may have been an adapta-

---

*Clearly, those in attendance felt they were a part of history at that moment, and a half a century later, the trowels that had been sold that day remain treasured as family heirlooms.

tion of the "Institutional Church"—to the rabbi's method of raising funds, were based not necessarily on pure originality, but on Goldstein's ability to examine a good idea, to improve upon it by enhancing its general appeal and marketability, and then by his ability to enthuse dynamic manpower and womanpower to sell it to masses of people whose resistance to religious affiliations was to prove, time and again, to be no match for I.S. campaigners' all-encompassing consciousness raising activities. An article entitled, "The Transcontinental Evolution of a Money Raising Idea," stated, in substantive part:

> The ice man started it. It was the president of a Los Angeles ice company, you will recall, who baited appeals for a hospital with brand new one dollar bills, and asked the recipients of his circular letter to match his donation with one of their own.* The bills, like bread on the waters, came back multiplied several times over....The iceman was...a man who had discovered a new method. [Other applications of this approach were then traced. Most of them were blatant imitations with only minor variations. The climax of the article, however, was a discussion of the idea once it reached the business capital of the country.]
>
> Then the idea came to New York. "What's the use," said New York, "of putting up all that ready money? Why not apply business methods?"
>
> So the particular New Yorker, seeking to raise $42,000.00 for a specific purpose, **wrote [quite a bit more than] a handful of checks for $10.00 cash, and sent them to as many prospects. They were honest-to-goodness checks, too, drawn on a well-known bank, each one payable to the institution concerned, and each regularly signed.*** The brief letter which enclosed the check stated the purpose of the fund, and called on the recipient to match the writer's check with his own, sending the one back with the other. If 4,199 public spirited citizens responded to the challenge, the fund would be secured.
>
> Since the checks could not be cashed, short of forgery, by anyone except the person who drew them, he alone controlling the institution's account, the risk of loss was negligible. And

*And to refrain from depositing his circular letter, unread, into the "circular file."

**The purpose was the final phase of the building drive of the I.S.

***Actually, the signing was slightly irregular. Both Clarence Liberman and Harold Kaplan recalled signing many of them, not only with permission, of course, but at the rabbi's request.

178

not a dollar in real money was put up!

Rabbi Goldstein confided that "only a rabbi could do this successfully, because if a layman would try it, people would say 'he's not giving enough' or 'I can give less.'" In an interview with the *New York Times*, Rabbi Goldstein illustrated his ability to turn seeming kinks in this scheme to his advantage:

> Sometimes. . .we have a little difficulty. For instance, a furrier on West Forty-second Street received my check in the morning mail, and through an error of his clerk deposited it in his bank. My bank notified me that the check had come through. I went instantly to the furrier and explained what he had done. He apologized, made good the check, and I added $50.00 more to our gymnasium fund. That was his contribution.

The *Times* referred to "numerous. . .letters endorsing his plan," singling out one in particular suggesting "had you entered the advertising business, you would have been even more successful than you have been as a rabbi." Percy S. Straus of Macy's, the world's largest department store, who later became its president, wrote:

> If for no other reason than for its originality, your letter enclosing your check, which I return herewith, deserves a response in kind.
> I take pleasure in enclosing my check. . . .

The ultimate compliment from the *Times* was never printed in its pages.

> Mr. Sulzberger [the publisher] of the *New York Times* was so impressed with Rabbi Goldstein's initiative and ingenuity, that he invited him to join their public relations staff, if he would give up the ministry.

> The *New York Times'* loss was American Jewry's continued gain.

Chapter 20

Unconventional Aspects Of Otherwise Conventional Fund Raisers

The authoritative work, *Jewish Community Organization in the United States*, could have used the I.S. as a model to illustrate its conclusion that

> It has been pretty well established that the process of fund raising for community needs is one of the best means of educating the community to an intelligent appreciation of its needs and problems as well as some of the factors giving rise to them.

I.S. bazaars, for example, were far from being mere business-like financial operations. Mrs. Goldstein's entry for one of the early bazaars records:

> ...The bazaar opened with the praying of *Mincha* [the afternoon service], a speech by [N.Y. State] Senator [Julius] Miller,* and then the praying of *Maariv* [the evening service] after which people came down from the balcony where they were all seated and began to buy....

In the course of the bazaar's first evening alone, that year, $743 came in. Over $300 was raised on each of the bazaar's six consecutive days, not to mention the sum raised when the remaining items were auctioned off after the bazaar itself had

---

*Miller had also spoken at the first I.S. bazaar. He was the Borough president-elect of Manhattan at the time, and later to become a New York Supreme Court judge. He also was a son-in-law of one of Rabbi Goldstein's half brothers.

ended.

The magnitude of a full-fledged I.S. bazaar can be perceived by the concept of a "volunteer rally" that the synagogue leaders felt had to be organized in 1924 simply to coordinate all the people who had already offered their services *before November 7th* for a bazaar first scheduled to begin on *December 14th*.

Like so many other I.S. activities, even a bazaar demonstrated that it could become an occasion for creativity and constructive competition:

> Perhaps one of the most novel and unique features of the bazaar this year will be the Trophy Contest. The idea involved in this contest is as follows:
>
> Each [participating] club will be allotted a night which will be designated in its name. That will mean that they will act as hosts and will be responsible for the attendance and for the program which will include some novel stunt for increasing the attendance and the proceeds from the sale of merchandise. The club which, in the opinion of the Bazaar Committee, has had the most successful evening, will be awarded the Bazaar Trophy for the year. When this trophy has been won by any individual organization three times, it will remain permanently in their possession.

Although she herself had had a comfortable upbringing, Mrs. Goldstein not only did not hold herself above participating in the I.S. bazaars, but her own dedication undoubtedly served as an inspiration on which no price tag could have been placed.*

From Sales to Sails

The annual synagogue benefit boat rides would periodically thrust added wind into the ever expanding I.S. sails. Mrs. Goldstein summed up an early excursion in May of 1920:

> Went with Herbert to the foot of 129th Street where we

---

*In preparation for the first two bazaars, she "Spent the whole [first] morning till 2 [notice her definition of "morning" for a positive cause] making [175 the first year, and] over 200 sandwiches for the bazaar [the second year], "each time assisted by at least one relative and one nonrelative. The following year, she was "in charge of the automobile division" coordinating "anyone who can spare their machine for a morning or afternoon to facilitate the collection of merchandise." Two years later, she was listed in the synagogue bulletin as *the* addressee of those answering the question "What I can do for the bazaar?" (She was the de facto chairperson.)

After the neighborhood was well into its radical change, rummage sales took the place of bazaars. Mrs. Goldstein climbed still a notch higher in her selfless dedication by reacting to a sore throat that bordered on laryngitis with the following "treatment": "With the assistance of Lillie Levine who did the phoning for me, I arranged for a sales force for the I.S. Rummage Sale for every morning."

boarded "The Seagate," the boat which the I.S. chartered for the day. The crowd was so big that many had to be left behind. I assisted in the making of sandwiches, of ice cream cones, in the selling of milk, candy etc. and enjoyed it immensely.* At 1:30 o'clock the boat landed at Newburgh and everybody got off for a while. Herbert and I took the train back to New York for Herbert had three weddings...

The following year's entry featured an added dimension—rain! But the I.S. was ready for it. Decades later, "one of the girls" recalled:"

One of our boys suggested that we insure [the venture against] the weather [more specifically, against the possibility of rain.] As long as a given amount of rain would fall by a certain hour of the day, the insured could collect for that particular boat ride day. Though an additional expense, we took his advice and God heard our previous day's prayer, for sure enough, early that Sunday morning, heavy clouds brought a downpour of enough rain to warrant collecting the sum insured for.** It was to have happened [the rain had to fall, in order for insurance to be collected] between the hours of 7 A.M. to 9 A.M. [This occurred], and, sure enough, before 9 A.M. the sun came out bright and hot enough to dry up the streets, and most of those who were in possession of their tickets turned up at the pier [contrary to the insurance company's standard calculation that an early rain would presumably discourage ticket holders even if the sun would come out later.] so [God let them *have* their cake and eat it too, and] that was a bumper year for profits.

A half a century earlier, Mrs. Goldstein had recorded this very incident in her diary:

Went with Herbert up to the Pier at 132nd Street to the boat "The Highlander" which the I.S. had taken for the day. It was raining very hard but 1,500 people came anyway and we started out two hours after schedule time. We went up to Pough-keepsie.... We then turned back and stopped for about half an

*Note that even *this* facet was enjoyed! In reading of the fond memories of "one of the girls," in a letter written over half a century later, one can sense the enjoyment of what people not immersed in this cause might consider to have been dreary "menial labor": "...and *how* we used to work below deck getting the sandwiches, candies, ice cream...ready and the selling of all those refreshments to add to our coffers!"

**"One of the boys" also recalled the idealism motivating them to prefer a financial windfall for the synagogue—and a meteorological *rain*fall for the whole countryside—rather than a good time on a boat ride on a beautiful day, by exclaiming, "We used to pray for rain"!

hour at Bear Mountain...got back to the city about 11:45 and Herbert was at the pier to meet us. He couldn't go along because he had six weddings.

From "Highland" to Dry Land

When the I.S. ran a theatre party, its problem was not so much selling its tickets—I.S. theatre parties regularly reached the S.R.O. (Standing Room Only) stage—as resisting the temptation to sell tickets to scalpers and to other "outsiders"! For some events, synagogue policy makers actually had to limit the number of tickets each club could sell. The following excerpts of a letter to Mr. Udell—the top ticket seller, who later became the first president of the West Side Institutional Synagogue—discussed this unique "problem":

I wonder if you, as well as some of our people, know what is actually going on in the theatre district in connection with the show "Broadway." Try and use all the influence you can and see if you can dig up a speculator in the whole city of New York that will sell you a pair of tickets during the next six weeks, price no object.*

...[W]hen you tied up the Broadhurst theatre management under contract for every seat in the house, and for two nights...then I say that Bernard Shaw ought to be ashamed of himself for accepting the Nobel Prize for the year.

No wonder you told me the other day that the Broadhurst management were sorry they sold the house for a theatre party, and would be happy if you would call it all off and [they could be released by agreeing to] pay you a small profit....The speculators are raising the devil.

Lester, I know that you could sell, yes, all your tickets at the I.S. prices to the speculators. But, of course, that is out of the question. It would be considered unethical on our part, and in any event, we would be in for a heap of criticism. Moreover, the fact that you made such a good buy—why should gouging

---

*He added:

Ordinarily, if someone were to tell me that speculators who invariably don't take anything but the first ten rows in the orchestra—center—are selling balcony seats at exorbitant prices, I admit I would be skeptical.

But Lester, on my word of honor as a gentleman...this is what actually took place. The other night, my brother was obliged to entertain a business friend who was very anxious to see "Broadway." All week he used every influence, ways and means, to get a pair of seats but was unsuccessful. Like a miracle, while visiting in a speculator's office, someone returned a pair of balcony seats, for which he had to make a grab...and on his way out he was offered a dollar profit....

183

head-hunting speculators get the benefit of it. Our people, I am sure, will appreciate it a great deal more.

They appreciated presentations on the celluloid screen as well. Motion pictures portraying a range of I.S. activities, from board meetings to swimming meets, were shown, at times, at I.S. theatre parties and at other I.S. events too.

Not *all* I.S. theatre parties featured ordinary full-length plays. Some were in the form of variety shows calling on talent specifically gathered together for the occasion—and *not* amateur talent, either. Thanks were extended, on one occasion, to:

> . . . those distinguished stars, Eddie Cantor, Belle Baker, "The Street Singer," also Harry Moss, who directed the show. . . the Jewish Theatrical Guild. . . .
> . . . The success of the Theatre Party can be attributed in part. . . to Lou G. Siegel [*the* Lou G. Siegel of the prominent pioneering midtown Manhattan kosher restaurant by that name], the terror of every actor on Broadway that night. . . . [I]t was the genial Lou G. Siegel who, hawk-like, pounced on stars in radio studios and other performances, and. . . made them appear at the I.S. entertainment.

Mrs. Lou G. Siegel was hostess to the entertainers backstage.

For years, the I.S. regularly printed weekly listings of its leaders in theatre party ticket sales and in sales of advertisements for the accompanying journal.* In one year, Mr. Udell alone personally took credit for the sale of 306 tickets for $1,521.50! The most commanding of individual leads, however, did not dampen but only whetted fund raising "appetites" of those who were not in the lead:

> It is not often that mature and serious-minded men of affairs show the enthusiasm and energy of youngsters at high school, but, in selling tickets for the I.S. Theatre Party, the traditional runners-up of the I.S. are vying one with the other. . . .**

Summer vacations are often "working vacations" for pulpit rabbis, but rarely for an inner city synagogue's *congregants.* One

---

*Although the journal ad sales played only a supporting role in the overall theatre party effort, they illustrated Mrs. Goldstein's involvement. One year, she came in fourth in the number of tickets sold, sixty-eight, with a value that was the third highest, $323, and she literally headed the list of ad sellers—which was dominated by women—by selling $249 worth of ads, more than the published figure representing the pooled efforts of the entire office staff, which ranked second!

**Note that even though Lester Udell was a foregone conclusion to conclude at the top, there was no letup in interest to be runner-up!

summer that the Goldsteins spent at Sea Cliff, their congregants vacationing at Far Rockaway organized a function to benefit the I.S. It was a theatre party which netted a clear profit of $2,000 at the local Columbia Theatre. Similarly, an entertainment at a Long Branch, New Jersey, hotel, in 1920, netted $3,000.

One of the most unusual ways of inspiring people to contribute to the synagogue was initiated not by any member of the I.S. staff or any officer, but by a bride on her wedding night. She was so enveloped in enthusiasm with respect to the synagogue, even at a time like that, that when she was married, in a *Brooklyn* synagogue, to one Mr. Herman Sachs, then a member of the I.S. board of directors, the former Miss E. M. Levy became the subject of two synagogue bulletin articles:

> . . . At that time most precious to man and woman, in the spirit of giving, in the knowledge that true happiness comes not merely in self-satisfaction but in helping others. . . the new Mrs. Sachs [signed] her name as such for the first time to a request invitation to the I.S. $100 dinner. We are glad to say that quite a number of those present followed suit.

The I.S.'s easiest and at the same time most lucrative fund-raising idea was implemented after the neighborhood had changed and after the center of activity of the synagogue had moved from Harlem. By this time—the 1930s—activities in the Harlem building were reduced and the huge *main* building was referred to as "the Harlem branch." The Board of Education of the City of New York rented "some" rooms for the use of a neighboring junior high school, "for at least 14 or 15 years." By the depression year of 1934, the phenomenal sum of $10,000 per year was taken in by the synagogue from this single source. Eventually, the point was reached where, long after Rabbi Goldstein had left Harlem for good, while the comparative handful of neighborhood diehards stayed on, "when *they* moved, [meaning, the high school] *we* [the people affiliated with the shell of the synagogue then remaining] had to move out."

Chapter 21

New Features In Still-Traditional Synagogue Prayer Services

They were not as glamorous as the gala anniversary dinners, not as electrifying as the mass revival meetings, and did not create the kind of a splash in the neighborhood that the sparkling new swimming pool did, but the synagogue services were the first programs to be run on a regular basis under the banner of the Institutional Synagogue—even before any I.S. program could be run under the roof of the then still to be renovated first I.S. building—and they remained the most consistent of all.

Although even before 1917 all those who wished to pray in Orthodox synagogues in Harlem could have been accommodated, the Institutional Synagogue met certain needs which many of the existing synagogues did not. On one hand, it answered the prayers of those who wished to pray at decorous services but were dissatisfied with the existing synagogues, and, on the other hand, it reached out to the subconscious yearning in "the unsynagogued" people who would not have approached any existing synagogue if the I.S. had not sought them out—and won them over.

We have already scanned the shortcomings of "provincial" synagogues *(shtieblach)* and their inward limiting thrusts. On the opposite extreme, in a sense, was the synagogue of the world famous Cantor Yossele Rosenblatt. Rosenblatt served as the cantor—when he was not on the concert tour circuit—of the prestigious Orthodox Congregation Ohab Zedek, known as "the first Hungarian synagogue," which was located right across the street from the Institutional Synagogue. The young Americanized type of Jew that Rabbi Goldstein appealed to, however, did not have the patience, the spiritual motivation, nor the musical inclination necessary to sit through the Ohab Zedek services or to pay for a cantorial opera singer's salary.*

The Institutional Synagogue services catered to the youth of America. Older people were accepted, to be sure, and their tangible assistance was indispensable, but the "boys" ran the show. The services were decorous, but not stuffy or ostentatious. Most significantly, Rabbi Goldstein popularized the ten-minute sermon. Without the aid of a microphone (prohibited for Sabbath use), he drove home his messages quickly and effectively, and did not sacrifice any eloquence or power in the process. He recognized the limited receptive parameters of the attention spans of many of the members of his young audiences, and did not attempt to expand them. As a result, his direct and to the point messages were delivered with intensity, and this, in turn, led to his audiences' return with regularity. The popularity of the Sabbath morning services was such that, at their peak, the two and one-half hour services regularly drew about one thousand people. Rabbi Goldstein commanded such respect that "In Harlem, when he stood up, no matter how many people were in the synagogue, they would all stand up."

The I.S. cantors were not opera stars.** Opera in the I.S. services in the Harlem days would not have fallen on deaf ears, but it would not have fallen on particularly appreciative ears either. The earliest I.S. cantors were naturally talented people who mastered the basic melodies of the services but were not considered full-time professional cantors. (Isadore Lauer was in the monument trade, Max Braun was in the catering business, and Rev. Samuel Taitz performed religious circumcisions.)

Even Cantor Zalmon Yavneh, who came to the synagogue in 1926 and remained with the synagogue in a professional capacity for over fifty years, after moving with most of the congregants to the West Side Institutional Synagogue, was known to remark that he was first and foremost only a *shliach tzibbur*, a humble representative of the people in prayer. Nevertheless, he was widely considered to be among the best in the profession, in his own unique way, and was recognized by his peers who elected him to the presidency of the Jewish Ministers Cantors Association of America.

Born in what is now the Soviet Union, Yavneh had been in the United States for only three or four years before he joined the Institutional Synagogue. As he tells it:

---

*To his eternal credit, Rosenblatt turned down positions in the opera that offered up to $2,000 per performance, since they invariably would have required him to violate the Jewish Sabbath.

**One congregant recalled that one year, a brother of the famous Cantor Rosenblatt, newly arrived from Europe, officiated at the I.S., yet there is no record of his ever having sung there again, and more significantly, nobody from the I.S. later contacted could even recall this performance, much less treasure it in their memories.

I first met Rabbi Goldstein when I came to visit my lawyer cousin Abe Eisenstadt in early 1926. . . . I was asked to *daven mussaf* [chant the prayers that get the most attention on a Saturday morning]. I said I would come again on *Pesach* [Passover] but I had to postpone it [and temporarily pass over the opportunity] till *Shavuot* [the next major Jewish holiday] because I had been engaged at the [Chassidic] Lubavitch *shul* [synagogue] of Rabbi Dachowitz. . . in Brownsville. . . On *Shavuot,* Rabbi Goldstein took me around warmly and said, "I'd like you to be our *chazzan.*" [Cantor. The decision was officially made later by the Board.] I had a lot of *Chassidic* melodies.*

. . . A thousand dollars a year they offered me. . . . At the end of the year, I was given a two-year contract at $2,000 a year.**

In order for the synagogue officials to develop a dynamic and decorous Hebrew-language prayer service for a congregation composed, in large measure, of young people who had never identified with a synagogue before, some form of education was needed. For this reason, it should have come as no surprise that one of the first priorities of the Institutional Synagogue, even before Rabbi Goldstein was released from his obligations to his previous synagogue, was a series of organized rehearsals of "congregational singing." Another series of such rehearsals was conducted in the warm environment of the Goldstein home in 1920, and in 1921 and 1922 at the synagogue itself.

Later, when Cantor Yavneh came, in 1926, he harmonized both socially and musically with the musically inclined members of the congregation; however, whatever formal teaching he did was not of his own choosing.

> In the Hebrew School, I went from class to class to teach congregational singing. They talked me into it. I'm not a teacher.***

*This can only be taken as a most modest remark, as if to say that these melodies were what had convinced the members of the I.S. to hire him. If anything, his newly acquired *American* melodies were more likely to have "sold" himself to them. The same way that many seemingly classic Jewish prayer tunes actually are adaptations by European cantors of local Russian or Polish melodies, so American tunes were applied by innovative I.S. "ringleaders" (*singleaders?*) to a selected few Hebrew chants, notably to the concluding chant of the service, the "*Adon Olam,* which was boisterously sung to "different American tunes every week."

**One must keep in mind the value of the dollar *then,* and the number of days per average week that the cantor actually "performs"—one. Even *that* day, of course, is an enforced day of abstention from work for observant Jews, so that the cantor's position in this period of the six-day work week was virtually the only professional position that an observant Jew who was not self-employed could take which could enable him to earn a living six days a week. A rabbi, of course, works seven.

***Whether or not he considered himself a teacher, he taught. In fact, on special occasions he even directed a Hebrew School choir.

The importance Rabbi Goldstein attached to congregational singing was demonstrated in his auspicious opening sermon at the West Side branch of the I.S.:

> ...I urge that less emphasis should be laid on the reproduction of operatic and vaudeville stunts in our religious services. Our service should be alive and wide awake through extensive congregational singing, where old and young lift up their voices in unison in public exaltation and praise of our Lord.
>
> Pedagogy employs self-activity as the best method for indelibly imprinting upon the mind the lesson to be taught. So, too, must we, if we are intent upon restoring once more our prayers as the outpouring of every soul spontaneously to his Maker, bring back to the worshiper in the pew, that emotional, soul-stirring and spiritual attunement between himself and the infinite.
>
> The leaders of every large congregation in our city should take to heart this need for a model...and ideal service which will not only appeal to the old but attract and hold the young people as well....

Even those who opted, on occasion, to walk out of the synagogue auditorium into the lobby during the services for a few minutes found that the synagogue was able to channel even *this* time to religious and Jewish cultural areas by setting up a bulletin board—originally called a "pasteboard"—to rivet the attention of those who sought diversion. The synagogue newspaper described it:

> [E]very week news items and magazines will be exhibited on a large pasteboard in the lobby. During intermission periods, or if the whim of the prayer should urge him to leave the House of worship for a few minutes, loitering in the lobby is made more pleasant by the reading of the news items on this pasteboard.
>
> *"Clearinghouse" of News*
>
> The items pertain chiefly to matters of Jewish interest. They are culled from a large variety of Jewish publications and newspapers. Regularly, the reading matter is replaced; live notes, as well as sustained interest, is thereby kept up at a maximum.
>
> The Librarian is charged with the first responsibility of keeping the pasteboard in proper condition and appeal.

Gradually, new dimensions were added:

> ...Here off, to a corner, are...the...announcements of

189

the...results of the various games (basketball, baseball, swimming, etc.), with...schedules of coming games and classes. Off to a side are two spread copies of the last "Institutional" [the synagogue newspaper] replete with news of the Building and news generally Jewish.

...The...atmosphere of the Building is breathed in the simple and almost severe style of the lobby's finish. Not a lounge for the idle, but rather a workshop for the busy, is the direct suggestion and conviction of this lobby.

...Occasionally...notwithstanding constant supervision, some one enterprising club...may courageously (perhaps selfishly) slap its gaudy pasteboard indifferently over the pictorial declamations of some other rival club...at times the Bulletin Boards represent a jamboree of clashing color, youthful effervescence...

Three bar mitzvahs in one day in a synagogue in a declining neighborhood would normally be a rare, if not unprecedented occurrence. The I.S., however, hosted *five* bar mitzvahs on *one* Saturday morning, and then, as if to prove that this was not just a freak occurrence, a headline in the synagogue newspaper a mere three weeks later almost *casually* announced, "Five More Lads to Be Confirmed in One Day at I.S." The synagogue publication explained:

Boys nowadays are beginning to take an interest in the question of the place where they are to be confirmed. The Harlem boy, in answer to any inquiry on this point, will always tell you that he wants to be confirmed at the I.S. Confirmation then has an added meaning to him.*

Rabbi Not Afraid of Being "Shown Up" Upon Inviting Top Guest Preachers

As time went on, the guest preachers at the I.S., particularly

---

*The names of the bar mitzvah boys were not merely listed. The *way* they were presented is significant:

On February 11th, five bright and strongminded lads will enter upon the honors of Bar Mitzvah at the I.S. [This expression clearly refers to the religious honor of being called to the Torah and *not* to a social ceremony.] Three of them, it will be noted, live on the same block. The names of the boys are: Aaron Horowitz, 6 East 117th Street (father, Abraham); Bernard Levine, 124 West 114th Street (father, Louis); Benjamin Rabinowitz, 15 East 116th Street (father, Joseph); Morris Siedelman, 8 East 117th Street (father, Aaron); and Philip Weinstein, 10 East 117th Street (father, Morris).

The boys were most certainly encouraged to savor the occasion. One may even get the feeling that the writer of this article took the trouble to print the youths' *fathers'* first names partly because the last names, by and large, were so indistinctive.

during synagogue anniversary celebrations, and during the periods when Rabbi Goldstein did not have an assistant rabbi, comprised almost a "Who's Who" of the leading American Orthodox rabbinate of the day, as well as a "who *will* be who" of future Orthodox leaders.*

One rabbi whose very presence as a guest at the I.S. may have been more unprecedented than all of the sermons delivered by all of the I.S.'s guest preachers was the subject of the following few words in the synagogue newspaper, in 1924:

> Rabbi Abraham Isaac Kook, Chief Rabbi of Palestine [long before the dawn of the jet age], paid the Institute a surprise visit on election day last. [The visit, to be sure, was *a*political!] He was shown through the building and expressed his appreciation of the work we are doing. The Rabbi blessed the building [meaning, the people in it and their organization] and wished us success.

All of the inspiration, rhetoric, and even, possibly, the blessings, of all of the guest rabbis would have been almost useless, of course, without at least the equivalent of the synagogue's down to earth *"Bedek Habbayit"* or "House Committee," which was "composed of [volunteer] carpenters, painters, glaziers, locksmiths, electricians, and plumbers." Clearly the synagogue engendered self-participation on all levels, from the mundane to the sublime.

---

*Some of the more familiar names of a group so prominent can only be mentioned alphabetically.

Rabbis Samuel Berliant, one-time president of the Rabbinical Council of America; William Berman, a martyr at the Hebron Massacre of 1929; Bernard Drachman, one of the first American-born rabbis of prominence to receive a traditional ordination (in Europe); Moses Hyamson, a one-time acting chief rabbi of the British Empire, a successor of Joseph Mayer Asher in the pulpit of Congregation Orach Chaim, and a predecessor of Rabbi Goldstein as president of the League for Safeguarding the Fixity of the Sabbath Against Possible Encroachment by Calendar Reform; and Leo Jung, the man that the prestigious Jewish Center found acceptable to replace the by then ideologically deviating founder of the synagogue, Mordecai Kaplan. Over a half a century later, Jung recalled, "The second sermon I ever preached in New York was at the Institutional Synagogue." Joseph Lookstein, a successor of Rabbi Goldstein at the Kehilath Jeshurun, and later Chancellor of the Bar Ilan University in Israel; Henry Pereira Mendes, co-founder with Sabato Morais of the originally-basically-Orthodox Jewish Theological Seminary, president of its Advisory Board, co-founder and first president of the Union of Orthodox Jewish Congregations of America (a position Goldstein later occupied), ranking professor of homiletics at the Rabbinical Seminary of Yeshiva University (a position Rabbi Goldstein later occupied), and rabbi of the oldest congregation in the United States (a position Goldstein was later offered); and Alex S. Rosenberg, the rabbinic administrator of the Kashruth department of the UOJCA. (This unprecedented department had been organized in Goldstein's administration.)

Chapter 22

How They Packed The House Sabbath Eves

No one can overemphasize the hardships that faced Orthodox Jews who merely wished to avoid violating religious Sabbath laws in the era of the six-day week that included early Friday evenings and entire Saturdays. Orthodox Jews were effectively closed out of virtually any position in any business not owned by another Orthodox Jew. Out of sheer necessity and the instinct for survival in virtually any job that did not involve self-employment, many otherwise pious Jews inevitably succumbed.

The I.S. Sunday morning rallies constituted a first step at least to those Jews who could not get to a synagogue on a Saturday morning. However, the I.S. leaders undertook still a greater challenge, in a sense, when they sought to compete with regular Friday night activities. Since the Jewish Sabbath extends from Friday before sunset to Saturday night, and since most typical Friday night activities involve infractions of both the letter and the spirit of the Sabbath period of rest, the added significance of the synagogue-sponsored alternative Friday evening activities was clear. The synagogue programs aimed not only to provide positive experiences on their own, but, also, to prevent the religiously compromised young people of the Harlem community from violating the Sabbath on Friday nights which they would normally spend in recreation, violating certain technical laws pertaining to the day of rest. For this reason, an old-timer recalled, "It was an important night."

The Goldsteins lost no time in making the most of it, both on an individual level and on an organizational one. On an individual level, they began, in a sense, *before* day one! Specifically, the weekend before the first Jewish New Year of the I.S.'s existence, the Goldsteins had "one of the I.S. boys" at their house for the festive

Friday night Sabbath dinner that often represents the emotional and spiritual high point of the week in traditional Jewish homes. Religiously traditional but socially "modern" homes were particularly hard to come by, and Mrs. Goldstein made a point of writing in her diary: "I mean to make it a practice to have one of the I.S. boys or girls with us for supper every Friday night as far as practicable." Sure enough, over fifty-seven years later, one of them fondly recalled: "Friday nights and Saturday afternoons Mrs. Goldstein always invited young people over, sometimes for the meal Friday nights and Saturdays after the meal. About five people would be over at a time, on the average."

On an organizational level, Mr. Louis Simon, one of the top two youth leaders of the synagogue in its earliest years, recalled:

> I was appointed by Rabbi Goldstein....My job was to conduct Friday night lectures. I started them at 112 West 116th Street [The first I.S. building]. The Friday Evening Circle it was called at first....The attendance was as many as could cram into the basement floor.

This kind of enthusiasm did not materialize by itself. Another early participant recalled the selectivity that went into the programming.

> Rabbi Goldstein was careful on guest speakers. He wanted down-to-earth people.* After each lecture there was a discussion. He always invited criticism.

The last thing Rabbi Goldstein would have ever done, however, would have been to approach these Friday evening gatherings as obvious attempts simply to limit Sabbath violation. He won the hearts of the youth of Harlem by presenting them with something that he was convinced was *better* than the alternative, something *different* from their nightly recreation, something that would fill a void in their spirit as people and as Jews, something that would truly create—or re-create—(as ordinary everyday *re*creation could *never* do) the most delightful hours of the week Jews have known and cherished throughout the ages—the Sabbath *atmosphere*. It cannot be described in words, but the Sabbath *experience*—like a traditional Jewish oasis in a world of purposeless drifters—binds Jewish families together with memories of emotional equanimity powerful enough to enable them to endure the most difficult

---

*In one month in 1921, for example, the Friday night programs featured both Dr. Samson Benderly, the backbone of New York's one-time world famous Kehilla (founded 1909), and Rabbi Meyer Berlin, the world famous president of the Mizrachi movement, acting president of what was to become Yeshiva College, and the person after whom Bar Ilan University is named.

hardships facing them in their eternal fight for the right to practice their religion undisturbed. No series of memories is as vivid in the life of the typical Orthodox child as his memories of his family around the traditional Sabbath table. For generations, and, in fact, until this very day, Orthodox Jews see their co-religionists as divided into two groups—Sabbath Observers and Sabbath Violators. No other single criterion of Jewish commitment is even remotely comparable.* While many Orthodox Jews keep their distance from Sabbath violators in order not to be tempted to join them in their transitory and less ethereal pleasures, Rabbi Goldstein sought to encourage them, gradually, to appreciate the Sabbath spirit to a point where they would eventually be willing to make personal "sacrifices," of their own accord, so that they, too, could experience this mystical day in all its special splendor.

If one were to isolate the single aspect of the I.S. that evoked the fondest memories of those who participated in these formative I.S. years, the impact of this Sabbath experience would invariably be the most powerful. One of the young ladies who had been active in the I.S. during this period wrote a letter from her residence in Israel a half a century later, which typified this perspective:

> I recall that brownstone, high stoop private house where we first gathered as a youth group and held Friday evening after supper *Oneg Shabbatot* [literally, "Joy of Sabbaths"— Sabbath gatherings], where we girls would see that hot tea was readied and we each took turns to furnish the cake or cookies, which was enjoyed with the lovely *zmirot* [special Sabbath melodies which both describe and reinforce the Sabbath spirit] and some interesting lecture, sometimes given by our own Rabbi Herbert S. Goldstein. . . .

Note that these Friday evening get-togethers were obviously the first activities to come to her mind when discussing the whole subject of the I.S. in general. Of course there were many other activities, but these were unique. Nothing comparable would take place at the "Y." These cozy gatherings in the intimate original building, in fact, served as an extension of the personal home, which was particularly essential since many of the homes of these young people had lost their authentic Orthodox flavor. In this setting, everyone would take seats around a large table with "a very pretty floral centerpiece and two candlesticks with lighted candles in them." (The latter is the symbol of an authentic Jewish home on a Friday night.) The festivities featured food for thought, food for the spirit, and food for the stomach, along with the camaraderie of

*Except Kosher laws, which require much less of a commitment and of a distinctive lifestyle.

a young fun-loving family as well as a genuine father figure and mother figure in the Goldsteins' communal home away from home.

As with most Jewish homes, the I.S. grew, and a different format had to be devised for the much larger quarters into which the synagogue would soon move. The new approach, begun in 1924, took root and flowered with particularly satisfactory results:

> [At] the first Friday Evening Circle of the season at the I.S. . . . there was an informal discussion as to the nature of the programs for the season. It was decided to make each club responsible for an evening.

It was apparent that no pressure tactics were used in the process of reaching the decision. Rabbi Goldstein was not above listening to others, no matter how young and inexperienced they may have been, and incorporating their constructive suggestions into the plans for which he was to assume ultimate responsibility. The following week's synagogue newspaper summarized the outcome of this meeting and set forth

> . . . the following method of conducting Home Night: Each Senior Club is to be assigned a Friday evening during which time it would act as host. The club would supply a topic for the evening of a Jewish nature; the topic to be outlined by someone designated to lead the discussion. Following this outline, there will be a round table discussion or open forum on the topic. Then a summary will be made of the discussion which will be published weekly in *The Institutional* [the synagogue newspaper]. After the discussion will come singing of Hebrew melodies and folk songs and the serving of refreshments.
>
> Rabbi Goldstein stressed the value of these Home Nights and publicly announced the offer of a trophy to the club that presents the best constructive and interesting program during the season.

The competition gradually broadened in scope. The judges later in the month were announced to be "Mrs. Goldstein for refreshments, Cantor Lauer for singing, and Mr. Max Schuchatowitz for the program." By December, the contestants found themselves judged in still another category, with the final breakdown "as follows: 60% for discussion, 20% for refreshments, 10% for singing, and 10% for attendance." Louis Simon estimated, "when we moved [from the small, overcrowded, original building into the huge, permanent one], from three-quarters to 100% of the auditorium would be filled" for a typical Friday evening program.

The wide range of views represented in the Friday Evening Forums was vividly illustrated in a public discussion on the topic, "What Comprises Judaism," in which the speakers ran the gamut from pure nationalistic Zionism to religious Zionism to religion without Zionism. The young women asserted themselves with programs on "What the Jewish Women have Done for Palestine," and even "The Contribution of the Jewish Women to Civilization." Other topics were as complex as they were long-winded, as, for example, "Why Does the Jew Coming from Europe Being So Well Educated in Europe in the Jewish Education Drift When Coming to America and Fail to Educate His Children Properly?"* and "The Laxity of the Jew in Keeping His Faith and What the Jew Has Done to Remedy This."**

After three years of this format, the clubs were able to maintain "their own Friday Home nights for the purpose of observing Friday evening in the spirit of the Sabbath." The Friday evening programs had completed a full cycle.

---

*Some faulted economics, and some, overemphasis on Talmudic law at the expense, allegedly, of Jewish philosophy.

**In the discussion of this latter topic,

One of the speakers told of [his] travels through the West [before the days of jet flights and 'T.V. dinners'] and how he managed to keep...his faith and observe the dietary laws. The importance of the New Kashruth Law and how it helped the Jew to be sure that he is eating strictly Kosher was also brought out.

Chapter 23

Hebrew School "A Haven" Rather Than A Hell

The amazing success story that the Institutional Synagogue represents is reflected in the tremendous emotional commitment and enthusiasm it instilled in young people for matters not usually associated with juvenile excitement. It would be difficult to conceive of an institution less likely to arouse favorable enthusiasm in children than a school, not to mention a school "imprisoning" them after regular secular school hours when other children have free time. Yet while generations of children, at some point in their young lives—and, sometimes, throughout their adulthood, as well—have viewed Jewish education as "an ogre from which a child used to [and still does] run," the I.S. Hebrew School came to be known as a "haven for the children."

Not only was the I.S. able to present an attractive atmosphere in its Hebrew School, precisely as Rabbi Goldstein had visualized, but it even was able to evoke so much enthusiasm that *students*, who ranged from six to fifteen years of age, voluntarily recruited *other* students from among their public school acquaintances to join, of their own volition.

This, in an era when, in Goldstein's pastoral words, many children were first sent to a Hebrew School, if at all:*

at ten, or even twelve years of age, and then we hope for the best. What would you think of the farmer who began to plant in August instead of May? In August, weeds have grown all

---

*In 1910, for example, only about 20 percent of the Jewish children of school age in New York City were receiving *any* Jewish education.

over the field and the ground has given its best to the weeds.

Of course, with all the good will in the world, the I.S. recruitment campaigns did not take place by themselves. Enrolled students were actively encouraged to bring their friends, and duly honored "for their efforts in bringing outside children..." in an honor list published in the synagogue newspaper.

The synagogue itself also attracted neighborhood Jewish children by organizing entertainment events for their amusement and by then appealing to them, directly, at these extravaganzas, to join the Hebrew School, of their own volition, without any parental intervention. Parental *dis*approval was unlikely, especially once parents were made fully aware of the goals and methods of the school, since the I.S. movement's ideals—if not the enthusiasm of dozens of its zealous recruiters—were not perceived as fanatical and since, unlike some church leaders who guide missionaries of certain other faiths, I.S. leaders levelled their attractive forces on members of their *own* faith only.

The neighborhood was saturated every year with posters in store windows and "thousands of leaflets." At the same time, no I.S. success was achieved without painstaking preparations behind the scenes. Mrs. Goldstein accompanied one woman at a time to local public schools "to copy lists of children for the Hebrew School," on at least one occasion getting access to actual roll books at P.S. 184. Some of the I.S. letters to parents were virtually irresistible:

DO YOU WANT
  To make your child more truly yours?
  To give your child a feeling of self-respect?
  To keep faith with your parents and forebears?
  To play fair with your child?
  To build up your child's character?
  To insure the future of Jewish life in America and
    elsewhere?
  To bring up a better American citizen?
  To provide your child with rich interests?
  To surround him with worthwhile select companions and
    friends?
  To make him aware of the romance of his people?

GIVE YOUR CHILD A JEWISH EDUCATION!

The most dramatic event in the recruitment campaigns, however, was aimed not at parents but directly at the children themselves. Long after the revival rallies in neighborhood theatres had been succeeded by specific activities in the I.S. in its role as a community center, the cavernous Mt. Morris Theatre—the scene of so many glorious I.S. successes in the past—was brought out of its religious "retirement" to host I.S. Hebrew School recruitment rallies to capacity audiences of 2,000 people. Without a doubt, these children came not to be lectured to, but to be entertained, and the I.S. was always ready. At one representative such event, motion pictures were shown in no fewer than *three* different categories—a comedy was shown for pure entertainment; films of "Palestine" blended entertainment with education; and motion pictures of I.S. activities blended entertainment with a very practical and exciting recruitment vehicle. The "on location" filming for this last set of pictures was particularly ingenious, since it motivated those *already* enrolled to encourage their friends to see *them* on the screen, and, of course, this resultant free advertising enhanced the prestige of the school. It was not without an element of retrospective symbolism that the synagogue had been founded in *Hollywood* Hall!

Some of the atmosphere of these recruitment rallies was captured in the synagogue newspaper:

> "Betcha million dollars I'm in the movies" or a cheaper saying, "Betcha ten cents I'm a star in the Mt. Morris Theatre."
>
> These jocular remarks were overheard when two of our pupils invited their friends to the moving picture performance given to the children of the neighborhood.
>
> Our pupils would positively win their wagers, as the feature attraction at the Mt. Morris Theatre next Sunday will be, "We're in the I.S. Now" [a take-off on the popular patriotic song "We're in the Army Now"].

No sacrifice was too demanding for the young I.S. movie stars in their eagerness to appear on the screen.* An I.S. newspaper writer reported:

> ...Many queries [that were] directed to this column on the question of why the [young children] were jumping around so much in the showers as depicted in the moving pictures may be answered...: The steam from hot water disturbs

---

*The excitement that surrounded this film was not lost on the older generation, either. Adults were filmed, too, and they received opportunities of their own to be entertained with showings of the visual productions at I.S. theatre parties:

It was quite interesting to watch the expressions of our Directors last week, when their moving pictures were being taken for the big film. Their attempts to appear unconcerned as the camera clicked in front of them, were the subject of much witticism among their own members. At any rate, we never had a Board Meeting before as *quick* as the one that appeared on the screen.

the camera lens—it was therefore necessary for them to turn on ice-cold water....

Once the theatre lights were turned back on at the recruitment receptions, a typical program included the distribution of awards for a *Rosh Hashanah* (Jewish New Year)—*Yom Kippur* (Day of Atonement) Question Contest, an address by Congressman Siegel pleading for daily reading of Psalms, and an appeal "to the children present" by Rabbi Goldstein to enroll in the Hebrew School.

The results were often spontaneous:

> ...So well did they instill the children with the I.S. spirit that the office was crowded immediately afterwards with applicants for admittance....

After the West Side branch was established, recruitment efforts were not diluted, but, to the contrary, were intensified:

> ...The campaign will run for three entire weeks and many special events will take place during this period. Special bulletins will be issued to each pupil daily, urging them to bring all of their friends...
>
> Registration devices depicting the progress of the campaign will be posted in conspicuous places throughout the buildings [of both branches]. Weekly assemblies will be held to which prospective pupils will be invited. Every pupil that enrolls another will receive a beautiful prize.

Once the students were lured into the I.S., the bait was *not* taken off the hook. The synagogue's next challenge was to hold and consolidate its gains. Classes with the highest attendance records were not only honored and singled out for praise in the synagogue newspaper, but they were also granted "the privilege of going...to the gym and pool as a reward."

Enrollment Unlike a Rolling Stone

The school began with one class of thirty children in the original modest I.S. brownstone building; however:

> ...the Hebrew School expanded so quickly that it was necessary to divide up the small auditorium by means of dropped curtains, in order to have sufficient room to accommodate the children who expressed a desire to attend.

By 1922, the Hebrew School boasted twenty-four classes,

twelve teachers, and about 700 students. The I.S. Hebrew School enrollment peaked at 1,000 in 1926,* and in 1927 the school had the most classes in its history—thirty-six. These numerical high points are all the more remarkable since these years came just after the first in which synagogue officials openly referred to the massive Jewish "exodus" from the suddenly rapidly changing neighborhood.

An explanation for this statistical paradox can be arrived at based on the backgrounds of the students in this period. As the neighborhood underwent its most dramatic metamorphosis during these years, wealthier Jews, if they were replaced at all, were replaced by those in economic difficulties. While ordinary non-publicly funded schools had to take a more demanding stand on tuition—or close down entirely, as many did, leaving their stranded remaining pupils well within the I.S.'s gravitational drawing power—the I.S., as the neighborhood's primary Jewish community center, accepted *every*body and was extremely flexible regarding—or *dis*regarding—tuition. In 1927, the year that the West Side branch became a reality—and a necessity—Rabbi Goldstein observed that his Harlem Hebrew School had more students on full scholarships "than ever before." A few years later, statistics were released to the effect that more than 70 percent of the Hebrew School students were *not* pressed for tuition. In the middle of the depression, the I.S. boasted:

> No child has ever been refused admittance...for failure to pay an admission fee. Our motto [or *one* of them, anyway] has always been: A religious education for every child, regardless of circumstances.

In the pivotal year of 1927, the synagogue was able to point with pride to its claim that:

> No other [Hebrew School] in Harlem can boast of such a satisfactory record of growth as our [Hebrew School]. Even at the present time, with the rapid decrease in attendance at the other institutions in Harlem, our Hebrew School flourishes constantly.

The I.S. Hebrew School was unique among even nearly comparable schools in that as part of a multi-faceted institution, it could indirectly draw on a variety of sources of support.**

*This figure is arrived at when the enrollment figure claimed by the synagogue in 1925—900 students—is calculated in conjunction with the official 1926 statement that "Comparing the registration to date with the [same] date of last year...we show an increase of 102 pupils...in spite of the constant state of 'moving' which is going on in this neighborhood."

**In 1927, the I.S. ran up a Hebrew School operating deficit of $11,844.52, yet it was able to recoup this sum through other means.

Furthermore, the I.S. was able to draw on the loyalties of the wealthy Jews who had left the neighborhood by this time and were already coalescing into a nucleus for a West Side branch, one of whose primary functions, at first, was to support the activities still taking place in the main building.

Eventually, the depletion of Harlem Jewry took its inevitable toll. In 1929, the I.S. Hebrew School enrollment figure was put at "over 500," and it continued to go down with the neighborhood in *inverse* proportion to the *rise* of the West Side branch.

A Pleasant Experience
Despite The Tough Curriculum

Although Rabbi Goldstein organized the Hebrew School, set its tone and was ultimately responsible for it, it was run, over the years, by three principals, each with a definite mind and approach of his own. The first of the principals was Rabbi Isadore Goodman, who later was to occupy pulpits at points as far west as Indianapolis and as far east as England. The last principal was another Goodman, Rabbi Philip, who later gained prominence in a high administrative position in the Jewish Welfare Board. The I.S. files disclose little about Joseph Datt, who was sandwiched in between, other than the fact that he was a disciplinarian and he was considered a good man with a *small* "g," as compared to the Rabbis Goodman with a *capital* "G" as well.*

The approaches the two Goodmans took might have seemed to some to have been diametrically opposed to each other. In rosy retrospect, this appears to indicate that, if well executed, either one of their approaches can work—although *not* to the total exclusion of the alternate approach—given the *other* attributes of the school and the synagogue under which it was organized. In a word, Isadore Goodman stressed good *content,* and Philip Goodman good *aims.* Isadore Goodman stressed textually measurable achievements and Philip Goodman emphasized intangible attitudes toward religion.**

---

*He was to maintain this low profile later in life, leaving the big city in favor of a farm.

**Most strikingly, whereas the study of the Talmud is often considered to be beyond the reach of Hebrew School aged children who attend only a few hours a week after their public school secular classes, Isadore Goodman's detailed six-tier curriculum called for the study of the Talmud in the first half of the *fifth* level, after the study of the Mishna leading up to it in the second half of the fourth. Philip Goodman's curriculum, on the other hand, referred to these advanced subjects indirectly at most, and certainly did not provide for a line-by-line chapter-by-chapter textual approach to them.

One of Rabbi Isadore Goodman's most basic subjects taught from the 1A level and on, was called not just "ceremonials" but "ceremonials and memory work." Clearly, he was interested in forcing his students not to take their Jewish education lightly, but, rather, to take it seriously enough to come out with something substantial. He even went so far in his written curriculum as to openly and matter-of-factly exhort the members of his staff to assign "much homework,"

We will see later how, even during *Isadore* Goodman's administration, the Hebew School had numerous other dimensions and gave the students many outlets for their energy, with diverse opportunities for a very well-rounded Jewish and social experience. However, it cannot be denied that Rabbi Isadore Goodman concentrated his pedagogic efforts on the intellect—the brains—of his students, without disregarding other areas, while Rabbi *Philip* Goodman's primary pitch was to the *hearts* of his students, although he too did not disregard other areas. Specific texts cited in Isadore Goodman's original curriculum were often replaced by Philip Goodman's directives to "imbue the children with love and respect for the Jewish people and to keep them interested...."*
Ironically, despite the fact that Philip Goodman's curriculum de-emphasized pure memory work in favor of an emphasis on broader aims, his curriculum *itself* was "guilty" of restating its aims excessively for virtually every subject at virtually every level!

In his guidelines on the study of Jewish law, Rabbi Philip Goodman was not interested, primarily, in the specific details that his predecessor would have emphasized, but, rather, he wrote:

> The object of this course should be to impress upon the children the beauty of Jewish customs and ceremonies: to expound the moral obligations of the children to God and others.

The aim of the study of history was not, in his eyes, to create walking Jewish encyclopedias, but, rather:

---

which, he maintained, "should be given to make up for shortness of periods in class." Although at the grade level at which this particular directive was issued seven and one-half hours of attendance per week were required, by the final year no fewer than ten hours were required. Isadore Goodman likewise recommended "frequent verbs to be written so many times daily," and similarly tedious assignments.

*The priority of positive attitudes over powerful memories was illustrated implicitly by Philip Goodman's curriculum for the subject of prayers. Teachers of the youngest classes worked with the following guideline:

> The aim of this course is not "reading" but to make the children appreciate the importance of prayers and to see that they pray at home and at the synagogue.

Note the mere one word addition that appears in the curriculum that guided teachers of the *oldest* classes:

> The aim of this course is not "reading" but to make the children appreciate the importance of prayers and to see that they pray *daily* [italics not in original] at home and at the synagogue.

Philip Goodman felt that if prayers would become part of their lives, students would inevitably get something lasting out of their studies, whereas rote memorization might forever turn them *away*.

The central idea which the teacher is to impress upon the child is the attempt on the part of the Jewish people to fashion and preserve its individuality and its distinctive institutions according to the law of God at the cost of many sacrifices.

Since the morale was high under both principals, it appears that the success of the Hebrew School must be attributed, at least in substantial part, to the other factors about to be discussed which were common to the Hebrew School under *all* its administrations.

The Total Experience

As important as the official curricula may have been, the vast body of material alone would not have moved without a soul, and the people entrusted with transmitting the material were the "prime movers." At a time when many teachers in other Orthodox Hebrew Schools were elderly or alien, and could not speak English fluently, Rabbi Goldstein "wanted young dynamic teachers. He took great care in choosing his staff," preferring college-educated people who could easily relate to and gain the confidence of their American-born students. More of a prerequisite, and the *only* one mentioned in an article during the period between the two Goodmans, was:

The faculty is recruited from young men and women who are deemed sufficiently qualified to properly instruct our children in an Orthodox spirit.*

Long before the benevolent "heart-oriented" Rabbi Philip Goodman came to the I.S., Rabbi Goldstein from above had imprinted the school with his basic philosophy. A prominent person close to the scene at the time recalled, years later: "He wanted the totality. He wanted a total Jew." The influence of the Hebrew School was not restricted to the classroom or even to the all-purpose building. The pupils were encouraged to "pledge...to observe the Sabbath and to keep the dietary laws," the most prominent hallmarks, through the ages, of Jewish commitment.

*Among the more popular teachers was one Miss Gertrude Schlang, a granddaughter of Rabbi Goldstein's former Senior Rabbi, "Ramaz" Margolies, "the dean of the American Orthodox rabbinate." When Miss Schlang announced her engagement to Rabbi Joseph Lookstein, a later-day successor to Rabbi Goldstein as associate rabbi of the Kehilath Jeshurun (Lookstein later became the senior rabbi), the I.S. newspaper unabashedly echoed the sentiments of its readers by candidly observing that the Hebrew School, "especially her pupils, would have all reasons to regret her engagement if it were not for the fact that she is not leaving immediately." As sad as the members of the I.S. family were to see her leave their ranks, they certainly shared her personal joy, with a party in her honor attended by "all the staff" as well as her fiancé and, of course, Rabbi Goldstein.

Such pledges were unenforceable, of course, and often virtually impossible for young children to maintain in homes that had already debilitatingly compromised their religion. But the Hebrew School staff was flexible enough to accommodate pupils in these types of dilemmas as well. Sabbath observance, for example, may be implemented on many levels. There are innumerable "do's" and "don'ts"—and they cannot realistically be "imposed" all at once. One of Rabbi Goldstein's sons recalled one incident that his father had recounted to him up in Harlem:

> He [referring to Rabbi Goldstein] had [Hebrew School] students pledge that on Saturdays they would not do specified things—for example, touch money. A secretary at the synagogue once noticed a student's mother leaning out a window and asking her child to go and buy something from a neighborhood store. The child said, "No; I promised the rabbi." The child's mother said she would "drop a dollar out the window and you'll *have* to."

The storyteller did not recall how the incident had ended and probably never knew whether the child's response was a resourceful excuse for not having to go on an errand or whether it was truly a sincere gesture. Either way, it demonstrates the type of commitment that the school sought to engender.

The boys, who were (and are) to wear *tzitzit* (special fringed undergarments) according to Jewish law, were actively encouraged to observe this tangible sign of Jewish identity. Rabbi Goldstein used to "come down to the gymnasium" and subtly apply peer pressure in the locker room when the boys' shirts were off, so that *wearing* the garment became the "in" thing to do. "He did this diplomatically. No boy felt offended." In fact, Rabbi Philip Goodman recalled: "Frequently, he asked the children to show him their *tzitzit*. Also teachers." Goldstein had enough confidence in the commitment of his teachers to take this risk. Even today, some Jews who call themselves Orthodox dispense with this tradition, but Goldstein expected his teachers to be up to a certain standard, and would surely have considered any teacher in his school who would fall below it to be intolerably hypocritical. He showed the students that, in Judaism, *no*body is above the law, and that the students were not being asked to do anything in the realm of religion that their teachers themselves did not do.

The Hebrew School was clearly not just a part of the Institutional *Synagogue* in name or affiliation, but in practice as well. Participation in the special children's services was not just another unenforceable requirement, but an activity that was participated in with enthusiasm. Unlike their parents, who felt economically pressured by the six-day work week to forego the

Jewish Sabbath prayer services, children were uninhibited from attending the special I.S. "Children's Synagogue" every Friday night, Saturday morning, and Saturday afternoon.* These three services *each* Sabbath day continued through all three Hebrew School administrations.** Under the relatively iron thumb of Rabbi Isadore Goodman, "[a]ll pupils of reading ability" were "required to attend and did so enthusiastically." The synagogue newspaper occasionally published a list of "the classes that distinguished themselves in the high attendance," both "among the boys' classes" as well as "among the girls' classes." In addition, prizes were conferred, some years, for "the class with the highest percentage of attendance." The services were set up to give the students an opportunity to "emulate their elders," and their simulations were most realistic, with young schoolchildren occupying "all the positions in the synagogue."***

Rabbi Isadore Goodman's departure from the I.S. scene did not slow down the momentum. A 1927 synagogue newspaper article described the "dilemma" that organizers elsewhere would wistfully dream about being "forced" to confront:

> The attendance in our children's *shule* [synagogue] is unceasingly increasing. When the scheduled time arrives, we are forced to close the doors of the already overcrowded [Children's Synagogue] and many a *"Minyan"* [quorum for religious purposes] can be seen outside striving to gain admittance.
>
> The inspiring services have become part of our pupils' lives....We venture to say that even the fear of a penalty would not keep the overflow home.
>
> The following conversation...took place between Mr. A. Levine and Mr. S. H. Reiss, [the top two] supervisors of the [children's services]:
>
> Mr. Reiss: "Why is our [synagogue] like Mussolini?"
> Mr. Levine: "Because both need expansion."

---

*Comparable children's services are normally conducted in other major synagogues once a week, at most.

**Back in 1919—and possibly earlier (our source is Volume I, Number I of the synagogue newspaper, which first appeared after the I.S. was well into its second season)—the children's services already were conducted Friday evenings at sundown and Sabbath mornings at 8:30 in the gymnasium. (It may be noted that in the *first* I.S. building, the "gymnasium" was little more than a modest relatively bare room with a basketball hoop.)

***These included the positions of the "cantor, *shammash* [administrator of sundry synagogue functions], *Gabbai* [dispenser of the honors, a role often appropriated by synagogue presidents], *ba'al korai* [reader of the Torah, the Five Books of Moses, from the actual parchment scrolls], etc."

Continuing to defy the population shifts, in 1928, at a time when Jews were leaving Harlem en masse, "so anxious were the pupils to attend [the Children's Synagogue] that overcrowding resulted" leading to the creation of a "Junior Synagogue" as an "offshoot of [the] larger Children's Synagogue." The amazing paradox was not lost on the synagogue newspaper's editor, who noted "the expansion of the venture during the flux in the Jewish population of Harlem, it [the Jewish population] being constantly on the decrease."

Still another solution was found some years later: "The room used for their services is being overcrowded and some of the older children are forced to attend the adult services." This was hardly a traumatic occasion. First of all, many of the "adults," still young themselves, were similarly Americanized, and presumably only moderately more mature versions of the official "junior" congregants. Secondly, the I.S. had a longstanding practice of "interrupting" the Children's Synagogue "in order to enable the children to pray together with their parents on the High Holidays." Some of the parents were "three times a year Jews" and others worshiped at other more conventional synagogues. An ultimate goal of the I.S. was to *bridge* the generation gap rather than to create tension. Furthermore, the Children's Synagogue was geared, in the long run, to making the children feel at home in the *adult* synagogue.

Fringe Benefits

The student organization of the school had two branches, straightforwardly named "Boys of the I.S." and "Girls of the I.S." The boys had the catchier acronym—B.O.I.S.—although the girls—who never called themselves G.O.I.S.*—could not have claimed any unfavorable discrimination in this regard (or in virtually any other, for that matter). The official purpose of the organization was: "...to fill out the scholastic work with recreation and social affairs." The scholastic work itself was not considered complete without the activities provided outside the classroom.

Although almost completely absent from many Harlem households, Jewish holidays, in season, were an integral part of life at the I.S. school. For example, the annual Chanukah entertainment created the following kind of excitement, according to the synagogue newspaper:

"Isn't December 19th ever comin' [sic]?" is the popular

*"Goy" happens to be a Jewish word for non-Jew.

question. Even the great hope of receiving Chanukah *gelt* [money traditionally given by parents to children on this holiday], has been overshadowed by the extraordinary anxiety displayed by the pupils in regard to the entertainment.

Unless another miracle occurs,* the enormous multitude expected will be unable to be accommodated even in so large an auditorium as ours. . . . [H]undreds. . . actually stormed our doors at the previous festivals and were turned away disappointedly for lack of space. . . .

First Come, First Served

The sole method of obtaining admittance is coming much earlier than the stipulated 8 o'clock. . . .

The world in 1928 had barely entered the era of the "talking" moving picture; yet, already at that time, the I.S.'s Chanukah celebrations featured still more exotic programs:

One of the feature presentations of the evening was the "*Menorah* [candelabrum] of Many Stars," the "*Menorah* of Many Colors," and the "*Menorah* in Motif," a composite of three numbers presented with the aid of brilliant and beautiful electrical effects. . . thanks to. . . the electrician who liberally furnished the supplies and constructed the effects.

The students themselves hardly sat back and let professionals run their program: "Over ninety-eight [Hebrew School] pupils helped to make the evening successful." Smaller scale events at the Hebrew School were "arranged for the entire week of the holiday."

The manner in which the school sought to integrate the atmosphere of the Jewish holidays into the lives of its pupils was illustrated meaningfully in a letter to all parents, co-signed by Rabbi Goldstein and Principal Datt, and published in the synagogue newspaper the day before Passover in 1930:

It is a beautiful custom to have the children participate as much as possible. They should not be passive. They should be active to the utmost degree.

You will find that we have done our very best to equip your child with all the knowledge required for the celebration of the holiday. He can chant the *Kiddush* [holiday blessing over wine], ask "the four questions" [that are recited, traditionally, by the youngest member of every Jewish household at the *seder,* the festive service at the Passover eve dinner table].

---

*The most colorful miracle of this holiday was that a cruse of oil that could normally have fueled a candelabrum for a single day lasted eight.

read with you the "Hagadah" [the text of this festive service], and possesses a fine knowledge of the history and of all the laws and customs [a slight exaggeration!] of Passover.

We hope that you will make your child happy and yourself proud of him by giving him a fair chance to participate. We hope that you will also award him with all the usual holiday spoils that go to the child, such as nuts to play [with, as substitutes for money, which may not be touched on key parts of such holidays according to Jewish law], and a prize for succeeding to hide the *"afikomen."**

The social activities of the Hebrew School were by no means limited to commemorations of holidays. The Hebrew School ran programs which ranged in scope and frequency from annual field day outings to the publication of a newspaper. The "elaborate program of extracurricular activities provide[d] ample opportunity to the children for self-expression along Jewish lines. The activities include[d]...Jewish Arts and Crafts, Jewish content games, dramatics, [and a] choir." In fact, the school boasted that:

> No week ever passes without some noticeable event occurring....Our regular special assemblies, our movie entertainments...as well as our social and athletic clubs, all have one aim, to make [the school] attractive to our children.

Under the auspices of the Hebrew School, in this spirit, "During the summer, the pupils [used to even] attend the baseball games."

As will also be seen later, the most consistent and effective means of stirring up excitement in synagogue activities could be summed up in one word—incentives. This device was certainly put to constructive use in the Hebrew School as well. Each week, a list was compiled "of pupils who have received honor cards for proficiency, scholarship, and conduct." On occasion—apparently at random times—these lists were published in the synagogue newspaper.** More than the recognition and the glory, those who received these honor cards also received "the privilege of enjoying an hour in the gymnasium each week." Quiz contests were arranged on different holidays, but contests were also arranged for those willing and able to demonstrate persistence rather than brilliance, notably by means of competitions conducted along the lines of the "reading contest" by which the first pupil to report,

---

*This is a half a matzo that children are encouraged to "steal" and then demand a "ransom" for. The entire "game" serves, intentionally, to maintain their interest in the unique long "dinner-table service" once they are motivated to remain awake throughout most of it.

**Two representative lists in 1926 recorded fifty-eight names averaging about two to a class one week and seventy-seven names of from one to five per class another week.

satisfactorily, on five Jewish-content books selected and read by him or her individually was declared the winner.

The I.S., obviously, did not sponsor the *only* Hebrew School that promoted competitions, but it certainly was in the forefront. The role of the I.S. in the Jewish Education Association's program described below was indicative:

> [A]ll the excellent pupils of Harlem, Yorkville, and Washington Heights will receive prizes [including the sponsors'] sending a number [of the pupils]...to a camp and distributing Bibles, medals, and certificates to the pupils who have a high attendance between 95 and 100 percent, A or B in progress, and A in conduct...
>
> The festival will take place in the Wadleigh High School....The I.S. is highly represented on this occasion. The main address will be delivered by our President, Hon. Isaac Siegel, and the prizes will be distributed by one of our directors....The Chairman of the Committee of Arrangement for this occasion is our principal, Mr. J. Datt....

Within the Hebrew School itself, the Parents' Association was actively involved in sustaining a competitive spirit, contributing "medals, books, and other prizes to encourage proficiency amongst the students," "scholarship and punctuality."

Parents As Involved As Their Children

Within about a month of the first service held at the permanent I.S. building, a parents' organization of the Hebrew School was organized "by Rabbi Goldstein." His personal involvement from its very inception was not just confined to paper titles like the rabbi's formally recognized position as "honorary president of the Parents' Association." Rabbi Goldstein's inspiration was both general and specific. At the initial meeting of the 1924 season:

> Rabbi Goldstein, in a stirring talk, thanked the members for their good work in the past and urged them to renewed efforts....He pointed out the many possibilities for improvement and suggested ways and means for increasing the activities of the organization.

The Parents' Association not only distributed an edible "treat" appropriate to virtually each Jewish holiday to each student, but it also distributed nonedible spiritual sustenance like "little prayer books" on the holiday of *Lag B'Omer* and, during one "Boys' Week," "a gift in the form of beautiful cards upon which the *Modeh Ani* morning prayer was printed, in both

210

Hebrew and English."

The Association promoted weekend religious activities by assisting "the social department in securing refreshments for the Friday Evening Forums" and sponsoring "Saturday afternoon parties...supplying refreshments for the...children every Sunday afternoon." It was no idle boast that "wherever the comfort of the...children was involved the Parents' Association...was ever present to lend a helping hand."

The independent fund-raising drives that were run in order to subsidize the Association's activities were regular and significant events in the synagogue calendar. "Among the many activities sponsored" were "annual theatre parties, luncheons, strawberry festivals and socials." These events did not merely draw the young parents themselves. A Purim (holiday) carnival and dance in 1926 drew "a large crowd of men and women, both young and old." A total of fifty new parents could be added to the membership rolls in a single membership drive, and 200 members and friends could gather to attend a single "koffee klotch."

Like vibrant vegetation in an Amazon jungle, I.S. sub-organizations constantly seemed to sprout additional offshoots, and the parents' organization, both because of its name and its example, was no exception. The enthusiasm and commitment of parents and younger siblings led to the creation of the "Junior League of the Parents' Association," which was geared to and composed of the Hebrew School children's parents' "sons and daughters between the ages of nineteen and over," plus, of course, the ubiquitous "Rabbi Herbert S. Goldstein, Honorary President." The Junior League's activities more than supplemented those of the parent Parents' Association. As reported in 1927:

> They have annual June walks for the children, and even supply clothing for the needy [Hebrew School] boys and girls. The spirit of the Junior League is an inspiration to the other organizations in the building.

Graduations Get Top Grades

If the day by day grind of studies could be transformed into an exciting experience at the Institutional Synagogue Hebrew School, one can easily imagine what the *graduation exercises* must have been like. The first graduation was conducted in June of 1922. The school, at this time, honored eleven children who had completed a course equivalent to five years of Hebrew and religious education.

Gradually, the Hebrew School graduations came to show, by the multitudes they drew, just how important the Hebrew School was considered by the rank and file synagogue membership. As late as 1928, the "record-breaking crowd" was described in unprecedented terms:

> Next to the size of the attendance that is usually present at the Institutional Synagogue during the High Holy Day Services, probably no event attracts the adults of Harlem to the work of the Building in such vast multitude as does that of the [Hebrew School] Graduation. This year's graduation was a brilliant demonstration in proof of this fact.
>
> It was necessary to summon the police in order to traffic the stupendous crowd that attended the graduation.

These ceremonies, of course, were not without the oratorical input of Rabbi Goldstein:

> "Next to being Americans, I would exhort you boys and girls to being great Jews," the rabbi said to the graduates. "It does not require an overmuch stock of qualities to make a professional man. With intelligence, pluck, and industry, any one of you might become a lawyer, doctor, or even minister. But it does require heaps of real courage and intellectual independence for you to be real and sincere Jews...."
>
> The rabbi quickened the sense of the graduates to their coming life. Especially did he impress upon them that their studies are far from over. "You are the future leaders and champions of the Jewish people," he added. "Do not compromise your name. Remember that you may be termed a Hebrew, an Israelite, or a Jew—nothing more nor different...."

Probably the Institutional Synagogue Hebrew School's graduation that is of more historic significance than any of the school's others is the one that took place in December of 1933. By this time, Harlem was rapidly becoming essentially a Black community. The Institutional Synagogue, as a liberal and idealistic institution not bound by prejudice, welcomed the Jewish Blacks in the community to its activities, and so it developed that Vertella S. Valentine became not only "the first Jewish Negress ever to be graduated from an American Hebrew School," but she actually did so as valedictorian. The photograph of this event was literally shown 'round the world. It was no mere token grandstand performance, either. A second Black graduated from the same class, and more were destined to graduate from later classes.*

Rabbi Philip Goodman, then the principal of the Hebrew

---

*Vertella, incidentally, continued in the synagogue's Hebrew High School and was active in it.

School, developed such a close sense of rapport with the Black Jews of that period who had attended his school, that fully forty years later, he was able to sit back and recall many of their names, fondly, from memory. Similarly, one Hebrew School teacher was still charmed, after a comparable lapse of time, by the four Blacks who "spoke Hebrew with a Southern accent" in one of her classes.

To many people, of course, the real graduation from a Hebrew School occurs, for boys, not at the formal graduation ceremonies at the end of the school year, but at the bar mitzvah party. To counter this tendency to misuse the bar mitzvah milestone by letting it block the path that leads to religious awareness and responsibility, the I.S. offered, for "bar mitzvah boys" only, a special adjunct class. The Hebrew School did *not* limit this class's curriculum to coverage of "the necessary knowledge toward the Bar Mitzvah ceremonies. [Rather, it also trained the "bar mitzvah boys"] in the putting on of *Tephilin* [religious articles donned in a special manner for weekday morning services] and the daily prayers." The *Tephilin* are not even worn during the bar mitzvah ceremony itself (when the ritual is conducted on the Sabbath, as is the usual custom), so the singling out of these two elements of the curriculum emphasized the stress placed at the I.S. on the long-range follow-up to the bar mitzvah experience. A Jewish boy's thirteenth birthday is supposed to signal the *beginning* of a full-fledged commitment to Judaism, rather than a farewell. Put differently, I.S. bar mitzvah preparations focused on the *mitzvah*—the religious obligation—and *not* the *bar*.

More significant than the graduations and the bar mitzvah classes were the enduring means that the I.S. used with which to imbue Jewish ideals and knowledge in young men and women as they crossed the threshold into adolescence and beyond—in the Hebrew High School.

Hebrew High School Is High-Water Mark

The I.S. Hebrew High *School* grew out of what was originally known as the mere I.S. High School *Department* whose unpretentious purpose, as defined in 1922, was "to rear a number of young men and women who will not be ignorant but [who will be] learned Jews and Jewesses and Pedagogues to teach in elementary Hebrew Schools." Curiously, while still humbly defined as only a high school *department*, the school—with Rabbi Goldstein himself on its faculty—conducted classes three times a week and attempted to train potential teachers. When it was referred to as a comparatively high and mighty "Hebrew High School" in 1934, it met for formal classwork only twice a week, and apparently abandoned all pretensions of training teachers, although extracurricular activities were expanded. Instead, its goal was redefined and its program was trimmed to the point where it offered a one-year course of study "after which time the students will be prepared to enter higher institutions of Jewish learning."* The instructors succeeded in cramming quite a bit of content into these two evenings a week, however, for by 1937 the curriculum included Bible with Rashi's commentary,** prophets, liturgy, Jewish history, and Jewish current events and problems. Furthermore, although the reading of English-Judaica books, as we have seen, became cultural grist for a quantitative reading contest in the Hebrew School, in the *high* school the reading of such books—"both fiction and nonfiction"—became "an integral part of the course of study."

The level of Hebrew comprehension of the students during the middle years of the existence of the school must have been quite satisfactory. Reporting on a high school class trip to see "the world famed Hebrew [language] troupe, 'The Habimah,'" an I.S. newspaper article described "the ease with which the students understood the spoken Hebrew." The contemporary post-Biblical Hebrew language, at that time, of course, enjoyed a microscopic amount of popularity among American Jews, generally (outside of the I.S.), compared to that which it can boast of in today's era of jet travel and a vibrant state of Israel.

Extracurricular activities were not by any means limited to passive, nonparticipatory ones like attending Hebrew-language theatrical productions. The typically comprehensive headline of a weekly column in the synagogue newspaper speaks for itself—and for the individuals involved: "Current Events in the Jewish World—Edited by the Students of the I.S. Hebrew School."

Probably the most novel project that the students undertook involved a book.*** The synagogue newspaper reported:

> Finding the available Jewish History textbooks unsuitable for their purposes, the students of the I.S. Hebrew High School are now engaged in the novel project of writing their own history textbook.
>
> Regular assignments are given by Rabbi Philip Goodman, principal, to the individual members of the class. The work of the students is then submitted to the Board of Editors who

---

*Such institutions beyond the high school level had not been readily available under Orthodox auspices before Yeshiva College was established in 1928.

**Rashi was the eleventh century author of what is almost universally regarded as the all-time "most popular commentary on the Bible and the Talmud."

***As novel a project as it may have been, it nevertheless never left the realm of nonfiction, however.

rewrite and revise the material to fit in with the general scheme of the book.

    Copies of completed chapters are given to every member of the class. Illustrations make the manuscripts attractive.

The result, according to an article written the following year, "was a very excellent volume of Jewish History." The objectivity of this statement is admittedly suspect, but the *idea* back in the 1930s speaks volumes on behalf of the constructive and creative atmosphere of the school.

The Most Direct Testimony
Comes from Students Themselves

    The best judges of the sense of kinship that the pupils felt in relation to the Hebrew School were the pupils themselves. Under the headlines, "What the I.S. Means," Laurel Rosenbaum, age ten, wrote:

> ...It gives me a good time when learning Hebrew and when they give plays about Jewish history or other plays about Jews....What comforts me is knowing I have friends in the I.S. and God lives there....

Ida Finfang, age twelve, under the same headline, had this to say:

> ...Our [Hebrew School] not only gives us a Jewish education but pleasure as well....I always loved our Hebrew, and always will. It is the best Hebrew School....I hope in the future to repay the Hebrew School for everything it has done for me.

Chapter 24

The Adults Had A
Lot To Learn, Too

Many community leaders make the mistake of concentrating virtually all of their educational efforts on children, and giving up on the involvement of adults. Even when adults are afforded the opportunity to study, their classes are usually geared to a specialized or an elderly group of people. This longstanding widespread sense of priorities made the innovative vibrant I.S. adult education program all the more remarkable.

One course in particular stood head and shoulders above all the others. It also *encompassed* many of the others in its broad scope. The only course that could have possibly met this description, of course, had to be the one in Rabbi Goldstein's specialty, the Bible. It was chaired by the rabbi virtually every single week from the very first season of the existence of the Institutional Synagogue and continued long after the West Side Institutional Synagogue formally came into being in 1937. Rabbi Goldstein's unique captivating style was the subject of an article that appeared in the synagogue newspaper about midway through this period:

> Fundamentalism and evolution appeared at the first session of the Bible Class last week, there to inflict dire damage to each other and to recall the age-worn hates and prejudices. They parted from the field of battle, smiling and friendly and with a "collation" to add zest to their mutually understanding positions.
>
> Novelty was the twist of the evening. Conspicuously absent from the session of learning was the pall usually present at any discussion of the Bible. Not one or two men did all the talking and theorizing; everybody present took an active and

sincere part in the exchange of ideas. There existed no fear of criticism or ridicule, such as sometimes is unpleasantly prevalent where technicians and laymen come together. Nor was there any attempt at rhetoric or chicanery. You either understood the point, or you did not; if you did not, you were emprivileged to courteously "break in" and offer your point of criticism or else put your question seeking explanation. . . .

Rabbi Holds Interest

Only a man like Rabbi Goldstein could have led the boys as he did. For the Rabbi is essentially a "regular" [as opposed to an aloof] fellow, and only a regular fellow could attract the boys from their homes, after a busy day's work, to study Bible and Torah in their application to the problems of the times. And the boys present were of the kind quick to discern any weakness or deficiency in learning or understanding; and unlike the run of fellows whom we ordinarily call "regular," the Rabbi is possessed of deep learning and profound human feelings—traits and qualities in which he has already proved his excellence time and again. . . .

. . . The purpose of these Bible Classes is to bring the Holy Book to the people. The Rabbinic interpretation of the various passages are given with the various commentaries from the Midrash [homiletical writings] and the Talmud. Rabbi Goldstein uses his own book, which he recently published, to supplement this traditional interpretation. . . .

The most striking and conclusive evidence of the widespread demand generated by and for Rabbi Goldstein's Bible Classes may be gleaned from a mere headline in a 1929 issue of the synagogue newspaper: ". . . Rabbi Goldstein Conducts Bible Classes at Conclusion of Meetings of Daughters [young women's group], Brothers [Men's Club], Women's League [sisterhood of the West Side Branch] and Parent Association [of the Hebrew School]." A different issue commented on this rare phenomenon:

At every meeting of the senior organizations of the Institutional Synagogue, one is sure to find that the outstanding feature is the Bible classes which have been conducted for the past few years by Rabbi Herbert S. Goldstein. And now, more than ever before, the popularity of these classes is supreme.

Despite the fact that the country at this time—the original era of jazz that led into the great stock market crash of the century—was wallowing in what was then considered its most ostentatious hour of materialism and prosperity, and despite the fact that the synagogue was in a neighborhood that by this time was decaying; nevertheless, all of the major adult organizations within the synagogue superstructure demanded Bible classes on a regular basis every time they met!

The devotion of the women's association of the synagogue to the rabbi's Bible class was manifested in particularly unique ways. For one thing, its roster of officers must have been one of the only synagogue sisterhood rosters in the world to consist of a president, two vice presidents, a treasurer, a secretary, and a "secretary of the Bible class."* When the class completed the study of the Book of Genesis, the women presented their teacher with a smoking jacket. Although there is no record of a complete wardrobe being assembled as they continued to complete the five books of Moses, the satisfaction all parties received in this monumental achievement more than compensated. The by-then-merged *American Hebrew and Jewish Tribune* announced, in 1935:

> For the first time in the history of Jewish women's activities in this country, a *Seeyum* [ceremonious celebration upon completing, originally, a Talmudic tractate (the concept has been extended, informally, to other holy books)] on the Five Books of Moses was celebrated by the Women's League of the Institutional Synagogue on Wednesday...

It took ten years to complete the study of the Pentateuch.

This course, in other words, had begun in Harlem. When the rabbi and many of the congregants moved to the West Side, an offshoot of the class was transplanted to the synagogue's West Side branch, picking up just where it had left off. The participants could desert their old neighborhood, but never their Bible class.

The endurance record of the Bible class is particularly impressive in light of the fact that this particular class first began long *after* 1919 when "Every Monday evening...Stereopticon Views on the Bible" were shown for children and every Wednesday evening for adults. These "Stereopticon Views" represented the ultimate in popular visual technology in 1919, seven years before sound effects and eight years before dialogue reached American movie houses, yet the Bible class outlasted them.

Goldstein never missed an opportunity to make his congregants feel at home with the Bible. By advocating Biblical names for their children, he sought to develop a sense of pride in and closer emotional feelings to their heritage during a period when Jews consciously sought to submerge their religious identity in order to "Americanize." He felt and immediately shared a particu-

---

*At that point, there was a charge for attending the Bible class.

lar sense of satisfaction when he could demonstrate that model American citizens *themselves* took pride in their Biblical association. The *New York Times* publicized his "plea that children receive Biblical names rather than the hybrid ones of today":

> The striking note of the family tree of the Coolidges [Calvin was then the United States president] is that they drew their inspiration, as the founding fathers of our country did, from the Bible. . . . I refer particularly to the names of Sarah A. Brewer, mother of Colonel Coolidge [the president's father], and Israel Brewer, grandfather. Further, in the list of great-grandparents you will find the names of Elihab, Hannah, Sarah, Rachel, David, Bezaleel, Obadiah and Josiah.

Practicing what he preached, he named his own four children Simeon, Gabriel, Josephine (for whom he went to the trouble of "feminizing" Joseph, the Hebrew name of his late father), and Naomi.

All of life was one informal Bible class to Rabbi Goldstein. One issue of the synagogue newspaper carried the following message in a box.

How to Use the Bible

When you have the blues, read Psalm 34.
When you are discouraged, read Isaiah 40.
When God seems far away, read Psalm 139.
When you are lonely or afraid, read Psalm 23.
When penitent, read Psalm 51.
When men fail you, read Psalm 27.
When you want courage, read Joshua 1.
When in danger, read Psalm 91.
When you want faith, read Psalm 73.
When in sorrow, read the Book of Job.
When leaving home, read Psalm 121.
When pondering over environment, read Psalm 1.
For prudence, read Proverbs.
For correction, read Isaiah 1.
The Ten Commandments, Exodus, chapter 20, vs. 1-17.
— From Rabbi Herbert S. Goldstein

Possibly his ultimate statement in favor of Bible classes was the one where he contrasted them with prayer and the classes came out ahead:

> Reading scriptures properly is the most sublime act of man. Bible reading is even more praiseworthy than praying.

When we delve into the Bible, we try to find out what *God* wants; when we pray, we declare what *we* want.

Although the Bible class—on *all* levels—was Rabbi Goldstein's special joy, classes for adults in this subject were also given by two other people, one of whom was a lay scholar, Mr. Sol Lamport, who had contributed more than mere scholarship to the I.S. at the cornerstone laying ceremony, as was seen earlier. By using the term *Chummash shiur* (Hebrew for "Bible class") for his Sabbath afternoon sessions, Lamport clearly appealed to more traditional elements in the synagogue. Goldstein, of course, was always reaching out, and drawing in, so his wide-ranging class was invariably referred to by its English classification as a "Bible" class, a term which, even when contrasted with that of Lamport's Hebrew-name class, was hardly "over-Americanized" either.

Although adult education courses were offered in many secular subjects in the over-all I.S. adult educational program, the emphasis was clearly on the Judaic. Rabbi Goldstein did not hold himself above teaching even the *rudiments* of the Hebrew language, a knowledge of which was indispensable to comfortable participation in the synagogue services. He found such teaching particularly essential at the time of the I.S.'s beginning, given the weak grounding, in this crucial area, even of many members of the synagogue's inner nucleus. Thus, even before the rabbi left his employ at his previous congregation, an early I.S. "committee meeting" produced the following transformation so essential to his overall plans, as described by his wife:

> At first some of the girls were a little indifferent, but later, those very girls expressed a desire to learn how to read Hebrew, and for this purpose Herbert is going to give a class in Hebrew at the Y.W.H.A. [before the I.S. moved into its building]... evenings.*

In this area, Goldstein's role as a *motivator* was even more significant than his role as an educator. While many different people, including laymen and laywomen, taught the Hebrew language on various levels over the years, Goldstein, even in later years, continued to motivate people who came to the synagogue with poor Hebrew backgrounds, by personally teaching, on occasion, "Hebrew reading for beginners."

---

*In so doing, he encouraged his students to use mnemonic devices, developing one, for example, that not only assisted in a fundamental of the Hebrew language but that also simultaneously reinforced the rabbi's moral preachings. The Hebrew alphabet has two letters that are identical except that one, the letter *shin*, has a dot at its upper *right* hand corner while the other, the letter *sin*, has a dot at its upper *left* hand corner. He taught the difference between the two by simply asking the rhetorical question: "Can a *sin* be *right?*"

Goldstein took his turn among the Talmud teachers, over the years, along with, among others, his *own* teacher, Dr. Zadok Kapner. The rabbi reached many more people, however, in his *Mishna* classes, teaching the basic principles—from the original Hebrew text—on which the Aramaic Talmud is based. This subject, unlike the Talmud itself, lends itself to pithy fifteen minute daily sessions which he taught right before the prayer services, as well as to weekly hour-long classes, which he taught as well. This—and *not* Bible—was the *only* subject taught at the I.S. which seems to have been in his domain alone, probably because most Talmudists preferred to treat the *Mishna* almost as an adjunct to the vast and intricate "sea of the Talmud" whereas the rabbi was effectively able to use the subject to whet people's academic appetites for the Talmud or to use it, so to speak, as an hors d'oeuvre before the daily evening service.

The study of "the [Biblical] Prophets" is often considered a discipline distinct from the Five Books of Moses, the latter of which are sometimes loosely but popularly known in Jewish circles as the Bible, since, among other reasons, the symbolic Torah scrolls consist only of these key five books. Because of this lower priority in relation to both the "Bible" and the panoramic Talmud, the prophets, many of whom were insulted and scorned in their *own* days, are often posthumously ignored in *our* times as well. The very title of Rabbi Goldstein's course is therefore particularly significant. Rather than stressing the historical or ethical aspects, he preferred announcing his intent to study the "Social Message of the Prophets," in order to get his *own* message across to the broadest audiences. One year, this idea was carried even further in the class on "Industrial and Social Problems as *Solved* [italics not in the original] by the Jewish Prophets."

The other courses that the versatile Rabbi Goldstein taught on the adult level, at one time or another during his twenty years in Harlem, included Jewish History, "General Jewish Knowledge," and "Codes"—of Jewish Law.

The only inherently Jewish subjects in the I.S. adult education program that Rabbi Goldstein did *not* teach were Jewish literature (which frequently is not even inherently Jewish but which often is *anti*-Jewish or merely written by misguided masochists who *happen* to be Jewish), congregational singing (led by four different cantors over the years), and the musical rules and notes of synagogue Bible chanting. The culturally well-rounded Dr. Samuel Nirenstein, who had a Ph.D. from Dropsie and an L.L.B. from Columbia, and who was appointed the first Orthodox Jewish Law Secretary of the New York State Supreme Court and eventually succeeded Rabbi Goldstein as president of the U.O.J.C.A., presumably knew enough about Jewish literature to concentrate on the wealth of positive and constructive Jewish literature available, in his I.S. lectures on the subject.

One cannot conclude a discussion of the I.S. Judaic adult education program without mentioning the Israel Friedlander classes. Professor Israel Friedlander (of the Jewish Theological Seminary), who was an influential intellectual giant of New York Jewry early in this century and chairman of the board of trustees of the Bureau of Jewish Education of the city's "Kehillah," was murdered by Ukranian bandits while he was "on a relief mission" in Russia in 1920.* After Friedlander's tragic death, a group of his admirers requested that the Seminary organize a "department of extension instruction...in Friedlander's name." It was a rather far-flung and heterogeneous arrangement of independent Jewish classes, but it *did* memorialize his name and the Seminary *did* subsidize them, so that by 1922, "Fully ten Friedlander Hebrew classes of varied nature were organized" in the I.S. This was virtually the only link Rabbi Goldstein had maintained with the identity-crisis-ridden Seminary since his dramatic departure, and it did not last long, but the funds the Seminary invested, however indirectly, into Goldstein's Orthodox organization in its critical building years did not go unappreciated.

The wide variety of non-Judaic classes offered at the I.S., over the years, included, in alphabetical order, classes in accounting, advertising, art appreciation, arts and crafts, bookkeeping, boxing (taught, at times, by the undefeated lightweight champion of the world), camp counseling, choral society, citizenship (for immigrant adults), club leadership, cooking, cultural talks, designing, debating, elocution, English to foreigners, fine arts, first aid, gymnastics, industrial arts (including decorative ornamental drawing and modeling, textile decoration, antique and stencil work, and wood carving), interior decorating, journalism, law, languages, novelties, piano, play production, poster work, psychology, public speaking, reducing, sciences, staging, swimming, and violin.

One would have to be stretching one's credibility to assert that there were unique attributes to these I.S. classes, but the sheer variety of the subject matter speaks for itself. The courses ranged the gamut from the religious to the practical to the intellectual to the athletic to the artistic.

One opportunity made available through the I.S., but never, apparently, realized to a significant degree, was the opportunity to enroll in extension courses in conjunction with Columbia Univer-

---

'By this time Goldstein had long-since divorced himself from the Jewish Theological Seminary, but he still was counted among Friedlander's many admirers. In turn, Friedlander, who felt that "the most urgent Jewish communal problem was the education of Jewish youth," had admired the work of his former student. So much so that, according to the biased impression of one who knew the two personally, Friedlander had "worshiped" him!

sity and the College of the City of New York. Columbia alone made 400 courses available at the I.S. building, by arrangement with the Metropolitan League of Jewish Community Associations.

The synagogue leadership aimed to smooth out every rough edge or loose end that could possibly develop in the educational lives of its members. Rabbi Goldstein conducted a regular "question box and forum," to handle individual problems. Club members who needed to be "coached" for tests in entire subjects were invited to consult staff members of the I.S. Individuals who sought career guidance for their entire futures were channeled to "I.S. workers otherwise engaged in the practice of law, medicine, social work, journalism, accounting, teaching, marketing, and other professional and commercial enterprises."

The personal knowledge of I.S. teachers and counselors was supplemented by a synagogue library. Like virtually everything else about the synagogue, the library had been assembled in a manner that was not only relatively painless but also enjoyable. A nucleus of books was acquired by means of a "book dance" conducted less than a month after the first I.S. building was put into service. Admission to the dance was "only on the presentation of a book." "A large number of books for the library were acquired in this way," until it contained—by virtue of this and *other* means, to be sure—about 1,500 books as well as "current magazines on file." The figure of 1,500 books may not have been overly impressive, but Rabbi Goldstein may have been influential in encouraging this seeming moderate priority rating, having once observed:

> ...It is paradoxical, but nevertheless true, that the curse of the present generation is the multitude of books in our libraries, or, as we read in the closing verses of *Ecclesiastes*, "the making of many books has no end."

What should we read first—the latest novel or magazine? My answer is that there is nothing wrong per se, perhaps, with the novel or magazine, but these would be described by our sages as "extra books," not those of prime importance.

The library was open daily. It employed a librarian willing and able to be of service, and it provided an atmosphere conducive to both scholarship and leisurely reading to many young people who would have otherwise grown up without having ever known either experience.

Chapter 25

Adult Groups
Not Just Social

Every adult social group in the synagogue had at least two purposes, to promote social relationships among its members, and to assist the synagogue. Many of these sub-groups of the synagogue, of course, served other purposes as well.

"The Brotherhood" Young Men—A Historic First

The American Hebrew credited Rabbi Goldstein with having organized "[t]he first Brotherhood connected with an Orthodox synagogue in New York City." This recognition undoubtedly was appreciated, but it equally undoubtedly was granted close to a decade late, even regarding the I.S., and it referred to a program totally unrelated to the brotherhood's original one. In fact, the first attempt at launching a social organization for the young adult men of the synagogue—a monthly supper meeting—had not caught on, and only in the Brotherhood's second season, under a different format, was it able to succeed.

In 1918, upon the opening of the second season of the Brotherhood, its members intuitively sensed that they had a winning idea, and they were proven to be correct. At the same time, the synagogue newspaper was candid enough to concede that the original pattern had *not* proven successful:

> The Brotherhood made a clean "somersault" at its first meeting of the season held the other night.
> Under the inspiration and guidance of Rabbi Goldstein, the Brotherhood, by the virtue of a plan which was evolved at the meeting, now bids fair to come back to its own. That plan would have the members of the Brotherhood dine, study, and play regularly at the I.S. once a week.

Instead of falling back upon the old practice of casual monthly suppers (a means which, by itself, has already demonstrated its futility in keeping the members of the Brotherhood together), the new Brotherhood plan would have the members of the organization have a light supper every Monday evening at the I.S. between the hours of 6 and 7. After the meal, to be furnished at cost, the members will hold their meeting; and, as soon as that is over, the members will resign themselves to the study of the Bible, under the leadership of Rabbi Goldstein. A gymnasium fest is then to follow after the mental session.

Nothing Forced

The members of the organization have seized upon the plan with striking enthusiasm. Here, at last, is a proposition that promises returns of interest, diversion, and education. Nothing forced about the requirements of the plan....*

The combination "dine-study-play" plan was largely suggested by Mr. Harry Burak, former President of the Brotherhood.

The boys have already negotiated for complete gymnasium outfits. Even Rabbi Goldstein, notable democrat, will mingle among the boys and play handball, basketball, and otherwise indulge in their physical exploits "downstairs."

One of the factors that may have been as significant as Goldstein's eloquence in his success as a rabbi was his status as "one of the boys." He could enjoy doing what they enjoyed doing, and was able to get them to enjoy doing some of the more spiritual things that *he* enjoyed doing. He did not hold himself above them. He was with them, all the way. Many years later, some of "the boys" recalled that he had not merely made *token* appearances on the basketball court to honor them with the momentary aura of his detached presence. To the contrary, "He used to play for a full hour. He played the whole game." Harry Ward, the only one of the early I.S. "boys" whose own inclination, combined with God's, enabled him to remain on the I.S. Board of Trustees—both that of the original I.S. and later of the West Side I.S.—until the country's bicentennial year, during which he passed away, vividly recalled those weekly "dine-study-play" days that culminated in the gym and the pool. Few incidents could have possibly said as much about the intensity of the rabbi's participation as the following one:

---

*The uninitiated might have assumed that the Bible study facet of the new plan was imposed by the rabbi or not fully approved of by the rank and file. For this reason, undoubtedly, the article made a point of stressing that the idea was not "forced."

Abe Eisenstadt [the cousin and "agent," as it turned out, of Cantor Yavneh], the rabbi, and I were in a basketball game. Abe bumped into the rabbi and his [the rabbi's] glasses broke. Rabbi Goldstein said, "Think nothing of it," and he kept on playing without his glasses!

We will see more of this appropriately named "Brotherhood" later.

Social Service League Follows Congregation Kehilath Jeshurun's Lead

On the last day of the first month of the first secular calendar new year that the I.S. celebrated (Jan. 31, 1918), the Social Service League came into being. As with the synagogue itself, the idea of organizing it came from a Goldstein, one of the most active workers was a Goldstein, and its first president was a Siegel, but unlike the situation with the synagogue itself, the rabbi's *wife* and the congressman's *wife*, respectively, filled these roles. The "New Temple League Plan," according to a headline in the *New York American*, was to "Save Boys And Girls from Crime-Infested Harlem." In a little more than a month's time, Mrs. Siegel was able to report:

> We have already evolved a plan to care for the delinquents. We have enlisted the aid of the Jewish Big Sister and Jewish Big Brother organizations toward this end. The delinquents will be taken in hand by capable men and women and shown the right road. Positions will be obtained for many of them and everything else done to make them good American citizens.

The league did not have to seek out problem cases. By this time, it had already been contacted by parents of children in trouble, and had already enlisted the cooperation of the "police department and detective bureau." The league was also mandated to:

> help . . . poor Jewish children to receive a religious education, to care for destitute children, to read for the blind . . . encourage club work among the young, and to do hospital work.

Over two weeks before the first Passover holiday following the league's formation, "the chief subject of discussion" at one of its meetings "was the distribution of matzohs to the poor of the neighborhood." Enough money was raised to enable the league, as a unit, to implement its idealistic plan most efficiently:

We used a store at 1658 Madison Avenue, which was selling matzohs anyway, as our distributing center [note that this "venue" served to minimize the trauma of accepting charity], and there, as each person came in, the owner of the store gave them as much as they needed, and finally reckoned up the entire amount distributed which was in the neighborhood of 400 pounds [180 kilos] including matzoh flour. We also distributed some cash to very needy cases.

The members of this league were unsung heroes, and most of the problem cases they tackled did not lend themselves to dramatic, long-term, or quick resolutions. An exception, however, involved the incident recorded in Mrs. Goldstein's diary early in May of that first year:

I...went over to the opening of the grocery store of Mr. Maltinsky whom the Social Service League of the I.S. put into business.

As was to be emphasized later, helping a person to set up a business represents the highest level of charity in the Jewish strata of priorities.

By 1924, the "Social Service League" had dropped the word "service" from its name, but the newly re-christened Social League still claimed to have "many of the original organizers...the same zeal...and the same functions." The major headline-catching functions were fund-raising "annual dances." It was not long before the renamed Social League dropped these two words also and merged into another synagogue organization. Apparently, when a "Social Service League" removes the word "service" from its identity, not much is left!

Young Folks League, a Stronger Force

This league was founded, at Mrs. Goldstein's invitation and encouragement, by "17 young folks." She, the eighteenth person, helped to breathe life into it.* Superficially, it may seem as if she made no conscious prediction regarding the viability of the new organization, but her typically casual diary entry made the prediction for her! When she, normally a paragon of patience, simply remarked that "they didn't leave till after 12," she thereby revealed that she herself expected or wanted them to leave earlier. The indication that she did not have to prod them to stay, and, if

---

*Each letter of the Hebrew alphabet has a numerical equivalent. The most popular two-letter combination spells the Hebrew word *chai*—life—whose numerical equivalent happens to be eighteen.

anything, might have prodded them to leave, augured well! She was also *treated* well by the group which, incidentally, grateful for her role, named her its "honorary president."

The Young Folks League was:

composed of young men and women of the ages of 21 years and over . . . their aims [were] for the mutual aid in time of need, united effort toward the moral and mental culture, the progress and the elevation of [its] members, and the friendly and faithful co-operation in the spirit of good fellowship, in order to assist the I.S. in all it [undertook].

In less than a year, the members' idealistically motivated activities and their constructive record of fund raising, mainly through bazaars and monthly "sociables," earned the superlative words of praise from Rabbi Goldstein that "the Young Folks League is the most essential and, perhaps, the most important organization in our midst." Goldstein's remark was taken verbatim from an unsigned article in the synagogue newspaper, with the exception of the careful rabbi's diplomatically added modifying word "perhaps"—that did not appear in the original. The synagogue newspaper stated that "the league's most important work . . . is to financially support the I.S." Rabbi Goldstein did not go quite that far in citing its priorities at the opening meeting of the 1924-1925 season. According to the synagogue newspaper:

The meeting was one splendid evening of enthusiasm. At least two hundred friends and members were present. . . . Rabbi Goldstein . . . bid them renew their activities on behalf of their own betterment and that of the institution. . . .

Another area in which they appeared to be better than many of their peers was alluded to in the "Around and About" synagogue newspaper gossip column:

One thing that strikes our fancy is the regularity of attendance of the [members] of the enterprising Young Folks League at our [prayer] services. . . .

In the middle of this 1924-1925 season the inevitable happened. The Social League amalgamated into the Young Folks League, and only the latter organization retained its name.

"Daughters of the I.S." Recognized As Such by Appreciative "Parents"

At a "Get Together Dinner" and reunion for over 200 people,

held at the I.S. on Washington's Birthday in 1926, Rabbi Goldstein "made a spirited plea for a new movement which would [re-]create a Brotherhood composed of young men and a similar organization for young women called the Daughters of the I.S., which would in a true sense develop and make for the members and directors* of the I.S. of tomorrow."

In this period, patriotism was still a near universally popular concept throughout the United States, as it certainly was among members of the I.S. It is possible, therefore, that the name "Daughters of the I.S." may have been a "take-off" on the Daughters of the American Revolution, which was founded by and open to women whose ancestors had aided the patriot cause in the American revolution, just as most of these I.S. daughters had promoted the "revolutionary" I.S. concept from its very inception!

At the opening meeting, each of the six committee chairmen (their wording!) appointed by Mrs. Goldstein, the founder, was a young Miss at the time. Not surprisingly, therefore, by the following month, Mrs. Goldstein, a young mother figure herself, casually referred to the "Daughters of the I.S. of which I am the mother." This informal feeling of kinship was mutual. The very first month of May after the Daughters had been formed, its members sent a symbolic Mother's Day card to Mrs. Goldstein on that holiday. Likewise, later-year New Year's Day visits to their "'mother'" (as Mrs. Goldstein recalled "they jocularly call me,") understandably "touched" her "by that feeling of devotion which has continued. . . ."

Another personal angle to the name "Daughters of the I.S." was that Mrs. Goldstein by this time had two natural sons and her longing for a daughter after over a decade of marriage was well known. She was blessed with her first natural daughter two years after her organizational "daughters" assumed their organizational identity. The chain was then simply extended by one link, as Mrs. Goldstein's new daughter was promptly "adopted" as a "sister" by Mrs. Goldstein's organizational daughters. The original daughters never forgot their leisurely Sabbath afternoons spent as invited guests in the Goldstein residence, almost as members of the family, "when the Goldsteins' son Simeon was the only one," which means literally wthin the very first few months of the existence of the synagogue.

Mrs. Goldstein made sure that everyone became involved. At an early meeting in her house:

> Twenty-two of my daughters were present. . . . We had election of officers and appointment of a number of committee

---

*This suggestion that women should be named to serve on a synagogue board of directors came not only before this was to become a reality in *Orthodox* congregations, but also long before it was to become a widespread practice in many "Reform" temples as well!

chairmen. Then each chairman appointed her committee so that everybody went home with some position....

The organization was officially formed to do "social, cultural, and philanthropic work." Most of the charter members, it may be noted, had already been almost indispensably active in the synagogue through other sub-organizations or as individuals involved in specific projects. As I.S. "Daughters," their activities included "supper meetings, theatre parties, and bridges for fund raising; a gym and swimming class and a Bible class... unbounded cooperation with every activity of the I.S. at all times." Mrs. Goldstein herself arranged the cultural aspects of the organization at first, to set its tone. She set an example for the young women by inviting accomplished *women* speakers to address them. One of the first was Mrs. Joseph Mayer Asher, the widow of the rabbi who had inspired Mrs. Goldstein more than any other in her developing years, and one of Rabbi Goldstein's chief inspirations as well. Mrs. Asher:

> read a paper to the girls on "The Symbols of Judaism." This made a deep impression on them and several of them asked for a copy of it so that they could have it with them and read it over occasionally.

At another early program, Miss Pearl Bernstein, who was conspicuously introduced as a graduate of the prestigious Barnard College, (most girls in this period did not attend *any* college), spoke on "The Chassidic Movement in Jewish History."

Although gradually most of the girls married and moved out of the community,* their ties to the I.S. remained strong. They met regularly even after the West Side Institutional Synagogue was created and when most of them had to "commute" to the meetings, some from as far away as Long Island. By 1937, the year all formal ties between the I.S. and the West Side I.S. were cut, a synagogue publication wrote:

> The chief function of this group is to preserve that beautiful bond of friendship which had grown up among the girls,....

In 1940, nearly a decade after even the Goldsteins themselves had moved out of Harlem, Mrs. Goldstein referred in her diary to the:

---

*By 1937, the year that the West Side branch became independent in its new neighborhood, at least three of the girls, in fact, had permanently settled in Israel (then Palestine) long before the idea of relocating in that country was to become "fashionable."

supper which I give every year for the Daughters of the
W.S.I.S. [the West Side Institutional Synagogue] at the
synagogue. About 25 attended. . . . This is a bond which I like
to keep up out of appreciation for the work these girls did
when we were up at the 116th Street building. . . .

On the first of the Goldsteins' annual visits to Israel that
began in 1949—at which time the Daughters were still meeting
"once a month"—Mrs. Goldstein's letter from Israel to the family
showed that the years and the distance had not strained these ties.

> May 27—One of the girls of my club. . . lives here in
> Jerusalem now. She has been waiting for our arrival to be of
> help to us, if necessary. I asked her to take Naomi [the younger
> Goldstein daughter] shopping. . . .
> June 1—. . .[M]y W.S.I.S. Daughter just brought us a
> cheese cake for [the holiday].
> July 7—. . .[A]n evening given in honor of Dad and me,
> by my W.S.I.S. "Daughter," Miriam Levow Rieder, at her home
> in Rechovia [the most elegant neighborhood in Jerusalem]. . . .

Brotherhood Suddenly an Example for Others

As leadership changes every few years, organizations frequently have their ups and downs. The year 1926 began as a down
year for the Brotherhood, until Rabbi Goldstein came up with an
appropriate way to give it a lift and revive two birds with one gold
stone.

Superficially, one might have assumed, the two organizations
he sought to inspire were the Daughters of the I.S. and its sibling,
the Brotherhood. Actually, still another organization was to
benefit from his consciousness-raising exercise, namely, the Union
of Orthodox Jewish Congregations of America (U.O.J.C.A.) of
which he was then national president. His own synagogue's
newspaper was not the only one to talk in grandiose terms about the
revived organization by stating that "the undertaking will assume
national proportions [although only indirectly, at most], and will
be fostered in other Jewish communities throughout the land
under the auspices of the U.O.J.C." The *American Hebrew* wrote
that "this movement is an effort in conjunction with the U.O.J.C.A.
to draw the young men closer to the religious life of their respective
communities." By stirring his *own* congregants to set an example
for others to follow, he clearly made the most of his efforts.

The Brotherhood program this time around apparently did
not adhere to a schedule as rigidly as it had in its early days. The
Bible class was a constant, but the dinner at times became a

231

"collation" and the recreation in the gym and pool was substituted, occasionally, by a "general get-together." Even when the men *did* retire to the gym after the rabbi's "inspiring and pedagogical" session in this period, the rhythm had apparently changed. Note the subtle nuance in this synagogue newspaper description:

> ...An active session in the gym then followed, with the rabbi hitting home runs "a la Babe Ruth," as one of the features.

In earlier years, a session in the gym had aspired to no special features. There had been regular games and everybody had simply participated as equals.

Although the full-fledged weekly dinner was not a *permanent* component of the Brotherhood events in this era, on those frequent occasions when there *was* such a repast, it was conducted in a Jewish spirit not otherwise generally experienced by a substantial number of the participants. According to one synagogue newspaper account:

> ...One of the excellent and usual features of the supper was the fact that all those present wore skullcaps and said grace from the little prayer books that were distributed around the table.

Rabbi Goldstein clearly did not limit his role at these gatherings to his Bible class or to sermonizing. In particular, he relished making announcements that he knew would generate excitement, as, for example, the time when:

> ...During the course of the evening, Rabbi Goldstein read a letter to the effect that Mayor Walker has promised to appear at one of the suppers when he returns from his vacation.

Sure enough, four months later, the mayor did indeed show up!* In those days, non-Jewish politicians did not wear Jewish religious articles of dress in front of Jewish audiences with quite the same frequency as they do today. For this reason, the following sequence must have seemed quite novel:

> The mayor, after promising not to discuss "serious topics," somehow touched upon religion. One of the members at the guest table passed the skullcap to him.
> The mayor took the silk hat eagerly and gingerly placed...the black silk skullcap...upon his head...at the

---

*This is not to suggest that the vacation lasted quite that long!

rakish and sporty angle he usually sets his grey fedora…
evok[ing] a spontaneous burst of cheers….

It was truly a captivating political appearance.

At about this point in time, the Brotherhood came out with its own newspaper, which, at four pages per issue, was as large as the synagogue's weekly but contained "about half the content." How the editorial staff justified this seeming reverse boast is not clear, unless it claimed that its primary aim was to entertain rather than to inform, which, under the circumstances, would have been reasonable enough!

Two years after the West Side branch was established in its comfortable neighborhood on the upswing, the Brotherhood chose to embrace its counterpart on the West Side in the most brotherly way possible—it gave up its own identity and merged into it.

Sisterhood Created BEFORE Day One!

Fully two weeks before Rabbi Goldstein was to complete his contractual obligations at his previous synagogue, a "Ladies Auxiliary" was already created for the nascent I.S. It took the ladies over a year, apparently, to decide on a less subservient-sounding name, the I.S. "Sisterhood," at which time "committees were appointed on constitution, nomination, war work, [the Hebrew School], War Relief, and Ways and Means." No matter how many committees may have existed on paper—or even in fact—they all paled next to the primary area the Sisterhood entered first, to wit, war relief.

It was only natural that a synagogue that claimed to have been founded the day the United States entered World War I and that had sent so many of its own sons to offer to make "the supreme sacrifice" would inspire a sisterhood whose number one priority, at first, was to contribute, in various ways, to the war effort. While the men sacrificed their very lives, wives sacrificed their sons and their husbands. The other major sacrifice that women were called upon to make was the sacrifice of their precious time. The most time-consuming activity in which they were to immerse themselves did not require nerves of steel but needles of steel and patience to endure the stillness of nights spent alone and without the opportunity to caress their loved ones while they could only sew together garments that could give those on the battlefields a bare minimum of comfort. So pervasive was the sewing circle that brought the women together in this critical period that the writer of the synagogue journal article on the Sisterhood, many years later, in recalling these early years, felt compelled to remark, "but our sisterhood was not *only* a sewing circle…." (italics were not in the original).

An overview of the Sisterhood after its first score of years described not how its first president had presided over the organization as a whole or chaired meetings in particular, but rather how "she [had] supervised the knitting of heavy sweaters and stockings for our boys in the trenches," as the hallmark of her administration! The women did not take an amateurish approach by any standard (except, of course, for their refusal to be paid for their efforts), but worked "in cooperation with the Council of Jewish Women," with two instructors from the Red Cross. During the war and its aftermath, the Sisterhood also worked in cooperation with the Jewish Welfare Board. Even the armistice agreement did not mark an end to these efforts. In 1919, months after the conclusion of the war, "under the auspices of our young ladies, garments [were] made for the wounded soldiers who...returned from 'over there.'"

Once the machinery had been set in motion, the close-knit sewing circle, in its new peacetime environment, did not hem and haw, "sew" to speak, but called on the synagogue membership to "send us your old and outgrown clothes. Help us keep the poor and needy families in our neighborhood warm and comfortable."

After the war, the Sisterhood felt free, at last, to focus on the synagogue itself, which was such an instant success that the need for larger quarters had been apparent at the I.S.'s very first services in its own first building. Accordingly, "all minds were centered on the thought of raising the funds necessary for larger quarters."

We have already seen the leading role played by the husband of the second Sisterhood president, Mrs. Samuel Silver, in support of the synagogue. If the Goldsteins were the synagogue's golden couple, surely the Silvers were the synagogue's silver lining. Beginning with Mrs. Silver's administration, the Sisterhood began to reach its potential in terms of its "chief function...to assist the directors in securing the necessary funds to carry on the building's activities."* The Sisterhood ran its own theatre parties, bridge parties, rummage sales, cake sales, package parties, and other events to raise funds—all this was in addition to the Sisterhood's indispensable support of general synagogue affairs.

---

*The next president, Mrs. Annie Morris, wife of the alderman, "...led the Sisterhood for years and [knew] the Sisterhood as no [other] member of that organization [did]." This knowledge gave additional significance to her remark, excerpted in the synagogue newspaper from her presidential message in 1925:

> ...[N]o thought was more pleasant to me than to look forward to the Sisterhood meeting when I knew, God willing, our Rebbitzen [rabbi's wife] would be present as an inspiration to us all.

The program that afternoon listed not merely a "Greeting" from Mrs. Goldstein but a "Greeting and Spiritual Message."

234

Although most of the Sisterhood's funds went directly to the synagogue and to offsetting its own expenses, occasionally it siphoned off some of its proceeds to benefit other synagogue arms—or mouths—directly.*

Never a Boring Moment at the I.S. Board

The I.S. board of directors, more than being merely an executive or administrative body, was as much a social organization as any of the other adult groupings. Every vertebra of this firm backbone of the I.S. administration was carefully welded together by the Goldsteins. The first four meetings of the board took place under their personal care in their own home.** The official "standards of election" to the board were high, consideration theoretically going to "standards of character, influential position, service, and general popularity and deserving." Membership was not taken lightly nor attained easily. Even such loyal general synagogue members as Abe Eisenstadt, Harold Kaplan, and Clarence Liberman found, after about ten full years with the institution, that they still were not considered "ripe" for full-fledged membership in the board itself, so associate director status was created for and conferred upon them with the following explanation:

> The idea of the Associate Directors is a novel one in the history of the I.S. The theory which supports this idea is that the members elected to the Associate Board, while otherwise most deserving and capable for direct election to the Board, are deemed still comparatively unfledged for full and senior service on the Board. A course of training is expected to be initiated for Associate Directors, so that when the proper time comes promotion may directly be made to the Board itself. The Associate Board has been likened to an ante-room which the associates must go through before they may take up equal voice and control in the main body of the I.S. In addition the Associate Board is hoped to work as a means of inducement for the associate members to devote themselves in order to reap the award of election to the main board.

Rabbi Goldstein, like most synagogue rabbis, was never formally designated a member of the board, but, unlike most rabbis, he not only attended virtually every board meeting, but

---

*As early as 1918, it "gave a Chanukah treat to each one of the children of the Hebrew School." (Later, such treats were to be meted out on a regular basis by the Parents' Association.)

**The first three meetings took place even before the rabbi had officially completed his contractual commitments to his prior synagogue.

took an active part in them as well. Since the rabbi had proven himself so successful on both the local and national scenes, no board member could treat any policy position he took very lightly. Cantor Yavneh, an outsider to these meetings, once called him "the power on the throne and behind the throne," although Congressman Siegel was not exactly a political novice who could be easily intimidated! The minutes of nearly every meeting for decades began: "The following were present: Rabbi Goldstein and [the names of the directors present in alphabetical order]." More significant was the lead he took in setting an example of personal sacrifice. Although we have seen how modest his synagogue salary had been, for a person of his stature, at the outset, the following meeting excerpt at the inception of the Great Depression was typical:

> A motion was duly made and carried that the directors advance $2,500 on notes which is to be paid [back]. . . .
> The following directors have volunteered to advance $500.00 each. Rabbi Goldstein, Messrs. Settel, Wartels, Udell, and Gluck.

Once again, it was the rabbi who set the tone and took the lead, not merely in abstract theory but also in concrete deed.

All the I.S. News That Was Fit to Print—And More!

Volume I, Number I of the synagogue newspaper, *The Institutional*, burst into print just over a year after the I.S. moved into its first building. Until that point, synagogue events had been publicized on billboards in the community and reported in an impressed local and Jewish press. According to the opening issue:

> . . . Our purpose in publishing this bulletin is to make known the activities of our Synagogue and to stimulate interest in our work of reviving and intensifying the faith of our fathers. . . .

Two years later, Rabbi Goldstein was called upon by the staff to crystallize the paper's aims. He responded, in part:

> . . . Any branch of our work must. . . contain this two-[f]old purpose [outlined above].
> Your magazine. . . must contain such articles that will give to the reader a knowledge of the faith and an exhortation for its practice. The paper must not be too intellectual nor must it be a "wishy-washy" sheet. It must serve the average and not either extreme. I believe there must be a sermonette in

every issue, an article on Jewish ethics, an article on Jewish law, and a question and answer column.*

Space should be given in our paper for civics and articles that will intensify the American spirit....

...I would like to see the *Institutional* contain the advantages of the *Literary Digest* and the *Saturday Evening Post* so that the magazine may be a literary and a popular one.

The newspaper was a monthly at first, and began with a staff of four equally ranked editors and three business managers.** Although the paper generally ran four pages in length, its page size varied greatly over the years. On rare occasions, the generally consistent format was tampered with, as was the case one week in 1921 when the whole issue consisted of two postal cards attached together, one with "this week's events" on one side and the addressee's address on the reverse side, while the other had "theatre party information" on one side and the synagogue's return address on the other.

The editors of the weekly paper underwent a healthy turnover, and on two occasions—spaced about a decade apart—the newspaper became a means of on-the-job training for aspiring journalists. In 1921, a "Press Club" was organized "with its main purpose that of editing successfully this little magazine." It also held meetings on a weekly basis "at which lectures, debates, and discussions" took place. Not until 1930 did the paper launch a recruitment effort and offer, with the following selling point, to convert itself once again into a model mini-school of journalism:

> The *Institutional* staff will receive intensive training in all phases of journalism. Lectures, visits to newspaper plants, practice in writing, proof-reading and lay-out, and sympathetic and intelligent criticism, will be some of the advantages accruing to those who make the grade.
>
> Mr. Allan Dennison, of the *Jewish Tribune*, and a frequent contributor of poetry and short stories to magazines, will be associated with the *Institutional* as literary advisor.

Some of the regular weekly features included personals, book reviews, articles on Jewish history, philosophy, curiosities, and humor, in addition to those quoted above that were proposed by Rabbi Goldstein, though not all of them appeared at any single point in time.

---

*At one time or another, the rabbi himself provided each one of these suggested features.

**Modestly in the sidelines, Mrs. Goldstein "went over the printer's proof of the *Institutional* with Herbert and the printer" for the second issue and "wrote up some articles" for the third.

In 1926, when the synagogue was near its peak, it claimed that its newspaper "actually reache[d] about ten thousand Jews." A more conservative and whimsical estimate of the readership of a given column was made with tongue in cheek five years later:

> There were sixteen readers of this column last week. We know there were sixteen readers because there were nine complaints for omission, three because names were included in this column, and four sensitive souls objected to the liberties we were taking with Mr. Webster's really fine opus.

Actually, of course, sixteen comments on a single column in less than a week in a synagogue newspaper point up a tip of a multithousand-eyed iceberg. The heat emanating from such a thorough and responsive readership was capable of putting a chill into any perfectionist's "vains," but at the *Institutional,* it was met only by the warm self-deprecating comment just quoted.

Occasionally, a special edition was put out featuring humor or junior talent. In fact, so many clubs put out publications of their own one year, that their simultaneous presence justified a full-fledged intra-synagogue "publication contest."

Sabbath Bureau Combats Six-Day Week

The six-day work week with the "wrong" seventh day was such a formidable obstacle to Orthodox Jewry that it prompted Rabbi Goldstein to discuss it in his resignation sermon from his previous synagogue, during which he formally outlined his immediate plans for the I.S.:

> I realize that at the present time on Sabbath morning, I cannot have the youth of Harlem or the youth anywhere in the City at a Sabbath Service, but I propose to ask the leading Jewish merchants who keep the Sabbath to remedy this by informing me when there is an opening in their firms for young men and young women who desire to keep the Sabbath. I propose that through the Institutional Synagogue, a strong, a thorough, a powerful Sabbath Employment Bureau will be established.

True to the rabbi's dream, Congressman Siegel was able to announce, at the first annual membership meeting of the synagogue in its first non-rented home, that the bureau was "already in operation." The service was extended "free to both employers and members."*

The following month, the synagogue, in conjunction with the Jewish Sabbath Association, officially "opened a Harlem branch of the Association's Employment Bureau." Whatever actual association there may have been thereafter with the Jewish Sabbath Association appears to have gone unmentioned, if it existed at all.

Volume I, Number I of the synagogue newspaper carried, in distinct articles, both a direct and a subtle reference to the Sabbath Employment Bureau. The direct appeal stated, in part:

> Rabbi Goldstein tells us constantly that all preaching for the observance of the Sabbath is theoretical unless it is backed up by practical work. Practical work for the Sabbath rests in the maintenance of an Employment Bureau. . . . Our Employment Bureau is open every day except Saturday.

Elsewhere in the same issue there was a description of the eight levels of charity as set forth by Maimonides. The highest is obtaining a job for an unemployed person. The article was entitled simply, "Practical Judaism."

One can imagine what the situation must have been like if even a few months *before* the Great Depression suddenly set in, Rabbi Goldstein could write:

> We have hundreds of calls from earnest and sincere Jews and Jewesses who want to keep the Sabbath properly.

The situation did not require dramatic pleas, but it is difficult to conceive of more touching case histories brought to the public's attention through the bureau than the one of a young man who:

> . . . at an early age . . . was forced to leave school and . . . support my widowed mother and sister. . . . I solemnly promised my father, on his deathbed, that I would observe the Sabbath in the same way as when he was living. . . .

It was not enough for the I.S. to inspire such promises. It also had to help to provide the means for them to be kept.

---

*Once the bureau was established for a few years, the Fischel Family Foundation, which was dedicated to promoting Orthodox Jewish values, contributed $350 on one occasion. These funds presumably went toward the bureau's advertising and general office expenses. Senator Albert Wald, a Fischel son-in-law, was duly appointed chairman of the Propaganda Committee of the Bureau. Harry Fischel's own rags-to-riches success story—including a description of the almost inhuman sacrifices he had had to make to keep the Sabbath at the expense of otherwise available employment—was documented extensively in the Fischel biography that Rabbi Goldstein wrote, and Fischel's munificence in treating his *own* Sabbath observant employees was legendary.

Social Service League without the League!

We have seen what happened to the Social Service League after it dropped the word Service from its name. In contrast, the I.S., as a whole, also had a wide range of activities under the category of "Social Service," and these activities, which were run without a special "league" to carry them out, were mainstays of the synagogue, in conjunction with existing multi-purpose synagogue organizations and with the cooperation of individuals.

The functions of these activities were self-explanatory, though far from self-executing! The projects included big brother work, big sister work, Boy Scouts, clothes for poor [Hebrew School] children, first aid courses, Girl Scouts, helping released prisoners, homes for destitute children, poor people's clothing closets, reading for the blind, and visiting hospitals.*

To tie up any loose ends, Rabbi Goldstein had a charity fund from which he personally made disbursements using his own discretion.

---

*In connection with the last activity mentioned, an "adult glee club" was organized "to sing at all festivities of the synagogue and also to help bring cheer to the inmates of the hospitals, homes, and asylums of the city. In a large glee club there is room even for those whose voices do not rank with the voices of the Levites of old." Who knows, but perhaps if the glee club sounded bad enough, it may have encouraged some hospital inmates to recover and escape in time to miss the next "concert"!

Chapter 26

If The Mountain Won't Come To Mohammed...

In 1925, Rabbi Goldstein, as president of the Union of Orthodox Jewish Congregations of America (U.O.J.C.A.), expressed his outrage and then his constructive proposals in reaction to the then-existing treatment of young Jewish children whose families could not afford to send them to camps in the cool New York or New England mountains to escape, at least temporarily, the merciless city heat waves that withered bodies and spirits, particularly in those pre-air conditioner days. The seemingly well-intentioned *New York Herald Tribune* and many other agencies sent "fresh air children" up to the mountains under the care of gracious *Christian* families and well-organized camps. The objectionable part of these arrangements, of course, was that many of the beneficiaries were impressionable, poor *Jewish* children from the Lower East Side. Rabbi Goldstein supplied his own answers to the rhetorical question he posed:

> What lasting good are we accomplishing...when thousands...of poor Jewish children are sent to these non-Jewish...and anti-Jewish camps?...The poor parent in many instances salves his or her conscience by saying "It is for the health of my child." Now, fellow delegates, it is high time that this yearly religious breakdown be halted. I ask for two concrete remedies. First, that wherever possible, Orthodox Jews who are away for the summer, volunteer to take a poor child in their home for a two weeks' vacation. [He practiced what he preached.] Secondly, I ask for...camp sites near the large cities to take care of the poor Jewish children. Camp life in the summer under auspices that are Orthodox, will do more good even than any of our [Hebrew Schools] can accomplish

in the winter, because here we can have the children practice the Jewish religious life which we teach the rest of the year. Daily prayers, Sabbath observance, grace before and after meals, etc., will be realities to be practiced through the rest of the year, and not merely abstract doctrines.

President Goldstein's resolution was adopted, and, accordingly, before the following summer set in:

> The U.O.J.C.A. . . . established a fresh air fund [to] assure hundreds of poor children a vacation in the country . . . entirely and strictly under Jewish auspices, religious influence, and kosher dietary laws.
> [At] a meeting [with this topic on the agenda] . . . all members present pledged their full support and a sufficient immediate sum [was] donated to the cause [to insure] a positive start [in the] summer [of 1926].
> . . . The first group of children was sent to the Central Jewish Institute Camp. The children came from . . . Montefiore Social Service, Committee of the Care of the Jewish Tubercular . . . Beth Israel Social Service, and Stuyvesant Neighborhood House. . . .

The groundwork for this project had clearly been laid in the I.S. two years earlier, though on a smaller provisional scale. The synagogue newspaper reported, at that time:

> We have arranged for space at the C.J.I. strictly kosher camp. Supervision of boys and girls, ages 6 to 15, under direction of I.S. Councillors [sic] located at Port Jervis, heart of the Catskills. . . .

An estimated $15.00 in those days could send a youngster to camp for a two-week period. A special "Camp Counselors Course" was given at the I.S. to make sure that I.S. ideals would be effectively transmitted. Apparently, they were—a "Send an I.S. Junior to Camp Fund" was destined to continue into the early 1930s, when the I.S. was to take another dramatic, giant step still further.

The I.S. Home Camp

The concept of a "home camp" evolved out of the Great Depression of the 1930s, when an increasing number of parents found themselves unable to afford to provide their children with a summer vacation "in the country." Community Centers and "Ys" attempted to simulate a summer camp atmosphere in the middle of the cities. As with most summer camp atmospheres, however, they

242

were usually devoid of an authentic *Jewish* spirit.

Until 1933, the I.S. Hebrew School operated on a "year 'round" basis. As soon as Rabbi Philip Goodman, its new principal, arrived on the scene, however, he realized that "in August the classes were almost empty. Sixty out of the 225 students attended.* This was when I got the idea of a day camp." According to Rabbi Goodman, the I.S. Home Camp was the first such inner city day camp under Orthodox Jewish auspices. He recalled that it drew German immigrants from as far away as Washington Heights.**

The first affair for the exclusive benefit of the "Home Camp Scholarship Fund" was an I.S. dramatic presentation in November of 1933. Eventually, the camp acquired a name, Camp *Ta-a-noog*, a transliteration of the Hebrew equivalent of enjoyment, pleasure, and delight. The hyphens in the transliteration gave it a taste of the traditional Native American flavor of many camps that sought, in this period, to reflect a romantic outdoor image in which the original inhabitants of this continent used to be stereotyped. The exotic Native American culture, however, hardly went any further than the name of the camp. Beyond that point, the Native American trappings went the way of the wigwam.

The *Jewish Daily Bulletin* carried a feature on Camp Ta-a-noog the summer that it opened:

> . . . You'll find Camp Ta-a-noog. . . perched on the roof of the Institutional Synagogue. Don't look for tents. There aren't any.
>
> You'll also find the camp down in the pool. In the arts and crafts room. In the classrooms, studying Hebrew. Or in the large, cool auditorium singing songs. And if it's on Wednesday, the camp just won't be anywhere around the building, inside or topside. To catch up with it, you'll have to go to. . . Yankee Stadium, to the Museum of Natural History, to Coney Island. For on Wednesdays the Camp Ta-a-noog, as well as the other home camps throughout the city, strike their imaginary tents and go on the march.

The camp was not set up to take the place of the Hebrew School but rather to give it a vacation type of an identity. According to Rabbi Goodman:

---

*During this scorchingly hot month, of course, public schools, which these same students normally attended during the better part of the school day, were closed entirely.

**"Including Rabbi Breuer's daughters!" Rabbi Breuer was the leader of the generally close-knit and insular community of recently-arrived Orthodox Jews of most pronounced German extraction.

...[It] was organized primarily to broaden the scope of the [Hebrew School], and to provide a recreational program for the children of our neighborhood during the summer months, in the same spirit and ideology governing the religious school, expanded to meet the opportunities afforded us in having the child for forty hours per week. We consciously set out to condition the whole camp program with Jewish values and import wherever it would naturally fit in.

...So as not to lose the continuity of the work of the [Hebrew School], during one period of each day, the entire camp was divided into graded classes with the regular teaching staff in charge. The informal curriculum include[d] reading, writing, prayers, Bible, laws and customs, and current events. The laws and customs deal[t] mostly with the prayers and blessings used in the camp, such as, the blessings for food and the grace after meals. Appropriate games of Jewish content were introduced. . . . An effort was also made to replace camp terminology with its Hebrew equivalent and met with some success.* Treasure hunts in which the clues contained Hebrew words prove[d] to be very exciting. The texts of Palestinian and traditional songs, included in the camp songster, [were] explained. Weekly reports showing the progress of each child [were] prepared by the Hebrew teachers. . . .

Fascinating stories of Biblical and post-Biblical times, as well as Jewish legends, [made] up the greater part of the story hour. . . .[T]he children also [were] urged to read stories of Jewish interest and to narrate them. . .a comprehensive list of stories [was] compiled. [The students "would study a chapter in the Bible, and then dramatize it."]

The weekly publication of the camp was also utilized by the campers for writing articles on Jewish current events, Herzl Day, Tisha B'Ab,** etc. A portion of the paper [was] devoted to contributions written by the children in Hebrew.***

The Jewish motif was also introduced in the arts and crafts workshop through soap and wood carving, raffia weaving, and stippling. Some of the objects made during the past season [1935] were scrolls, the Tablets of the Ten Commandments, the Holy Ark, the *Magen David* [Star of David], and Hebrew letters

*The following year, this was described as "usually meeting with success."

**This is a holy day commemorating the destruction of both Jewish Temples in Jerusalem.

***The *Ta-a-noog Shofar*, a weekly publication containing news and gossip of the camp, was edited by the campers. One year "a 30 page Farewell Edition" was issued!

244

Tisha B'Ab [a fast day] [was] observed in accordance with tradition. The entire day's program [was] rearranged to conform with the fast. In the morning an assembly [was] held, for which a special service containing prayers in Hebrew and English [was organized].

Every Friday afternoon the campers themselves...[conducted] services in the synagogue. A regular feature of the services [was] the narration of a Sabbath story. [In fact, daily morning services were held for all campers who were "approaching the Bar Mitzvah age" and beyond. Although counselors attended too, they were officially present "to supervise." The services were conducted "solely by the campers."* Following the prayers, and undoubtedly as an added incentive to attend, breakfast was served.]

The success of the Jewish content program that [was] executed was due to the fact that it [was] not considered a special activity to be heralded by a fanfare of bugles, but, rather as a normal integrated part of the daily camp routine...Jewish living [was] not confined to the four walls of the classroom, but rather it [was] carefully portrayed as the pervading spirit of every action and thought of the Jew.

Creativity was not only encouraged among individuals, but in group projects as well. For example, in 1936:

As a result of an all-summer project, a miniature synagogue, complete in every detail, was constructed. Practically everybody in the camp had a hand in this endeavor.

Another season, a model miniature *succah* (religious "tabernacle") was constructed.

Possibly the most enchanting of all the imaginative ideas developed at the camp in these Depression days before the creation of the State of Israel and the jet plane was "an imaginary trip to Palestine" taken by one group of I.S. girls:

...A special room was set aside with pictures, maps, books and crafts materials, all selected in terms of conditioning the group with a curiosity about Palestine. As a result of discussion, and interest aroused by the counselor, the girls decided to make the journey. Local trips were taken to a travel agency, department stores, the Jewish Museum, the Zionist Organization, Hadassah Headquarters, and a steamship. Several people who lived in Palestine were invited to help

*A well-publicized photograph on one occasion even showed "[a] *minyan* [religious service] on the banks of the Hudson during an overnight hike."

conduct the tour. A diary of the preparations and the trip including souvenirs of the places visited, is a proud possession of the group. A special Palestinian program comprised of dances, drills, songs, and plays was presented for all the campers and their parents. Inspired by the work of Hadassah in the Holy Land, the group wrote and produced an original play on this theme. In connection with the visit to Tel Aviv, a miniature Maccabiah [sports competition] was held in which the entire camp participated.

The intra-camp "miniature Maccabiah" (Olympic-type competition) was considered miniature only because it was compared to international "Maccabiahs" held in what is now called Israel. Closer to home, on an intra-city scale, the I.S. did far more than follow a pattern. The very summer of its own miniature Maccabiah, we read that, by no coincidence:

> For the first time in the history of Home Camps, an Inter-Camp Maccabiah was held on August 5th, at Van Cortlandt Park. The idea of this project originated at the I.S., [which was] the most prominent in the entire proceedings.

The program included:

> a grand parade of participants, mass drills by each camp, and the Maccabiah invocation and pledge. Each camp [was to] present a pageant symbolic of the city in Palestine it [was to] represent. [The] Washington Heights "Y" [was to] present Haifa, the port of Immigration for persecuted Jews. [During this period, German Jews were escaping Hitler-dominated Germany and settling, in large numbers, in Washington Heights.] The Schiff Center [was to] portray Tel Aviv, the Levant Fair, representative of the industrial wealth and growth of Palestine. [Jacob Schiff was famous for his own industry and wealth.] The Institutional Synagogue [was to] present Jerusalem, the city of learning. [This choice likewise appears not to have been a coincidence, and speaks loudly on behalf of the priorities of I.S. decision makers.]
> Following the pageant, a comprehensive program of track and field events [was to] be conducted, in the same manner as the [regular Israeli] Maccabiah games [were] held.

So comprehensive was the camp's program, in general, that a "camp alphabet" was published to dramatize its diversity!

Athletics	Motion pictures
Breakfast	Nature study
Crafts	Overnight hikes
Daily morning services	Physical examinations
Entertainments	Quiet games
Friday night services	Rest period
Group singing	Swimming
Hebrew classes	Theatricals
Inter-camp activities	Unusual projects
Journalism	Visits to historic places
Kindergartening	Weekly outings
Luncheon	

The medical attention given to each camper and the general hygienic atmosphere that was promoted were more than token gestures to the campers in these Depression years in a decaying neighborhood. This aspect of the camp went far beyond the thorough physical examinations administered to each camper, before the season began, by the "camp physician," who at one time was the familiar "Maimonides of the I.S.," Dr. Zadok Kapner.

> Health teaching [was] integrated in the program as an incidental rather than as direct subject matter. Aspects of health and hygiene [were] brought out in actual practices. . . . A very effective opportunity for health teaching, as well as health building, [was] the midday lunch, which the children often help[ed] to plan, buy, prepare, and serve ["under the supervision of an experienced dietician"].
> This meal [became] a real experience in social living. The children [sat] in small groups at attractively set tables. Group table service and its amenities of consideration and courtesy, wholesome attitudes toward food and eating. . .[were] educational by-products. . .The service of afternoon milk [and crackers] constitute[d] another pleasant, relaxing interlude in the day's activity, combining health with social routine.

Rabbi Goodman recalled that the camp ran for nine seasons, with from about 100 to 170 children. The camp "charged $12.00 for eight weeks, and we didn't have 10 people paying the full price!" In addition to drawing on fund raising aid from within the synagogue, the camp also received direct assistance from at least seventeen food concerns ranging from the Great Atlantic and Pacific Tea Company (the A & P) to Horowitz Bros. & Margareten.

Most important, the morale was high. At the farewell banquet marking the successful conclusion of the camp's third season, no fewer than forty-two campers were presented with awards for outstanding achievements. Earlier, at the first camp reunion—

which was held a little more than a month after the conclusion of the first camp season—practically all of the campers attended, leading to the following positive course of action:

> A plan for the continuation of camp activities throughout the entire year and the formation of a Club Ta-a-noog was advanced and eagerly accepted. The various *"shevatim"* or "tribes" will hold their organization meeting within the very near future and will begin their activities.

Perhaps the greatest tribute to the success of the camp was paid not by the polished I.S. public relations machine, but rather by our earlier acquaintance, Laurel Rosenbaum, at age ten, who wrote, in an essay on "What the I.S. Means":

> ...The camp is the good time in the summer. I'd rather go to this camp than to the country. That's what the I.S. means to me.

Chapter 27

The Multi-dimensional Young People's Programs

No matter how advanced the I.S. Hebrew School may have been, and no matter how palatable to "modern American youth" the main synagogue prayer services may have seemed, the I.S. could never have made the impact that it did in an American scene dominated by constant Whys, majestic "Y's," and Rabbi Stephen Wise, had it not been for the ability of the I.S. to hold its own with the best of them as far as its social and recreational program was concerned. On this universally respected platform, the I.S. was able to introduce educational and religious planks with greater intensity than the less religiously-oriented superstructures against which it was invariably contrasted.

The Social Department's beginnings necessarily had to be humble, since all it had to work with in the original I.S. building was a social room and five meeting rooms. "Inter-club activities" were run, at first, under the supervision of a "Senior Club Council." A year after the synagogue moved into the large renovated building that was to be its permanent home, however, "the clubs increased to the extent that it was necessary to engage a director solely for senior club activities."*

...In that year the I.S.'s [first] much heralded one-week Boys and Girls Weeks Campaign was held. During that time the message of the Institutional Synagogue, by means of moving pictures, dramatics, and every other available advertising medium, was spread throughout the vicinity. In the following year, educational classes were introduced and the

---

*The new I.S. "social director" was a former "assistant superintendent of the Y.M.H.A., at 92nd Street."

department assumed a regular place in the Building activities under the new name of Social and Educational Department.

The social and educational director, who had been appointed in 1924, was succeeded three years later by a person who was required to take on the additional responsibility of editing the synagogue newspaper. Continuing the trend toward increased responsibilities, the director in 1930 found his department extended in scope "to include social welfare and communal activities." In 1933, Rabbi Philip Goodman became the *de facto rabbi*—by this time, Rabbi Goldstein's base of operations had shifted almost entirely to the West Side branch. Simultaneously, this same Rabbi Goodman was saddled with the roles of the editor of the newspaper, Hebrew School principal, *and* director of the "Department of Center Activities"!

The titles of the members of the staff of the "Social-Educational Department" in a single non-peak year give a good indication of the department's scope. In addition to the synagogue's executive director and the head of the department, otherwise sometimes known as the "headworker," the staff included an assistant headworker, a registrar, a medical examiner, two religious directors, a boys worker, a girls worker, a director of girls athletics,* two librarians, and three junior workers, in addition to personnel specifically assigned to boys' problems,** a music department,*** domestic science, advertising, journalism, literary projects, and dramatics. Three scoutmasters and numerous club leaders rounded out the staff. Many of these leaders were looked up to for their accomplishments outside of the synagogue as well as those they accumulated within the building's decorated walls. One year, the staff was comprised of:

a number of I.S workers otherwise engaged in the practice of Law, Medicine, Social work, Journalism, Accounting, Teaching, Marketing, and other professional and commercial enterprises.

The field of law was considered particularly desirable in this period, which made the composition of the staff all the more

*The boys' athletics "directorship" was a responsibility of one or more of the other members of the staff.

**No comparable problems were anticipated that year, apparently, from the incomparable I.S. girls.

***In which the exciting and popular Cantor Yavneh was a rather reluctant pedagogue, and fortunately had a more pedagogically inclined woman counterpart whose exclusive responsibilities were within the music department.

250

impressive. In a single issue of the synagogue newspaper, a social column mentioned the names of three staff members who had just opened offices for the practice of law, and a columnist in an issue a month earlier had already remarked that "The staff is soon going to resemble a branch of the Bar Association."

The accomplished, cooperative, and highly motivated staff sought "to add what polish it possibly [could] in the way of lasting veneer for those boys and girls who [did] not secure the maximum of right home training."

Dramatic Rise of a Drama Department

The drama department was not in the exclusive domain of the synagogue clubs or of the Hebrew School for the simple reason that *each* of these organs of the synagogue had its *own independent* drama department. Generally "never did the twain meet," but even when they finally did, in 1931, they did not merge, although they *did* perform in front of the same audience, one after the other. The cast of the Hebrew School's production alone was comprised of seventy-five members. Such was the single-minded dedication of some staff members that one theatrical director became so involved in sets and costumes, as well as a play itself, that she actually deferred her annual vacation from her regular job, "which comes about Chanukah," for a synagogue production. Even the *New York Times* was enthused enough with the advance reviews of at least one production to send a photographer.

One-act plays became so popular that, one year, no fewer than nine clubs competed independently in an intra-synagogue "one-act play contest." For three consecutive Sunday evenings, three teams competed, and on the fourth, the three victors vied for the title in a "playoff." The I.S. Thespians did not stop there, however. On at least two occasions, they won the Manhattan-wide tournament conducted by the Metropolitan League of Jewish Community Centers.

When the Depression set in, the I.S. let some professionals perform on its stage in cooperation with the Federal Theatre Project of the Works Progress Administration. One of their weekly presentations—Jacob Gordin's *The Jewish King Lear*—was actually produced "under the personal direction of the world-famous Boris Thomashefsky."*

---

*Years later, a prominent New York City rabbi recalled that, when he had been a seminary student, unable to afford commercial entertainment, he had escorted to the I.S. the girl who later became his wife. The rabbinical student had taken her to the building not in order to attend the synagogue's prayer services but rather for its Federal Theatre Project presentations.

Operettas Opening at the I.S.

I.S. operettas apparently tolerated no "imported" performers, although, to their credit, at least some of the operettas were conducted under the supervision of people with actual experience in Broadway theatres. I.S. members even formed their own "operatic guild." Objective reviews of their productions are not available, but the fact that their promotional *previews* were preserved is quite understandable....

...[T]he rehearsals of the 'H.M.S. Pinafore' are sailing over calm waters. The sailors and officers of the cast are faithfully performing their duties to insure the arrival of the ship into the port of success.

The fair Captain...is standing at the helm of the ship guiding its destiny. Her knowledge of musical compasses is standing her in good stead in avoiding the dangerous reefs and other nautical terrors that abound in the dangerous waters of light operetta production.

...The dock will undoubtedly be filled to capacity, so secure your visitors' pass to the ship in advance.

There was nothing hasty or slipshod about it. Not until two months later was:

[t]he "H.M.S. Pinafore"...sighted making its way into the friendly shores of Island Institutional.

Music in the Synagogue Leads to Harmony
or
Musical Chords and Social Accord

Included in the first general I.S. checklist of activities—circulated even before the synagogue's first building was to be occupied—was a single purely musical activity, one that could appeal to the broadest base of people, and that would not only service individuals but would, as a practical matter, benefit the synagogue as well. It did not focus on any specific instrument or promote rare virtuosity. It was an orchestra. A year and a half after the first orchestra had been proposed, an "orchestra of children" was formed, and a half a year later, the I.S. orchestra was polished enough to play as a unit at local and national events!

The benefits that *individuals* could derive from I.S. musical programs were even greater. For a couple of seasons, at least, the I.S. offered "free...individual instruction in piano and vocal studies." In addition to these studies, the I.S. also offered violin lessons, "choral work, voice training, and music appreciation," all free of charge under the direction of a Concert Master of the Symphony Orchestra of the Educational Alliance and of a prominent graduate of the Vienna Conservatory of Music. Instruction was also offered, some years, in various string and bass instruments, and, at times, every single class offered by the music department was free of charge, at both the main and the West Side branches.

The training was not without visible—and audible—results. Members representing the I.S. won intra-city awards as violin and piano soloists. I.S. virtuosos did not hold themselves above joining musically together either, presenting annual concerts featuring classical, old English, and operatic music. One of the concerts had what was billed as "the only choir of Colored Jews in the City of New York."

A Time to Beat And a Time to Meet

We have already seen the widespread attitude that existed, even among many people who otherwise considered themselves Orthodox, on the issue of permitting social dancing among men and women not married to each other. A permissive attitude prevailed even in branches of the two largest Orthodox national synagogue-based organizations, the Union of Orthodox Jewish Congregations of America (U.O.J.C.A.) and the Young Israel. In fact, even the Orthodox Rabbinical Council of America, in a full-fledged meeting, responded in 1939 "to the question whether or not Jewish organizations are permitted to arrange for functions at which dancing of boys and girls takes place" by referring this straightforward question to a committee. The U.O.J.C.A. actually considered itself *victorious* when it convinced public high school officials to switch dance events away from the holy Sabbath eve to other evenings of the week, presumably so Jewish students could attend (or, in the case of the I.S., to win an opportunity to introduce the young people to alternative Friday evening programs geared for their participation).

The policy permitting "mixed dancing," which has long since been discountenanced by contemporary "modern Orthodox" leaders, obviously existed long before Rabbi Goldstein took a public stand on the issue. Although he personally repudiated it, it was too firmly imbedded in too many otherwise Orthodox people (particularly in Manhattan, the center of New York City and of the city's Jewish community as a whole when he was in his prime) for him to try to ban it, and he certainly could not reasonably have been expected to *eliminate* it from the social life of the irreligious people he was trying to bring closer to religion.* What Rabbi Goldstein *could* and *did* do, however, was to make sure that the dances did not turn into ends in themselves, but were limited to being *means* to keep the participants involved in the other synagogue activities, and, ideally, to draw them to multi-faceted events which themselves had unequivocably redeeming educational or religious components, as did so many of the events described in these chapters. Actually, in this period of widespread assimilation and intermarriage, Mrs. Goldstein once remarked that it was an achievement in itself just "to keep Jewish boys dancing with Jewish girls" as a first step back toward their heritage.**

The first regularly scheduled dance in the original I.S. building was run over a year after the first service, and the first dance in the permanent I.S. building was run more than half a year after the first service, so the priorities discussed earlier were consistently followed. In addition to the synagogue programs associated with and popularized by the dances, these social functions also served to raise funds for and attract members to the synagogue. Some of the dances drew such large turnouts that it became "nigh impossible for those who desired to practice the terpsichorean art to do so, until late in the evening." This, of course, was a blessing only partly in disguise!

---

*The migration from Eastern Europe to the United States in the wake of World War II was destined to change this climate.

**Incidentally, although some non-Jews were permitted to use some of the synagogue's facilities, it was tacitly understood that they were not to participate in I.S. dances.

Chapter 28

67 Clubs At One Time

In terms of sheer magnitude and variety, the club program at the I.S. stood head and shoulders above virtually all its other regular activities. The ground rules were simple:

> Any fifteen members of the Building in good standing may apply for the privilege of using a room for meeting purposes, provided this organization conforms to the regulations of the Department and submits an approved Constitution. These clubs will be permitted to meet at least once a week and are entitled to admission to the respective Council in whose membership lists they are classified, either Juniors, Intermediates, or Seniors.

"In 1917," the year the I.S. was founded, "with a social room and five meeting rooms to work with," the institution had a proud record of about ten clubs meeting in the building. Less than a year after the I.S. was founded—and only about a quarter of a year after the first I.S. building was occupied—Congressman Siegel was able to announce, at the very first annual I.S. membership meeting that, as of January, 1918, thirty clubs were already in existence, and "many clubs were waiting admission, by reason of lack of room." The pioneering spirit was continued in the much larger quarters that the I.S. later occupied, even before the renovation was completed in the early 1920s. "When the clubs originally began to meet in the new building, the rooms did not contain concrete flooring. Doorways were mere holes in the wall." By 1927, as the synagogue celebrated its tenth anniversary, the synagogue newspaper claimed that the synagogue's Social and Educational Department had 63 clubs including 945 boys and girls—the calculation appears to have been based on an *average* of fifteen active members per club. The *American Hebrew* at least once credited the synagogue with "67 literary, athletic, and social clubs."

The tone for the I.S. clubs was set by the Maccabees, a network of clubs named after the Jewish patriots who became the heroes of the holiday of Chanukah. The network, originally formed by "the juniors" in 1918, "at one time had 22 branches meeting in the Building." Jacob Marrus recalled how he had founded these groups:

> I was asked by Rabbi Goldstein to lead some clubs. It started off with my leading a *minyan* [prayer service] for youngsters. I spoke on occasion. I had some boys preach. I made some youngsters club leaders. Every leader served without pay, including me. The leaders generally ranged in age from about 16 to 27, and the club members from 8 to 16.*

The Maccabee branches were patterned "on similar lines with the A.N.I. [clubs]** of the Harlem Hebrew Institute."*** In fact, they had so much in common that at least two A.N.I. branches actually met in the I.S. as well. Each of the Maccabee chapters "was primarily interested in fostering religious spirit," which manifested itself in "religious activity, religious thought, Zionist thought, etc.," as well as in a quarterly magazine.**** The A.N.I. branches took their individual chapter names from Arabic numerals, so the Maccabees chose to take their names from letters of the alphabet.

Louis Simon, one of the leading Maccabees, recalled a curious incident where the name of the organization served a unique function:

> The I.S. wanted to schedule a field day at Macombs Dam Park. The I.S. wrote to the Parks Department in the Bronx for a permit for a certain Sunday. They received a negative reply. So [suspecting anti-Semitism may have been a factor] someone got the idea for the Maccabees to write again for that permit. It

---

*He added: "My wife was a leader of one of the senior clubs...My wife, incidentally, was 15½ when she became a leader."

**This stood for Agudath Naarei Israel, which translates, loosely, into the United Groups of Young Jewish boys.

***Otherwise known as the Uptown Talmud Torah.

****Their activities also included athletics.

was granted. They thought we were Irish! [from the "prefix" Mac!]

Possibly the most lasting monument of the Maccabees stemmed from founder Jacob Marrus' feelings toward Israel. "I was interested in Zionism," he recalled, "so I affiliated the Mizrachi Hatzoir [literally, "young Mizrachi"]* . . . It [the "young Mizrachi"] was born through the sons and daughters of the Maccabees." Marrus, of course, didn't quite do it alone. "A few groups from different parts of the city came together to form the Mizrachi Hatzoir." But at or about the year 1925, "the first so-called convention. . .was at the Institutional Synagogue."

After Gentle Pushes, Leaders Led, As I.S. Ideals and They Were Wed

The snowballing increase in the number of clubs created a corresponding need for additional club leaders. By 1924, fifty-two leaders led clubs on a voluntary basis!** During its peak years, the I.S. openly recruited club leaders from its adult membership, even for "one night a week." A typical appeal went something like this:

> No one of us. . .has the right to criticize the youth of today, unless we have done at least one outstanding bit of good. Let. . .us. . .ask ourselves, "What have I done. . .to help the coming generation realize its responsibilities to the future generations?"

A typical response:

> For the past week, Mr. Philip Simpson of the electrical firm of that name, who has been a good friend to the I.S. and a prominent member of this community, has answered our call for club leaders.
> He is now planning an excellent program of activity on behalf of the Orioles, a Juniors boys club. . . .

The dynamism and resourcefulness of the club department one of the years it had over sixty clubs was illustrated by this report

---

*The Mizrachi movement itself later acquired its greatest influence through its Israeli branch that is now known as the National Religious Party.

**This high level of selfless devotion was not to be taken for granted. After two conferences, in this pivotal year, and "a great deal of discussion, the leaders decided, of their own accord, that they did not wish to be compensated for their work and asked that they still be classified as voluntary workers." The fact that nine club leaders were listed on the staff in 1930, when dozens of clubs still existed, may imply that at times some leaders were financially compensated, nevertheless.

excerpt:

> ...April usually is the month when the decreases start and we find that the remarkable registration of *twelve new clubs* appears on the record. So many new Junior clubs came into the building that we had to draft Intermediates to act as club leaders....

A special title of "leader-in-training" was devised for these situations. Like so many other features of the I.S., club leadership training became not only an end in itself but an exciting social pastime as well. One phase of the ever regenerating "Leaders Council" was traced in the following lines:

> In the early part of the 1932 season a group of young people, interested in community center work, were gathered together for a *Sukkot* [holiday] celebration. From that meeting there emerged an organization that was destined to become one of the most active groups in the history of the I.S.
>
> In the beginning, only members of the staff of the Department of Centre Activities, former members, and club leaders were admitted to membership. With the passage of time, it became evident that there were many young people who were interested in the work carried on by this group who did not fall in either of these categories. It was decided, therefore, to admit these young people to membership...their main project was securing funds for the organization and maintenance of the first season of the Home Camp....Practically every meeting during that season was devoted in part to learning something about the camp they were sponsoring. Lectures were delivered by outstanding members of the Jewish Welfare Board and other authorities in this field.
>
> The second year...the Leaders' Council widened the scope of its activities. It...undertook a program of lectures, discussions, debates, forums....social activities....[P]roblems that face[d] the individual club-leader [were] brought up for group discussion and remedies were suggested....

The I.S. also did not miss the opportunity of pointing out what the leaders *themselves* could derive out of I.S. work professionally, in addition to personal satisfaction and an uplifted feeling:

> ...Some of the I.S. club members, using I.S. training...as a background, are employed as Social Entertainers, positions carrying substantial salaries.

Probably the most effective method of generating enthusiasm

was by example. At one time or another, both Rabbi Goldstein and Congressman Siegel led clubs themselves. The Goldsteins had also hosted early meetings of club leaders in their own residence. Rabbi Goldstein's personal involvement with the clubs, however, added up to more than token gestures. One club member later recalled that the rabbi "visited every club periodically—*every* club in the building from top to bottom. He always had a coterie of people around him. I remember when he saw me acting and said, 'very nice, Irene.'* He took a personal interest in all of us." An official who had been in charge of the building activities recalled:

> I would make the rounds with him. . .about once or twice a week, maybe with a director, too. He would come into a meeting and make some remark, or tell a story, or a joke. No speeches. He left them alone. He showed an interest. He would observe. . . .

He would also *participate*. The original I.S. building had:

> . . .a game room, where Rabbi Goldstein could be found most evenings [although many times only for limited appearances] playing chess or checkers with the young people, thus drawing them closer to him and to the synagogue.

This relationship was not forced. He thoroughly enjoyed playing checkers, and used to delight in playing against two or three people at a time! Notice that he did not try to extend his role as a teacher to disciplines outside of a Jewish framework.**

Not Content Without Jewish Content

The Goldsteins were quick to find out that their own ideal conception of what a synagogue club should be did not, at first, by any means, jibe with the conception of the available club *leaders*, let alone club *members*. The synagogue was only a few months old when Mrs. Goldstein observed, from a vantage point on a committee organized "to draw up a set of programs for junior and senior clubs," that:

---

*There may not have been anything memorable about the comment other than the fact that his having made it could evoke such a vivid recollection so many decades later.

**On a single occasion when he *did*, it was with regard to checkers, and only in answer to a specific request. On a ship bound for Israel, he was part of a "captive audience" when, according to a letter written by his wife to his children:

> . . .Dad, at the request of Mrs. M.— [a member of his synagogue], gave Mr. M— a lesson in checker playing. Dad is the recognized champion checker player on the boat.

Our great difficulty lies in the fact that we are trying to inculcate something Jewish into every club and most of them are so constituted that things Jewish do not appeal to them. I believe, however, that time and careful attention will solve our problem.

The necessary time and attention were invested, and the anticipated interest was eventually returned.

When the I.S. Department of Center Activities issued a pamphlet on "The Club Meeting" to illustrate "the procedure of conducting a business meeting," the only article within the publication to be singled out by the synagogue newspaper for specific mention was the one entitled "Jewish Content in the Club Program." We will soon see the very real and pervasive presence of this influence on a far more steady basis than celebrations "in every club" that commemorated every major Jewish holiday.

The commitment to "inculcate" Jewish content into the clubs was no idle or merely theoretical ideal to be relegated to the recesses of the brain of the synagogue's mastermind. To the contrary, the I.S. decided *not* to rely on only the rabbi and his wife or the social director for direct religious influence on the clubs, but it engaged a religious director whose exclusive responsibility was described, at the time:

> to induct a Jewish program into the work of all the Clubs in the building. He will hold Jewish Festival parties and by the medium of slides and moving pictures, explain the significance of various holidays. He will organize the Friday Evening Home Night at which time the members will give up their evening to the discussion of things Jewish, of singing Hebrew melodies and to listening to interesting sermons. He will organize Hebrew study circles for those of our members who are interested in taking up Hebrew studies and haven't very much time otherwise at their disposal. He will permeate the ideals of a Jewish culture through a medium of our various other activities.

In time, the religious director had his own staff, and the "Religious staff" (with a capital "R") had its own committee!

Some of the clubs adopted Jewish or Hebrew names,* but most of the clubs expressed Jewish identity in their *actions* rather than their *names*.

One of the peak years in club membership, 1926, was *at the same time* one of the peak years in terms of Jewish content in club activities. In this year, for example, "all of the clubs" were

---

*E.g., *Jeshurun*, Jewish Stars, and *Shomrim*.

"required to open their meetings by reading a portion of the Bible, which was outlined in advance." The synagogue newspaper published the specific weekly selections.

But if 1926 was *a* peak year, 1927 was probably *the* year in which the synagogue had both more clubs and more Jewish content *in* the clubs than it had at any other point in its history. A *sample* month's schedule—not a *special* month dedicated to Jewish programs but a *typical* month—in the *middle* of the 1926-1927 season, divided the clubs of one division into groups that incorporated into their club meetings the following programs:

X GROUP

1st Week

Jewish Education and Culture—discussion of weekly current events of present importance in the Jewish world. Content from *Jewish Tribune, American Hebrew, Jewish Daily Tribune*, etc. Papers to be prepared by club members. Club discussions.

2nd Week

Dramatic Expression—for Juniors and Intermediates—interpreting short plays—Readings.

3rd Week

Jewish History—play is made on reiterating stories of Jewish heroes, both men and women, as the case may be—by Religious Director.

4th Week

Camp Fire Circle for Juniors and Intermediates.
a. —songs, American and Hebrew.
b. —story telling.
c. —nature discussion.

Last Week

The Holy Bible—Talks by Religious Director in historical sequence showing the purpose and merits of the various Books.

Y GROUP

1st Week

[same as above]

2nd Week

Hat Talks—Purpose [—or, rather, the format] of these talks is to submit slips in a hat asking questions concerning present interesting discussion of the week, each member speaking extemporaneously: all participate.

3rd Week

[same as "Last Week" above]

4th Week

Intra-Club debates—Monthly—Discussing current topics— one boy or girl on each side and then general discussion.

Last Week

[same as 3rd Week above]

Other variations included declamation contests, poetry programs (including readings and discussion), discussions of Jewish holidays, readings of one-act plays (plus discussion), and Bible story contests "to act as a climax for the Bible discussions carried on in the various clubs during the season."

Rabbi Goldstein personally launched a "Judaica discussion group" characterized by "informal discussion," geared to the older members of the young people's clubs.

Religion a Part of Their Lives

The I.S. never claimed that it had persuaded all of its club members to participate in group prayer services three times a day but it *did* claim to create general positive attitudes toward religion to the point where frequently, of their own volition, club members would interrupt their meetings so that unannounced visitors:

> would see a group of youths [praying] *Maariv* [the evening prayer service], or perhaps *Mincha* [the afternoon prayer service] (depending on the time of day), with an earnestness

and sincerity that is surprising. Most of the boys [women are privileged, in Jewish law, not to be obligated to interrupt their top priority activities in order to participate in group services] frankly admit that it has been many years since they last held a [prayer book] in their hands. Some can recall Bar Mitzvah as the eventful occasion. The parents of the young men have reported some instances where praying has become a part of the life of the boys.

After Prayer, a Message

After the prayers, punctuated with group chanting at appropriate places, the boys usually listen to a short message, not more than four or five minutes in duration, from Rabbi Goldstein, Mr. Hauer, or Mr. Shapiro. Thus inspired, the business meeting continues, and, curiously, with much more being accomplished.

Some clubs even ran their own services on Saturday afternoons. After-dinner prayers may be recited quietly or, ideally, in unison with certain passages sung together. When the clubs participated in a joint banquet:

Rabbi Goldstein officiated at both the grace before and after meals, and it was with a gusto that the clubs sang the melodies.

One of the clubs was motivated to amend its constitution, formally:

regarding the question of admitting members. The new amendment state[d] that all new members must wear *Tzitzit* [religious apparel] and [pray] every morning.

Zionism Even Before It Was Fashionable

Solidarity rallies in support of the right of Jews to settle in the Promised Land of what is now Israel existed long *before* the *state* of Israel came into being. As early as 1919, the I.S. Orchestra played under the auspices of the Zion Advancement League of the I.S. at a "Monster [meaning, "large"] Zionist Mass Meeting" which Rabbi Goldstein addressed.

We have already seen the strong role Zionist thought played in the Maccabees whose name did not even reflect Zionism per se. The influence of Zionism was apparent in the very names of other clubs, such as the one named after the founder of "modern Zionism," [Theodore] Herzl, the Palestine Travel Club, the Girls of Blue and White (now the colors of the Israeli Flag), the Star of Zion Club, the Young Lovers of Zion, and the Zionist Advancement Club, otherwise known as the Zionist Advancement League.* Some equally sincere clubs, of course, did without a Zionist name and without dramatic events, but nevertheless somehow managed to spend their time together in such mundane but useful—and no less unselfishly Zionistic—occupations as "sewing caps for Palestinian children."

The orientation of the I.S. Zionists was to "religious Zionism," as opposed to "secular Zionism." Religious Zionism stands for the totality of a full and distinctively Jewish way of life in the land of Israel whereas secular Zionism, promoted by many nonreligious Jews, stands for what many people consider to be the shallow existence of nationalists for the sake of purposeless empty nationalism, and the right to be left alone rather than to participate in a historic divine mission. To most Jewish American Yankees, religious Zionism is personified by the Religious Zionists of America, otherwise known as the Mizrachi, whose youth group's roots were traced, earlier, to the I.S. Maccabees.**

Club Trivia

At one time or another, within the score of years that Rabbi Goldstein was affiliated with the I.S. in Harlem, no fewer than 245 names of clubs appeared on the synagogue's roster. (If one were to take into account the Maccabee Clubs individually, the Boy Scout troops, and other clubs with identical generic names, the total would reach 272.) Dues were fixed according to age levels. For example, in 1924, seniors over twenty-one paid $5; intermediates, $3; and juniors, $2, entitling them "to participate in all activities exclusive of the gymnasium and pool, [Dues] also include[d] the receipt of the *Institutional* [synagogue newspaper] once a week."

If the clubs that chose Jewish names stressed Jewish activities and those that chose Zionist names stressed Zionist activities, one might be tempted to assume that those clubs that selected Greek letters to symbolize their identities, as college fraternities did, abandoned the Jewish culture in favor of the Hellenic. Both the basic assumption and therefore the logical deduction based on it would be inaccurate. *All* of the clubs had Jewish features, and many of the Greek letter clubs were no more fanatical about the

---

*This last organization was organized "by a handful of enthusiastic Zionists" and quickly attracted a membership of forty. Probably its most dramatic meeting was the one "at which [the league] presented the I.S. with a big woolen Zionist flag and Meyer Berlin [charismatic leader of the Mizrachi] spoke on the Carlsbad Zionist convention."

**Rabbi Goldstein's roles in both the Mizrachi and the rival Agudath Israel will be discussed later.

Greek culture than the *original Maccabees* two millenia earlier had been, when they had become martyrs fighting against that culture which had been tyranically thrust *upon* them! It is true that some I.S. clubs had names as tongue twisting as *delta iota rho, omega alpha phi,* and *phi alpha sigma,* but an I.S. club like the *Epsilon Omega Sigma* club was so demonstrably Jewish that it was not content with keeping its own religious zeal to itself, but chose to use its platform at one of the Friday evening forums to "stress the importance at this time of 'Teaching Jewish Education More Extensively.'" Clubs like the *alpha* and *gamma sigma pi* regularly entertained children of the Hebrew Orphan Asylum and showered them with gifts and treats that could be appreciated in *any* language!

It would take a book in itself to document all the activities of all of the clubs, so the balance of this chapter will just highlight some of the unusual features of the nineteen clubs (in alphabetical order) that had particularly out-of-the-ordinary characteristics:

AGUDATH NAAREI ISRAEL CLUBS (literally, the United Group of Young Jewish Boys). The clubs bearing this name were among the *only* clubs that operated at the I.S. while simultaneously owing partial allegiance to a different institution, the Harlem Hebrew Institute. Mac Shenken, the president of the "A.N.I."—as the movement was popularly known—sounded the harmonious tone of cooperation that was to exist between the A.N.I. and the I.S. by sending a letter containing more than just words to the head of the Social and Educational Department of the I.S., who promptly arranged for it to be published in the synagogue newspaper for all to see. Its most striking feature, in light of the fact that it came from a competitor of a sort, follows:*

> Enclosed you will find a small contribution, which we hope you can use for the furtherance of the A.N.I. policy in your institution.

At least two chapters of the A.N.I.—numbers 18 and 24—were based at the I.S., at one time or another. The first was "initiated... largely by means of Saturday afternoon [prayer] services" which were supplemented by "regular discussion groups, community singing, and an occasional [festive Sabbath afternoon meal]."

It is not clear whether the cause was restlessness, faithlessness

---

*The preceding paragraphs of the letter stated:

It is indeed with great pleasure that we hear of the kind cooperation extended by you and your staff to the A.N.I. group recently organized at your institution.

The A.N.I. has for its purpose the fostering of Jewish ideals, and the encouragement of Jewish youth to live according to Orthodox principles.

to its roots, or idealism, but the apparently peripatetic A.N.I. branch #24 was the only I.S. club to react to the munificence of the synagogue's number one benefactress by renaming itself in her memory—becoming, in 1932, the Hennings social, religious, and athletic club.

ALI CLUB. This was "the honor organization of the building." The club's members, who were elected "on the basis of character and service," assumed the responsibility of helping, at one point, to "take charge of nearly all the social functions of the building." They did *not*, of course, do all of this alone.

ARAGON CLUB. "In the summer, [this] club [arranged] many excursions into the country and usually [rented] a bungalow at some seashore."

BENNY LEONARD CLUB. Before focusing on Benny Leonard's personal role as an unpaid morale booster within the synagogue and as an active participant in the club that was named after him, we will take note of an excerpt from the most unusual biographical sketch of this undefeated lightweight champion of the world, as published in the *Universal Jewish Encyclopedia:*

> He reached the peak of accomplishment in 1923, when he successfully defended his title... in the most widely publicized and best attended match in the history of lightweight prize fighting. The following year Leonard retired... because his mother, an Orthodox Jewess, did not like him to fight. His love of family and his clean living did much to rehabilitate the good name of the pugilistic profession....
>
> Leonard was considered by many experts the greatest Jewish athlete of all time. According to Arthur Brisbane, he did more than any books or lectures in combatting anti-Semitism by the strength of his example....

Matter of factly, the I.S. newspaper mentioned, one week in 1926, that "The popular fighter came to the building with his brother, Joey Leonard, who is an officer in the Benny Leonard Club." Without any ceremony, "He got into a regular gym outfit and had a workout with the club's basketball team." His affiliation with the I.S. was no one-time publicity stunt. The very next week, the I.S. newspaper reported:

> ...[H]e appeared twice again in gym togs on our gym floor last week. To the edification and amusement of our members, he boxed a few rounds with our better athletes. The varying cries of "Come on, Benny, please knock him out" kind of discouraged these enthusiastic sparring partners, however....

Mr. Leonard's chief purpose in coming to our building is to popularize this dean of clean sports amongst the youth of Harlem....Personally, he would like to see more of our Jewish boys interest themselves in athletics as a whole....We shall...anticipate his regular attendance here hereafter on Tuesday and Thursday evenings and on Sunday mornings.

A great deal of his athletic training is done with the Benny Leonard Club. [The training there was "for real." He returned to the ring as a welterweight a few years later.]

"He usually [wound] up the evening with a few rounds of boxing with the members of the...club," and even played basketball on its team in at least one I.S. inter-club competition.

Most appropriately, this model American Jewish sportsman personally presented all the athletic awards at an I.S. "award night" one year, sending "the crowd...wild with delight when the guest of the evening was introduced—not to fight but to speak."

BOY SCOUTS. Their role in the I.S. went back to the very first rally organized by Rabbi Goldstein, even before he left his prior position: "Two companies of boy scouts were stationed in the assembly room to aid in seating the people." At one time or another, the Boy Scouts of America were represented at the I.S. by no fewer than *seven* troops.

The last of these troops formally received its charter at a ceremony marked by the participation of the district marshal, a representative of the headquarters of the Boy Scouts of America and of the Jewish Advisory Committee on Scouting. Rabbi Goldstein, instead of dwelling principally on a Biblical reference, chose at that time to "express the hope that the troop would live up to Scout Law No. 12, namely, a Scout is reverent to God and faithful in his religious beliefs."

CRESCENT CLUB. This club created such a strong feeling of identity that when one of its former presidents moved to San Francisco, the club back in New York was enabled not merely to inform the I.S. of the East Coast's loss, but to "startle" the newspaper's staff "with the announcement that a branch of their organization" was to "be opened in San Francisco, Cal."

FRACARA CLUB. This club was able to organize an entire orchestra without having to recruit a single person from outside its own membership.

GIRL SCOUTS. There may not have been quite as many girl scout troops—only two—as boy scout troops organized in the I.S., but the girls may have compensated in quality for what they may have lacked in quantity. Not only did they occasionally focus *all* their attention on a Jewish holiday-connected program, but "Through all their activities the Jewish motif predominate[d]."

In Brownie Pack #14, consisting of eight-year-old relative "toddlers," the girl scouts apparently began their character building training at an earlier age than the I.S. boys, who did not formally organize a corresponding "pack" of "cub scouts."

JESTER CLUB. "In spite of the facetious implication of their name," the members of this group were described as "very serious," the only Harlem-based I.S. club, in fact, serious enough to "conduct a radio program through station W.P.C.H. [which was destined to feature many programs "starring" Rabbi Goldstein] under the auspices of the Social-Educational Department."

NAVAL NURSE CLUB. (Naval as in "bell bottom"; not navel as in "belly button," that is.) Nobody ever turned the tide at the I.S. against its forthright policy of maintaining the sex-role distinctions within the synagogue that Jews throughout the ages have accepted as God's will, and that some nineteenth century Jews took it upon themselves to toss overboard, considering themselves to have been smarter than God and/or those mortals whom Judaism has traditionally considered to have been God's historic agents. The I.S., however, always drew a firm line between what the misguided majority of American Jews, passively adhering to outmoded nineteenth century "reform" thought, perceive as an "inferiority" regarding the role of women in Jewish law, and what universally respected and university educated Jewish legal scholars through the ages have recognized and continue to recognize as a progressive division of labor and religious responsibility in a specialized and ordered civilized society.

It was only natural, therefore, that the I.S. did nothing to discourage the unusual club (particularly in this pre-"feminist" period) that fostered an atmosphere more often associated with men's inclinations as long as the club did not sail against religious currents:

> ...[T]he order maintained [at the Naval Nurse Club's first meeting] was very impressive...[B]efore securing permission to speak, each girl had to salute in order to be recognized.
>
> The...ever present motto is service, and in pursuance of this, the girls will learn the elementary principles of first aid, always useful knowledge. In addition, information concerning the plan and layout of a naval vessel and seamanship will be given. It seems that boys have no monopoly on the desire to learn about this...
>
> [U]niforms will soon be in evidence...blue capes and

white caps [were designated] the official regalia....

OUTDOOR GIRLS CLUB. These girls likewise "showed up" the boys, who, though stereotyped as members of a sex more the "outdoor type," had no counterpart "Outdoor *Boys*" club per se!*
PALAIS CLUB. This club dramatically drew attention to the drawing power of the I.S. in that "[p]ractically all" of its members were "Bronx boys." Not only is the Bronx in a different neighborhood but it is also in a different borough of the huge metropolis that New York City was even then.
PAWNEE CLUB. This group attracted not only individuals or even a mere entire club, but it "brought with them the entire membership of the Independent League," which, from then on became *de*pendent, at least to a degree, on the I.S.
POSTER CLUB. On the initiative of a single "art student of long standing" who decided to become an "instructress," this creative club was itself created, against the following backdrop:

> The various groups...are always in need of signs and posters. Now they will be able to secure these from a specializing group at a cost price. This organization will serve to make two factions happy. Those who want to learn commercial art under professional guidance and those who need the products of their efforts.

REUS CLUB. This was the club that Mrs. Goldstein personally led, at first. Naturally, therefore, when it began, during World War I, its program was a model one:

> We begin our meeting with a reading from the Bible, then we have some Jewish history, which I tell the girls, then we discuss our business, read from Mark Twain's "Innocents Abroad," do some war work which now consists [of] winding up 3½ yard bundles of cord which is sent across to the soldiers. We retire reluctantly a little after 10.

SPADE CLUB. This club won an I.S. inter-club newspaper contest for the publication of its prophetically named "Ace of Spades," which "consisted of eight mimeographed pages containing articles about Jewish news events, a Jewish 'Hall of Fame,' and club news and activities."
SUNSHINE GIRLS CLUB. The "sunshine girls" shined in quite a few different seasons at the I.S. and in quite a few different ways,

---

*It could be counter-argued, however, that since the boys had many clubs featuring outdoor activities, it would have been inappropriate to single out only a single club with this name.

but most importantly, they made the sun shine for those less fortunate than themselves. Their club was in the forefront of those clubs that spent their precious free time dressing dolls, for example, "for the orphan children of the day nurseries," and involving themselves in other forms of "charitable endeavor," like filling baskets of food on Thanksgiving Day and "distributing them to needy families in the immediate neighborhood."

U.O.J.C.A. CLUBS. (Union of Orthodox Jewish Congregations of America.) The national presidents of the U.O.J.C.A. and of its Women's Branch, respectively (Rabbi and Mrs. Goldstein), shortly after assuming office, began to organize high school and college branches. Never one to let an opportunity slip by his fingers, the rabbi grafted some of the local young high school branches into his own synagogue for the mutual benefit of all concerned. Both the High School of Commerce and the Julia Richman chapters, in fact, were among the U.O.J.C.A. clubs that became full-fledged members of the I.S. "Intermediate Council" as well.

YOUNG ISRAEL CLUB. Although this club participated in an "interclub debating tourney," for example, within the I.S., its name makes its own roots subject to a possible claim by another obvious source—the national Young Israel movement. Undoubtedly, this particular club would have felt at home in both and like a stepchild in neither.

ZENITHIAN CLUB. This club clearly went against the trend prevailing in the I.S. in the early 1920s at a time when the I.S. was still only approaching its own organizational "zenith."

> The Zenithian Club, one of the oldest groups of the building, having emigrated with the rest of us from our old quarters at 112 West 116th Street, has decided to disband and will amalgamate themselves into the Order of Knights of Pythias. Although they will hereafter be known as the Zenithian Lodge, they promise, as individual members of the building, their full cooperation in all of the building's undertakings.

An explanation for this change of status may be deduced from the very fact of the club's having been with the I.S. from its earliest days. Some of the club's members may have simply jumped onto the exciting bandwagon without fully realizing where it was going!

Although the parting promise of continued loyalty, as individuals, to the I.S. may have a noble ring to it, somehow the thought most likely to be ringing in readers' ears as they retrospectively contemplate the shift in the allegiance of the members of the original Zenithian club is loud and clear: Last in the alphabet and last in I.S. hearts.

Chapter 29

Athletics—Last But In A Sense First

We have seen, earlier, the strategic reasons for allowing the athletic department to become the last of the four cornerstones in the I.S. to be fully developed. Physical fitness, however, was far from being a stepchild of the institution, and was definitely promoted by the synagogue as an end in itself, one which received strong encouragement. Since the I.S. was founded at the outbreak of the United States' entry into World War I, it comes as no surprise that the synagogue made the most of this military campaign. It did so not only by emphasizing the special link I.S. servicemen had to the general I.S. motto of "Service to God and Country," but also by drawing some lasting lesson for the limb as well as for the soul, out of the shattering war effort:

> The revelations of the War Department Draft Examinations concerning national physical deficiency came as a shock to the general public. The average run of men were found to be in deplorable condition. Today the old order is changed; everybody wants to be fit for action!
> ...As part of the general program in promoting Jewish Community activities, the building up of the body is an essential element....

The synagogue made a strong point of safeguarding the health of all of those who were to use its facilities, before permitting the indiscriminate use of its equipment for short-term enjoyment. When the new facilities were being phased in, no fewer than four doctors were "on the job every Thursday night giving physical examinations to new members," with Dr. Benjamin Goldstein—who was *not* a relative—of the Board of Directors, "the...chairman of the examining committee." This policy was still in effect long after Rabbi Goldstein moved to the West Side.

In the midst of the bleak Depression years, the gym was pictured as both a bright spot and an economy measure to *lighten* the burdens weighing heavily upon so many drooping shoulders.

> The winter months are the unhealthiest months of the year. Most sicknesses and deaths occur during January, February, and March. How will *you* fare this winter?
>
> Your health is one of your most valuable possessions. It represents more than . . . freedom from sickness or disease. It is a positive, constructive condition of your body and mind that permits you to realize your highest possibilities physically, mentally, and spiritually. It is essential to your success. Health increases your quantity of life as well as its quality. It makes your growth more perfect, your decay less rapid, your life more vigorous and your death more remote. [Facts on expanded life expectancies followed.]
>
> [T]he average annual cost of illness per person in the United States is about $131 or $567 per family. . . . It amounts to 16 billion dollars a year in the United States.
>
> Health is Purchasable! Within natural limitations. . . . An investment in gym dues is a wise economy.

Indeed, the physical fitness program seemed to work wonders. A synagogue official reported, in 1926:

> I am proud to state that most of our members who have joined with physical defects, such as spinal curvatures, overweight, underweight, flat feet, etc., have shown marked improvement.

The synagogue put together an elaborate health exhibition one year, drawing on the "cooperation and aid [of] the New York Tuberculosis and Health Association, the Metropolitan Life Insurance Company, the Department of Health, the Board of Education, the [Union of Orthodox Jewish Congregations of America,] U.O.J.C.A., and the Child Study Association of America." The exhibition was so successful that "the initial supply of literature concerning health soon was exhausted and it was necessary to obtain an additional supply before the exhibition ended." No fewer than 2,300 people took the trouble of signing the register, and "all the students of the Cooper Junior High School visited the exhibition."

Another indication of the stress on personal hygiene and health care was the "KKK Campaign" launched by the juniors. As described in the synagogue newspaper:

> The KKK Campaign, called the campaign with a "K" or a "kick," means clean, quiet, courteous. [The "K's" obviously, were only phonetic.] The juniors feel that if they can get their members to be clean, quiet, and courteous, they will have accomplished their object.

Athletics before the Gym

> The gymnasium in the old building [the first, small one] was unique both in arrangement and in content. The [basketball] baskets in the 5 x 25 foot [1.524 x 4.572 meter] gymnasium consisted of two barrel hoops which served their purpose more or less, usually less. The "building up" [body building] apparatus consisted of one solid oak boxing bag support and a paper-stuffed boxing bag. There were, however, five or six hot and cold showers, all with nice, clear, cold water.

The contrast vis-a-vis the dream gymnasium that climaxed the construction of the new building needs no further elaboration here, but it demonstrates that the interest and participation in physical recreation was there from the outset, and that there was enough room for improvement to make the long struggle worthwhile! There was also enough drive on the part of I.S. members in the intervening years to foster a "Junior Basketball Team...[which,] using Evening Recreation Center 184 for its home grounds, remained undefeated for a period of two years."

The major organized activity to take place in the fully equipped and modern gym was, predictably enough, basketball.*

The major athletic attraction in the building, and as far as many I.S. members were concerned, in the entire community, was, of course, the modern fully-equipped heated swimming pool. It was geared to *all* levels.

The same "physical director" who was able to describe the wonders of the physical fitness program earlier, had an equally rosy report about even the lowest level of I.S. fledgling swimmers:

> I am proud to state that 95 percent of all those members of our department who were unable to swim have learnt to do so here and the other 5 percent have been unable to attend regularly.

---

*See Chapter 30.

By this time, these 95 percent were eligible to try to qualify for a "formal" swimming club.

> In order for one to join this club, it will be necessary to swim a given distance in a specified time. If you feel you can swim or dive, come to the swimming pool, where your faults will be corrected, your form will be improved, and your "repertoire" of dives will be increased.

The next step up the ladder was taken by those who made the biggest splashes of all, the members of the swimming teams that will be discussed in the chapter on competition. Finally, "life-saving tests" were "given to those interested in securing positions as life guard" and "to members who desire their Red Cross emblem and diploma." As comprehensive as the swimming programs were, however, the underlying aim from the administration's point of view was to get the swimmers "from the pool to the *shool*"! (*Shool* is Yiddish for "synagogue.") It is by the successes in *this* area that the swimming programs must ultimately be judged.

At one time or another, Rabbi Goldstein personally participated in basketball, "indoor baseball" (his role in the more conventional *outdoor* baseball was active but from a point *off* the field),* handball, and ping-pong in the I.S. gym. In fact, the only land sport not generally limited to field day competition in which we have no record of his participation was badminton, presumably not solely because he was known to try to look only for the *good* in people, but because in 1936 it was "the latest sport to be introduced among the gymnasium members," and by that time Rabbi Goldstein had left Harlem for the West Side. Had the game been introduced earlier, he undoubtedly would have participated, if his participation in tennis in the mountains during summer vacations was any indication!

Women in Sports

As was the case with so many other characteristics of the I.S. that now seem to have been ahead of their time, the I.S.'s athletic department had a progressive attitude toward *sportswomen*. The women, of course, needed no prodding. Unlike many women today who insist they are "fulfilled" only when they are doing precisely what men do, the I.S. women were mature and liberated enough to participate in the activities of their own choice, whether or not they happened to coincide with those of the men. Thus, in the peak year of 1927:

---

*This involvement was discussed in Chapter 3.

In our Women's Department, we find the formation of teams and classes. Much stress has been laid on the reducing class. The women will run their own swimming meet. . . . The girls have also successfully participated in ice skating parties and outdoor hikes.

Celebrities Help Celebrate Physical Feats

The athletic department, as did all the other departments in the I.S., sought to give recognition, periodically, to its high achievers. Its "athletic carnivals" were often highlighted by the presence of role models. One such carnival was graced by the active participation of George Kojak, a world Olympic champion swimmer, as a referee in one of the boxing bouts, and, as we have seen, Benny Leonard, the undefeated lightweight boxing champion of the world, as a story teller! The *real* stars on the I.S. athletic horizon, however, were the young men and women who made the most of the I.S. facilities on a regular basis regardless of special events and featured guests.

Chapter 30

Constant Competition Within The Synagogue

Virtually no phase of the I.S.—with the exception of religious prayers—was left untouched by the frenzied atmosphere of friendly competition that heightened the excitement in each activity. We have already seen how the competitive instinct gave immeasurable impetus to the membership and fund-raising drives that turned the Institutional Synagogue concept into a reality. We have seen how it helped motivate the Hebrew School students to draw their public school peers *into* it rather than to "play hooky" *from* it. We will now see its role in the other major institutions of the synagogue—the athletic, recreational, cultural, and social activities that constituted Rabbi Goldstein's neutralizer to the major drawing cards of the "Y."

**An Athlete Without Competition
Is Like an Election in a One-Party Country**

The top competitive sport to dominate the I.S. gymnasium, as most other gyms, was basketball. There were so many organized teams within the synagogue complex that a "Round Robin" tournament was needed just to determine who would represent the intermediate division's clubs, for example, in inter-organizational competitions. Even without a gym of its own, we have seen, the junior basketball team put together two undefeated seasons, laying the groundwork for the season of 1925 when the I.S. seniors "won the championship of the Community League of New York City." A few years later, one and the same person captained both a Columbia University and an I.S. team. Yet probably the greatest team act of heroism on the court came in defeat, when the regular team inexplicably did not appear for one particular scheduled game. The rather comprehensive synagogue newspaper headline says it all:

> I.S. Impromptu Basketball Team Goes Down in Glorious Defeat before Superior Odds of Bronx "Y" Team—Rather Than Have Forfeiture Declared against I.S., Boys Scrape Together Impromptu Team to Fight Certain Defeat

The I.S. swimming team was in a class by itself in two striking respects: First, it belonged to what may have been the first Orthodox synagogue serving any community in the world with a swimming pool of its own; second, it was often in a class by itself simply in that it was *so good!*

The coaches of the swimming team, during its championship seasons, had such outstanding credentials that had teaching by example been the only pedagogic method in use, they could have produced *automatic* winners. Harold Florence was "the United States record holder for [the] Medley Swim, [the] Metropolitan 100-yard swimming champion, [a] member of the team that [toppled a] Yale championship team, [and a] Teacher of Swimming for the Board of Education." His successor, Jake Silverman, had quite an act to follow, and proved himself equal to the challenge. He had been "the runner-up in the National Swimming Championships," he had smashed six records when he had raced Walter Spence, "the national champion," and, appropriately enough, he had about ninety trophies to his silver name. In addition, he had been a board of education teacher and Red Cross lifesaving examiner.

The captain of the I.S. swimming team, at least at one point, was, as in the case of the captain of the I.S. basketball team, simultaneously also the captain of the team of a secular school, in this case the De Witt Clinton High School.

No matter how good a swimmer the coach or the captain may be in his own right, what counts in judging a team is what one sees when looking at the record—and seeing how regularly records are broken. No dust could have ever collected for long on the ever-expanding I.S. record book. After winning the championship of the Community League in 1925, the I.S. swimming team proceeded to win the championship of the Metropolitan League for four consecutive years. In one of these championship meets, the I.S. team amassed more than double the number of points credited to its nearest competitor—the 92nd Street "Y," and more than four times the number credited to the third-place finishers.*

One sport that rarely made headlines as an intra-city team

---

*That happened to represent the Schiff Center. In light of the circumstances outlined earlier, this total dominance must have been particularly devastating.

sport was handball, but when it did, the I.S. handily rose to the occasion, at one time sharing the championship of the Metropolitan League in this area.

Even those teams that did not play against other institutions were well organized into intra-I.S. tournaments. Baseball tournaments were held both indoors and out. Although presumably the equipment used for the two types of baseball tournaments were as similar as a golf ball is to a marshmallow, practice for the outdoor tournament was conducted, on at least one occasion, in the gym, which may have broken some well established precedents, not to mention windows. Rabbi Goldstein frequently offered incentives in the form of prizes for a variety of synagogue events, but baseball was the only *sport* for which the winning team was annually awarded a victory cup by the rabbi. Less taxing on the physique but no less taxing on the nerves were the regular tournaments in ping-pong, chess, and checkers.

The "All-[a]Round Indoor Championships" were physical marathons that occupied several hundred members every week for an entire season. The first time this arrangement was tried, it was described in language conjuring up an ideal model of democracy in a very real world composed of people with unequal talents:

> A novel all-[a]round athletic contest is being conducted in the Gymnasium consisting of a series of events held once each week in which *every* member participates. The scoring system is such that no matter how poor a performance is made, each man may score points in each event....[Different divisions competed on different days (on Sundays)—or nights—of the week.]
>
> The list of activities is as follows: Athletics, standing broad jump, pull-ups, foul shooting, eight-pound shotput, running high jump, potato race, baskets in thirty seconds, springboard high jump, rope climb, bar vault. Swimming: Plate fetch, ducking for time, one lap freestyle, one lap breast stroke, fancy dive, three lap freestyle, one lap under water, one lap backstroke, plunge for distance, two lap breast stroke, medley, three laps free, back and breast strokes.
>
> Those who have missed events will be given an opportunity to make them up.

One can readily understand, given the hundreds of people involved, how the competitions took a whole season.

This "gymnasium contest" was completely independent of the annual outdoor field days. The synagogue newspaper was not guilty of distortion when it predicted, in advance, that not just the athletic children but that even the comparatively flabby adults—the "Brotherhood, the Daughters, the Sisterhood, and the Board of

Directors [—] will join the Club and Gym members in a day of healthy outdoor sport." The basic program was similar to that of the indoor event, except it included more running and dashing, fewer events in general, and no swimming. To cram into a single day what had been done indoors in the course of an entire season would have been impossible, so for entry into each event, a nominal fee was charged, graded according to the relative earning capacity—or "allowance"—of the members of each general age bracket. (This system, built as it was on a nominal fee scale, did not discriminate in favor of the *privileged interests*, but, rather, it served to weed out those *not really interested* in the *privilege*.)

A "Special Program" supplemented the more straightforward athletic competition, under the following unusually pleasant terms:

No entry will be charged for
special events, but prizes will be given.

1. 50 yard dash for members of Board of Directors.
2. Potato and Spoon Race for I.S. Sisterhood.
3. Husband and Wife Strolling Race.
4. Fat Men vs. Skinny Men Relay
   (Board of Directors).
5. 50 yard dash for I.S. Brotherhood.
6. Piggy-back Race, I.S. Brotherhood.
7. Basketball Throws for I.S. Daughters.
8. 140 yard relay, Young Folks' League vs. I.S. Daughters
   (4 girls each running 35 yards).
9. 140 yard Relay [Hebrew School] (1 team from each grade),
   4 boys on team, 35 yards each.
10. Several Novelty Relays for [Hebrew School] boys.

Cultural competitions were encouraged to an equal degree; in fact, probably to a *greater* degree, since cultural pursuits do not lend themselves to competitions as naturally as do team sports. One cultural activity that stands out as an exception to this rule—and that certainly does not only lend itself to but *requires* competition—is a debate. Here, again, the junior I.S. team outshone the seniors, and, in fact, all other city challengers as well, running up an undefeated record in its first ten years of existence. When the members of one of the final winning teams of this dynasty of juniors graduated to the I.S. senior team, they promptly proceeded to catapult the seniors to the championship of the Metropolitan League as well, so that the I.S. stood "supreme as the debating institution among some twenty-seven Jewish community centers in Brooklyn, Manhattan, the Bronx, and

Westchester."* Five years later, the senior team was still able to go into the Bronx-Manhattan championship debate undefeated and emerge the winner.

Contests in religion, (e.g., on holiday laws and customs in the appropriate seasons), Bible (some years organized around the weekly Biblical portions, a different one of which is read in the synagogue thrice a week, every week of the year), and Jewish essays, were given prominent attention as well. The latter category of contests was judged by a panel consisting of no lesser lights in the I.S. religious constellation than Rabbi Goldstein as "Chairman of the Board," Congressman Siegel, Dr. Zadok Kapner, and Rabbi Philip Goodman. The Bible contest *awards* were undoubtedly of more general interest than the *awardees*, no matter how talented the contestants may have been, including, in a single contest:

> ...a set of "Bible Comments for Home Reading," by Rabbi Goldstein; "The Jewish Library," edited by Rabbi Leo Jung; "Religious Parties in Israel," by Rabbi Abraham Burstein; "Choice of Pearls," by Solomon Ibn Gabirol,**and many other books....

The cultural competitions promoted by the I.S. had universal as well as Jewish dimensions. Many I.S. members won prizes under the synagogue banner "in intra-city contests in musical and literary fields." All other considerations being equal, however, the I.S. constantly tried to inject a Jewish angle into its activities. This was not always possible, especially within the confines of rules imposed by intra-city league officials. The topic that the I.S. team was required to debate in one of its championship winning performances in the Metropolitan League, for example, had about as many Jewish overtones as would a local election in Outer Mongolia: "Resolved: That the United States [in 1926] should enter into an agreement with the allied powers for the mutual cancellation of inter-allied war debts." In stark contrast, the winning topics at a typical annual essay contest *within* the I.S. were: "Anti-Semitism," first place; "Jews in the History of America," second place; "Zionism," honorable mention. Again, the relative importance that the synagogue wanted this type of contest to reflect merited a "Board of Judges headed by Rabbi Goldstein" himself. (It also included Rabbi Abraham Burstein and Philip Goodman.)

---

*The Jewish communities in the two New York City boroughs not mentioned were negligible at the time.

**The last one mentioned preceded the others chronologically by nearly a millenium so he was not in a position to express justified outrage for being placed at the end of the list.

Nobody could have accused the I.S. judges of male chauvinist favoritism. All three of the winners of the "junior declamation contest," although performing "in the true Ciceronian sense," were girls. They each represented different clubs.

Reference has already been made in earlier chapters to I.S. team successes in inter-organizational dramatic tournaments, and to the intra-organizational reading contests and Friday Evening Forums.

The annual award nights drew so many people and involved the distribution of so many medals, plaques, and caps that, some years, two evenings had to be set aside for this occasion in the huge I.S. auditorium, and, at times, tickets were required for entrance. There seems to have been a divergence of opinion in different years as to which was "the most treasured of all prizes," the character medal or the service award ("for individual improvement and for service"), but one point remained constant, according to Rabbi Goldstein: "There is nothing more honorable than knowing that we have given our best to come in first place, even though we were not victorious. It is the attempt to do the right thing that is so laudable." One man—Abraham M. Davis—was so enthused with the activities of the I.S. that, some years, he singlehandedly not only chaired the Committee on Social and Educational Activities, but more than matched the prizes awarded by the entire Parents Association of the Hebrew School, serving in the capacity of "benefactor of the evening" while the "P.A. *also* contributed [italics not in the original] a number of [Hebrew School] medals."

At one point, during the Depression, a point system was instituted to promote greater participation by individuals as well as clubs. The greatest incentive of all, however, was most eloquently described by one Maurice Spanbock in an essay published when he was thirteen years old:

> *The Institutional Synagogue has placed before me a book, as it were, and tried to show me why it is urgent that the book be read, why it is absolutely necessary for me to understand the glorious history of the Jewish race through the ages* [italics not in original]. They have tried to aid my family in bringing me, as they have brought hundreds of other Jewish boys and girls, to the religion which contains the most perfect Code of Laws ever set down. And they have, I believe, succeeded in executing this exceedingly difficult thing, for it is difficult while we are in exile, in a most noble manner.
>
> *The I.S. has laid for me a foundation upon which to construct the building of my life, for I shall attempt to always build my life along an Orthodox Jewish manner. They have given me an incentive always to be a religious Jew. This above all else, I believe, is the most important thing that any Jewish institution can do.*

Chapter 31

Populists, Democrats, And Republicans

Two threads that were woven into the I.S. from its very inception were the broad principles of democracy and patriotism. An early I.S. leader illustrated how the first of these ideals can be applied within the framework of a synagogue's day -to- day operation:

> The young people were disappointed [before the I.S. was created for them] with the way the existing synagogues were run—with *misheberakhs* [extensive public blessings rendered on behalf of the family and friends of recipients of honors that were awarded, to a great extent, on the basis of the size of the anticipated financial "honorariums" to the synagogue and/or its employees. Jewish law specifically sets forth priorities for such honors, which have nothing to do with money, although it does leave some slots subject to discretion] and [they were "disappointed," likewise, with] drawn out *chazzanut* [cantorial renditions]. The people wanted democracy, where young people would have the responsibility of running the synagogue, so they would become interested in the synagogue and other communal work.

This sentiment coincides precisely with that of the I.S. literature that had appeared on the back of the activities checklists distributed at the very first mass rally held on behalf of the I.S. after Rabbi Goldstein had become free to devote his full time to it:

> The Institutional Synagogue is a democratic organization and we earnestly solicit any practical suggestions or recommendations that you may have to offer for its welfare and

success.... "Do your bit" and enlist now in the Suggestion Army.

In a sense, the most all-pervasive evidence of the democratic way in which the synagogue was run was illustrated by the emphasis on competition that we have just seen in the previous chapter, promoting individual initiative. *Any* person could rise to the top at the I.S.; *any* person could succeed; *any* person could win. Personal recognition was not reserved for the few or the wealthy; it was reserved for the most industrious and for the best.

In a seeming anomaly, the membership policy had the Marxian feature of encouraging all members to give according to their means and accept the services the I.S. offered according to their needs and inclinations, yet at the same time it rose above the inherent weaknesses of a socialistic system by encouraging personal initiative and achievement both on behalf of oneself *and* the cause.

One person who most dramatically filled this double bill was the I.S.'s first man to reach Washington's Capitol Hill. Congressman Siegel won friends and influenced people while occupying the synagogue's highest elective lay office not by *accepting* favors but by *granting* them; not by *"milking"* charities but by *building* them. If a politician's role is to influence colleagues in a political body, then the most highly qualified Orthodox politician any American institution could reasonably hope to obtain would be an incumbent member of the United States Congress.

Two anecdotes centering around Rabbi Goldstein's wealthy and influential father-in-law illustrate the centrality of fairness and democracy in I.S. policy. Reuben Metchik, the British-born-and-bred printer who had helped to give the I.S. the minimal cosmopolitan touch it had in its early years, recalled:

> I donated the first *parochet* [ornamental curtain hung in front of the ark] to the I.S., but as it turned out, Harry Fischel had donated the first ark, and [having assumed that the donation included the customary ornamental curtain], he didn't like the idea of having *his* ark covered by a *parochet* that somebody else had donated. There was quite a big fuss about the matter, but finally it was decided that since *I* had made good on my pledge of the *parochet*, it would go up in my name.

With the principal people involved now unavailable for comment, it would be impossible to determine precisely what representations had been made to Mr. Fischel, so although we cannot weigh the merits of the decision, we *can* point to the obvious fact that the heavy weight of Mr. Fischel's personal influence was *not* permitted to turn aside a judgment arrived at in a democratic manner.

On another occasion, a prominent synagogue official publicly made a disparaging personal remark about the recognition Mr. Fischel expected for his charitable contributions. (Since his contributions were so numerous and so extensive, the recognition he received from countless national and local organizations was legion.) Rabbi Goldstein saw the insult as a personal attack on his father-in-law's character, and announced from the pulpit that something had just been said that hurt him—the rabbi—deeply, and that he would resign from his own position if the statement would not be withdrawn. It was withdrawn, and the abuse of freedom of speech—as negative a concept as its opposite is positive—was held in check.

He who whitens the face of [embarrasses] his friend in public is as if he spilled blood—Talmud, *Baba Metziah* 58-B.

Patriotism—From the Right to Citizenship
...To the Supreme Sacrifice

Although a person has to be a resident of the United States for five years to become a citizen, the I.S. as an *institution* was located in Harlem for less than half of that period of time before Rabbi Goldstein became the chairman of a local Americanization and Naturalization Meeting whose purpose was to try to make new American citizens feel as at home with their new country—without renouncing their old religion—as Rabbi Goldstein undoubtedly felt in his newer neighborhood. No small-scale event, the meeting was convened at the now-familiar Mount Morris Theatre. Appropriately—and coincidentally—enough, after the I.S. was in its own neighborhood for just over five years, during which period it had developed an ongoing program of naturalization work, Congressman Siegel was able to have the following remarks—although only excerpted here—inserted, in full, into the *Congressional Record:*

MR. SIEGEL. Mr. Speaker, on the evening of June 15 there was held at the auditorium of the Institutional Synagogue...a welcome to 522 newly naturalized citizens,..from 14 different countries. In addition...500 American citizens were present....

The following remarks were made by me in introducing Secretary [of Labor, James J.] Davis [of the United States Cabinet]:

For the first time [sic] in the history of New York City invitations have been extended to those who have become naturalized during the past few months to attend a welcome at the new citizens' meeting. It is fitting that the highest public official of the United States, who not only is in charge of the enforcement of the law in regard to the admission of immigrants but who also looks after the naturalization of aliens, should have come here to deliver a message on such an occasion. . . .

REMARKS OF SECRETARY OF LABOR JAMES J. DAVIS

. . . It is a privilege to meet the Congressman's friends personally. We hear a great deal from him about you in Washington. He must be personally acquainted with everybody hereabouts. Early and late he is at the Department of Labor pleading for the rights of someone or the other of you. When he has gone to everybody in the office with a difficult case he finds his way as a last resort to the Secretary of Labor personally. Usually he gets what he wants. . . .

We have seen some areas of Congressman Siegel's personal involvement in immigration problems in an earlier chapter, clearly reinforcing Davis' "testimony." Formally, Siegel had served in 1921, for example, as Chairman of the Committee to Investigate Immigration Conditions on the Pacific Coast, but what he consistently did, informally, on the Atlantic Coast and in the nation's capital may have been even more important.

The I.S. did not stop its immigration work at merely giving "greenbacks" to "greenhorns," or "naturalization aid and information on citizenship to new immigrants."* Rather, the synagogue stressed long-range and far-reaching solutions for the plight of immigrants, with particular emphasis on an early mastery of the English language. An I.S. instructor wrote:

The immigrant coming to this country is in a different position from that of the American going to Europe to live. The American would naturally settle in the English-speaking quarter and at the same time get right to the task of learning to speak and write the language of the country.

Up to about five years ago, the direct opposite of the above was a typical case of the foreigner who landed on our shores. He found his group of people who were tucked away in a small section of a big metropolis. He worked with people who spoke the only tongue with which he was familiar. . . . He was thrifty. His standard of living was no higher than [it had been] on the other side [of the Atlantic Ocean]. . . . His lack of knowledge of the new language was the cause of this. After he had saved a few thousand dollars, he would either send for his sweetheart in Europe or go across and bring her to the new country. He called it his home, but it was really only the

*Such work continued, incidentally, straight through to the World War II period.

community in which he lived which was "home" to him. He did not venture outside for any distance because he knew so little English. . . .

The emphasis in Mrs. Goldstein's diary three and one-half years earlier reflects total agreement as to this key underlying problem, and a direct commitment to combat it:

> I went to a meeting of the Immigrant Aid Committee at the I.S. We are planning to cooperate with the Council of Jewish Women in visiting immigrant families and befriending them. The first visit will be paid in the company of a trained social worker and later we will try to persuade them to come to learn English.

Classes were eventually given twice a week, with no age limit, and, of course, no charge.

Patriotic Holidays Holy Too!*

An article on "Jewish Americanization Agencies," written for the *American Jewish Yearbook* before the I.S.'s permanent building was even renovated and ready for full use, already gave the I.S. number one rating, in a sense, among synagogues with direct "Americanization" programs. Although the article singled out the I.S. as one of the two most prominent synagogue "centers," and although it gave the Jewish Center the edge in terms of "social opportunities," it mentioned nothing about direct patriotic programs of the Jewish Center, while specifically spelling out the fact that the all-embracing I.S. program included "lectures, meetings and celebrations promotive of American ideals."

Commemorations of American holidays took place both in large celebrations in the synagogue auditorium or gymnasium as well as in smaller forums convened by individual clubs. Nothing was taken for granted, however. On certain holidays, like Armistice Day, bulletins were "distributed among the various clubs, outlining a typical program," which the clubs, in turn, "manifested a

---

*We have chosen to sprinkle allusions to the special brand of rhetoric that focused on Americanism combined with Judaism, in various locations throughout this book rather than to lump them all together in one place because this spread-out approach was essentially the approach taken by the I.S. itself. Patriotic fervor and Jewish commitment were both so well integrated into the I.S. philosophy and programs that cramming all of the patriotic references within the I.S. into one area would take the essence out of the underlying approach of the multifaceted institution much as if one were to attempt to fasten many facets of a diamond together on one side of it. We shall make an exception here, however, by devoting an independent section to American holidays, and a separate chapter to Jewish ones.

keen desire to follow."

Memorial Day ceremonies at the I.S. not only bridged the abyss between the living and the dead, but they also bridged the sometimes even greater generation gap among the living as well. One year's ceremonies drew 500 people to an evening under the joint auspices of the Institutional Synagogue and the Manhattan Post of the Hebrew Veterans of the Wars of the Republic:

> Three generations were represented in the veterans of the Civil War, the Spanish-American War, and the World War [I]. . . . [I]t might be said four generations, for the Boy Scouts of America and the Girls Scouts of America were represented by some 200 members. . . .

Synagogue-wide celebrations were held to commemorate the birthdays of at least three different United States presidents: Washington, Lincoln, and Theodore Roosevelt. In the same spirit, no fewer than three I.S. clubs opted to adopt the names of three U.S. presidents permanently: Washington, Lincoln, and Madison. The synagogue newspaper once reprinted an entire article that Congressman Siegel had written which had been published in Emanuel Hertz's *Abraham Lincoln, the Tribute of the Synagogue*. Stories like that which highlighted this article* instilled pride in the impressionable young people—both in their religion and in their country.

When it came to Thanksgiving Day, the I.S. in general and the Goldsteins in particular had much to be thankful for. In addition, the I.S.'s grasp succeeded in touching people at both ends of the economic spectrum. We have seen, earlier, how the synagogue clubs made Thanksgiving Day meaningful for those less fortunate than their own members. One man *more* fortunate than they, Nathan Straus, the famous philanthropist of Macy's fame, surprised everybody at the I.S. in the synagogue's very first season by attending its first joint Thanksgiving Day celebration, coming "uninvited, just from having read about it in the *New York Times*."

---

*An excerpt:

Lincoln. . .left Springfield, Illinois. . .Feb. 11, 1861, never to return. . . .[J]ust as Lincoln was about to deliver his farewell words to those who gathered to say good-bye, Abraham Kohn presented to him a silk American flag upon which there was embroidered the words taken from Joshua which read:

"Be strong and be of good courage; be not afraid, neither be thou dismayed; for the Lord. . .is with thee. . . ."

Many years afterwards, President McKinley referred to this incident as one that he had heard had given to Lincoln the greatest possible courage during the trying days of the Civil War. . . .

[in retrospect]. . .The Battle had been fought and the victory was his, but, like Moses, he was not destined to reap the harvest.

287

The ultimate Thanksgiving Day tribut   e I.S. came, most appropriately, from the director of America's Goodwill Union, in an open letter to Rabbi Goldstein published in the *New York World*, and widely reprinted:

> When I called at your place of worship this morning to give you the invitation of the Rev. Dr. A. Edwin Keignin to the quiet private dinner at the Faculty Club to which he is asking a dozen rabbis and a dozen clergymen of as many denominations...what I saw in your synagogue amazed me.
>
> ...The sight would astound our Christian ministers and congregations. It told more than volumes of "Books by the Best Authors" could tell of the valuable contribution which Judaism is making to all that is best in our American life.
>
> A great audience filled with children of the neighborhood at a Thanksgiving Day service, listened with rapt attention to an address on Godliness, Americanism and cleanliness.
>
> Tell us Christians how you do it, for I think IT IS A SAFE TEN TO ONE WAGER THAT IN ALL OF OUR PROTESTANT CHURCHES IN OUR GREAT CITY THERE WERE NOT AS MANY CHILDREN AS I SAW IN YOUR ONE SYNAGOGUE. [Capitalization not in original]
>
> ...I saw a better painting than the famous masterpiece of the story of the lost boy of twelve years found after three days in the Temple of Jerusalem.

The I.S., as a composite of three institutions, had a right to claim more than one motto. According to Congressman Siegel, however, all its other slogans went by the wayside in comparison with the one that referred to patriotism. In his Flag Day address of 1926 he commented:

> The Institutional Synagogue has always stood for the best in Judaism and Americanism—exemplified by our motto, "For God and Country."

Mottos were not enough. I.S. boys were called upon to make sacrifices for their country, and even the supreme sacrifice. We have seen earlier how they were encouraged by the synagogue to do so, and how they did indeed make this ultimate sacrifice, as both an American and a religious duty.

Chapter 32

Holidays As Spirited...
As They Were Spiritual

If the I.S. leadership felt that the synagogue was an appropriate place for celebrating patriotic holidays and running Americanization programs, it does not require too much imagination to picture its conception of the role of *Jewish* holidays in synagogue life. Nevertheless, most imaginations would never have conceived of some of the variations from the norm injected into celebrating Jewish holidays at the I.S. Although the I.S. did not by any means neglect everyday—or every holiday—aspects of holidays, these features will be ignored here, since the purpose of this book is *not* to catalogue the ordinary or the mundane, especially in *this* chapter (on the *Holy* Days)!

The High Holy Days are the three days of the year on which many otherwise-nonobservant Jews attend a synagogue. Consequently, for reasons of supply and demand—and out of fiscal necessity—synagogues generally feel obliged to charge for tickets to defray the expenses for an operation that is open morning and night, 365 days of the year. One policy that distinguished the stand taken regarding seating at I.S. High Holy Day services from that of most synagogues was the synagogue's determination not only not to charge for, but, "as usual," to "reserve seats for members of the Fire Department, Police Department, the War Veterans, Municipal workers and other communal agencies."

Yom Kippur, the holiest of the High Holy Days, is the only day of the year when the professional cantor, in many congregations, is replaced by the rabbi for an entire service (out of five for the day), known as the *N'ila*. This *N'ila* service is the climactic final one of the long tedious fast day, in which the spiritual level of the rabbi is often considered high enough to compensate for his lack of musicality in the final plea for his people that is uttered from the cantor's rostrum.

In recalling Rabbi Goldstein's chanting of this service in his early years, the mellifluous Cantor Yavneh was not alone in his analysis of the rabbi's musical expertise—or lack of it: "He had no melody." Another candid one-time confidant recalled that "He shouted every word at N'ila [sentimental smile]. He wasn't very musical." The very same Cantor Yavneh, however, conceded that the rabbi's chanting left a rather memorable impression: "His *davening* [praying] was very emotional. We knew Rabbi Goldstein would go into his ecstasy." One woman raved about the I.S. services in general and Rabbi Goldstein's sermons in particular, closing with a reference to his rendition of the *N'ila:*

> ...A fitting climax...was the unforgettable *N'ila* service which he read [sic] this evening. In all of my experience of hearing that sacred service read, there has been none to equal it. It is impossible to describe the religious fervor, the divine exaltation, the effacement of self that one felt throughout that service, the being brought in close communion with our merciful Father Himself. The inspiration of that service will live with me always.

The physically taxing exertion clearly took its toll on the fasting rabbi. His sisters "used to sit there [in the balcony] and worry how he would be after that." His wife used to *know*: "Herbert was all knocked out from the two sermons and the N'ila...."*

Possibly the most dramatic High Holy Day services in the history of the I.S. took place not in New York City but in Long Beach, Long Island. The year was 1926, when the I.S. was at its peak in terms of activity while, on the other hand, the Harlem Jewish community that had supported the I.S. so generously was beginning to deteriorate. The financial squeeze this created was nothing short of demoralizing, particularly since this was a full year before the West Side branch was destined to be opened to assist the main branch.

The High Holy Days, calculated according to the lunar calendar, came out "early"** in this particular pre-airconditioning year of 1926, and the synagogue had many active members who vacationed in this Long Island seacoast resort of Long Beach for the entire summer. It was not surprising, therefore, that a number of

---

*The expression "knocked out" was strong language coming from this usually soft-spoken source. It must have *really been* a draining experience!

**In the first rather than the second half of September.

them proposed organizing High Holy Day services out on this refreshing and breezy shore, under the auspices of the I.S. Accordingly, the ever helpful Clarence Liberman "took the train over to Long Beach every night, except Friday and Saturday, for a 2 or 3 week period to sell tickets, staying until 9 or 10 o'clock."

Some of the directors argued that if Rabbi Goldstein himself would conduct the services in Long Beach on *Rosh Hashanah*, the Jewish New Year holiday—constituting the first two of the High Holy Days—he could attract many additional worshipers not affiliated with the I.S. The Harlem congregants, they felt, would attend the I.S. services in New York City regardless of who would lead them. At the same time, the I.S. without Rabbi Goldstein in the pulpit on the High Holy Days must have seemed unthinkable. The debate raged unresolved within the I.S. board of directors until the first early morning hour of the last full day before the holiday was to begin. Mrs. Goldstein's entry for the meeting that had begun the previous evening stated, in cryptic form:

> Great uncertainty as to the advisability of Herbert's going to Long Beach for *Rosh Hashanah*. New York directors said "no"; Long Beach directors said "yes." Final decision that we should go was made at 12:30 [A.M.].

Her diary excerpts for the three days* spent in Long Beach speak for themselves:

> Thursday, September 9. 1st day of Rosh Hashanah . . . Fair sized crowd at our services which were held in the vestry room of the Beth Israel Temple and from which we were to derive half the proceeds of the sale of seats—after we had paid the expenses. . . .
>
> Friday, September 10. 2nd Day Rosh Hashanah. . . . Herbert made a splendid appeal which brought in about $4,000. We were all very elated about it. Many people from the Temple upstairs came down and many from other places in town who heard of Herbert's presence here also came. . . . Herbert made such a wonderful impression that the Temple authorities agreed to *waive* their share of the rental of our seats and give us the entire proceeds.
>
> *Victory* number 1. After dinner, the I.S. delegation was on hand again to hold a thanksgiving celebration. They also went to see some more people—possible donors. The reports of Herbert's excellent talk spread and a demand arose for him to speak upstairs in the Temple. He said, of course, that a

---

*The holiday ended Friday night, so, not being permitted by Jewish Law to drive on Saturday, they stayed till the end of the Saturday Sabbath.

$1,000,000.00 check couldn't persuade him to do that, unless the sexes were divided.

Saturday, September 11. During our *Schacharit* [morning] service, the Rabbi of the Temple [Norman Goldberg] came down purposely to invite Herbert to speak upstairs at the request of the upstairs congregation, assuring Herbert at the same time that the sexes were divided.

Victory number 2. The entire downstairs congregation was also invited upstairs and it was a regular *triumphal march* when we all walked upstairs.

Victory number 3, and most wonderful of all, Herbert delivered a sermon that was a masterpiece in thought, delivery, and inspirational power. Everybody went wild about him and he stirred the audience to such a pitch that many suggested that a portion of the money raised for the Temple should be given to us. Utilizing this high pitch of enthusiasm, Herbert and his faithful committee visited a few people this afternoon and evening and got almost $1,000. in additional pledges. . . . One man gave $500.

Sunday, September 12. Herbert [after returning to New York City] went back to Long Beach at the request of some of our directors, this morning, to see some possible donors. He came back at 1 o'clock with $250.

Friday, September 17 [as Yom Kippur eve approached]. The Al-mighty is certainly showing us His miracle and rewarding Herbert for his unselfish devotion to the cause of Orthodox Judaism. In these days, when conditions look so bad in Harlem, when so many people are moving away and we have been overwhelmed with fear as to the possibility of raising our budget, the Long Beach project turns out to be such a howling success. . . . Things like this are encouraging not only to Herbert and me but to all those who are still working for the I.S. . . . .

While the Institutional Synagogue observances of the many other Jewish holidays of the year could not quite match those of the High Holidays, each colorful holiday on the traditional Jewish calendar* was lit up at the I.S. by its own distinctive highlights.

Observances of the holiday of *Sukkot*, or Tabernacles, requires the construction of temporary huts simulating the living quarters of wandering Jews in the Sinai desert after the Exodus. The I.S.

---

*Incredibly, pseudo-Reformers, under the assumed name of "purifiers" of Jewish traditions, have simply eliminated some of these holidays. In so doing—or *undoing*—they have even further bankrupted their padded religious accounts by the criteria applied in classical Jewish ledgers.

Sukkah, or "hut," which accommodated about 300 people, was hardly a humble abode, however, in terms of size.* Nevertheless, the throngs that streamed into it after each main service of the holiday, for the religious benedictions over a cup of wine and a piece of cake,** actually had to be served in shifts.

From Holiday Booth. . . To Party Sweet Tooth

The distinctive feature of the *Shemini Atzeret* holiday, which comes at the conclusion of the *Sukkot* holiday, was the annual *"Shemini Atzeret* Party" thrown by the Goldsteins who opened both their hearth and their hearts to the congregation. These parties at the Goldstein home were not characterized by small talk or gossip, but by speeches, Hebrew songs, good cheer, "the dainties and refreshments of Mrs. Goldstein," and "the usual ready wit of our beloved rabbi and *rebbetzin* [rabbi's wife]." In later years, for those "[a]mong the happy gathering who had walked from Washington Heights and from the West Side, it was in the nature of a 'pilgrimage.'"

This annual afternoon party led right into the joyous *Simchat Torah* holiday which features processions around the synagogue with the Torah scrolls and high-spirited levity. At the I.S., these processions began before the people even reached the synagogue and before they even touched the Torah scrolls. The rabbi and the other synagogue officials undoubtedly sailed into the I.S. from the party in high physical spirits as they led a lively nucleus into the synagogue.*** Theirs was truly a once-a-year type of "preparation" for the normally otherworldly and religious brand of spirituality generally associated with synagogue and holiday prayers. The boys "dressed up with beards, to look like *chassidim,*"****according to one of them, and "old men," according to the more objective Mrs. Goldstein. They also "acted as a choir," which is quite a far—and shrill—cry from mere participation in congregational singing which only involves chanting along, ideally in unison, with the cantor. One can get the "feel," if not, thankfully, the *sound,* of the medley that ensued, by the comment that "everybody, especially the youngsters who sang away for dear life, had a great

---

*However, in terms of furnishing, it was hardly a palace either. The first year of its use in the main building, the flags and bunting were not even bought, anew, but they were merely collected from "the old I.S. building" and brought over by Clarence and Mrs. Goldstein.

**Some years, *challah*—special braided bread—and fruit were also available.

***The rabbi himself, it is authoritatively reported, was *not* "under the influence."

****Chassidim are Jews who are most prominently characterized by their retention of the outward appearance and dress of their ancestors in Eastern Europe, and their inward devotion to a religious leader or "rebbe."

time."

For many years, every *Simchat Torah* holiday at the I.S. was marked by Clarence Liberman's patented routine in which he "went through his annual comical take-off" of Rabbi Goldstein, "impersonating him," according to Mrs. Goldstein, "to a T," and *she* should surely have known, as nobody else! Not content to deliver a mere sermon, Clarence also, on occasion, spiced up his delivery with "a mock appeal for funds," which, by Mrs. Goldstein's assessment, "was great," and on another occasion addressed "the [mock] 'Bar Mitzvah' boy, who in this case was our [veteran] Cantor, Mr. Lauer,"—hardly a thirteen-year old Bar Mitzvah boy!*

When the synagogue branch was established on the West Side, Clarence, like a good soldier, spoke there as well. By 1929, Clarence's last year at the I.S., the rabbi's son Simeon, who was fourteen by then, and who was being eased into some of Clarence's roles, delivered his maiden "sermon" at the main synagogue, while Clarence spoke at the branch. The synagogue newspaper captured some of the theater of the occasion:

> Simeon punctuated his remarks with fidelity to his famed father's mannerisms and gestures. His mode of expression and his speaking with deep faith and understanding reminded everyone of the Rabbi. The adjustment of the *Talit* [prayer shawl] about his shoulders, his kissing the *parochet* [the ornamental curtain resting on the holy ark (this gesture is often made as a religious token of respect for what is behind it)], his movement and pacings of the body, all served to heighten the premeditated imitation of our beloved Rabbi in action, to the delight of the knowing congregation, and Rabbi Goldstein who was present.

Nobody could say that the atmosphere of this unusual holiday service did not go to the heads of those who enlivened the proceedings so animatedly. On one occasion, the cantor "had on an elaborate headdress and used a *lulav* [palm branch saved from its quite different use on the *Sukkot* holiday] as a baton" with which he "conducted" the "choir."

From Holiday of Lightheadedness...To "Festival of Lights"

Chanukah holiday celebrations organized by every I.S. club and organization were as festive as would be expected, and need no

---

*The amiable Cantor Lauer preceded and then assisted the professional Cantor Yavneh for many years.

elaboration. What *might* have stood out, though, was the Goldsteins' preoccupation both with the holiday and with I.S. members even when the Goldsteins were out of town and on vacation. The day after they arrived at Atlantic City one year, Rabbi and Mrs. Goldstein went out on the boardwalk for a quiet and leisurely walk by themselves. Sure enough, when they returned, it was not before they had "picked up a number of the I.S. girls who [came] back to the Hotel with us [wrote Mrs. Goldstein] and [all the women present] listened to [the rabbi recite the appropriate blessings over his] Chanukah candles" before joining him in singing the traditional holiday melodies.

Escape from Darkness followed by Escape from Slavery

The most outstanding I.S. function centering around the holiday of Passover was to be *completed* each year even *before* the eight-day holiday was actually to begin! A self-imposed responsibility undertaken by the synagogue each year was that of seeing to it that the needy members of the community would be able to enter the holiday—which commemorates the freedom of the Jewish people from slavery and servility—as people who would not experience slavery and servility to a severely limited budget. In other words, the I.S. supplied the needy with enough food and clothing to celebrate this holiday, commemorating renewed Jewish dignity, in a dignified manner!

We have seen earlier how the Social Service League took full charge of this project in a modest way the first year of the synagogue's existence. Beginning with the following year, this project, too big for those who had initiated it so admirably, was taken over by the Sisterhood itself. This "senior"—though *itself* less than two-year old—organization staffed the building every evening over an extended period of time, with women "ready to accept contributions." The Sisterhood also was in a position to call from its ranks women with "machines" (automobiles) to solicit donations of matzo from matzo factories. One year, no fewer than 190 pounds (86.18 kilos) of matzo were obtained from this single set of sources (seasonal businesses at the peak of their only real season) two weeks before the holiday was to begin! The very first year that the Sisterhood ran this project, it disposed of about a thousand pounds (450 kilos) of matzo, as well as an unspecified amount of clothing.

In 1926, "six large organizations," noting "from past experience...that there [had] been much duplication, due to [which] many worthy families had to be overlooked...volunteered to pool their funds and clear their lists." The formalities were arranged, with the aid of the Harlem District of the United Hebrew Charities of the City of New York, at a meeting which was held at the

Y.W.H.A. on the ides of March, an "auspicious" a time as any to create "the Harlem Joint Passover Relief Fund." Since by this time, according to the chairperson of the Harlem District, the I.S. was considered "the Harlem community center, it was decided that this would be the most advantageous point for the granting of relief." To solidify the grip of the I.S. on this joint venture still further, its first treasurer was Mrs. Annie Morris, the I.S. Sisterhood president who was described more than a decade later as having personally been "always in the vanguard of our Passover relief work...."

Two years later:

> Under the auspices of the...Fund, 540 Jewish families were given substantial and material aid at the I.S....
> $2,000. in cash was distributed in varying amounts; 3,000 pounds (1,350 kilos] of matzos and matzo meal, [unspecified amounts of other food items], clothing, and tickets entitling obtainment of chicken at designated butcher shops, were among the forms of relief distributed.*

From Mountains of Food...To Mountains of Sinai

The night that the Ten Commandments were given to Moses on Mount Sinai is commemorated by the holiday of *Shavuot*, "The Feast of Weeks."** Most appropriately, many people follow the custom of staying up all night to study selected Biblical writings and prepare for figuratively renewing their acceptance of them. Many of these people, however, expend their energies entirely on the limited goal of trying to pass the time away without falling

---

*These were pre-Depression figures. After the Great Depression had set in and four additional years of Jewish "flight" and neighborhood deterioration had taken their toll, the figures did not drop nearly as dramatically as may have been expected. Although the major donors were lucky if they had not been ruined financially *themselves* in the interim, and there was no shortage of *recipients* even as far back as 1922 when reference had been made not to a neat statistical breakdown but to "a mob of cases," the Depression figures were remarkably respectable:

Approximately 276 families were taken care of in Harlem; Cash received and spent, $1,249.50, Matzos and Meal, 2,500 pounds [1125 kilos]; Sugar, 480 pounds [216 kilos]; Salt, 480 bxs. [boxes], Tea, 50 pkgs. [packages]; Candles, 20 bxs. (72 in box); Nuts, 50 pounds [23 kilos]; Apples, 3 bbls. [barrels].

An astounding point of comparison is that in the pre-Depression figures cited, "25 percent of the cases were 'foreign'" to Harlem, coming "from various downtown centers and from the Bronx," whereas the Depression funds were channeled exclusively back into the Harlem community, which means that more pounds of matzo were donated by members of the severely depleted Harlem community to Harlem families during the Depression than went to them the year before the bubble burst in the "roaring twenties"!

**The holiday is so named because of the special religious significance of—and the formal count-down during—the seven-week period between Passover and this holiday.

asleep rather than trying to pass the chain of Biblical knowledge on to others without its falling apart.

The first *Shavuot* at the I.S. featured "an all night session and party according to the tradition." The *session* came first. Exactly how "traditional" the party was can be questioned. Since the holy day is called the *Feast* of Weeks, however, a properly conducted "party" *following* an all night study vigil and early morning prayer service would surely pass near-universal muster. Nevertheless, by the fourth season, only the study session and *not* the party remained!*

Tu Bishvat, "the Jewish Arbor Day," may have seemed to some to receive a disproportionately large measure of attention at the I.S. compared to the attention it was and is generally given elsewhere. On an otherwise ordinary Monday evening, a celebration of this minor holiday drew "more than one thousand [Hebrew School] children" to the I.S. auditorium.** The event was highlighted by a showing of "the stereopticon views of Palestine taken by Rabbi Goldstein" and narrated by Rabbi Goodman. Of greater significance, from a young child's point of view, was the day's designation by the Parents' Association as a holiday worthy of being celebrated with the distribution of cookies and candies.

Try as one might, it would be difficult to find anything particularly out of the ordinary, beyond pure numbers of participants, about the I.S. celebrations of the holidays of *Purim* (commemorating Queen Esther's lead role in the deliverance of Persian Jewry from a general massacre) and *Lag B'Omer**** (observed, inter alia, as a reminder of the cessation of a plague which threatened to destroy the multitude of prominent students of the first century Rabbi Akiba).**** Each of these two holidays is so unique in its own right that by their very nature they lend themselves to programs that stand out wherever they are celebrated. The joyous holiday of *Purim* is distinguished by masquerades all over the world, so the I.S. masquerades, on a relative basis, produced no particularly unprecedented novelties. As to *Lag B'Omer*, the members of the I.S. generally had a field day, both literally and

---

*The advance publicity by that time was limited to the statement that "Rabbi Goldstein has invited Mr. Pearlman, the scholar, to deliver a discourse from mid-night to the break of day, Friday, and at the conclusion of *Shacharit* [the morning prayer]."

**Notice that the evening timing meant the house would be packed even after regular Hebrew School hours.

***Although we have seen examples of celebrations of each of these holidays in earlier chapters and in different contexts.

****An outline of this rabbi's love affair with a beautiful woman and with a classic tradition appears in Chapter 33.

figuratively, on this holiday.* Even without a formal program, however, this particular holiday has almost a built-in guarantee of a good time, since it comes as an oasis of joy on the Jewish calendar, so to speak, interrupting a long period of semi-mourning, so anything pleasant arranged for this day only naturally gives vent to nearly unrestrained pleasure and frivolity!

*This was in line with the custom to have field days on this holiday for a variety of reasons. The least mystic reason is that on this day the author of the mystic Zohar passed away, but at his death he is alleged to have revealed to his pupils many illuminating thoughts that "filled the world with light." The day is therefore celebrated in Israel by pilgrimages to his grave in the northern part of the country. Once there, they also go—and have gone, for centuries—into the nearby countryside to "celebrate."

Chapter 33

Icing On The Birthday Cakes

If the I.S., as we have just seen, had the capacity to bring its members close to Jewish and American holidays alike, it would not require too much imagination to speculate on how close the members of the I.S. must have felt to the annual celebration of their *own* collective birthday. Nevertheless, some of these annual anniversary celebrations of the synagogue had features that would defy imaginations as they practically glowed with the mutual signs of respect that emanated from rabbi to synagogue to community and then back again in a noble cycle of reciprocal recognition and appreciation.

A special "Fifth Anniversary Sermon" was delivered at the I.S. by Dr. Moses Hyamson, who for two years had served as the Acting Chief Rabbi of the British Empire—when there had still been an Empire to speak of. On this particular occasion, he spoke of the attributes of both the I.S. and its rabbi. If his post-service visit to the Goldstein home was any indication of the longstanding rapport that united the two rabbis, his praise was more than perfunctory. Mrs. Goldstein recorded: "Dr. Hyamson came home with us for dinner [after the service, which ended about noon], and stayed with us till 4:30 *schmusing* [chatting informally]."

The banquet the following evening featured, according to its coverage in the Jewish press, the participation of seven individuals who were, or were destined to become, judges, five prominent rabbis, and "the most popular cantor of his age" (by the judgment of the *Universal Jewish Encyclopedia*), Joseph Rosenblatt, who sang at least twice in the course of the multi-course dinner. The most personal nuggets of the celebration, predictably enough, were tucked away in Mrs. Goldstein's diary:

> [When her husband was introduced, he] got a most
> wonderful ovation. . . . Everybody stood up, and the boys sang,
> "For He's a Jolly Good Fellow."*. . . .[O]n behalf of the Board
> of Directors, [her husband] was presented a most gorgeous
> sterling silver 6-piece tea service. Herbert responded. . . by
> saying that he did not like to take any gift for his service, but as
> long as they did want to give him something, he was glad they
> picked something which I could enjoy and appreciate, for he
> said all that he is and that he has done he owes to me. He also
> told, in this connection, the story of Rabbi Akiba and his
> wife.** Then there was a cheer and a "She's a Jolly Good
> Fellow" for me. . . .Papa [the philanthropist who certainly
> knew the meaning of money] said he wouldn't take
> $10,000,000.00 for the occasion.***
>
> [W]e [Rabbi and Mrs. Goldstein] both felt prayerful and
> thankful to God for His great kindness and goodness to us,
> that he privileged us to live to see the beginning of the
> complete realization of our dream of 5 years ago. It just goes to
> show that our guiding principle was correct—namely, any-
> thing undertaken "lishmaw," [with the intent of fulfilling
> God's wishes, above all, rather than only one's personal
> desires], in sincerity, must succeed.

The egalitarian nature of the synagogue could be detected by
even a cursory analysis of the seating arrangements. The congress-
man-president and his party were not ensconced at a dais or even a
"table number one," but at a modest table number seventeen, and
the rabbi and his party were at table thirteen, a number that
superstitious Americans avoid with such tenacity that the designers
of some skyscrapers, in designating floor numbers, throw the laws
of physics—and gravity—to the wind and "skip" from the
twelfth floor to the fourteenth. Anybody seated at the table with
the synagogue's spiritual head, of course, even if not at a head table
per se, could not possibly have felt slighted.

Normally, of course, Rabbi Goldstein could anticipate only

---

*Note that it was this relationship of fellowship, rather than an attempt at personal
lordship, vis-a-vis his followers, that sustained his success.

**In a nutshell, Akiba was an ignorant shepherd who fell in love with the daughter of the
wealthy owner of the flock under his control. With her self-effacing encouragement, he went off
to study the Talmud from scratch when he was forty years old. Notwithstanding his late start, he
developed into "the father of rabbinical Judaism" and the undisputed leader of another
"flock"—of admiring rabbinical students—in his own lifetime and for posterity.

***Note that the largest public cash donation to the I.S. announced in his name was $500,
so he certainly was not one to steamroll his son-in-law to success on a silver platter—or even a
silver tea service!

300

honor and glory at the I.S. anniversary dinners, but even on the single occasion when all he could have anticipated, had he participated, was physical discomfort, he absorbed as much punishment as he could possibly endure, for the sake of the success of the synagogue affair. According to the synagogue's first lady's first person account:

> Herbert developed a stiff neck and was in excruciating pain. He screwed up all his energy and went to the *9th annual I.S. dinner, at the Hotel Astor*. He was in such terrible pain, however, that we had to go home after the first course.

A cloud hung over the tenth anniversary dinner as well, although *this* time the anguish the rabbi endured was *emotional* and the constraint on his attendance was *legal*. Jewish law forbids a person who is in mourning for a parent to listen to music, and the year of mourning for Rabbi Goldstein's father was at its midpoint. The directors of the synagogue felt, however, that the ten-year milestone dinner could have the broadest appeal possible only if it would be held in honor of Rabbi Goldstein himself. Thus, his wife wrote, "Of course Herbert had only consented to be personally honored at the dinner, during this, his year of mourning for his father, because he felt it would help the Institutional Synagogue, and it certainly did."

There was to be an appeal for funds at this affair, so the synagogue, in *not* counting on dinner ticket sales for a significant percentage of its projected revenue, was in a position to make the dinner within the financial means of a broad range of its—and the rabbi's—admirers. Its low price policy certainly succeeded in eliciting the desired results. Mrs. Goldstein wrote: "It was surely a tribute to Herbert, for over 700 people [1,000* by a newspaper estimate] from all parts of the city and all walks of life came specifically to do him honor."

In due observance of his mourning status, the rabbi "was escorted in by all those seated on the dais. He just sat at the table a few minutes and then left the hall for the greater part of the dinner, as there was a musical programme during the dinner. When he returned to the hall, the speaking part of the programme began." Rabbi Goldstein said nothing unpredictable in his own address, which he closed with the plea:

> "that any appreciation to [him] could be shown best by the maintaining and perpetuating of [his] ideals in the Institu-

---

*The apparent discrepancy in the estimates may be easily reconciled. The seating list provided for 72 tables of ten people per table, and the I.S. customarily provided for the young unmarrieds to be present for the program and entertainment without being required to obtain a ticket for the dinner itself.

tional Synagogue."

Then came the answer. First, Supreme Court Judge Hon. Aaron J. Levy, humored those present with anecdotes, and...pleaded for the actual pledges, as an answer to the rabbi's challenge. The rabbi arose to announce the presence of the "greatest philanthropist—collector of the day"—and you can believe the statement of the writer that the person so described merited his title. It was none other than Judge Gustave Hartman, who arose to make the appeal. His wholehearted enthusiasm stirred the audience in every sense of the word. Whole tables began an intensive competition to outdo each other in contributing to this cause. The diners arose in applauding tribute to Judge Hartman as he concluded the drive with the announcement of the proceeds that had been collected.

Mrs. Goldstein's account was more crisp and candid:

...Judge Aaron Levy followed with a glowing tribute to Herbert and a weak appeal for the I.S.

Judge Hartman then "went to the bat" and did Herculean work in pulling out $25,000.00 from the assembled guests. It was just thrilling.

The rabbi received encouragement of a practical nature in a non-monetary medium as well, according to the synagogue newspaper:

...[O]ne of the directors surprised the rabbi by presenting him with a tremendous and beautiful traveling bag, on behalf of the directors. The bag is to be used by the rabbi in his trip to California this summer to address the B'nai B'rith Convention.*

Too surprised by the presentation of the traveling bag, however, the rabbi did not appear to have been, since immediately thereafter, he revealed that he was at least a collaborator of sorts in a seemingly related presentation, when "[he] then sprang a further surprise [sic] by presenting another traveling bag to our president...."

The bipartisan but equally strong support the I.S. received from political figures in both of the country's major political

---

*This cross-country trip, incidentally, was utilized by the resourceful rabbi, then president of the Union of Orthodox Jewish Congregations of America, as the basis of a far-reaching "tour of the country in behalf of Orthodox Judaism" in general and the U.O.J.C.A. in particular.

parties was demonstrated most evenhandedly when, despite the fact that the president of the synagogue was a *Republican* former congressman, members of the Owasco *Democratic* Club mustered up a "large attendance at the dinner," and "they donated $250.00 to the building."

The anniversary dinner two years later was dedicated to the *Democratic* incumbent congressman and member of the I.S. Board, the Hon. Sol Bloom, yet the speakers who came to honor him included the Hon. John Q. Tillson, the *Republican* leader of the House of Representatives.

The twentieth anniversary celebration in 1937 was not only the most extensive in the history of the I.S., but it was the last to be held before Rabbi Goldstein and the members of the West Side branch left to create the independent West Side Institutional Synagogue. As if everybody involved subconsciously knew that this celebration would go down in I.S. annals as their last united "hurrah," the synagogue planners not only outdid themselves in relation to all of their past celebrations, but they even delivered more than they had dared to promise. Although normally politicians and other people in the public eye who are particularly anxious to please are notorious for overpromising and then not fully delivering, the I.S., on this occasion, as on others before it, still had the internal strength actually to produce *more* than it had promised, and it did *not* offer modest proposals either. In this climactic year, the I.S. did not simply invite a prominent orator to deliver a guest anniversary sermon the Saturday morning before its large anniversary banquet, but it publicized an anniversary *week* celebration with a different event to highlight *each day* of the week, and then proceeded to schedule special "anniversary week" events for nine consecutive and often multi-event days.

Fully a month before the last of the joint anniversary celebrations were to take place:

> The combination tickets [which] sold for the nominal sum of 50 cents including admission to all of the week's activities [were in such] great demand [that] the first one thousand tickets that [had been] printed [were] completely distributed and additional tickets [had to be] ordered [with so much time still remaining] to meet the unprecedented requests.

The highlights of this nine-day "week" included, on the first Saturday night, graduation exercises of the Hebrew School; on the first Sunday, an inter-city debate, an athletic carnival, a basketball game and a popular orchestra; Monday was "Bible Class Night"; Tuesday, a theatrical event (Sinclair Lewis' *It Can't Happen Here*), in Yiddish, and a patriotic service in commemoration of the 20th anniversary of the United States' entry into the World War;

303

Wednesday, a Parents' Association social; Thursday, a motion picture entertainment; Saturday, anniversary sermons at each branch in the morning, a youth symposium in the afternoon, and an inter-club one-act play contest in the evening; Sunday, the annual dinner.

The climactic annual dinner featured the Joe Moss Orchestra, triumphant from its recent performance "by special request...at a dance given by President and Mrs. Franklin D. Roosevelt at the White House." In addition, for the third time during the week, part of their program was broadcast on the air, providing:

> The most thrilling moment of the evening...when the announcer's voice was heard saying, "This is station WHN broadcasting from the ballroom of the Savoy Plaza Hotel, where the Institutional Synagogue is celebrating its 20th anniversary...."

Thousands of people participated in a series of events destined never to be duplicated in the throbbing Jewish heart of the waning middle-class Harlem community.

Chapter 34

The I. S. Moses Leads The Exodus From Harlem

Ironically and tragically, neighborhoods change so rapidly in America in general and New York City in particular that as soon as a neighborhood approaches its full development, its dominant members often feel compelled to move. Unfortunately for the I.S., Harlem was destined to win the rating of the New York City community "most radically revamped" among all New York neighborhoods in the 1920s. It was in mid-1925 that Congressman Siegel acknowledged outright, for the first time, that "The real rich men and those who have given freely have moved away from Harlem." Until that point, I.S. publications had been brimming with unbounded optimism. Ironically, the strains of the celebration marking the final phase of the renovation of the I.S.'s main building had barely begun to recede just a single month before the close of 1924. And so if 1925 was the turning point, the fully completed I.S. had no more than half a year to count its blessings before it began, nervously, to count the Jews who were streaming out of the community. The trend, however, had been apparent earlier.

Although superficially the dramatic change of the neighborhood was seen by many as a two-dimensional black-and-white matter, careful analysis points to other considerations as well. On one hand, there is no getting away from the figures that show that between 1920 and 1930, 188,792 white people left the neighborhood and 87,417 blacks arrived, and that by 1930, 72 percent of Manhattan's blacks and most of the entire city's 45,000 Puerto Ricans lived in Harlem. These figures, however, by no means tell the whole story. These statistics can only be seen in their true perspective if they are taken, as they *have* been by authoritative sources, side-by-side with the less tangible but no less compelling consideration that the children of immigrant parents traditionally find the general life-styles of their parents unacceptable. Harlem was settled *to begin with* by immigrant parents who *themselves* had moved up to Harlem because they were dissatisfied with conditions on the still more blatantly immigrant-dominated Lower East Side, and because they *themselves* were obsessed with goals leading to upward social mobility. It was thus only natural that *their* children would take the next logical step—and the next available moving van—on to still *more* "Americanized" areas of the city.

To suggest that the Jewish flight from Harlem was based only on skin color would be to flay the Jews unfairly. It was apparent to people of all shades of opinion that at least *some* of the causes for the radical change in the complexion of the neighborhood were rooted in the stark realities that the community suddenly and simultaneously was becoming overwhelmed by people whose presence purportedly brought real estate prices down and physical crime statistics up. We have just looked at the motives of the young to abandon Harlem irrespective of new neighbors who might be left behind, as long as these new neighbors would be no higher in the social world than their own immigrant Jewish parents. Older Jews had an equally compelling motive to move, as newcomers engulfed their neighborhood, and this motive, too, would have been potent no matter who their new neighbors might have been. It may be noted that their own ghettos in Europe, ironically, were not at all hewn by hands cuffed in iron. To the contrary, their ancestors had originally locked themselves *into* communities voluntarily, creating ghettos by choice in Europe.* Once in the American land of opportunity, many Jews, due in part to their strong sense of community, moved, out of their own free will, into neighborhoods that outsiders considered no better than ghettos. As a result, the snowballing movement of Jews out of the "Hell of Harlem" was no more of an affront to the new residents, in a way, than the Jews' decision not to move to or live in any other neighborhood which could not provide them with—or which threatened—their cherished sense of "community."

On the other, more unfortunate, regrettable and contemporary side of the world picture, many ghettos of Europe evolved, in the course of centuries, to a point where discrimination against their Jewish inhabitants-by-choice came to be imposed *by law*. Once-captivating ghettos were suddenly used *against* Jews and converted into virtual community prisons of captivity, in a manner that was

---

*Only later did the ghettos turn into virtual prisons. Bible followers will recall that Joseph's brothers' families went through a similar experience, coming to Goshen to live in Egypt as the Pharaohs' invited residents before being doomed to literal slavery and finally breaking free.

far more stiflingly all embracing than that of the often unlawful discrimination associated with the artificial "ghettos" which are now built, in some places, around blacks against, at least, the spirit of the law in the long "emancipated" United States.

Jews, as a long-suffering minority, have historically borne more than their due share of "racial" discrimination in their *own* right—and others' wrongs. So, had all other factors been equal, they certainly would have been *more* likely than most other groups to identify *with* the plight of other minorities. Many Jews who felt they *were* their black brothers' keepers identified most dramatically as they "kept the faith" in the Civil Rights movement of the 1960s which they had helped to organize, and in which many marched shoulder to shoulder with the black "civil disobedient" leaders in the critical confrontations in the seething American South.

Notwithstanding all the good will and common problems of persecution, however, open anti-Semitism within the black community cannot, unfortunately, be dismissed. Even the author who probed *Inside Black America*—and wrote a book so entitled—concluding that black anti-Semitism was based on "artificial" foundations and revolved around "manufactured enemies," could not deny that the problem was unquestionably "very real." He dated this sorry situation, curiously, to the year of Hitler's rise to power, coinciding with the Great Depression, the arrival of Jewish refugees from Germany, and the allegation, which even this authority conceded was false, that these refugees would have more than an "infinitesimal" impact on the job market as it affected blacks. Yet "Captain" Carlos Cook, a Harlem "race missionary," was not alone when he would address local rallies and refer to Hitler with the open observation that, "What he's trying to do, we're trying to do!"

A far more likely explanation for the anti-Semitism is that it was basically "an anti-white manifestation," and the Jew in Harlem was the black's most visible white with whom he had contact as landlord, merchant, employer, and "professional."

Still another view is that anti-Semitism was promoted by "unscrupulous Negroes" who sought to "exploit the Negro community's legitimate grievances" and cast the Jews in their traditional scapegoat role.

It seems clear that religious differences were not at the heart of whatever black anti-Semitism may have existed.* It also seems clear that many of the reasons advanced to try to explain the existence of black anti-Semitism apply to the 1930s, and the Jewish "exodus" was well on its way in the mid-1920s, so we are left with the conclusion that anti-Semitism was not really a key factor in the

---

*One "proof" advanced for this negative thesis is that black Jews would otherwise have been among the first victims.

307

early neighborhood change that touched off the great exodus.

The relationship of the I.S. with the blacks in its community was almost *too* harmonious for the good of either! We have already seen how well the blacks were integrated into the Hebrew School. The reception blacks received was *so* warm, however, that many began to come whom Rabbi Goodman, the school's principal, suspected were not even Jewish. We have already seen in the discussion on revivalism that, unlike Christians, Jews not only consider themselves too busy—trying to strengthen the religion of their co-religionists—to spend time and energy trying to find people outside of their faith to "enlighten" or impose their will upon, but Jews are even required by their code of law to *discourage* conversions not only *from* but even *to* their religion.* Sure enough, on one occasion, fourteen black adults came to the I.S. to study Hebrew. Rabbi Goodman had some qualms about the nature of their professed Jewish roots and prepared a questionnaire for them to fill out so he could determine the authenticity of their claims. On the basis of the replies, he felt compelled to cancel the special class that they had asked the synagogue to start on their behalf.

Those blacks whose Jewish roots were found to have been legitimate, however, unquestionably "participated in all activities." In addition, once "it was determined" that those who had not been born Jewish had authentically converted to Judaism in the past, they, along with born-Jewish blacks, were all accepted with no further questions asked—"including former slaves."

A lady with an Irish name recalled her conversations with Rabbi Goldstein who happened to have inspired her on one of his many radio programs. She recalled visiting the I.S. to see the rabbi in person, and commented:

> . . . There were many young black boys attending it, and I could see that Rabbi Goldstein was helping them in material as well as spiritual ways.—In fact, while I was talking to Rabbi Goldstein, one of the boys interrupted to thank him for the new shoes he had received.

No matter to how minimal a degree anti-Semitism may have festered at first, and no matter how well Jewish blacks may have been received at the I.S., there was simply no getting away from the fact that Jews were moving away from Harlem not just as individuals but on a community-wide scale. By 1926, the synagogue that was across the street from the I.S., the First Hungarian Congregation Ohab Zedek—the home base of the great Cantor

---

*Witness the Biblical *Book of Ruth.*

308

Rosenblatt—found it "necessary," for "the fifth time in a little more than half a century...to select a new house of worship" in a different neighborhood. In this same year, the I.S. found it necessary to launch its daring one-time sensationally successful high holiday venture into Long Beach because its leadership was "overwhelmed with fear as to...raising the budget."

By 1927, the first I.S. appeal for funds at the West Side *branch* in its first season netted more than the Yom Kippur appeal for funds at the *main* branch in Harlem. By 1928, the synagogue newspaper casually mentioned that "the substantial element" had moved away, and by September of 1929, the Saturday morning attendance dipped to as low as a hundred people on one occasion.*

There was no question that the West Side Branch, almost as soon as it was founded, became the main means of support of the "main" branch in Harlem. Rabbi Goldstein, accordingly, devoted an increasing proportion of his time to the new branch, even though he did not personally move out of Harlem until 1932. In 1930, Mrs. Goldstein was moved to remark, after a holiday service at the West Side branch, "Fine congregation—great contrast to the scarcity of *Bal Habatim* [heads of household] at the 116th Street building."

All of these statistics and comparisons do not by any means mean that the building on 116th Street became an empty shell. Far from it! Although the numbers may have been decreasing, we have seen that the I.S. stubbornly resisted the downward trend of the Jewish population like an automobile going down a long and winding mountain road in low gear, with maximum traction—and, in the case of the I.S., attraction—giving its passengers as much of the atmosphere and scenery of the summit as possible for as long as possible.

Although many of the members and the donors gradually slipped away, the *need* for the activities of the I.S. in Harlem remained for the hundreds of people the synagogue *continued to service* as long as Rabbi Goldstein was affiliated with it. In 1928, the I.S. line became:

> Ours is certainly not a local movement. It can no longer look to the people of the neighborhood of Harlem for support...It is now a communal problem and responsibility....**

The "radical change in the type of members" simply put the Harlem I.S., in the eyes of its leaders, "on the basis of pure

---

*This was admittedly on the border of the summer vacation season.

**The "community," in their eyes, of course, became expanded to include the "West Side."

SETTLEMENT [social] work rather than the former Jewish Community Center functions, to which it traditionally held." "Functions" here seems like a poor choice of words. The *functions* the I.S. served throughout these difficult years remained constant, as did the synagogue's basic goals and activities. What changed were the venues—and the sources of the revenues—of the leading fund-raising functions. (The main shift was not so much in the way funds were *spent* as in the way, and locations in which, they were *acquired*.) The growing branch on the West Side was obviously thriving in what were rapidly developing into greener pastures. Even without photosynthesis, however, it brought sunshine to the main frame in Harlem, and tangible sustenance back to the roots that had nurtured the whole complex into being.

Great Depression Hits...And I.S. Hits Back

The Great Depression did not hit Harlem significantly harder than it hit any other community. The exodus and the budget deficit had begun long before the crash of 1929, and Harlem's gradual shift to the status of a black community had a far greater impact on the I.S. than had Black September. But the Depression did not exactly *help* matters.

In 1931, the teachers and staff members had four months of unpaid salaries to fret about, but, in retrospect, they would have been relatively content with this situation, since half a year later, "due to [then] present conditions," the board unilaterally reduced all salaries retroactively by five percent. By today's labor union standards, of course, this would be outrageous, but the "conditions" of the Depression, by *anybody's* standards, were no less outrageous! There is no available record of any firings for economic cause, and the retroactivity only extended four days back, so as terrible as the action may have sounded, its impact on the programs at the I.S. was *still* far less significant than the over-all loss of financial support within the community caused by the exodus of the 1920s.

The measures taken by the I.S. board of directors to keep the I.S. afloat were all the more remarkable because they were voluntary. In 1930, the directors voted to impose on each and every one of themselves an obligation to raise $200 in one two and one-half month period. The following year, nineteen members of the board further obligated themselves to raise the additional sum of $250 within a two-month period. What makes these sacrifices so noteworthy is the consideration that unlike the members of the I.S.'s paid staff, each individual director was free to drop out of the scene at any time with no personal loss, and, if anything, with the loss of only a financial *burden*, yet they chose of their own free will to *stay*, and to sacrifice.

Most significantly, "eventually," every single person on the I.S. payroll in this painful period "got paid to the last penny"—and this is the testimony not of a public relations department official but of the office secretary who was behind the scenes and on top of the situation.

While other organizations—certainly nonprofit ones—cut back their operations and the services offered during the Depression, the I.S. considered itself more indispensable than ever. While drawing its primary support from afar, the I.S. published these words of encouragement for those who felt close to it, and for those who felt close to despair:

IN TIMES OF DEPRESSION

In Times of Depression . . .

The I.S. extends its social welfare work and its facilities; [Hebrew School] tuition is offered free; Social-Educational facilities are offered free; physical recreation department program activities are offered free.

In Times of Depression . . .

It is most incumbent that the I.S. should play a significant part in sustaining the morale of our young people now unemployed.

In Times of Depression . . .

Unemployment—the serious depletion in family incomes—bills must be paid—the morale of the family unit must be preserved—rent—food—clothing—winter weather, unoccupied time—Pool Parlors and Dives provide a glamorous escape from troubles for young men—questionable dance resorts offer a tinsled escape for young girls.

Then Does the I.S. Offer a Haven!

An encouragement; an uplifting atmosphere; a genial and most Friendly Aid . . .

After a majority of Harlem's Jews had pulled up their stakes, after the Depression had set in, and after Rabbi Goldstein had begun to focus most of his attention on the West Side branch, those members of the I.S. who remained needed a strong stabilizing influence. They got it in Rabbi Philip Goodman, who came to the I.S. with an unusual and solid educational and religious background, having attended the Teachers Institute of Yeshiva University, while simultaneously attending the City College of New York, then having been ordained two years later at the prestigious a of Rabbi Kook, the Chief Rabbi of Israel, in Jerusalem.

More importantly, Rabbi Goodman was practical, creative, and resourceful. He wrote a number of manuals and anthologies for youth programming, which were duly recognized by establishment organizations.*

Rabbi Goodman did *not* come to the I.S. in 1933 with a pessimistic attitude. By no means was he resigned to preside over its agonizing demise in the aftermath of the mass of relocations of the 1920's and in the midst of the economic hardships of the 1930s. Rabbi Goodman not only creatively stamped his own imprint onto the I.S. Hebrew School, as we have seen, but he pioneered the concept of an Orthodox Home Camp as well. Although the congregation he led was never as large as it had been in the 1920s, a daily service was maintained in the 116th Street building throughout the years of cooperation between the Harlem and West Side branches of the I.S., and even for the duration of the Harlem branch's existence after the rift.

As long as Rabbi Goldstein and the West Side branch had been working together with and supporting the "main" branch in Harlem, Goodman had labored under his senior rabbinical colleague's ubiquitous shadow. Although on paper it was the West Side *branch* that became independent in 1937, in actuality the *main* branch in Harlem was the entity that felt the responsibilities of financial independence most tellingly at that juncture—or disjuncture—while only then did Rabbi Goodman first don the mantle of pastoral independence. After this point, he recalled, "Rabbi Goldstein had nothing to do with the I.S." Harlem branch.** Curiously, for the first five years of Goodman's tenure, his title in the official synagogue newspaper was listed as "executive director" while Rabbi Goldstein was listed as "rabbi,"*** although even by the beginning of this period, Rabbi Goldstein—who had moved to the West Side in 1932—had long since established his primary personal base of operations outside of Harlem. In fact, while Rabbi Goodman regularly occupied the pulpit during this period—and beyond—his occasional co-occupant of the pulpit was not even Rabbi Goldstein, but, rather, the loyal "Maimonides" of the I.S., Rabbi Goldstein's own mentor, Dr. Kapner! In the unusual relationship that existed

---

*In the course of his career, he was appointed administrative secretary of the World Federation of Y.M.H.A.'s and Jewish Community Centers, and director of Jewish Education of the Jewish Center Division of the Jewish Welfare Board.

**In fact, this was far from a hard and fast rule.

***Rabbi Goldstein's name and title remained on the masthead of the Harlem-based synagogue newspaper for a year after the West Side branch had broken off, during which time the newspaper reflected the new realities by halving its number of pages, although it never publicly mentioned the creation of the West Side Institutional Synagogue or the causes of the complete break between the two former branches.

between the I.S. and the gifted radiologist—who, according to the synagogue newspaper, "radiate[d] a loftiness of spirit and a creative intelligence that was contagious"—Dr. Kapner was in a position to deliver a sermon, during these years, "in Yiddish, whenever he felt like it!"* Dr. Kapner, who had delivered the annual pre-Passover special learned lecture ("*Shabbat Hagadol pilpul*") at the Harlem synagogue since at least the early 1920s, had no trouble dictating his own schedule at will. He was recognized and appreciated as a person who "epitomize[d], in his person and temperament, the ideal, classic Jew...scholar and saint, teacher and healer, mature yet buoyant...."

The West Side branch, likewise, was able to draw on both Goodman and Kapner, in the two scholars' own particular areas of strength and utility. Rabbi Goodman served as principal of "both Hebrew Schools—at both branches"—and Dr. Kapner delivered his special pre-Passover intricate Talmudic discourses not only at the West Side branch—sometimes the very afternoon of his morning sermon in Harlem—but even at the West Side Institutional Synagogue after it was to declare its independence.

In April of 1937, just before the West Side Institutional Synagogue shed its branch status, took its leave of Harlem, and formally assumed its own independent identity, Lester Udell, then destined to become the first president of the W.S.I.S., actually "raised the question" at a meeting of the board of directors of the *original* I.S., "about the advisability of continuing to maintain the 116th Street building" at all. The Harlem branch hung on gamely, no longer as "a lighthouse" but, in a sense, as an island for the lighthouse to occupy as well, in its changed community, for another five years, until Congressman Siegel met his untimely death. A bank to which the I.S. had become mortgaged then made its due claim, and eventually sold the I.S. building to a Baptist Church.** The spirit of the synagogue itself, ironically, was destined to be "reincarnated" on the West Side in a building purchased by the W.S.I.S. from a church and then renovated for its own purposes.***The residual funds from the sale of the Harlem building—funds that had not been consumed by the mortgage obligations—were allotted, by an I.S. Goldstein-less committee****

---

*A similar arrangement had been in effect whereby he had spoken at his pleasure—and *to* the I.S. congregants' pleasure—on those weeks when Rabbi Goldstein had been on the West Side during the period when he (Rabbi Goldstein) had alternated between the two branches.

**Jewish law generally forbids the direct sale of a synagogue for any non-synagogue-related use, but at this point the I.S. building was no longer in Jewish hands.

***This act *is* encouraged in Jewish tradition, just as its converse is *discouraged.*

****He was no longer connected with the original I.S.—or even its "ghost."

to a host of organizations in the Jewish community. The annual
income of a designated portion of the synagogue's investments
was distributed according to decisions reached in regular meetings
that continued for decades in the presence of both Rabbi Goodman
and Congressman Siegel's widow. The W.S.I.S. inherited none of
these physical assets, and the *spiritual* assets it came away with
were never the same—and could never have been quite the same—
as they had been in the Harlem heydays and their spiritual
paydays.

Chapter 35

The West Side Branch Takes Root

We have seen that by 1926 it was apparent that the I.S. could not support itself any longer solely from the resources available in the transformed Harlem community. In that year, the I.S.'s most prosperous neighboring synagogue had relocated elsewhere, and the I.S. had to turn an ordinary summer resort, temporarily, into a *last* resort, for fund-raising purposes, with uncanny, unprecedented, and unrepeatable success. By the second month of 1927, the time was unquestionably ripe for the formation of a committee to find an answer to the pressing "question of establishing a West Side branch." Four months later, the committee was authorized to lease the space that was to become the first base for the new branch.

The rooms that were leased in Leslie Hall, at 260 West 83rd Street, were adequate for the purposes to which they were put at first, but they clearly had their limitations, not the least of which was the one recalled by Cantor Yavneh, who understandably did not like to be rushed, particularly since he chanted at a relatively brisk pace—for a professional cantor—already. "We had to be through at a certain time," he remembered, ruefully, "because the place was already reserved for rehearsals for a night club"!

The branch was *not* set up for a grandstand act or a mere series of High Holy Day services. As outlined by Congressman Siegel in his announcement of the creation of the branch, it was to be the scene of:

> ...daily, Sabbath, and High Holy Day services [note the order used] beginning Friday evening, September 9 [more than half a month before the first of the High Holy Days]. Rabbi Herbert S. Goldstein...will preach alternately at the West

Side and Harlem branches [as he indeed did during the first few years of the transition].

The first weekend's services at the West Side branch set the pace for the transition period—and many paces were involved, since those who came down (from Harlem) to the West Side each week for the express purpose of setting up a viable Saturday set of services, made up to three three-mile round trips per Sabbath day—one on Friday night and two on Saturday—all on foot! Jewish law, of course, forbids vehicular traffic in the normal course of events on this day. The option *was* available to them, however, to travel *to* the first service and *from* the last in a vehicle, before and after the prescribed period of time, from Friday before sunset until Saturday night.

By the second round trip of the first Sabbath of the new venture—and the only round trip that had to be made on foot both ways—Mrs. Goldstein, who had *not* joined the trek down, took the long march in stride.

This morning, Herbert, accompanied by some of the I.S. folks, walked down to the West Side Branch again and got home (quite overheated) at 12:45.*

Although Congressman Siegel had announced that the rabbi would speak at the West Side only on alternate weeks, and although the rabbi—then thirty-seven years old—was obviously tempted to let his younger associates bear the brunt of the fatiguing physical hikes involved in getting the new branch on its feet, he took more than his full designated share of the footwork—not to mention the oratorical pressures—with the same youthful enthusiasm that he had summoned for his earlier projects. After the second weekend was over, his wife recorded:

Friday, September 16. [At night] Herbert was down at the West Side Branch of the I.S. for services, and came home quite over-heated, although he maintained that he was not tired.
Saturday, September 17. Herbert went down to the West Side I.S. again this morning and said there were twice as many people this week as last. Thus ventures grow...[while on the home front in Harlem] The boys (Sim and Gaby) [her sons] and I went to the I.S. where there was a fair attendance, considering the change in the neighborhood, and where Congressman Siegel spoke on Constitution Day.

---

*A mere forty-five minutes after high noon on a sweltering summer day, they had a *right* to be overheated!

Although Yom Kippur is a fast day, Rosh Hashanah, the first of the High Holidays, is not. Rabbi Goldstein thus appears to have been unrestricted in his determination, on that two-day holiday, to have his cake and eat it too, or, less figuratively stated, though with an accountant's figures in mind, to cater to *all* his congregants, past, present, and future, by "delivering"—in his case, a sermon—at both congregations. His wife recorded:

> Rosh Hashanah. After supper, Herbert and Clarence walked down to Hotel Greystone on 91st Street, where they stayed overnight, as it was easier to walk after supper than to get up at 5 A.M. to be at services at 6.

Over 400 people attended the first High Holy Day services of the West Side branch, and much of the credit went to the same Sam Silver who had worked such wonders for the early I.S. membership drives in Harlem. Others quickly joined the religious bandwagon, but it is to the credit of the early leaders of the original I.S. that the "magic" had not deserted them in a new neighborhood and in a new decade.

The new undertaking did not take place without generating its tensions, though, between different elements of the synagogue. The Harlem chauvinists fiercely opposed I.S. activities' taking place outside of their community, correctly sensing that this policy would promote a trend toward the placing of increased emphasis on Manhattan's Jewish population center of the future rather than on that of the past. The I.S. pragmatists favored doing the greatest amount of good for the greatest number of people, and further pointed out that even in order to benefit the Harlemites themselves, they would have to involve people from elsewhere. The most effective way of winning over non-Harlemites—given no realistic chance of *bringing* them over, or back, to Harlem— would be to let them see for themselves what the I.S. could do.

The "tug of war" between these two factions of directors had been pronounced in the debates precipitating the Long Branch enterprise—notwithstanding its attendant *financial* prize—and even in the reluctance of some to accept the almost inevitable decision to set up a branch. Rabbi Goldstein's decision to be on the West Side for *more* than half of his key appearances the first couple of weeks undoubtedly did not sit well with many of those who had chosen or felt compelled to stay behind in Harlem. The game of rotating "musical cantors" that was played even on the first High Holidays may have produced some *dis*cord as well. Only one of the cantors, after all was said and sung, was a professional in every sense of the term. The system of alternating cantors continued throughout the early years of the transition period. It was a system that could not possibly satisfy all the people all the time. Three years later, the matter was still a point of contention. The tide gradually shifted with the powerful winds of the west:

> The question of the *chazzanim* [cantors] to officiate for the coming High Holy Days was discussed [at a board meeting] and a motion [was] made, seconded, and carried that Cantor Yavneh officiate at Harlem. A motion [was] made, seconded, and carried that Cantor Yavneh hereafter perform his services as follows: 75 percent for the West Side and 25 percent at Harlem.

Cantor Yavneh dutifully cooperated, of course, and recalled the numerous round trips he made down to the West Side "with the rabbi," but from his point of view, the whole arrangement, "never worked out" to his complete personal satisfaction. He was a family man, and unlike the rabbi he did not have influence on the board comparable to that enjoyed by Rabbi Goldstein, who was considered to be more than just an "employee." Also, as a European by birth and breeding, the cantor quite understandably did not feel quite as "at home" on these adventurous and pioneering forays as did his companions, who were basically, in his eyes, American—or at least "Americanized"—Yankees and his employers.

There is no doubt that the cooperation of the synagogue's employees was important, but what was equally—if not more— essential to the success of the new undertaking was the positive state of the morale of the contingent from Harlem dedicated to creating a new nucleus on the West Side. Spirits were high as the young selfstarters marched down to the territory they were in the process of "conquering"; their religious spirits were reinforced at the actual services; and they may have attained their highest spirits, emotionally, on their triumphant marches home. They were encouraged not only by their continuing string of organizational successes, but also by their regular stopovers en route, at the home of one of the famous "three G's" of clothing manufacturing fame:

> [After going down to the West Side] to establish a *minyan*, [one of them recounted,] we would then go back up [to Harlem.] On the way home, we used to stop off at Isaac Goldman's house on 92nd Street. The room was filled with every brandy you could think of...cake and *schnapps* [the Yiddish and German generic term for any strong liquor].
>
> We would then come back in the afternoon to "make *Mincha*." [Idiomatically, this would normally mean "to be in time for," or to "catch" the late afternoon prayer of *Mincha*. In *this* case it could have been stated literally as well. The young people from Harlem literally helped to *make* the service]...We

would go in any weather, rain or shine.

Harold Kaplan, one of Rabbi Goldstein's earliest and most loyal young followers, recalled these round trips of his youth, with particular reference to his position in the "procession." Both he and Clarence Liberman were in the "big strapping fellow" category, and the two used to flank Rabbi Goldstein on some of those trips and act as "bodyguards." Not only was the walk a long one, but the route went through some neighborhoods that even then were not the friendliest to Jews who did not try to hide their Jewishness. Nobody, but nobody, could ever accuse Rabbi Goldstein of trying to hide his Jewishness. On Saturday mornings, in an era when dignity was still looked upon positively by young people, Rabbi Goldstein regularly dressed up in a formal cutaway and top hat, attire not unusual among style-conscious Jews of large cities in this period. "That hat," Kaplan recalled, "made a rather tempting target, but with Clarence and me around, nobody would dare throw a snowball at the rabbi!"*

The rise of the West Side branch could be measured in inverse proportion to the decline of the Harlem operation, and was so measured, in fact, by the traditionally most objective indicator— money. The synagogue, however, in not overly glorifying the largest contributors to its cause, thereby encouraged contributors of lesser sums to come forward as well. The emphasis was generally on the *cumulative* amount raised either by individuals or by the synagogue. For this reason, open appeals to the general membership assumed greater importance when compared to those held at other institutions that could count on a handful of individuals with open checkbooks ready to wipe out any deficits. Mention has already been made of how the very first Yom Kippur appeal on the West Side already edged out the results of the Harlem appeal for first place. By the second one, in 1928, the West Side branch nearly *doubled* the pledges of the Harlem branch, and by 1929, the West Side branch literally more than *quadrupled* the pledges of the Harlem die-hards.

After the I.S. had used rented quarters on the West Side for two years, the community demographic die was cast, by 1929, for the synagogue to cast a new building in the image of the one it had molded so painstakingly up in Harlem. Accordingly, the directors let their lease at 83rd Street expire, and bought the "L"-shaped Knights of Columbus building at 148 West 85th Street. The building was almost immediately taken over by *Jewish* knights in shining religious armor, figuratively speaking, and was soon thereafter to be occupied, literally, days and nights. The building's first religious function took place four nights after its purchase

*Notice the type of "weapons" people had to "worry" about in those days!

was officially announced at a board meeting. The next day's opening Sabbath service received the following I.S. history-repeating opening night review:

> The auditorium which was used for the services, was crowded to capacity by a congenial and distinguished congregation. Almost everyone on our Board of Directors [was] present....
> Although the auditorium will seat three hundred souls, so encouraging was the attendance at the first services that there are expectations of increasing the capacity of the synagogue.

If "almost everyone on the [by now only titularly Harlem-based] Board of Directors" could attend this opening West Side Sabbath service, presumably without violating the Sabbath to do so (i.e., they arrived on foot), it is no wonder that even on a weekday evening (when vehicular travel *is* permitted) before the first High Holidays in the new building, the I.S. itself, which was still officially based in Harlem, could and *would* hold a "regular meeting of the board" at the West Side branch.

The overwhelming dominance of the West Side branch only a year after it had acquired a building of its very own can be seen in at least four different nuances of one brief excerpt from the minutes of a pre-High Holiday board meeting in 1930:

> It was decided to have our president, Honorable Isaac Siegel, speak on Kol Nidre night [of Yom Kippur], to be followed by Rabbi Goldstein and that Mr. Sanders was to help in the appeal, and that at the Harlem branch, an appeal was to be had at the Memorial Service [on Yom Kippur *day*] and that Rabbi Goldstein was to speak and be assisted by Mr. Udell.

Without any attempt at subtlety, the minutes made it clear that (1) Of the two appeals, the one on the West Side was not referred to as the one on the West Side but as "the appeal," period. (2) Only the *Harlem* appeal was thought to be conducted at a "branch"—another indication that the "branch" on the West Side had become, de facto, the *trunk*. (3) The appeal on the West Side was mentioned first and had more speakers. (4) The president of the synagogue himself—even despite his strong Harlem chauvinism—spoke on the West Side, while the person who was destined years later to become the first president of the independent West Side I.S. was relegated to speak up in Harlem.

By 1934, even the congregants at the *overflow* "upstairs West Side service" produced more revenue from seats than did all of the worshipers at the Harlem branch. In addition, even when the figures are rounded off charitably to the advantage of the Harlem branch, the participants at the *main* West Side service outdid their counterparts in Harlem with respect to revenue from seat reservations by a ratio in excess of ten to one and out-pledged them (in terms of additional donations) by seventeen to one! Despite these figures, the comparatively wealthy West Side branch never approached its financially less affluent branch in the scope of its activities. The Harlem branch, in fact, "milked" its fat and content counterpart and grew ever richer culturally, spiritually, and athletically at the expense of those who, taken as a whole, were rarely hungry enough to take their own full measure of what the I.S. had to offer.

For starters, the basic Hebrew School program that was to set in motion the Jewish educational process of each I.S. child met, after public school hours, only thrice a week, at most, on the West Side, compared to every weekday up in Harlem.* Also, instead of having one central aim with many youth clubs to realize it, the West Side branch, for a substantial period of time, developed, for its young people, one central club, primarily, with a turnover of many *names*. All of the names had at least two noticeable features in common. The I.S. League, The Young People's Conference, and the Young Folks League were all names equally devoid of color and of particularly Jewish flavor! The league, by whatever name, and its eventual counterparts were *not*, however, devoid of Jewish *content*. In fact, in 1934,

> Rabbi Goldstein met with a group of enthusiastic boys...and organized them into two chapters of the Junior Council of the I.S.
> Rabbi Goldstein presented a plan for religious activities to be centralized about the Saturday afternoon service. The Junior Council, beginning [with the week of] *Shabbat B'raishit* [the first Biblical portion of the world-wide annual weekly synagogue Bible-reading cycle], will conduct the entire Saturday afternoon service of the West Side Branch. In addition, a program of educational and social activities was also presented....

The Saturday afternoon arrangement became such a permanent feature that the youth domination of the main Saturday

---

*This was eventually more than compensated for, however, shortly after the independent West Side Institutional Synagogue was founded in 1937. In 1939, Rabbi Goldstein, without Congressman Siegel to oppose the idea, implemented his long deep-frozen plan for a school that rapidly evolved into the full-time nationally-known Manhattan Day School. M.D.S. was quickly expanded to serve the entire community. It encompassed not just a fully-developed religious department but a comprehensive "double curriculum" of Jewish and secular subjects.

afternoon services continued throughout the remaining years of Rabbi Goldstein's long life and beyond. The precise extent of the young people's participation varied from year to year, but the prayers and the Bible readings were always in their exclusive province, from the year the experiment began. The idea caught on so well that the maximum level of their participation was attained for the first time as early as their second season:

> ...Rabbi Goldstein has already made arrangements with the boys to assume definite assignments. Every participant has been given a topic on which to speak as well as a list of references.
>
> ...An added feature of the Saturday afternoon services will be a *Seudah Shilishit* [closing Sabbath dinner] to be given by the recently organized "Sabbath Afternoon Circle" [of girls who hosted these events].
>
> Preceding the *Mincha* [afternoon services] Simeon H. F. Goldstein [the rabbi's eldest son] will present a series of talks on "Outstanding Events of Jewish History."

One of the few areas that received an equal impetus at both synagogue branches, in addition to the Men's Club and the Women's League, was the junior congregation, which enabled the young people in their formative years to feel at home in the synagogue. As if to demonstrate the equal importance attached to this concept, two popular brothers ran these mini-congregations simultaneously one year, Lester Rhine in Harlem and Abe Rhine near the bank of the Hudson. Boys Weeks services likewise were carried over downstream from the bank of the Harlem River, although in later years the West Side Institutional Synagogue, unlike the I.S., did not necessarily attempt to harmonize its Boys Week events with President Roosevelt's declarations of national Boys Weeks.

Ironically, although the main branch building in Harlem had far more of an identity with the I.S. in all its glory than did the West Side branch building of only a few years (before the members of the West Side branch moved still a bit *further* downtown and formed the West Side Institutional Synagogue), the *Harlem* building, as has been pointed out, was destined to be sold by a bank to a non-Jewish church, yet the West Side *branch* building was sold, in precisely the opposite religious direction, to one Rabbi Yisroel Stamm's absolutely traditional synagogue!

Chapter 36

Amalgamation Requests And Ultimate Tributes

A tree does not grow a branch until it has a trunk to support it. A typical organization is not moved to become a subservient branch until it sees a sufficient movement in the primary organization to sustain it. The I.S., however, unsolicited, somehow managed to be "invited" to accept not merely an *olive* branch from its neighbors but a community center branch before it even moved into its own first, even semi-permanent, headquarters. In May of 1917, before Rabbi Goldstein had officially left the employ of his previous congregation to devote his full time to the I.S., the Washington Heights Y.M.H.A. had already invited him personally to become its "religious leader and advisor" while *it* proposed to become a "branch of the I.S." Rabbi Goldstein could hardly have discouraged its leaders by agreeing to launch their Friday night religious meeting series after the branch proposal had been extended. An I.S. "branch" *was* established over two miles north of the synagogue center, at 2005 Amsterdam Avenue in Washington Heights, by the following month, while the I.S. itself was still using the facilities of the Harlem 110th Street Y.W.H.A. on a most temporary basis.

The other independent group that seriously considered establishing a branch per se under the I.S. did so within the first year of the creation of the I.S. Ironically, this initiative came from Yorkville, precisely the community from which Rabbi Goldstein had just moved. Although there is no available record of this group's ever even *claiming* to be a full-fledged branch, it must be conceded, in all fairness, that even if it did, neither the formal branch nor the proposed branch ever rustled its leaves as a branch very audibly.

The feelers extended to the I.S. in favor of "amalgamation" were far more serious, although only one ever resulted in anything concrete. Formal "papers of amalgamation" were actually drawn up with representatives of both the I.S. of Harlem as well as the theoretical "I.S. of the Bronx." There were enough lawyers, judges, and businessmen in the I.S. community, however, to keep the I.S. from being duped, naively, into a deal not worth its while. Sure enough, ten days after the papers had been drawn up, the Harlem I.S. representatives discovered what appeared to be the immediate and underlying motive of the proposed "Bronx I.S." for the suggested "amalgamation." As of that point in time, they found out:

> . . .the building intended for the I.S. of the Bronx cannot be purchased unless $30,000 more is given than offered. That put. . .that matter in abeyance and [relieved Rabbi Goldstein's] mind of the question whether the I.S. was losing an opportunity or not.

The I.S. board had not been sleeping. The day *before* this information leaked out, it had already collectively decided *not* to "amalgamate with the Bronx till they are stronger financially," but the specifics they found out the next day clinched their decision. The original I.S. base within Harlem was small, but the momentum of its growth was steady, and the I.S. was not about to siphon off precious resources before finalizing its purchase of its *own* permanent building.

The momentum was *so* strong that barely a month after the I.S. bought its new and huge building on 116th Street the following year, the next delegation to visit the Goldstein residence seeking amalgamation came from no less august an institution than the Ohab Zedek itself, the synagogue then boasting such titans on the American Jewish scene as Rabbis Philip Klein and Bernard Drachman, as well as the operatic cantorial virtuoso, Joseph Rosenblatt. Although nothing of any permanent substance ever came out of this meeting, the fact that such an established synagogue could even *consider* an amalgamation with the then-two-year-old I.S. to be in its *own* best interests, is astounding. The timing of the meeting seems to indicate that once the Ohab Zedek saw that the I.S., having just purchased its own building independently, was on the brink of actually realizing Rabbi Goldstein's grandiose dream, it was time for the established synagogue to offer to absorb the upstart. Notwithstanding the observation that the sentiment in favor of amalgamating was "quite strong" among the twenty participants of this joint meeting, the I.S. chose to "go it alone" organizationally—although it certainly never felt alone when it came to *individuals'* participation.

The only proposed amalgamation that the I.S. actually consummated* was with one Congregation Adath Jeshurun.** This restructuring took place in 1925, with the I.S. at its peak and clearly in the driver's seat in the negotiations. The I.S. absorbed the other synagogue's members and its "valuable Hebrew library," among other benefits, in return for which it dedicated "a room in honor of the congregation."

Tributes from the "Competition"

The recognition the I.S. received within the Orthodox community was obvious. What set it apart from so many of its "competitors" was the superlative acclaim it received even from its *non*-Orthodox "competitors."

Goldstein's leading "Conservative" counterpart, Dr. Israel Goldstein, presented a paper at the educational session of a convention of the Metropolitan League of Jewish Community Associations, which paper was published in the Jewish Welfare Board quarterly, *The Jewish Center*, in which he referred to the I.S. as:

> The outstanding institution [not just synagogue, but institution—a much broader term] in the Orthodox ranks whose purpose and program are addressed to the Jewish youth....

Louis Marshall, one of the leading American Jewish community spokesmen of all time, and president of the most prestigious "Reform" temple in the country, Temple Emmanuel, delivered an address at the I.S., in which he—a man among "men of the world"—stated, in part:

> In ancient days, the synagogue was the center of the life of the Jews. In hours of joy, in hours of sorrow and trouble and in days of oppression, they all repaired to the synagogue. It performed a three-fold function. It was a *Beth Hakneseth* (House of Gathering and Assembly); a *Beth Tefilah* (House of Prayer); a *Beth Hamidrash* (House of Learning). Old and young, men and women came there for spiritual sustenance and intellectual improvement, for salvation and advice....
> ...I am very happy to observe...the synagogue is now becoming what it was—in its origin...the synagogue is

*But please see the special note about a **W.S.I.S.** development, at page 327.

**Although its name was virtually synonymous with that of Goldstein's career's launching pad, the *Kehilath* Jeshurun, whose orientation was Orthodox, that is about where the similarities ended.

visited every day and almost every hour....

...I was very impressed when I heard Rabbi Goldstein call your attention to the many activities which are constantly in operation in this house. It is most encouraging. It indicates that this synagogue is performing...all of the functions that the synagogue of old occupied and performed in the lives of the Jews. It is a great institution, this synagogue of yours....

One can only speculate as to what might have been had Marshall spoken so piously in front of his *own* "Reform" congregants about returning to the practices of the "synagogue of old!"

From the outset of the I.S., Goldstein recognized that "what is needed...is the environment in the home and...outside the home. The Institutional Synagogue...represents all the activities outside the home." An estimated 2,400 to 3,000 people entered the synagogue daily, and to many who lacked an ideal Jewish home life, the I.S. was clearly a Jewish "home away from home." Its comprehensive mottos in this regard were "Always Open" and "The place for every member of the family." We also saw, most notably in chapter 22, how the I.S. at times even simulated religious activities generally considered indigenous to the home itself.

A recurring question raised by critics of the I.S. related to the priority of and the amount of attention given to the synagogue and Jewish culture within the multi-purpose building. Almost all the chapters in this book dealing with the I.S. answer this question, in some measure. Even for those who did *not* consider the synagogue and its values to be important, at first, Rabbi Goldstein often cited one of his favorite analogies, and he even did so, perhaps for the last time, in his autobiographical sketch:

> The Institutional Synagogue is comparable as a university would be toward the college. The following illustration will perhaps help to make my point clearer. If a man goes to the College of the City of New York and desires to see a School of Mines, he must make a special effort and a special trip to Columbia University which has a School of Mines. However, a student of a university need not necessarily be moved by a desire to see a School of Mines or make a special trip to accomplish this purpose. As he crosses the campus each day, the School of Mines is located right on the premises, and if he has any curiosity whatsoever, he will very likely enter the building and learn something about what it offers for study.
>
> Similarly, when a young man, attending a social center, is requested to attend the synagogue, he must make a special effort and a special trip, to a different building, perhaps to some other part of the district. This additional effort he will

not expend unless he has a strong inclination to do so.

On the other hand, the youngster who attends the Institutional Synagogue, its gymnasium, its library, its study classes, or the wholesome social functions, because they are all before his very eyes, it does not require very much extra effort to take advantage of any one of these opportunities. Man is so constituted that he naturally takes the path of least resistance. The Institutional Synagogue will offer this path for the furtherance of the best religious, moral, social, and physical ends.

For those who were too weak or unimaginative even to take the path of *least* resistance, Goldstein recalled:

...from personal experience, that in our case if the members of the various clubs did not come to the synagogue, the synagogue came to them.

No matter how persistently a synagogue will invite, it will not find its invitations answered unless it itself is perceived as an inviting and genuinely attractive place. Possibly the greatest achievement of the I.S. was its simplest one—it quashed "the ever increasing impression of the young, that the synagogue spoils the fun, that the synagogue constantly wears a frown." Every Saturday evening, the world over, Jews traditionally chant the triumphant refrain from the Book of Esther (8.16), "The Jews had light and joy, bliss and dignity. So be it with us." So *was* it with the members of the I.S.!

Special note: As the second edition of this book went to press, members of the Jewish community throughout Metropolitan New York were still reacting to what may have been the most unique synagogue merger proposal ever seriously negotiated, in that it involved synagogues with comparably spectacular and dramatic early instant successes. The officers of the West Side Institutional Synagogue and of the Lincoln Square Synagogue had agreed, in principle, by this time, to recommend to their respective boards that the synagogues should consider merging, and, thereby, establishing still another precedent for each precedent-setting institution. Under the initial merger proposals, all of the facilities of each synagogue would be put to maximum use under the auspices of a combined entity to be known as the Lincoln Square-Institutional Synagogue (with only the future fate of the hyphen unresolved). Although, unlike the Biblical Moses, the founding rabbi of each synagogue had seen the Promised Land (Rabbi Goldstein figuratively at the original I.S. and then at the W.S.I.S., and literally on annual visits to Israel in the 1950s, and Rabbi Steven (Shlomo) Riskin figuratively in the L.S.S., and literally then in his second year of full-time residency in Israel), when fate beckoned, their immediate successors were the rabbis who agreed to attempt to help their congregants see the promised merger become a reality if both boards and memberships would approve—with Rabbi O. Asher Reichel (of the W.S.I.S.) to become Sr. Rabbi, and Rabbi Saul Berman (of the L.S.S.) to become Rabbi of the new combined entity.

After the second edition of this book went into production, the two synagogues decided to maintain their separate identities. Rabbi Reichel became Rabbi Emeritus, and Rabbi Moshe Morduchowitz, former Acting Rabbi of the L.S.S., was elected to succeed Rabbi Reichel as the spiritual leader of the W.S.I.S.

Part Four
A CAPSULATED LOOK AHEAD

Chapter 37

One Dimension... And All We Need Mention

In spotlighting the Institutional Synagogue, the major im-mediate forces that led up to it, and all its principal components, we have seen virtually all of that which really matters concerning the achievement that put Rabbi Goldstein on the American Jewish communal map. The reader has *not* as yet seen, however, what Rabbi Goldstein did to *maintain* his preeminent position in American Jewish life for the next third of a century. What the rabbi later did would fill a book in itself and what *we* will do in this chapter is outline this as yet unpublished book. Both the book this chapter now completes and our soon-to-be published follow-up book are independent entities in themselves. Consider this chapter both a dessert to this book and an appetizer for the next. None of the highlights of the rabbi's life will be omitted from either, and each book in itself will mention virtually all of the achievements necessary to see Rabbi Goldstein's life in the perspective in which he was placed by the monumental *Encyclopedia Judaica:*

> [The caption next to his photograph identifies him not only as a professional rabbi but as a "rabbinic leader," a rabbi's rabbi. The widely cross-referenced entry itself closes with the observation that:] Despite the fact that he was a graduate of the ["Conservative"] Jewish Theological Seminary, Goldstein was a strictly Orthodox rabbi, belonging to the right wing of the English-speaking Orthodox rabbinate, and in this respect was unique.

Rabbi Goldstein taught public speaking, homiletics (ser-monics), and practical rabbinics to the first rabbinical students of Yeshiva University. He continued to expound on these subjects right on through to the university's rabbinical school's first two generations of rabbis, covering a span of close to half a century, heading the homiletics department for most of this period and thus setting his imprint on most of the "modern Orthodox" American rabbinate in its formative years. (*Other* people's prints, of course, tampered with his negative, and negated some of the ideas *he* considered to be positive.)

As president of the Union of Orthodox Jewish Congregations of America, Rabbi Goldstein transformed the U.O.J.C.A. from its widely recognized original status as a "paper organization," which did little more between occasional crises than hold conventions and issue resounding proclamations, into a vibrant action-oriented organization. During his decade in office, the historic O.U. Kosher food endorsement department was created, revolutionizing the eating habits of American Kosher-law-abiding Jewry. Women's, collegiate, and high school branches were organized within the O.U. for the first time during his tenure as well.

The relatively right-wing "ultra-Orthodox" Union of Orthodox Rabbis (Agudat Harabanim) not only made peace with, but actually worked *together* with, the U.O.J.C.A. on matters of Kosher food supervision during Goldstein's unprecedented harmony-promoting years in office. The rabbi served as a catalytic agent, too, in the creation of the national Young Israel movement. His personal encouragement of the founders of this movement supplemented the influence of the example he set for them up in Harlem. What is particularly striking about this personal interest is that it was manifested even though the Y.I. gradually evolved into a competing network, in a sense, to the O.U.

Possibly the most stunning instance of all of Goldstein's submersions of the apparent short-term interests of the O.U. as an organization in favor of the long-term interests of the Jewish community and its ultimate unity involves the oldest liberal arts university under Jewish auspices. The very university status of what is now known as Yeshiva University, which status was acquired by virtue of the university's full-fledged recognition by the Board of Regents of the State of New York, came about largely because of Goldstein's daring decision to throw the financial weight of the entire U.O.J.C.A. behind it, thereby risking that organization's very destiny in order to set the unique university on its feet.

The rabbi periodically launched personal, neighborhood, and legal crusades against unscrupulous butchers defrauding the Kosher community. We have alluded, earlier, to his most far-reaching and dramatic, however indirect, role in this area.

Rabbi Goldstein served as president of the League for the Safeguarding of the Fixity of the Sabbath Against Possible

Encroachment by Calendar Reform. Under the proposed seemingly harmless system that this league was formed to nip in the bud, a roving Sabbath day (or a "blank" day or days) was to be inserted into a restructured or simplified calendar, with the not incidental effect of undermining the *true* historic Sabbath day.*

No Jewish law was too little known or generally disregarded to draw the rabbi into a consciousness-raising position. He even served as president of an organization dedicated to preserving, by voluntary sophisticated scientific inspection techniques, the law prohibiting the mixture of wool and linen in clothing.

So significant was every law to the rabbi that he literally wrote a book outlining suggested reasons for the importance of each and every one of the 613 Biblical laws. Earlier, Rabbi Goldstein had written a full-length biography of Harry Fischel, the rabbi's famous father-in-law. Goldstein also compiled one of the first popular volumes—if not *the* first—to appear in an American's English summarizing the major classic commentaries on the Bible's basic Five Books of Moses. In addition, he authored a similar work on the book of Joshua, and an earlier, smaller-scale work on the pithy *Ethics of the Fathers*.

His greatest influence was attained, however, by the medium of the spoken word. The very unique dramatic quality of his booming voice—as well as the message it invariably carried—was perfectly suited to the medium of radio, where his instant appeal to the masses was electrifying. He conducted his own radio program for many years, and spoke countless times over various stations in numerous formats.

When Goldstein was in his prime, his influence on politicians and legislation on Jewish issues in American life may have been unsurpassed among his colleagues in the Orthodox rabbinate. He exercised this influence most notably in the area of kosher food legislation, policies of accommodation with respect to Sabbath observant individuals, and immigration decisions during World War II, when many of the Jews streaming out of Nazi-dominated Europe depended, for their survival, on the pressure he and other people were able to bring to bear on political people in high places. His impact on ordinary civilians was no less significant in the quiet and unheralded World War II European refugee rescue operation that was spearheaded by Orthodox Jewish leaders. Only individual civilians could sign vital visas and guarantee employment or support. Goldstein made numerous such guarantees,

*Specifically, under the internationally publicized proposal—which periodically surfaces in various forms—the actual Sabbath day on which Jews are required to refrain from work (which cannot be changed by any new calendar) would no longer always be Saturday, but would vary each year from one day of the week to another day of the week, on the secular calendar. This would severely aggravate the difficulties involved in holding a job or operating a business for any true Sabbath observer.

himself, and actively persuaded many other people to do likewise.

Goldstein's role on the Jewish Welfare Board (J.W.B.) was renewed and intensified during this Second World War. Jews were so directly singled out by the enemy that they hardly needed a comparable degree of inspiration to offer assistance to their fellow Jews as they may have needed during the first great war of this century. Instead of personally coming to deliver religious messages this time around, Goldstein took an active and independent stand from his vantage point on numerous J.W.B. committees to fight within the committees for the religious rights and needs of Jewish soldiers. In his position on the J.W.B. committee that was set up to advise draft boards concerning individuals' applications for deferments as clergymen or as future members of the clergy, he often was the only rabbi to promote the classic Jewish position that young Talmudic scholars are deemed to be bona fide rabbinical students of the highest order even when their motivation is limited to *Torah lishmah*—Bible study in the fulfillment of a religious ideal, rather than for the sake of maintaining salaried pulpit positions.

Rabbi Goldstein was a strong fighter for the working man, joining forces in particular with the labor leaders who advocated the five-day work week (when six was the norm) which eventually freed Sabbath-observing Jews from the dead-end positions to which so many of them had been relegated under the pro-Christian unfairly applied six-day work week. In fact, he was so highly regarded in the labor community that he was called upon to mediate and to arbitrate purely commercial disputes with no religious overtones whatsoever!*

The most skillful, dramatic, and unprecedented manifestation of his uncanny knack of developing the trust and confidence of two seemingly irreconcilable groups of people involved the so-called "ultra-Orthodox" world Agudah (Agudath Israel) and the so-called more "modern-Orthodox" Mizrachi (Religious Zionist) movements. Both movements have always claimed to represent true Orthodoxy as it was meant to be lived from time immemorial, and both fiercely reject many basic points in each other's philosophy. Each movement views the other as an impediment to the progress of Orthodoxy. Yet, incredibly, Rabbi Goldstein managed not only to feel close to the leaders of both movements, both in the United States and in Israel, and not only to assume leadership positions himself in both, but he was "claimed" by leaders of *each* of these movements and political parties as having been *basically* one of their own, even to the day of his death—and then posthumously! We will let the evidence—and the suspense—

---

*This was unrelated to his community service as a judge on the Jewish Conciliation Court, which certainly *did* very frequently have religious overtones.

continue to accumulate on this point, for the moment, and will merely mention some of his strongest links to each.

During one of Rabbi Goldstein's peak years at the I.S. and the U.O.J.C.A. he dramatically resigned from his position on the executive of the Mizrachi and urged his followers to join him at the Agudah! After the issue that had prompted his resignation became moot, he rejoined the Mizrachi, publicly pointed with pride to his membership in *both* organizations, and actively assumed leadership roles once again in both spheres.

Rabbi Goldstein co-founded the World Academy* in Jerusalem with Israeli Chief Rabbi Herzog, a Mizrachi leader, and the two served together as chancellor and president, respectively.**

The first Chief Rabbi of Israel, Rabbi Abraham Hakohen Kook, who has come to be regarded as a popular symbol of Mizrachi leadership, although he was never even a formal member, himself, first conceived of the idea of the Harry Fischel Institute, which he helped to institute well before the State of Israel was founded. For decades, half of all the religious court judges in the entire country were graduates of this elite institution, of which Rabbi Goldstein became the Chancellor, a post he occupied until the day he died. Goldstein's son-in-law, Rabbi Shear Yashuv Cohen, was the director of the Institute, while at one point simultaneously serving as Deputy Mayor of Jerusalem after his election to the City Council on the Mizrachi ticket. Both of the "Ashkenazik" Chief Rabbis of Israel (representing all of Israeli Jewry of Russian and European origin) from 1948 until Rabbi Goldstein's death served as presidents of the Institute, and both were leading Mizrachi personalities. The next Chief Rabbi—who assumed both the chief rabbinate and the presidency of the Institute after 1970—was the philosophical antithesis, within Orthodox Jewry, of the "ultra-Orthodox" Agudah, and a brother-in-law of Rabbi Goldstein's own daughter, Naomi.

On the Agudah side of the spectrum, Rabbi Goldstein left the purely academic institutions totally in the hands of their incumbent leaders who were successfully transplanting their great European world-famous seminaries both in America and in Israel. Goldstein clearly saw no need to establish new types of academies or institutes for *them.* He therefore focused his consciousness-raising and fund-raising on behalf of the day care centers and homes in which young, often orphaned students were cared for*** and prepared for entrance into schools for advanced studies.

---

*This leading research center is most widely known and respected for its ongoing publication of the *Encyclopedia Talmudica*.

**After Herzog's death, it was renamed the Yad Harav Herzog.

***One of his daughters, Mrs. Josephine Reichel, played a similar role as president, for 21 years, of the Agudah Women of America.

General Israeli politics, in Goldstein's lifetime, was always dominated by irreligious and anti-religious people who often channeled philosophically pliable and naive religious immigrants from war-torn Europe and increasingly hostile Arab countries into their own well-financed and well-connected kibbutzim and other settlements, with particularly chilling effectiveness with respect to—or, rather with *disrespect* to—the religious identity of hapless and helpless orphans. Goldstein therefore established the Homes for Children in Israel, on behalf of the Agudah, to ward off this enforced demoralizing "de-religionizing" process by providing alternatives that were religiously *as well as* physically wholesome. Not content to serve as a figurehead president, he vowed, at the mid-twentieth century mark when he founded this agency, not to permit a day to go by in his life without at least *asking* somebody to contribute to this cause.

Before the State of Israel was founded, the rabbi served as president of the *Keren Hayishuv*, the American Religious Palestine Fund, the main Israeli-oriented fund-raising arm of the pre-state Agudath Israel, and of the Save-A-Child Foundation, which evolved into the Homes for Children in Israel. When the state was founded, he immediately became the president of an ad hoc funding organization for the religious needs of Israeli soldiers, known as the Religious Defense Corps of the Haganah. The responsibility for most of the Agudah's major Israel-oriented fund raising then rapidly shifted to its *Israeli* leaders, who suddenly found themselves in possession of an added aura of prestige in their roles as full-fledged members of the newly constituted Israeli Parliament. Rabbi Goldstein remained one of their principal American contacts, and they hosted each other as a matter of course on their frequent intercontinental visits.

On the internal American Jewish scene, but far removed in many ways from the Agudath Israel of America, Rabbi Goldstein co-founded the Rabbinical Council of America (R.C.A.), which was composed of the former constituents of the rabbinical organizations of Yeshiva University and of the U.O.J.C.A. Immediately, he was elected to the presidium of the newly-merged organization, and, among the members of the presidium, he represented the three as the official president.

He also co-founded the Synagogue Council of America (S.C.A.), and became its president. Coincidentally, he was immediately preceded in this office by the "Conservative" Israel Goldstein—with whom he was sometimes confused. The Synagogue Council is an "umbrella organization" composed of the two leading rabbinic and lay groups of each of the three "branches" of Judaism. Each of the six founding and enduring constituent bodies—including the U.O.J.C.A. and the R.C.A. for the Orthodox—has a guaranteed veto power over all substantive decisions, so that for many years, Rabbi Goldstein considered the organization, in effect, tantamount to being Orthodox itself!

Shortly before he was hit by his first stroke, however, he had a dramatic change of heart when the leading Orthodox scholarly nonpulpit rabbis and heads of rabbinical academies renewed their opposition to support of and participation in the Synagogue Council of America on an organizational level and the New York Board of Rabbis on an individual level. This opposition focused on the issue of recognition, by the Orthodox, of "deviant" religious "branches" in Judaism. Goldstein took the unprecedented action, in an unusual demonstration of humility, of becoming the first leading "modern Orthodox" pulpit rabbi to express, publicly, his adherence to these nonpulpit rabbis' legal decision. As activist and modern as he may have been as a pulpit rabbi and community leader, he would never dare cross the acknowledged leading full-time Talmudic scholars, once he was convinced that their decision was of a legal and not a political nature. Goldstein abided by this allegiance even when it meant, in this unusual instance, swallowing his own pride and sentimental affiliation. The magnitude of sacrifice is demonstrated by the fact that his life work had been dedicated to harmonizing the Orthodox way of life with the diverse elements around him so that Orthodox Jews would be as comfortable as possible *with* their outside environment.

Goldstein was both a founder and a member of the original board of directors of the National Conference of Christians and Jews. His participation in the World Fellowship of Faiths was even more outstanding. He was the only rabbi among the organization's ten Regional Council chairmen. All of this fellowship did not save the world, of course, but it *does* illustrate tangible commitments in the ecumenical spirit that pervaded his character.

The West Side Institutional Synagogue that grew out of the West Side branch of the original Harlem-based Institutional Synagogue in 1937 became, in its prime, one of the generally acknowledged three most influential Orthodox synagogues in New York City. Generally, West Side Jews tended to be older, more established, and more affluent. The housing market became so tight after World War II that young families, by and large, found the otherwise-suitable—and most desirable—housing on the West Side prohibitive in cost. Rabbi Goldstein, therefore, looked elsewhere for additional outlets for his creative energy.

Rabbi Goldstein's reputation and oratorical abilities, along with his sincerity and dedication, made him a much sought-after fund raiser and after-dinner speaker. It was a role that others spurned, but one from which he derived constant satisfaction. He undoubtedly told dozens of audiences the mythical tale of how his mother had been told by a heavenly angel that she would give birth to a son destined to become a *schnorrer*—a beggar. After pleading for a modification of this heavenly decree, she was granted a partial reprieve—her son would indeed be a *schnorrer*, but for *others*, for vital "causes." And so, Rabbi Goldstein would tell countless audiences, he was named "Herbert S."—the 'S' stands for 'Schnorrer'—for others." He saw his role as a heavenly calling—or a debt to pay back for all of the bounties that God had bestowed upon him in his long and richly rewarding career.

In one way or another, Rabbi Goldstein supplemented his activities on behalf of all of the other charitable enterprises mentioned in this book by personally raising funds for literally dozens of additional organizations.*

Throughout their lives, Rabbi and Mrs. Goldstein were fortunate in being blessed with both the time and the means for extensive vacations, but their excursions never became vacations from God. True to his schoolboy nickname of *"Mincha* Goldstein," the rabbi had a compulsion not just to attend but to *establish* a *minyan*—an organized public prayer service—in his immediate vacation environment no matter what it may have been like. Not only did he bear the title "rabbi," but he conducted himself accordingly wherever he went. The most noteworthy illustration of his tendency to get as much religious mileage as possible out of his vacations came about as a result of a single invitation he once received to deliver a single keynote address at a B'nai B'rith convention out on the West Coast. He resourcefully converted this invitation into an opportunity to take his family on a national crusade on behalf of Orthodox Judaism in general and the Union of Orthodox Jewish Congregations of America in particular. Again he did not limit himself simply to addressing public rallies, but at every major city at which his train stopped, en route, he strove to establish new—and strengthen old—ongoing branches.

Many who knew the rabbi from his early years observed that he could never have achieved what he did without the able assistance of his wife and helpmeet, Rebecca Fischel Goldstein.

*The Allied Jewish Campaign (for "needy Jews of Eastern Europe and Palestine"), American Talmudical Institute in Israel, Army and Navy Kosher Food Service Committee, Beth Hamedrash Hagadol, Beth Medrash Gavoha, B'nai B'rith (for the specific purpose of influencing it to install a kosher kitchen in a home for the aged it sponsored), Camp Metifta, Chevra Kadisha (burial society) in Israel, Chofetz Chayim Yeshiva, Crusade for Children, Ezrat Torah, Hebrew Hay Fever Home in Bethlehem (New Hampshire), Jewish National Fund, Joint Distribution Committee, Lakewood Yeshiva, Lubavitch Yeshiva, Manhattan Day School, Mirrer Yeshiva, North Hudson Jewish Community Center, Ozar Hatorah, Palestine Emergency Relief, Ponevez Yeshiva, Steerage [passenger ad hoc] fund (on an ocean voyage, for indigent immigrants' expenses), Torah Umesorah, Torah V'daat, and the United Jewish Appeal.

In addition, Rabbi Goldstein waged and won heated verbal battles within his own synagogue board meetings to ensure the perpetuation of synagogue appeals for the following yeshivas—and others—jointly: Beth Joseph, Etz Chayim (Jerusalem), Grodno, Hebron, Kamenetz, Kelm (as opposed to Chelm), Kletzk, Lomza, Mitefta (Warsaw), Ohel Torah (Baranowitz), Slonim, and Universal (Merkaz Harav, in Jerusalem).

Not only did she follow up on details and troubleshoot on all pastoral fronts with her soothing and calming influence, but she also was a high achiever in her own right. In the years preceding, during, and following the rabbi's reign as president of the Union of Orthodox Jewish Congregations of America, she was the president of its Women's Branch. A Barnard graduate and former Columbia University student herself, she also founded the Union's Collegiate Branch. Among other positions, she served as Chairman of the Committee on Religion of the Council of Jewish Women. She was Honorary President of the Institutional Synagogue's Sisterhood, which, in its changed location bears her name to this day as the Rebecca F. Goldstein Women's League of the West Side Institutional Synagogue.

Shortly after Rabbi Goldstein's celebration of his seventieth birthday, the rabbi set sail on his last annual pilgrimage to Israel with his wife of nearly half a century. While on one of his many religious missions, he was smitten by a stroke, and both he and his wife returned to the United States in wheelchairs. The following year, his wife passed away—Rebecca Fischel Goldstein, a saintly woman whom he had described, in print, as "one in a generation."

After the year of mourning, Rabbi Goldstein married the former Mrs. Regina ("Rexie") Schumer Krengel, with whom he spent his twilight years, until his death on January 2, 1970. She had been active in Jewish organizations and had served as National President of Yeshiva University Women's Organization.

Although Rabbi Goldstein was succeeded by his son-in-law, Rabbi O. Asher Reichel, as the official rabbi of the West Side Institutional Synagogue, Rabbi Goldstein, first as Senior Rabbi and then as Rabbi Emeritus, occasionally occupied the pulpit of his synagogue until the very year he went to a hospital for the last time.

Rabbi Goldstein was in the midst of two literary works when he passed away. One of these works was his own autobiographical sketch which we are attempting to flesh out in this opus. His life, however, was too full to allow us to do it justice with the thoroughness it merits, in a single manageably readable volume. Accordingly, we chose not to sacrifice due consideration in this book of any of the significant factors relating to the crowning achievement of his early years—the Institutional Synagogue—which was his most comprehensive and historic model creation for future generations. We eagerly look forward to elaborate, in the very near future, on the highlights of this closing chapter 37, representing his equally productive middle and later years.

BIBLIOGRAPHY

American Jewish Yearbook. Philadelphia: Jewish Publication Society, 1914, 1921.

Central Jewish Institute, Social Welfare Circle pamphlets and programs.

Drachman, Bernard. *The Unfailing Light.* New York: Rabbinical Council of America, 1948.

Encyclopedia Judaica. Jerusalem: Keter and MacMillan, 1969.

Epstein, Joseph. *The Early History of the Central Jewish Institute— The Emergence of a Jewish Community Center* (unpublished Masters' thesis, Bernard Revel Graduate School, available for viewing at Gottesman Library of Yeshiva University). New York, 1978.

Glazer, Nathan. *American Judaism.* Chicago: University of Chicago Press, 1957.

Goldstein, Herbert S. *Autobiography* (unpublished). New York, circa 1969.

Goldstein, Herbert S. *Forty Years of Struggle for a Principle— The Biography of Harry Fischel.* New York: Bloch Publishing Co., 1928.

Goldstein, Herbert S. *Torahcratic The True Zionism* (reprint). New York: The Jewish Forum, 1943.

Goldstein, Rebecca F. *Diaries,* 1909-1937.

Goldstein, Rebecca F. *Scrapbooks* (on activities of Herbert S. Goldstein), 1913-1937.

Goldstein, Sidney, and Goldscheider, Calvin. *Jewish Americans—Three Generations in a Jewish Community.* Englewood Cliffs, New Jersey: Prentice-Hall, Inc., 1968.

Gurock, Jeffrey S. *When Harlem Was Jewish 1870-1930.* New York: Columbia University Press, 1979.

Institutional (four-page official weekly news organ of the Institutional Synagogue), 1918-1941.

Institutional Synagogue, *Certificate of Incorporation,* October 30, 1917.

Institutional Synagogue programs, souvenir dinner journals, and minutes of meetings of Board of Directors.

Janowsky, Oscar I. *The Jewish Welfare Board Survey.* New York: Dial, 1948.

Jewish Theological Seminary. *Students' Annual.* New York, 1914.

Karpf, Maurice J. *Jewish Community Organization in the United States.* New York: Bloch, 1938.

Klaperman, Gilbert. *The Story of Yeshiva University.* Toronto, New York, and London: MacMillan and Collier-MacMillan, Ltd., 1969.

Morris, Lloyd. *Incredible New York.* New York: Random House, 1951.

Osofsky, Gilbert. *Harlem: The Making of a Ghetto—Negro New York, 1890-1930.* New York: Harper & Row, 1966.

Ottley, Roi. *The New World A-Coming—Inside Black America.* Boston and Cambridge: Houghton-Mifflin Co., and the Riverside Press, 1943.

Ovington, Mary White. *The Walls Come Tumbling Down.* New York: Harcourt, Brace & Co., 1947.

Reichel, Aaron I. *An American Experiment—The Institutional Synagogue During Its First Score of Years, 1917-1937* (unpublished Master's thesis, Bernard Revel Graduate School, available for viewing at Gottesman Library of Yeshiva University). New York, 1974.

Reichel, Aaron I. "When Harlem Was Jewish," *Tradition,* Vol. 18, No. 4, Winter 1980, p. 374.

Rischin, Moses. *The Promised City—New York's Jews 1870-1914.* Cambridge: Harvard University Press, 1962.

Simonhoff, Harry. *Jewish Notables in America 1776-1865.* New York: Greenberg, 1956.

Schoener, Alon. *Harlem on My Mind—Cultural Capital of Black America 1900-1968.* New York: Random House, 1968, and Dell, 1979.

Universal Jewish Encyclopedia. New York, 1941.

Wiernik, Peter. *History of the Jews in America.* New York: Jewish History Publishing Co., 1931.

PERIODICALS

American Hebrew, American Hebrew and Jewish Tribune, American Jewish Chronicle, Atlanta Journal (Georgia), *Baltimore Jewish Comment, Better Times, B'nai B'rith News, Bronx Jewish Chronicle, Congressional Record, Courier, Daily Press* (Newport News, Virginia), *Evening Journal, Evening Sun, Evening Telegram, Harlem Home News, Hebrew Standard, Hudson Dispatch* (Jersey City), *Indiana Jewish Chronicle, Institutional, Israel-Hebdomadaire Juif Independant, Jewish Daily Bulletin, Jewish Daily News, Jewish Exponent* (Philadelphia), *Jewish Forum, Jewish Guardian, Jewish Independent* (Cleveland, Ohio), *Jewish Independent* (New Jersey), *Jewish Post* (Paterson, New Jersey), *Jewish Press, Jewish Review, Jewish Transcript* (Seattle), *Jewish Tribune, Jewish World* (Philadelphia), *Journal of Jewish Music and Liturgy, Light of Israel, New York American, New York Evening Journal, New York Globe, New York Herald, New York Herald Tribune, New York Jewish News, New York Journal, New York Journal and American, New York Sun, New York Telegram, New York Times, New York Tribune, New York World Telegram, Orthodox Union (of Union of Orthodox Jewish Congregations of America), Ottawa Jewish Community Centre Bulletin, Reform Advocate* (Chicago, Illinois), *Sentinel* (Chicago, Illinois), *Spartanburg Herald* (South Carolina), *Tageblatt, Tradition, West Side Institutional Review, Wisconsin Jewish Chronicle, World, World Magazine, Yorkville Home News,* and *Young Israel Viewpoint.*

Most of the above periodicals were published in New York City, unless otherwise specified.

INTERVIEWEES

Samuel K. Beier, Rabbi Louis Bernstein, Harry Block, Irving Bunim, Max Caplow, Herman H. Cohen, Irene Liberman Cohen, Dr. Naomi Cohen, Chief Rabbi Shear-Yashuv Cohen, Diana Darabaner, Isidor Epstein, Joseph Epstein, Professor Louis Finkelstein, Diane Friedenberg, Mrs. Harry Fromberg, Leon J. Gell, Molly Gertz, Dr. and Mrs. Braham Golden, Rabbi Tuvya Goldman, Gabriel F. Goldstein, Regina K. Goldstein, Simeon H. F. Goldstein, Rabbi Philip Goodman, Dean Simeon L. Guterman, Rabbi Leo Jung, Rabbi Joseph Kaminetsky, Harold Kaplan, Professor Mordecai Kaplan, Ned Kirsh, Lillian Levine, Clarence Liberman, Rabbi Joseph Lookstein, Fred Margareten, Jacob Marrus, Reuben Metchik, Bertha Rafsky, Josephine G. Reichel, Rabbi O. Asher Reichel, Rose Berger Segelstein, Mrs. Isaac Siegel, Louis Simon, Harry Ward, Cantor Zalmon Yavneh.

TECHNICAL NOTES

Most of the long indented first person quotations are either from Rabbi Goldstein's autobiographical sketch, or from Mrs. Goldstein's diary. Readers who cannot determine the authorship of any quotations from the context are invited to contact the author, whose address appears in the Acknowledgments.

Hebrew words are generally translated into English, but on the rare occasions when they are only transliterated, they are generally transliterated according to the pronunciation prevalent subsequent to the establishment of the State of Israel. Although Rabbi Goldstein used an "Americanized" pronunciation when he spoke Hebrew among Americans, we are nonetheless using the modern Israeli pronunciation, retroactively, since this is the pronunciation with which most contemporary Hebrew conversationalists feel comfortable. Finally, as to the selected footnotes, please see the explanation under that heading.

SELECTED FOOTNOTES

While the author has documentation for virtually every statement in this book, he has spared the general reader from the distraction of intimidating or overbearing footnote numbers that traditionally interfere with the natural flow of the narrative and that often make the conscientious reader feel obliged to wade through a sea of citations. Instead, when the reader comes across a claim or observation in the text that cries out for substantiation, especially if dealing with the rabbi or the synagogue directly, the reader is invited to look it up below, or, for further information, to contact the author.

Note: When counting lines, please include lines taken up by chapter headings and subheadings.

Chapter One

Page 17, line 22: Harry Simonhoff, *Jewish Notables in America 1766-1865* (New York: Greenberg 1956) p. 53; Michael N. Dobrowski, "A Bicentennial Assessment of the History, Contributions and Achievements of the American Cantorate," *Journal of Jewish Music and Liturgy*, Vol 1, No. 1, June 1976, p. 14.

Page 18, line 2: "Two Rabbis Urge U.S. to Let in Child Refugees—Herbert Goldstein Pledges Homes for 1000," *New York Herald Tribune*, April 23, 1939, page 4; "Getting Personal," *Institutional*, Jan. 17, 1941, p. 4, mentioning "Rabbi Goldstein made a rush trip to Washington...on one of his many errands of mercy for our persecuted brethren abroad."

Page 18, line 3: "Kosher Law Sustained in the U.S. Supreme Court," *Institutional*, Jan. 16, 1925, p. 1. Sometimes religious interests rested on preventing the passage of legislation. E.g., "President's Statement to Synagogue Council Meeting," by Dr. Israel Goldstein, at the Waldorf Astoria Hotel, March 10, 1943: "The Synagogue Council may take satisfaction in the knowledge that its intervention has been chiefly responsible for the failure of the Young-Milmoe bill to become a law. The representations which (sic) were made at Albany by Rabbi Herbert S. Goldstein, the chairman of our Religious Observance Committee, and his vigilant attentiveness throughout...resulted in the virtual withdrawal of the bill in spite of the fact that it had been passed by both branches of the state legislature."

Page 18, line 13: "Jewish Billy Sunday Begins $500,000 Drive for New Synagogue," *New York American*, March 9, 1919.

Page 18, line 16: Printed announcement, "The Program of the Sixty-Fourth Annual Grand Lodge Session of District No. 4, I.O.B.B. will be broadcast over K.F.O.N., operating on 241.8 meters Monday, June 27, 1927."

Chapter Three

Page 29, line 10: Dian Friedenberg interview, June 27, 1974.

Page 33, line 18: "Rabbi Herbert S. Goldstein," *The Jewish Forum*, October 1927. (The Master's degree to which reference was made was conferred in 1912.)

Chapter Five

Page 44, line 21: Bernard Drachman, *The Unfailing Light* (New York: 1948), p. 181. The cited statement of purpose was preceded by the following observation by Rabbi Dr. Bernard Drachman, a member of its first teaching staff, and later, dean of the faculty: "Although a certain proportion of the organizing delegates and participating rabbis belonged to the Conservative wing of Judaism, the principles of the seminary, as declared in its charter of incorporation, granted by the Legislature of the State of New York on the ninth of May, 1886, were those of uncompromising adherence to the tenets of Orthodox Judaism."

Page 44, line 43: "Social Notes," *The Hebrew Standard*, Nov. 27, 1914.

Page 45, line 6: "Rabbi H. S. Goldstein, Pioneer with Young Israel, Dies at Age 79," *Young Israel Viewpoint*, Jan. 30, 1970, p. 3. Also: Gilbert Klaperman (author of *The Story of Yeshiva University*), at Memorial Meeting for Rabbi Herbert S. Goldstein, Feb. 8, 1970, p. 11.

Page 46, line 31: "Seminary Graduates," *The American Hebrew*, June 19, 1914.

Page 47, line 17: Herbert S. Goldstein, President, "Report of Morais-Blumenthal Society," *Students' Annual—Jewish Theological Seminary of America*, 1914, page 51.

Page 49, line 47: Herbert S. Goldstein, Deposition in *Katz* v. *Goldman*, Ohio case, 1927.

Page 50, line 9: Louis Finkelstein, interview with author in Dr. Finkelstein's office at the Jewish Theological Seminary, July 21, 1975.

Page 50, line 19: Herbert S. Goldstein, "As *R'Chash* Sees It—The Right to Doubt—A Message to College Students," *West Side Institutional Synagogue Review*, Oct. 20, 1939, p. 2.

Page 51, line 20: Mordecai M. Kaplan, handwritten letter to the author, Dec. 13, 1976.

Page 52, line 40: Herbert S. Goldstein, letter to the individuals named in the footnote at the text, Oct. 10, 1934.

Page 52, line 45: Cyrus Adler, in letter to Rabbi Herbert S. Goldstein, Oct. 16, 1934. Adler quoted the same statement of purpose quoted by Drachman above.

Page 52, line 30: "Warns Judaism of Disruptive Perils," *New York Journal*, June 8, 1914.

Page 55, line 6: Jewish Telegraphic Agency (JTA) release, "Rabbi Yaffe, Leading Orthodox Rabbi, Dead," *Wisconsin Jewish Chronicle*, Nov. 23, 1923.

Page 55, line 8: "Rabbi S. E. Yaffe Dies Last Night at Age 65" (in Yiddish), *Jewish Daily News*, Nov. 16, 1923.

Page 55, line 9: "Union of Orthodox Rabbis of the United States and Canada (Agudath Harabbonim)," *Universal Jewish Encyclopedia* (1943) Volume 10, p. 347.

Page 56, line 19: Gilbert Klaperman, *The Story of Yeshiva University* (Toronto, New York, and London: MacMillan and Collier-MacMillan), 1969.

Chapter Six

Page 57, line 17: *The American Hebrew*, Oct. 10, 1913.

Page 57, line 24: Bertha Fischel Rafsky, interview in her home, Oct. 16, 1972.

Page 57, line 25: Id.

Page 57, line 32: Joseph H. Lookstein, letter to Rabbi Herbert S. Goldstein, Nov. 22, 1949.

Page 58, line 25: Joseph Epstein, interview, March 29, 1977.

Page 58, line 27: Joseph Epstein, *The Early History of the Central Jewish Institute—The Emergence of a Jewish Community Center* (Master's thesis, on file at Yeshiva University) (New York: 1978), p. 21, n. 15, citing, inter alia, Lookstein, *Yesteryears*, p. 24, and Kaplan, *Influences*, p. 30.

Page 60, line 33: "Congregation Kehilath Jeshurun," *The American Hebrew*, Jan. 9, 1914.

Page 60, line 39: *Hebrew Standard*, May 29, 1914.

Page 62, line 34: "Welfare Circles Unite—Auxiliary Societies of Orach Chaim and Kehilath Jeshurun Amalgamate," *The American*

Hebrew, Feb. 18, 1916.

Page 63, line 9: "Congregation Kehilath Jeshurun," *The American Hebrew,* Jan. 9, 1914.

Page 63, line 14: Id.

Chapter Seven

Page 65, line 3: Joseph Epstein, *The Early History,* p. 27.

Page 65, line 20: *Program-Journal* of First Anniversary Dance of Social Welfare Circle, Feb. 21, 1915.

Page 65, line 23: Joseph Epstein, *The Early History,* p. 33.

Page 65, line 25: Frederick Margareten, former president of Congregation Kehilath Jeshurun, interview at Margareten Park, Hunter, New York, July 19, 1972.

Page 65, line 35: Rebecca F. Goldstein, diary, April 13, 1914.

Page 65, line 40: Rebecca F. Goldstein, diary, Jan. 20, 1916.

Page 65, line 44: Joseph Epstein, *The Early History,* p. 33.

Page 65, line 42: Theodore R. Nathan, "Champion of Orthodoxy."

Page 66, line 5: "To Dedicate Jewish Institute," *The American Hebrew,* April 7, 1916, p. 621.

Page 66, line 32: Rebecca F. Goldstein, diary, Jan. 20, 1916.

Page 66, line 34: Rebecca F. Goldstein, diary, April 13, 1914.

Page 66, line 38: Minutes of meeting of Board of Trustees of Congregation Kehilath Jeshurun, Oct. 14, 1916.

Page 67, line 2: Mordecai M. Kaplan, handwritten letter to the author, Dec. 13, 1976.

Page 67, line 28: "Warburg Lays Cornerstone," *The New York Sun,* May 17, 1915.

Page 67, line 31: Joseph Epstein, *The Early History,* p. 35.

Page 67, line 34: "Motto: Judaism and Patriotism," *Dinner Journal* of Social Welfare Circle, Feb. 20, 1916.

Page 68, line 14: "Teachers Inspect Jewish Institute," *New York Tribune,* July 3, 1916.

Page 70, line 6: Herbert S. Goldstein, letter to Felix M. Warburg, March 4, 1917.

Chapter Eight

Page 76, line 27: Herbert S. Goldstein, "Torahcratic the True Zionism," *The Jewish Forum,* May 1943.

Page 77, line 17: "To Welcome Jews in 77th," *New York Times,* March 27, 1919.

Page 77, line 19: "What Our Lodges Are Doing," *B'Nai B'Rith News,* September 1917.

Page 79, line 12: M. Scheinbaum, president of Reines Mizrachi Zionist Society, Atlanta, Ga., letter to Herbert S. Goldstein, August

14, 1918.

Page 80, line 21: "Which Ten Jews Have Done the Most for America?" *Jewish Tribune,* Nov. 13, 1925, p. 12.

Page 81, line 29: Harry Ward, interview, July 23, 1975.

Page 82, line 16: "Rabbis Sound Note of Loyalty Here," *New York Times,* Sept. 18, 1917.

Page 82, line 25: "Whitman Lauds Loyal Jewry—Governor Unfurls 66-Star Service Flag of Institutional Synagogue at Theatre," *New York American,* Feb. 4, 1918.

Page 83, line 7: Rebecca F. Goldstein, diary, March, 10, 1922.

Page 83, line 20: *Harlem Home News,* Nov. 19, 1922.

Page 83, line 29: "250 from All Parts of U.S. Named Directors of J.D.C.," *Jewish Daily Bulletin,* March 25, 1931.

Page 83, line 33: "Getting Personal," *West Side Institutional Review,* Jan. 20, 1961, p. 4; Jan. 31, 1964, p. 4.

Page 84, line 15: Joint Distribution Committee radio announcement, Sept. 9, 1936.

Page 84, line 3: Frederick Margareten, interview with author at Margareten Park, Hunter, New York. Aug. 26, 1971.

Page 84, line 4: Id.

Chapter Ten

Page 94, line 29: Herbert S. Goldstein, "The Institutional Synagogue," *The Hebrew Standard,* Vol. 68, No. 8, Sept. 15, 1916, page 1.

Page 94, line 42: Oscar I. Janowsky, *The Jewish Welfare Board Survey* (New York, New York, Dial Press, 1948), p. 247.

Page 95, line 7: Jeffrey S. Gurock, *When Harlem Was Jewish, 1870-1930* (New York, New York: Columbia University Press, 1979), p. 116.

Page 95, line 15: Janowsky, *Welfare Board,* p. 244.

Page 95, line 23: "Reclamation of 1,000 Jews Rabbi's Aim," *New York American,* Sept. 23, 1917.

Page 96, line 8: Mordecai M. Kaplan, "The Jewish Center," *The American Hebrew,* March 22, 1918, p. 529.

Page 96, line 20: Joseph H. Lookstein, remarks upon conferring Doctor of Divinity degree on Herbert S. Goldstein, at Yeshiva University, June 19, 1941.

Page 96, line 28: Mordecai M. Kaplan, interview with author on telephone, Nov. 2, 1971.

Page 96, line 41: Leo Jung, "Goldstein, Herbert Samuel," *The Universal Jewish Encyclopedia,* Vol. 5 (New York, 1941), p. 37.

Page 97, line 4: "Brotherhood Forum Successful," *The Institutional,* Feb. 4, 1927.

Page 97, line 11: Julia Stitch, interview, June 18, 1974.

Page 97, line 28: "Many Notables to Honor Rabbi at Huge

Fest," *New York Evening Journal,* March 25, 1927.

Chapter Eleven

Page 98, line 23: Oscar Gruen, "The Laymen's Institute of Jewish Studies—An Interview with Rabbi Herbert S. Goldstein, Principal," *The American Hebrew,* Nov. 15, 1940, p. 7.

Page 98, line 25: E.g., " 'Jewish Billy Sunday' to Speak at Forum," *New York American,* Dec. 22, 1918; George Dugan, "Flock to Acclaim Pioneering Rabbi," *The New York Times,* April 18, 1959; Gilbert Klaperman, *Yeshiva University,* p. 154.

Page 99, line 9: "Jewish Billy Sunday," *The World Magazine,* June 22, 1919.

Page 99, line 20: "Plans Jewish Revival—Rabbi Herbert S. Goldstein Resigns Pulpit to Conduct New Work," *The American Hebrew,* April 13, 1917.

Page 99, line 33: Herbert S. Goldstein, manuscript of draft of letter to editor of *American Jewish Chronicle* in response to critical editorial of June 15, 1917.

Page 101, line 9: Id.

Chapter Twelve

Page 102, line 25: "Dinner to Rabbi Aids Institutional Synagogue," *New York Evening Sun,* April 7, 1927.

Page 103, line 7: Isaac Siegel, "From Our President," *The Institutional,* April 8, 1927.

Page 103, line 10: "Shemini Atzereth and Simchas Torah Celebrated with Mirth and Joviality at Both Main and West Side Buildings—Simeon Hai Fischel Goldstein and Clarence Lieberman Preach—Former's Debut as 'Rabbi'," *The Institutional,* Nov. 1, 1929.

Page 103, line 19: "Finds Number of Jews in Prison Sinking," *Institutional,* Nov. 20, 1931, p. 3.

Page 103, line 27: "Synagogue Stone Laid—Rabbi Goldstein in Address Calls Religion a Sure Crime Preventive," *The New York Times,* May 10, 1926.

Page 103, line 34: "Fourth Study 'R' Asked—Dr. Goldstein Would Add Religion to Reading, Writing and Arithmetic," *The New York Times,* June 1, 1931.

Page 105, line 3: "Rabbi Goldstein Condemns Police—Says There Are 40 Poolrooms Between 96th Street and 116th—Asks Citizens to Act—Pastor Of Institutional Synagogue Calls for Moral Purification of City," *The New York Times,* March 19, 1922.

Page 105, line 13: "Ordinance Urged to Close Places at 11 P.M. and to Bar Youth Under 18," *New York Evening Journal,* Jan. 12, 1926.

Chapter Thirteen

Page 108, line 16: "Rabbi Goldstein Leads New Revival Movement," *The Tageblatt*, April 11, 1917, first page of English section.

Page 108, line 23: Stephen S. Wise, letter to Herbert S. Goldstein, Nov. 6, 1916.

Page 108, line 31: Rebecca F. Goldstein, diary, Jan. 26, 1918.

Page 111, line 18: Rebecca F. Goldstein, diary, Nov. 15, 1916.

Page 112, line 26: Rebecca F. Goldstein, diary, Dec. 26, 1916.

Page 112, line 29: Rebecca F. Goldstein, diary, Feb. 18, 1917.

Page 114, line 43: "The Parish and Mission Department," *Federation*, published by the Federation of Churches and Christian Organizations in New York City, Vol. VI, Bulletin 5, Sept. 9, 1909.

Page 115, line 34: Rebecca F. Goldstein, diary, March 6, 1917.

Page 121, line 24: "Rabbi Herbert S. Goldstein to Head Institutional Synagogue," *The Hebrew Standard*, April 13, 1917.

Page 123, line 2: "The Awakening" (an editorial), *The Jewish Daily News*, April 11, 1917, p. 1 of English section.

Page 123, line 9: "To Lead Jewish Revival in Harlem," *The New York Times*, May 4, 1917.

Page 123, line 18: *Constitution*, Institutional Synagogue, Art. 3, sec. 2; art. 6, sec. 1.

Page 123, line 33: Rebecca F. Goldstein, diary, April 29, 1917.

Page 123, line 36: Rebecca F. Goldstein, diary, May 10, 1917.

Page 123, line 41: "House for Institutional Synagogue," *The New York Times*, May 15, 1917.

Page 124, line 2: Rebecca F. Goldstein, diary, May 13, 1917.

Page 124, line 8: "Y.W.H.A. Notes," *American Hebrew*, June 8, 1917.

Page 124, line 16: *Certificate of Incorporation*, Institutional Synagogue, Oct. 30, 1917.

Chapter Fourteen

Page 125, line 11: Harold Kaplan, interview, Jan. 31, 1975.

Page 126, line 5: Rebecca F. Goldstein, diary, June 1, 1917.

Page 126, line 26: "Rabbi Calls on Jews to Rejoin Faith," *New York American*, June 10, 1917.

Page 127, line 19: Rebecca F. Goldstein, diary, Nov. 3, 1917.

Chapter Fifteen

Page 132, line 8: "Highlights from Rabbi Herbert S. Goldstein's 45 Years in the Ministry," *Souvenir Album*, West Side Institutional Synagogue, April 19, 1959.

Page 132, line 22: "700 'Go Over the Top' in Institutional Synagogue Drive for 1000 Members," *New York American*, Dec. 9,

1917.

Page 133, line 12: "Jewish 'Billy Sunday' Begins $500,000 Drive for New Synagogue," *New York American*, March 9, 1919.

Page 134, line 15: "Ten Years Work of Harlem Institution," *Jewish Daily News*, Dec. 15, 1927.

Chapter Sixteen

Page 139, line 17, *Reform Advocate*, Chicago, Illinois, Nov. 26, 1921.

Page 139, line 41: Rebecca F. Goldstein, diary, Nov. 18, 1921.

Page 151, line 15: "Self Abnegation" (Editorial), *Hebrew Standard*, Dec. 9, 1921.

Chapter Seventeen

Page 152, line 17: Rebecca F. Goldstein, diary, Nov. 29, 1917.

Page 154, line 33: Rebecca F. Goldstein, diary, Dec. 20, 1917.

Page 155, line 6: "Jewish 'Billy Sunday' Begins $500,000 Drive for New Synagogue," *New York American*, March 9, 1919.

Page 158, line 19: Herbert S. Goldstein, "Why Synagogue Centers Fail," *Jewish Post*, Paterson, New Jersey, July 6, 1929.

Chapter Eighteen

Page 170, line 30: *New York Times*, June 9, 1919.

Page 171, line 9: "Form A—Jewish Welfare Board, 71 West 47th Street, New York, New York," *Survey of Institutional Synagogue*, May 1938.

Page 171, line 13: Id.

Chapter Nineteen

Page 174, line 2: "$300,000 Is Sought for Synagogue," *New York American*, June 1, 1919.

Chapter Twenty

Page 183, line 3: Rebecca F. Goldstein, diary, June 26, 1921.

Chapter Twenty-One

Page 190, line 28: "Five More Lads to be Confirmed in One Day at I.S.," *Institutional*, Feb. 3, 1928, p. 3.

Page 191, line 16: "Chief Rabbi Kook Pays I.S. Surprise Visit," *Institutional*, Nov. 21, 1924, p. 4.

Chapter Twenty-Two

Page 193, line 18: Louis Simon, interview, Aug 8, 1974.

Page 195, line 33: "Home Night Enthusiasts Arrange Season's Program—Rabbi Goldstein Offers Prize," *The Institutional*, Nov. 7, 1924.

Chapter Twenty-Three

Page 197, line 15: "Parents' Association Delights 'Kiddies' with Festive Celebration—Another Reason Why the I.S. Attracts and Holds Its Children," *The Institutional*, Oct. 12, 1928.

Page 197, line 19: "The Talmud Torah," *The Institutional*, Jan. 24, 1919, p. 2.

Page 198, line 6: "Talmud Torah Opens New Classrooms," *The Institutional*, Nov. 19, 1922.

Page 198, line 38: "Making the New Year New," *The Institutional*, Sept. 16, 1936, p. 3.

Page 199, line 5: "Talmud Torah Conducts Annual Drive," *The Institutional*, Nov. 19, 1926, p. 3.

Page 199, line 12: "Capacity Audience Enjoys Movies—Congressman Siegel and Rabbi Goldstein Speak," *The Institutional*, Oct. 11, 1933.

Page 200, line 13: "Talmud Torah Truly the Institutional Synagogue Asset," *The Institutional*, Dec. 9, 1932.

Page 200, line 24: "Talmud Torah Starts Drive for New Pupils—Broad Registration Campaign Features Many Varied Activities," *The Institutional*, Oct. 7, 1936, p. 1.

Page 201, line 1: "Talmud Torah Opens New Classrooms—Registration Over 700," *The Institutional*, Nov. 19, 1922.

Page 201, line 40: Isadore Goodman, "Our Talmud Torah," *The Institutional*, May 15, 1925, p. 2.

Page 201, line 42: "Talmud Torah Notes," *Institutional*, Oct. 15, 1926, p. 3.

Page 201, line 3: Outline of Activities of Institutional Synagogue (folded card), 1927-1928.

Page 201, line 21: "From Our Rabbi," *Institutional*, April 8, 1927, p. 3.

Page 201, line 23: "Greetings from Our Rabbi," *The Institutional*, April 13, 1934, p. 1.

Page 201, line 28: "Outline of the Scope of Talmud Torah," *Institutional*, April 17, 1936, p. 3.

Page 201, line 23: "Greetings from Our Rabbi," *The Institutional*, April 13, 1934, p. 1.

Page 204, line, 31: The synagogue's actual claim was more sweeping: "The pupils are pledged to observe the Sabbath and to keep the dietary laws,"—"The Talmud Torah Department," *The Institutional*, April 8, 1927, p. 6.

Page 207, line 5: Id., March 2, 1928, p. 4.

Page 212, line 35: *American Hebrew and Jewish Tribune,* Dec. 15, 1933.

Page 212, line 35: Id.

Page 212, line 36: E.g., *"Une Negresse Juive A L'Honneur,"* Israel *Hebdomadaire Juif Independant,* Jan. 12, 1934, p. 1.

Page 212, line 38: Rebecca F. Goldstein, diary, Dec. 17, 1933.

Page 212, line 42: "Hebrew High School News," *Institutional,* Jan. 4, 1935, p. 4.

Page 213, line 38: "Friedlander Classes Now in Session," *The Institutional,* Vol. 2, No. 1, Nov. 19, 1922.

Page 213, line 40: "Our Classes," *Institutional Synagogue Bulletin,* Dec., 1921, p. 4.

Page 214, line 4: "Hebrew High School Course Newly Organized," *Institutional,* Jan. 19, 1934, p. 1.

Page 214, line 8: *Twentieth Anniversary Souvenir Program,* Institutional Synagogue, 1937.

Page 215, line 4: "H.H.S. Engages in Novel Jewish History Project," *Institutional,* April 24, 1936, p. 3.

Chapter Twenty-Four

Page 217, line 25: "Popularity of Bible Classes Among Sisterhood, Parents Ass'n, Daughters, Brotherhood and Women's League Due to Rabbi Goldstein—Giving of Traditional Interpretation of Bible to People Is Purpose," *The Institutional,* Nov. 8, 1929.

Page 218, line 24: "Women Conduct Seeyum," *American Hebrew and Jewish Tribune,* May 24, 1935, p. 43.

Page 219, line 36: Herbert S. Goldstein, "How to Use the Bible," *Institutional,* May 21, 1926, p. 3.

Page 223, line 3: "Professors of Columbia University and CCNY to Come to I.S. to Teach—Over 400 Courses Made Available; Full College Credits to Be Given," *Institutional,* Nov. 11, 1927, p. 1.

Chapter Twenty-Five

Page 224, line 10: "Institutional Synagogue Brotherhood," *American Hebrew,* March 19, 1926.

Page 225, line 23: "Brotherhood Promises to Come Back to Its Own Through Means of 'Dine-Study-Play' Plan—Constituency Seizes Eagerly At Idea—Rabbi Goldstein the Inspirer," *The Institutional,* Nov. 21, 1918.

Chapter Twenty-Six

Page 243, line 35: Hy Wishengrad, "Camp Ta-A-Noog Perched on Roof of the Institutional Synagogue," *Jewish Daily Bulletin,* July 30, 1934.

Page 246, line 19: "Institutional Synagogue Camp Ta-A-Noog Completes Third Successful Season Today," *Institutional*, Aug. 28, 1936, p. 1.

Chapter Twenty-Seven

Page 251, line 32: E.g., "Institutional Synagogue Wins Metropolitan-Manhattan Dramatic Tournament," *Institutional*, June 3, 1932, p. 1.

Page 253, line 11: "Institutional Representatives Take Second in Metropolitan League Contest—Are Successful in Violin and Piano Contest," *Institutional*, May 21, 1926, p. 2.

Page 253, line 15: "Music Department to Present Third Annual Concert," *Institutional*, June 1, 1934, p. 1.

Page 253, line 23: "Collegiate Branch to Hold Dance—At St. Regis April 4th," *Institutional*, March 13, 1925, p. 4.

Page 253, line 23: "Basketball Team to Meet Young Israel— Will Play Sunday Evening, Feb. 8," *Institutional*, Jan. 30, 1925, p. 1.

Page 253, line 28: Minutes, Rabbinical Council of America meeting conducted at West Side Institutional Synagogue, April 13, 1939, p. 2.

Page 253, line 31: "Orthodox Union Cancels Friday Dancing," *Institutional*, May 16, 1924, p. 2.

Page 254, line 27: Harry Ward, interview, July 23, 1975.

Chapter Twenty-Eight

Page 255, line 21: "The Institutional Synagogue Shows Remarkable Growth," *Hebrew Standard*, Jan. 25, 1918.

Page 255, line 29: "Some Facts and Figures About Our Building," *The Institutional*, April 8, 1927, p. 4.

Page 256, line 4: "Institutional Synagogue of New York Celebrates Tenth Anniversary," *American Hebrew*, April 8, 1927.

Page 256, line 9: "Social & Educational Department," *The Institutional*, April 8, 1927, p. 7. An earlier article referred to twenty separate branches meeting in the building: "Jacob Marrus Recuperating from Illness," *The Institutional*, April 17, 1925, p. 4.

Page 257, line 11: Isidor Epstein (a cousin of Isidore Goodman), interview with author, Mar. 18, 1976.

Page 260, line 13: "Bulletin Issued on 'The Club Meeting,'" *The Institutional*, Jan. 4, 1935, p. 4.

Page 262, line 15: "Social and Educational Department January Program—Clubs Programs for Junior Groups," *Institutional*, Jan. 7, 1927, p. 2.

Page 270, line 17: "Intermediate Department Holds Chanuka Entertainment—UOJCA Adds Two Branches," *Institutional*, Jan. 2, 1925, p. 1.

Page 270, line 19: "Orators to Show Skill Sunday—Inter-Club Debating Tourney Arouses Keen Enthusiasm," *Institutional*, Nov. 20, 1936, p. 1.

Chapter Twenty-Nine

Page 272, line 41: "Thousands View I.S. Health Exhibition," *Institutional*, Nov. 3, 1933.

Page 273, line 24: "Physical Education Department," *The Institutional*, April 8, 1927, p. 6.

Chapter Thirty

Page 276, line 26: Id.

Page 277, line 36: Id.

Page 277, line 38: "Benny Leonard Helps Distribute Awards Earned During Eventful and Memorable Season," *Institutional*, June 28, 1929, p. 1.

Page 278, line 3: "Activities of Institutional Synagogue Gym Indicate Its Growing Popularity," *The Institutional*, May 7, 1928.

Page 279, line 38: "Social & Educational Department," *The Institutional*, April 8, 1927, p. 7.

Page 280, line 1: "Institutional Synagogue Wins Metropolitan Debating Championship," *Institutional*, Nov. 26, 1926, p. 1.

Chapter Thirty-One

Page 286, line 26: Charles S. Bernheimer, "Jewish Americanization Agencies," *The American Jewish Yearbook* (Philadelphia: Jewish Publication Society, 1921) p. 92.

Page 288, line 23: Edward Lawrence Hunt, Director of America's Goodwill Union, in an open letter published throughout the country; e.g., "Director of America's Goodwill Union Voices Remarkable Tribute to Jewish Children of New York," *Jewish Independent*, Cleveland, Ohio, Dec. 4, 1925.

Chapter Thirty-Two

Page 289, line 24: "Inspiring Holy Day Services Planned for Both Congregations," *Institutional*, Sept. 19, 1930, p. 1.

Chapter Thirty-Four

Page 307, line 20: Roi Ottley, *The New World A-Coming— Inside Black America* (Boston and Cambridge: Houghton Mifflin Co. and The Riverside Press, 1943) pp. 122-123.

Page 307, line 27: Id.

Page 307, line 30: Id., at pp. 128-129.

Page 307, line 34: Id., at pp. 122-123.

Page 307, line 37: Id., at pp. 128-129.

Page 307, line 46: Id., at p. 136.

Page 308, line 23: "Games, Gymnastics, Swimming, Art and Study Stressed at Rabbi Goldstein's Harlem Institutional Synagogue," *New York World Telegram,* Dec. 19, 1935.

Page 308, line 26: Id.

Page 310, line 38: Minutes, Board of Directors Meeting, Institutional Synagogue, May 14, 1930.

Page 310, line 40: Minutes, Board of Directors Meeting, Institutional Synagogue, Feb. 10, 1931.

Page 311, line 2: Molly Gertz, interview with author, Aug. 2, 1973.

Chapter Thirty-Five

Page 317, line 13: "Congregation Enjoys Inspiring Services at Institute and at Branch—Full Audience Expected at Both Services for Kol Nidre," *The Institutional,* Oct. 7, 1927.

Chapter Thirty-Six

Page 323, line 15: "Institutional Synagogue Expanding to Washington Heights," *Hebrew Standard,* May 11, 1917.

Page 323, line 20: "Rabbi Calls on Jews to Rejoin Faith," *New York American,* June 10, 1917.

Page 324, line 29: Rebecca F. Goldstein, diary, May 17, 1919.

Page 325, line 2: "Synagogue Amalgamation," *Jewish Tribune,* Nov. 20, 1925.

Page 325, line 7: Isaac Siegel, printed letter on a postcard to members and friends of the Institutional Synagogue, postmarked Nov. 5, 1925, regarding "reunion" scheduled for Nov. 11, 1925.

Page 325, line 22: Israel Goldstein, "The Synagogue and the Youth," (from a paper presented at the educational session of the convention of the Metropolitan League of Jewish Community Associations, Nov. 27, 1927), *The Jewish Center,* March, 1928.

Page 326, line 7: Louis Marshall, "Our Youth—The Greatest Problem of American Jewry," address delivered at the Institutional Synagogue, and reprinted in the synagogue's Twentieth Anniversary Souvenir Program, 1937.

Page 326, line 14: Congressman Isaac Siegel, "Congratulations and Best Wishes From," *Institutional,* April 6, 1924.

Page 326, line 14: *Program at Eighth Annual Banquet,* Institutional Synagogue, April 6, 1924.

Chapter Thirty-Seven

Page 330, line 26: Actually Rabbi Goldstein would be described more accurately as slightly to the right of center, if not right at the center, of the Orthodox rabbinate during most of his career. The writer of this encyclopedia entry knew Rabbi Goldstein only toward the end of Rabbi Goldstein's career, when the latter was clearly moving to the right, which was most clearly apparent by his having renounced the Synagogue Council of America over which he had once presided.

Page 330, line 29: *Hebrew Standard*, Oct. 8, 1915.

Page 331, line 3: Joseph H. Lookstein, "Dr. Revel and Homiletics: A Page of Yeshiva Memoirs," *Hedenu*, 62, cited in Gilbert Klaperman, *Yeshiva University*, p. 230, fn. 35.

Page 331, line 14: Ish-Shahar, "The Revival of Orthodoxy," *Light of Israel*, June 20, 1924.

Page 331, line 25: "Union of Orthodox Jewish Congregations Holds Convention," *The Jewish Tribune*, Oct. 30, 1925.

Page 331, line 28: Irving Bunim, interview with author, Jan. 4, 1976; also: "Rabbi Herbert S. Goldstein, Pioneer with Young Israel, Dies at Age 79," *Young Israel Viewpoint*, Jan. 30, 1970, p. 3.

Page 331, line 43: Gilbert Klaperman, *Yeshiva University*, p. 154, citing, inter alia, *The New York Times*, Dec. 3, 1923.

Page 332, line 20: Most of these books are mentioned in the Acknowledgments section of this book.

Page 334, line 24: Rabbi Cohen, now the Chief Rabbi of Haifa, heads not only the Fischel Institute, but also the entire umbrella organization known as ARIEL.

Page 335, line 36: "Rabbinical Groups Merge—Orthodox Council and Yeshivah Association Vote in Jersey," *New York Times*, July 4, 1935.

Page 335, line 37: Herbert S. Goldstein, first Presidium Report to Rabbinical Council of America, July 1936; "Rabbinical Council to Convene June 28-29-30," *Orthodox Union*, April 1937.

Page 335, line 38: "American Synagogue Council Formed," *The Sentinel*, Chicago, May 21, 1926.

Page 335, line 39: "Heads Synagogue Group—Rabbi Herbert S. Goldstein is New Council President," *New York Times*, June 10, 1944, p. 10.

Page 336, line 27: Everett R. Clinchy, "Human Relations—Then and Now," in Harry Schneiderman, *Two Generations in Perspective—Notable Events and Trends 1896-1956* (New York: Monde, 1957) p. 327.

Page 336, line 29: George C. O. Hass, Director, The World Fellowship of Faiths, letter on the organization's stationery. Oct. 14, 1951.

INDEX

Young People's League, 227, 228
lecturers, 230
newspaper, sexist stereotypes
reversed, 252
prayers, 206
roles, inroads against stereotypes,
268, 269
seeyum, Pentateuch, 218
silk-stocking advocates'
opposition neutralized, 154
Sisterhood, subservient-sounding
name rejected, 233
sports, 274, 275, 279
student organization, parallel with
boys, 207
Marriage, Rebecca F. Goldstein's
role in, 36, 41
World Academy, 334
World Fellowship of Faiths, 336
World War I, 74-84, 233, 234

Y
Yad Harav Herzog, 334
Yavneh, Cantor Zalmon, 187, 188, 250,
290, 315, 318
Yeshiva U., 29, 311, 330-331, 335, 340
doctorate, 56, 96
homiletics, 18, 330, 331
practical rabbinics, 18, 330, 331
Rabbinical College, 29, 45, 53, 55,
115, 137
Teacher's Institute, 50
Women's Organization, 338
Yeshiva College, 214
Yorkville Talmud Torah. *See* Central
Jewish Institute
Young Israel, 47, 119, 122, 253, 270, 331
Young Judeans, 47, 76
Young Men's Hebrew Associations, 65,
90-94, 117
Harlem, 71, 112, 119, 122, 125
Washington Heights, 323
Young Men's Heb. Orthodox League,
112, 113, 115, 119, 122, 123, 125
Young Women's Hebrew Association,
117, 123-125, 128, 220, 296, 323

Z
Zichron Ephraim, Cong., 142
Zionism, 76, 230, 231, 244, 245, 246,
256, 257, 263, 264, 280, 339

Aaron I. Reichel is a rabbi, a lawyer, and an editor. He was ordained at the rabbinical seminary affiliated with Yeshiva University, the oldest and largest university under Jewish auspices, and served for a number of years as the editor of the *Yeshiva College Alumni Bulletin*. After earning a law degree at Fordham University, he was admitted to the bar in New York and in New Jersey. He is affiliated with Prentice-Hall, one of the world's largest business and information publishers, at which he is an attorney editor, where he has been in charge of information services.

The author's writings on Judaica have appeared in periodicals ranging from *Tradition*, of the Rabbinical Council of America, to *The Jewish Press* and *The Jewish Week*, the most widely circulated Anglo-Jewish newspapers. His writings on legal subjects have appeared in periodicals ranging from *The National Law Journal* to *The Corporation Law Review*, and have been reprinted by various publishers, including a subcommittee of the U.S. Senate.

Reichel was the national president of Yavneh, when it was the only organization of its type with chapters from coast to coast, and the first chairperson of the Student Committee of Orthodox Organization Presidents. He is in Marquis' *Who's Who in Religion* and *Who's Who in the Law*.